THE
classic
CINEMA

ESSAYS IN CRITICISM

THE CLASSIC CINEMA

ESSAYS IN CRITICISM

EDITED BY

STANLEY J. SOLOMON
Iona College

HBJ

HARCOURT BRACE JOVANOVICH, INC.

New York   Chicago   San Francisco   Atlanta

ISBN: 0-15-507629-9

Library of Congress Catalog Card Number: 72-94995

Printed in the United States of America

PICTURE CREDITS

Cover: Frame engraving, Culver Pictures

page
11 *Intolerance,* Museum of Modern Art/Film Stills Archive
39 *The Cabinet of Dr. Caligari,* Museum of Modern Art/Film Stills Archive
65 *Potemkin,* Rosa Madell Film Library
89 *The Gold Rush,* Museum of Modern Art/Film Stills Archive
109 *The Passion of Joan of Arc,* The Museum of Modern Art/Film Stills Archive
129 *M,* courtesy Janus Films
149 *Rules of the Game,* courtesy Janus Films
171 *Citizen Kane,* Copyrighted 1941—RKO Radio Pictures, a Division of RKO General, Inc.
199 *The Bicycle Thief,* Richard Feiner and Company, Inc.
223 *The Seventh Seal,* courtesy Janus Films
247 *Vertigo,* copyright Alfred Hitchcock. Reprinted by permission.
273 *The Red Desert,* Cinemation Indústries, Inc.
295 *Belle De Jour,* Allied Artists
317 *Satyricon,* copyright 1970 by Produzione Europée Associates S.P.A.S. 1970. All rights reserved.

for my mother and father

PREFACE

The phrase "classic work of art" connotes innumerable qualities to each of us. This is true in regard to other art forms as well as to film, but with film the difficulty is compounded because it is an entirely contemporary experience. With older art forms, almost any work that has "survived" in the general esteem, that is still admired by a sizable portion of those interested in the art form, is readily labeled a classic. However, in attributing greatness to any particular film, no one can point to a generally accepted body of works by which the conventions of a classic film have been established. Yet this consideration seems never to have stopped anyone from presuming to interpret the classic cinema as it might appear to future generations. This practice is surely a legitimate function of criticism; it may be even more important to articulate such evaluations early in the development of an artistic tradition than to do so later on. It is valuable to distinguish between the forty or fifty "unforgettable hits" of every season and the one or two films of the year that might plausibly outlast their reviews and move audiences profoundly in a subsequent decade.

Of course, we already have a substantial body of cinematic works cherished by segments of the critical public, who bear witness to their greatness from time to time in countless lists of "the greatest films ever" variety. The lists never jibe, but when collated into a critics' poll they represent a kind of art by consensus, more amusing than controversial, for the massing of opinion toward the election of films to a figurative hall of fame never clarifies the grounds on which particular choices were made.

There are no universal, objective criteria for the evaluation of art other than the test of time, and that criterion cannot yet be applied to the cinema. Still, everyone knows intuitively that the standard of greatness for any narrative art is the capacity to deal profoundly with human experience through the technical and structural mastery of the distinctive artistic elements of the medium. Critics differ on the nature of the achievement of specific films, since criticism is itself an art, descriptive not only of the work perceived but also of the perceiver's mind, of his ability to respond to the selection and arrangement of the observable data of a work of art. A great work of art will invariably lead to a multiplicity of interpretations, because the vividness and force of the data it provides evoke complex responses at various stages during and after observation.

For this reason critics always affirm that a true classic "improves" with increased familiarity—that is, as the conflicting range of our responses to a work narrows on repeated observation, we become able to evaluate more justly the design of the whole and the depth implicit in the data. This experience does not suggest another objective criterion, but rather relates to the same one, the test of time, but now in the personal rather than the historical sense. A classic film in this basic sense is one that wears well, that strikes deeper levels of our awareness at the third viewing than at the first.

The fourteen films studied in this volume are intended to *represent* the classic tradition in the cinema or, more specifically, the Western world's part in that tradition. They are by no means anyone's list of the fourteen best films ever made, nor are they necessarily the best works by each of the filmmakers included. They are great films chosen from a much larger group of memorable films because they represent a variety of distinctive stylistic and historical developments within the major tradition in narrative film. Even so, it might be argued that, for example, an omitted work such as F. W. Murnau's *The Last Laugh* is representative of the same era as *The Cabinet of Dr. Caligari* and is artistically superior to it. The validity of such a claim, nevertheless, need not outweigh other considerations. Once it has been established (by general opinion, by personal attitudes, by precedents, by the views of authorities) that a film attains a high level of artistic achievement, other concerns such as time, place, influence, and popularity become decisive.

The purpose of this book is to point out the classic tradition, not to arouse controversy over the particular examples deemed significant within it. In selecting relatively recent films, then, an additional criterion was the general reputation of the filmmaker's other works; that was one obvious way of balancing personal taste and objective evaluation in an area too frequently governed by polemics. The choice of critical studies was based almost entirely on the contribution each piece makes to an understanding of one of the films; it was not based at all on predetermined critical assumptions or "schools." Nor was there any attempt to select articles for the sake of controversy, though critics occasionally dispute the interpretations of other critics and frequently point out flaws that other critics consider virtues.

I want to thank the staff of the New York Public Library at Lincoln Center for their assistance. The Iona College Library, Alexander F. Thomas, C.F.C., Chief Librarian, provided great help, and special thanks are owed to Lillian Doris Viacava, who obtained a great deal of material for me. Audio-Brandon Films as usual showed much consideration for the cause of scholarship.

STANLEY J. SOLOMON

CONTENTS

PREFACE   *vi*

INTRODUCTION   ᴛᴏᴡᴀʀᴅ ᴀ ᴛʜᴇᴏʀʏ ᴏf fɪʟᴍ ʜɪsᴛᴏʀʏ   *1*

GRIFFITH

INTOLERANCE   *11*

Credits   *12*
Introduction   *12*
IRIS BARRY AND EILEEN BOWSER
   The Scope of *Intolerance*   *15*
LILLIAN GISH
   Griffith at Work   *19*
LEWIS JACOBS
   Technique in *Intolerance*   *24*
PAUL O'DELL
   The Modern Story in *Intolerance*   *27*

WIENE, MAYER, JANOWITZ

THE CABINET OF
DR. CALIGARI   *39*

Credits   *40*
Introduction   *40*
SIEGFRIED KRACAUER
   The Making of *Caligari*   *43*
LOTTE H. EISNER
   The Beginnings of the Expressionist Film   *51*
ARTHUR LENNIG
   Caligari as a Film Classic   *56*

EISENSTEIN

pOTEMkiN 65

Credits 66
Introduction 66
JAY LEYDA
    Theory into Practice 69
SERGEI EISENSTEIN
    Image and Structure in *Potemkin* 76
A. R. FULTON
    Montage in *Potemkin* 82

CHAPLIN

THE Gold Rush 89

Credits 90
Introduction 90
ROBERT PAYNE
    The Frozen Hills 92
ERNEST CALLENBACH
    Classics Revisited: *The Gold Rush* 97
JOHN HOWARD LAWSON
    Premise and Progression in *The Gold Rush* 102
GERALD MAST
    Chaplin's Comedy of Character 104

DREYER

THE pASSiON of JOAN of ARC 109

Credits 110
Introduction 110
ROGER MANVELL
    Psychological Intensity in *The Passion of
    Joan of Arc* 112

x

Contents

TOM MILNE
The World Beyond 115
RICHARD ROWLAND
Carl Dreyer's World 122

LANG

M 129

Credits 130
Introduction 130
SIEGFRIED KRACAUER
Murderer Among Us 133
PAUL JENSEN
Encounters with Sound 136
ERIC RHODE
Fritz Lang (The German Period, 1919–1935) 144

RENOIR

RULES OF THE GAME 149

Credits 150
Introduction 150
PIERRE LEPROHON
from Three Masterworks 153
JACQUES JOLY
Between Theater and Life: Jean Renoir
and *Rules of the Game* 157
R. J. GARLICK
External Appearances in *Rules of the Game* 166

WELLES

CITIZEN KANE 171

Credits 172
Introduction 172

CHARLES HIGHAM
Composition, Imagery, and Music in
Citizen Kane   175
DAVID BORDWELL
The Dual Cinematic Tradition in
Citizen Kane   181
PAULINE KAEL
from Raising *Kane*   191

DE SICA

THE bicycle Thief

199

Credits   200
Introduction   200
BARBARA H. SOLOMON
Father and Son in De Sica's *The Bicycle
Thief*   203
ANDRÉ BAZIN
Neorealism and Pure Cinema: *The Bicycle
Thief*   208
GIAN-LORENZO DARRETTA
Vittorio De Sica's Vision of Cycles   218

BERGMAN

THE SEVENTH SEAL

223

Credits   224
Introduction   224
PETER COWIE
Milieu and Texture in *The Seventh Seal*   227
NORMAN N. HOLLAND
The Seventh Seal: The Film as Iconography   233
JORN DONNER
The Role of Jöns in *The Seventh Seal*   238

Contents

HITCHCOCK

VERTIGO   247

Credits   248
Introduction   248
DAVID THOMSON
    Narrative Viewpoint in *Vertigo*   251
ROBIN WOOD
    Thematic Structure in *Vertigo*   254
DONALD M. SPOTO
    Vertigo: The Cure Is Worse Than the Dis-Ease   266

ANTONIONI

THE RED DESERT   273

Credits   274
Introduction   274
STANLEY KAUFFMANN
    The Achievement of *The Red Desert*   277
RICHARD ROUD
    The Red Desert: The Triple Split   282
JOHN S. BRAGIN
    Meaning and Image in *The Red Desert*   288

BUÑUEL

belle de jour   295

Credits   296
Introduction   296
RAYMOND DURGNAT
    Fantasy and Reality in *Belle de Jour*   299
ELLIOT STEIN
    Buñuel's Golden Bowl   306
ANDREW SARRIS
    The Beauty of *Belle de Jour*   311

FELLINI

SATYRICON 317

Credits 318
Introduction 318
FEDERICO FELLINI
Preface to the Screen Treatment of
Satyricon 321
MARSHA KINDER AND BEVERLE HOUSTON
A Film from Fellini's Mythology 324
NEAL OXENHANDLER
The Distancing Perspective in *Satyricon* 328
JANET C. DOSS
Fellini's Demythologized World 332

APPENDIX **filmoqraphies and selected biblioqraphies** 339

INDEX 351

INTRODUCTION

toward a theory of film history

Although the entire history of motion pictures is so brief that it is en-
compassed within the lifetimes of many people living today, very little
has been done to distinguish the significant forces that led to the art of
the cinema as we know it now. Perhaps cultural history can be written
only after the mass of factual material has been fixed in the record books;
nevertheless, the process of sorting out the significant events from the
ordinary, of establishing the major contributions, and of clarifying the
essential methodology of the art has already begun. The time now seems
appropriate to attempt some appraisal of the landmarks in the history of
the cinema, not just in terms of a dozen or even a hundred great films,
but in regard to the shaping of esthetic principles and the development
of a classic tradition within the art form that has become the distinctive
medium of our age.

The motion picture began as a response to the mechanical, techno-
logical, and innovative sensibilities of nineteenth-century men who theorized that it would function to record and reproduce information; and
indeed, early film did serve as what would now be called a storage and
retrieval system. However, unlike present-day computer and copying
technologies, the motion picture developed in the 1880's and 1890's not
so much from the need to accommodate commercial enterprises as from
the driving impulse of the nineteenth century to expand all the possibilities of human communication. For the industrial applications of the
motion picture were not widely understood, and no large sums of money
were expended. Tireless inventors tinkered with various processes simply
because they were inventors, imaginative artists with a mechanical bent,
not because they anticipated fantastic riches. Some succeeded, but very
few made their fortunes through their efforts. Many years passed after
men like the Lumière brothers in France, William Dickson in America,
and R. W. Paul in England had demonstrated the feasibility of the in-

ventions before commercial interests began to generate significant capital for the creation of a new industry.

Fortunately for the concerns of art, the only real commercial use of the motion picture at that time was not in industry nor in education nor in news reporting, but in the production of film stories. Perhaps motion pictures became an entertainment business so quickly only because, coincidentally, other important applications had not yet been derived. Although invariably crude and frequently inept, short fictional narratives had become the main product of the primitive cinema by 1900; thus, the new medium had adapted itself to the narrative tradition years before its first great artist, D. W. Griffith, began in 1908 to give shape to the amorphous materials prepared by his ambitious predecessors.

The basic problem that confronted the nineteenth-century pioneers of the art of cinematic narrative was that of translating a primarily verbal mode of expression (fiction, drama, and narrative poetry) into a visual one. During the first twenty years of cinematic narrative, the problem was attacked in two ways, neither of which retained any lasting significance. The first was by performing a little story or anecdote in front of a camera, using mime, gestures, and physical action. All the material was usually recorded in a single shot, so that the viewing time was identical to the actual time elapsing within the story. Most films of the 1890's ran only a minute or two and very few ran more than five minutes. This placed severe limitations on the ability of the early filmmakers to convey anything above the level of sheer physical action. Even the stringing together of various scenes, which allowed for greater complexity in the plot line, failed to produce material any more complex than a fairy tale. Within each scene, this same limitation, together with a strict adherence to the depiction of real time (as distinct from dramatic time), prevented any serious attempt at communicating ideas or states of mind.

The second way early filmmakers approached cinematic narrative is best illustrated by the works of Georges Méliès. His contribution was to design narrative materials in specifically visual forms; in other words, rather than merely transferring a verbal story to a visual medium, Méliès created material suitable for film. Even before 1900 his short works, most of which dealt with fantasy, science fiction, or magic, stressed through "trick photography" the imposition of the visually deceptive upon the ordinary and the real. In these films plot frequently consists of the piecing together of incidents, each one amusing or surprising in its unraveling, but seldom directed toward the progress of a story. Even in his longer films, such as A Trip to the Moon (1902) and From Paris to Monte Carlo (1905), which were about fifteen minutes long and were shot in several scenes, plot is simply a means of getting from one point to another, rather than a narrative progression. Méliès ought to be credited with having introduced cinematic style and having taught audiences to perceive cinematic meaning in terms of the conflicting movements of objects and people. In the fantasy world of his films, plot literally explodes from the elements of the environment; movement is everything, and time is nothing.

But until it was learned how the film could compete with other art forms on its common ground—storytelling—the new medium could never hope to generate the prestige, resources, and serious following that it needed to become more than just a low-level form of mass entertainment. In the first years of the twentieth century, audiences were still curious enough to be drawn into the nickelodeons to see basic cinema: the recording of parades, the appearance of celebrities, and the slapstick collision of running men. With Edwin Porter's *The Great Train Robbery* (1903), however, exciting new possibilities became apparent. The fact that audiences have continued to appreciate this film for years indicates how the public can respond intuitively to a great leap forward in art. Although at the time no one clearly articulated the nature of the leap, *The Great Train Robbery* departed boldly from the traditional sequential movement of narrative, which had been a step by step progression over a precisely delineated space in continuous chronological order. This is not to say that prior to Porter's film the time and space depicted had corresponded exactly to real time and to the actual space. Méliès, for example, would show a rocket ship taking off from the earth and landing on the moon without recording the whole space or indicating the amount of time that passed on the journey. But the direction and the implicit logical connection of every point in such a journey was always demonstrated or acknowledged in his films in some self-evident way.

Porter, however, contributed the innovation of cinematic time and space, thus enabling the fledgling medium to take narrative flight beyond even the imagination of Méliès. What Porter did in this film, rather simply, was to transport his robbers to a point where they seemed on their way to an easy escape and then cut to a scene in which the railroad telegrapher is freed from the ropes tied around him by the robbers. The telegrapher is then shown informing others of the robbery, which is apparently taking place at the same moment. The implication of simultaneous action (we had previously witnessed every step of the robbery in the usual chronological order) is reinforced by the next shot, which reveals the posse almost caught up with the robbers. In this shot, Porter's camera has simply traversed an undescribed terrain in an exhibition of discontinuous time, and though this was new for the cinema, audiences had little difficulty in adjusting to the premise and grasping the connections. Time and space had undergone cinematic transformation. At last, the motion picture had been liberated from the imposition of theatrical logic and was on its way to experimenting with cinematic associationalism.

Strangely, after having prepared the way for a true cinematic art, Porter went no further in his exploration of filmic structure. Although he continued to experiment in film fantasy, documentary, comedy, and sociological studies his later contributions were to subject matter rather than to form and have not been examined very closely. It is clear, however, that neither Porter nor any of the men who followed him in the next five years produced any significant breakthroughs in the development of narrative expressiveness. When we look at the careers of such pioneers as Edwin Porter, Sigmund Lubin, Wallace McCutcheon, J. Stuart Blackton, G. A. Smith, James Williamson, Cecil Hepworth, and those few others who are only barely remembered, we find practically no films that retain serious claims to our interest (except in the sense that historical curios or primitive antiques remain of value). The medium was still awaiting its seminal genius.

David Wark Griffith began his career as an actor in a Porter film entitled *Rescued from an Eagle's Nest* (1908), a work that shows no sign of any technical advances over those made in *The Great Train Robbery*. Nor, for that matter, does *The Adventures of Dolly*, the first film that Griffith directed, though it is a more interesting work. It does demonstrate, however, that from the start Griffith had some ideas about how to make an ordinary event into a somewhat complex story in order to derive certain melodramatic values—but this is exactly the sort of thinking one would expect from a would-be playwright who was never to overcome his preference for romantic melodrama.

Griffith worked thoughtfully in the film medium, though at first he had no respect for its artistic potential; he even changed his name, perhaps because he was embarrassed by his connection with a popular entertainment medium that had no artistic standing and hoped someday to write a memorable play and return to the theater, where he had suffered a setback. In the meantime, the voracious appetite of the public for more and more films enabled Griffith to try out new techniques amid the frantic pace of a production schedule that is almost incomprehensible today. In his first year he directed more than 140 one-reelers, the equivalent of 20 full-length films. The advantage of such a schedule was that Griffith did not have to feel that he staked himself on any one production. If he had tried something that did not work on Monday, on Thursday he would be working on another film and trying something else. This trial and error method does not account for his genius, of course, but it does explain his rapid development.

In the course of that development, Griffith established the process that became basic to all future cinematic narrative. Prior to Griffith, the cinema had pursued the conventions established by its inventors: films were essentially visual records of movement; whatever passed in front of the camera was duplicated on the screen, and the relationship between the original material and its reproduced image was very clear. The pre-Griffith film could describe the external reality of events very well, especially when the subject matter was artistically arranged by Méliès or presented by Porter as selected scenes within a narrative structure. But what the pre-Griffith film could not do well was to transcend the literalness of each photographed image: ideas were simplistic and motivations were confined to the graphically demonstrable (which explains the facial contortions and the frantic gesturing and arm-flailing in these early films—it was all part of the search for expressiveness).

Griffith's breakthrough consisted in relegating the image (the individual shot) to a predominantly informational level. With Porter, the single shot had become the ideological base of the film. Every shot presented a section of the action: all relevant characterization, plot development, and theme went into one shot until the narrative required a change of scenery; then a similar amount of material was crammed into the next shot. The result was consistent superficiality (though Porter, who has never received much credit for esthetic sensibility, was actually an engrossing filmmaker, humorous on occasion, highly versatile, and capable of truly artistic camera set-ups).

By 1912 Griffith had demonstrated repeatedly that restricting the weight of information conveyed by any particular shot would actually increase the implicit meaning of his new structural unit. That unit, which is now called the sequence, consisted of a related series of shots that could be construed as a separate element of the narrative structure and was usually unified by location or by incident—it was the equivalent of a scene in a stage play. Griffith fragmentized the narrative action because he realized that action presented whole is explicitly descriptive, whereas action fragmented into its constituent parts results in associative implications that almost always go beyond the surface level. Intercutting long shots, medium shots, and close-ups, Griffith provided audiences with pieces of descriptive information. If we look at consecutive shots of a group of soldiers menacing a crowd, then a raised rifle, and then a terrified face, we inevitably make psychological associations regarding the significance of the images. Griffith found that he could control these associations with an infinite range of subtle possibilities by conveying different degrees of both the threat and the terrified reaction. He had discovered the way to depict inner life and abstract ideas—not through the accumulation of diverse materials within a single shot, but through the intellectual associations viewers would make from one shot containing limited specifications to another. Filmmaking became a matter of selecting the best images to film and assembling them in the most coherent and suggestive manner. Film could become a major art form only after it left behind the constraints of descriptive filming, of recording the total reality in the vicinity of the camera. Griffith made the camera an interpreter of reality, not merely a recorder of it, and produced the first masterpieces of narrative film, *The Birth of a Nation* (1915) and *Intolerance* (1916).

At the same time that Griffith had been perfecting his sense of what the shot ought to be, a huge audience had been developing its perceptive capacity, and a great many directors, performers, and cameramen had been working out the techniques of the art. Griffith had brought out the meaningful implications of action by incorporating human responses and attitudes into what, in Porter's work, had merely been portrayals of human activities. After Griffith, virtually every film was to be an *edited* film, conceived in terms of sequences created by the association of shots.

While surprisingly few attempts have been made to rebel against Griffith's procedure (Hitchcock's *Rope* in 1948 is about the only film remembered, though few consider it a successful attempt), a great deal of theoretical discussion has centered on two alternatives to editing: the use of a moving camera and the use of deep-focus photography. In practice, neither process has been found to be a viable substitute for cutting from shot to shot. The theory of non-edited films as it appears in the writings of otherwise excellent critics such as André Bazin probably arose as a reaction to the premises of Sergei Eisenstein. Eisenstein's early films (*Strike,* 1924; *Potemkin,* 1925) and essays seemed to urge a cinema so totally devoted to fitting together short lengths of film that almost the whole weight of the finished product was determined in the editing room. If Griffith and Eisenstein had proved that shots suddenly take on far-reaching implications through their collision with other shots in a sequence, then the most logical argument to offer in opposition seemed to be that the discontinuity of their images, when perceived as fragments of the total scene, created a sense of artificiality. This argument assumes, against historical fact, that Griffith did not alter the nature of the cinema by his discoveries, that the cinema is rooted in its ability to present the illusion of continuous movement, and that this illusion is destroyed by cutting.

Yet what is the real alternative to cutting? It is absolutely misleading to suggest, for example, as many anti-editing theorists do, that in their use of deep focus Renoir and Welles present an effective substitute for Griffith's and Eisenstein's editing. No major director, Renoir and Welles included, relies primarily on deep focus, on expanding the number of elements within a single shot so as to eliminate the need for shifting to other views. Certainly no director avoids the hundreds of shots needed to make his film expressive of all the nuances perceptible only by rigid exclusion of material from the frame. In fact, it was not Renoir or Welles who first made extensive use of deep-focus photography, but Edwin Porter; and it was also Porter who made the moving camera a feature of narrative filming. Porter needed these devices because he had not worked out a means of describing reality in narrative form within the fifteen-minute format of his era. Even with deep focus and moving cameras, Porter was never able to get beyond surfaces, to imply more than was shown on the screen; nor is the illusion of reality as convincing in his work as in Griffith's.

Thus, film has progressed historically along the path that Griffith laid out. In the 1920's the sense of mastering a new medium and harnessing the suggestive power of images through editing no doubt led some film-makers to emphasize that part of their craft. We see evidence of this tendency in the work of not only Griffith and Eisenstein but also Pudov-kin, Pabst, Dupont, Seastrom, Lang, Dreyer, and many others. They produced great films in this style, and yet it is interesting to note that every other director of merit, particularly Chaplin, Stroheim, and Keaton, also produced fully edited films, though they never exploited the extremes of associationalism of shots characteristic of *Intolerance* or *Potemkin*. All filmmakers since Griffith have committed themselves to cutting within the sequence, though the fragmented nature of *Intolerance*, which re-sulted in more than 1700 shots, is far removed in degree from Renoir's *Rules of the Game*, with its 337 shots (which is still an average of only 20 seconds per shot); in any case, these two films are obviously much closer to each other in their editing than to *The Great Train Robbery*, which has only 14 shots.

The introduction of the synchronized-dialogue film in the late 1920's had almost as great an impact on the development of the narrative film as did Griffith's introduction of the sequence. By the early 1930's, the sound film had made the silent film virtually obsolete—which is only an historical evaluation, certainly not an esthetic one. Art is capable of in-finite stages of formal evolution, of structural and thematic change, but unlike technology, art does not advance in qualitative leaps. Once an art develops past the initial stages in the formulation of its conventions and achieves a single example of greatness—that is, from the time of its first "classic"—it can only repeat or modify that formulation, expanding upon it to create other examples of greatness. A great work of art grows out of—and is then absorbed into—the tradition of the medium; all later works can only adapt its conventions or those modifications of its conven-tions that other artists have adapted through the years. Griffith's modifica-tions of Porter's conventions actually *altered* the basic nature of the cinema, which was possible at that moment in history because the cinema had not reached a significant plateau in the development of its artistic capacities. But after an impressive tradition of classic silent films, begin-ning with *The Birth of a Nation* and *Intolerance* and including such works as *The Cabinet of Dr. Caligari*, *The Gold Rush*, *The General*, *Greed*, *Mother*, *Potemkin*, *The Last Laugh*, *The Passion of Joan of Arc*, and dozens of others, the introduction of synchronized sound, revolutionary as it was, did not lead to a total revision of the essential nature of the classic cinema.

Sound did force many modifications: it changed the emphasis a great deal, so that the visual portion, which in silent films had merely been interrupted by insert titles to indicate dialogue, now had to accommodate spoken dialogue as a partner in the communication of the film's meaning. The discontinuity of the film image jarred somewhat with human speech, because language communicates through logical connections and is therefore primarily continuous. It took a number of experiments to discover how to harmonize discontinuous visual images with coherent dialogue, but it did not take as long as some textbooks imply; in the early 1930's several major directors of the silent era, including René Clair, Ernst Lubitsch, John Ford, and Alfred Hitchcock, worked out a variety of solutions for continuing the narrative tradition in its newly modified form. One of the most brilliant explorations of the possibilities of the sound film was Fritz Lang's *M* (1931), which, in its virtuoso handling of background sounds and of synchronized, asynchronized, and voice-over dialogue, as well as its incredibly suggestive use of silence, delineated all the meaningful variations still being experimented with today.

The impressive number of memorable silent films may cause us to forget that only fifteen years or so elapsed between *The Birth of a Nation* and the virtual end of the silent era; it is similarly remarkable that after only fifteen more years the sound film itself was thoroughly modified. At the end of the Second World War, the cinematic tradition again underwent crucial changes, but this time more in content than in form. The rise of the Italian cinema to its current artistic prominence began when it placed a new emphasis on the predicaments of ordinary people: in a film like Vittorio De Sica's *The Bicycle Thief* (1948), the story was so totally devoid of glamor and high adventure that it posed a challenge to the then-leading international industry in Hollywood, the "glamor capital," the "dream machine." The new realism became fashionable in all countries and in Hollywood too, and though the style was modified after a few years, it left its impact on future filming in at least two ways: it educated the public to demand films that dealt with social themes, films about people on the fringes of society, and films that criticized the institutions and structures of the modern world; and it also led to a new development in cinematic form.

This development was essentially a breaking away from the typical cinematic plotting found in a dramatic structure such as that of Ingmar Bergman's *The Seventh Seal* (1956) or in a suspense-story format such as that of Alfred Hitchcock's *Vertigo* (1958). The best-known representatives of this new style of plotting, François Truffaut, Jean-Luc Godard, and Michelangelo Antonioni, frequently derive whatever plot there is from the general condition of their characters. In Antonioni's *The Red Desert* (1964), the plot develops out of the neurotic psychological state of the central character: her feelings even seem capable of influencing the décor as recorded by the camera, since the colors of the walls change to reflect her perceptions of reality. Bergman and Hitchcock themselves contributed to the dissolution of the audience's customary plot expectations in such works as *Persona* (1966) and *The Birds* (1963).

Once the audience had acclimated itself to the kind of cinema in which the situation could seem either formless or arbitrarily imposed (but in both cases neither conventional nor Aristotelian), filmmakers were encouraged to depart from the classic cinema's usual clear delineation between the real and the unreal. Bergman's *The Seventh Seal*, in spite of its controlled dramatic plot, was a blending of the naturalistic level of imagery with representations of the imagination that was relatively rare in the 1950's. But in the 1960's, the willingness of the audience to accept or at least to tolerate new styles and structures allowed many filmmakers to combine fantasy and realism. Buñuel in *Simon of the Desert, Belle de Jour,* and *The Milky Way;* Fellini in *8½, Juliet of the Spirits,* and *Satyricon;* Antonioni in *Zabriskie Point;* Pasolini in *Teorema;* Bergman in *Hour of the Wolf;* and many others. Ironically, but logically, the success of postwar Italian neorealism exerted an influence on cinema to move beyond the real and to accommodate the imaginative experience within the realm of the ordinary.

Obviously, there are other ways of looking at the historical development of the cinema than by viewing it in terms of the classic tradition. One could concentrate on style, content, genres, characteristics of different national film industries, or cultural patterns as reflected in films. However, any historical evaluation of the narrative cinema must acknowledge the relationship of each film to the larger tradition, both to the works that followed and to those that preceded. A classic film is produced not only from the inner resources of a great artist and his collaborators but from their comprehension of the traditions of the art form. To reject or modify artistic conventions requires a profound knowledge of the previous uses of those conventions. The study of film, then, does call for a sense of historical perspective, a capacity to see change in its relationship to a tradition. In fact, change frequently serves to clarify the tradition: we often discover that those elements superseded by the new were less vital than they once appeared, whereas those that survive in the face of continuous development do so because they have become essential to the very nature of the classic cinema.

GRIFFITH

INTOLERANCE

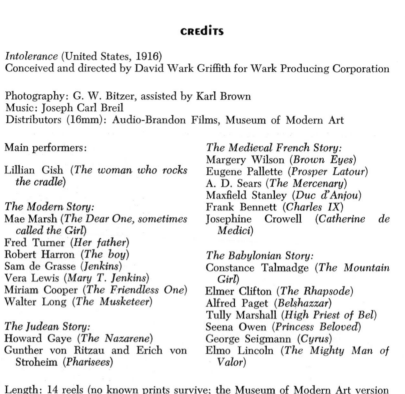

CREDITS

Intolerance (United States, 1916)
Conceived and directed by David Wark Griffith for Wark Producing Corporation

Photography: G. W. Bitzer, assisted by Karl Brown
Music: Joseph Carl Breil
Distributors (16mm): Audio-Brandon Films, Museum of Modern Art

Main performers:

Lillian Gish (*The woman who rocks the cradle*)

The Modern Story:
Mae Marsh (*The Dear One, sometimes called the Girl*)
Fred Turner (*Her father*)
Robert Harron (*The boy*)
Sam de Grasse (*Jenkins*)
Vera Lewis (*Mary T. Jenkins*)
Miriam Cooper (*The Friendless One*)
Walter Long (*The Musketeer*)

The Judean Story:
Howard Gaye (*The Nazarene*)
Gunther von Ritzau and Erich von Stroheim (*Pharisees*)

The Medieval French Story:
Margery Wilson (*Brown Eyes*)
Eugene Pallette (*Prosper Latour*)
A. D. Sears (*The Mercenary*)
Maxfield Stanley (*Duc d'Anjou*)
Frank Bennett (*Charles IX*)
Josephine Crowell (*Catherine de Medici*)

The Babylonian Story:
Constance Talmadge (*The Mountain Girl*)
Elmer Clifton (*The Rhapsode*)
Alfred Paget (*Belshazzar*)
Tully Marshall (*High Priest of Bel*)
Seena Owen (*Princess Beloved*)
George Seigmann (*Cyrus*)
Elmo Lincoln (*The Mighty Man of Valor*)

Length: 14 reels (no known prints survive; the Museum of Modern Art version consists of 13 reels with 1,716 shots, not including insert titles)

The current revival of interest in D. W. Griffith attests to a desire on the part of critics and historians to rescue the world's first great filmmaker from his own reputation of greatness. Paradoxically, Griffith has suffered as a film artist to the same extent that he has been exalted as a film pioneer. His position as the "father" of narrative cinematic technique has for nearly fifty years obscured his enduring importance as a creator of great films. Audiences, aware of the respect owed him as the originator of one cinematic device or another, have sometimes looked at his films as one looks at primitive artifacts in a museum. Furthermore, like all old films, Griffith's works display the surface styles (dress, cars, occupations, and so on) of an outmoded era as well as the superficial cultural interests of a remote time with its fashionable ideals, dated social concerns, and standardized plots. As a result, Griffith's films fell into neglect for a number of years, until a new generation of moviegoers, not overawed by Griffith's reputation and able to overlook the "old-fashioned" aspects of his films, began to rediscover the artistry and emotional power of the films themselves.

Although never as popular or as controversial as *The Birth of a Nation* (1915), *Intolerance* has gradually attained the eminence of that earlier Griffith masterpiece. In its scope and intellectual complexity, *Intolerance* is the greater achievement; it remains the most ambitious film concept ever attempted and perhaps the grandest spectacle ever achieved. Tracing the pervasive evils of narrow-mindedness and the tyrannical exercise of power (two related themes that Griffith unites under his dubious title) in four different periods of history—ancient Babylon, Judea at the time of Jesus, France in 1572, and contemporary America—Griffith confounded his original audiences by presenting much more than they could comfortably absorb in one sitting. The adverse criticism and commercial failure of the film forced him to curb his contending inclinations toward the mammoth assemblage of details and the embodiment of abstract ideas so that for the rest of his career, even in his later epics, such as *Orphans of the Storm* (1921) and *America* (1924), he scaled his material down to manageable proportions. So varied were his talents that he readily excelled at the opposite kind of film too: the domestic or rural drama, for example *True Heart Susie* (1919), *Broken Blossoms* (1919), and *The Love Flower* (1920). Even in longer films like *Way Down East* (1920) and *Hearts of the World* (1918), Griffith focused primarily on human conflicts rather than returning to the dramatization of cultural and social conflicts that make *Intolerance* so memorable an accomplishment.

Despite all its spectacle, *Intolerance* resembles his later films in its method of concentrating not on the history of an era, but on the problems and emotions of ordinary individuals who reflect the values and attitudes of their culture. Griffith's procedure of parallel editing enables him to combine the human element with the massive sweep of an historical movement; as we watch the Persian assault on the walls of Babylon or the massacre of the innocents on St. Bartholomew's Day, for example, we are always aware of a particular individual's gallant struggle to stand against the dehumanizing forces of his age. Parallel editing functions as a unifying stylistic device, not only among the four stories but also within each particular story. As we move back and forth between the general and the particular, one element illuminates the other. The meaning of the destruction of Babylon is made intelligible on the human level by the Mountain Girl's loyal but futile defense of her prince and the mutual sacrifice of the prince and princess; at the same time, the huge cast and the stupendous set allow Griffith to convey the general sense of a cultural disaster.

Intolerance is a flawed film. Its commercial failure cannot be attributed solely to the fact that it demanded too much from the mass audience of its day. The film's diffuseness and intricacy would bring almost any large audience in any age to emotional and intellectual satiety: while we are still assimilating one part, the film plunges us into another; and when we finally do comprehend the broad outlines of the whole, Griffith disperses our sympathies in different directions over situations of unequal significance. Still the film seems better on repeated viewings, but it always requires much more from the spectator than three hours of passive indulgence. *Intolerance* sometimes stimulates and sometimes irritates, but it never slows down, and finally it remains in the imagination as one of the great visual experiences of the classic cinema.

The Scope of Intolerance

IRIS BARRY and EILEEN BOWSER

Before *The Birth of a Nation* was released Griffith had almost completed a new picture, *The Mother and the Law,* a modern story which bleakly revealed the wrongs inflicted by a pious factory owner on his employees and the injustices of which the law may sometimes be capable. Suddenly the new picture seemed to him an insufficiently violent attack on prejudice and cruelty, so that he decided to weave in with his modern story three parallel stories of injustice and prejudice in other ages and so make of the film an epic sermon. The slums of today, sixteenth-century France, ancient Babylon and Calvary itself should speak of the evil which the self-righteous have perpetrated through the centuries. He flung up sets of a size hitherto unimagined, hired players by the hundreds, shot miles of film. Into this gigantic undertaking poured his profits from *The Birth of a Nation.* His employees were aghast when he ordered them to construct walls so broad that an army could march round the tops of them, palace halls so vast that the crowds in them were reduced to antlike proportions. Hollywood rang with rumors. The film was two years in the making, yet out of all this footage, extravagance and passion emerged a film of unmistakable greatness and originality called *Intolerance.*

The film *Intolerance* is of extreme importance in the history of the cinema. It is the end and justification of that whole school of American cinematography based on the terse cutting and disjunctive assembly of lengths of film, which began with *The Great Train Robbery* and culminated in *The Birth of a Nation* and in this. All the old and many new technical devices are employed in it—brief, enormous close-ups not only of faces but of hands and of objects; the "eye-opener" focus to introduce vast panoramas; the use of only part of the screen's area for certain shots; camera angles and tracking shots such as are commonly supposed to have been introduced by German producers years later; and rapid crosscutting the like of which was not seen again until *Potemkin.*

The sociological implications of the modern episode seem, perhaps, more pointed now than they did in 1916. They undoubtedly account for the fact that Lenin early in 1919 arranged to have *Intolerance* toured throughout the U.S.S.R., where it ran almost continuously for ten years. The film was not merely seen there; it was also used as study material for

FROM *D. W. Griffith: American Film Master* by Iris Barry, with an annotated list of films by Eileen Bowser, pp. 23–27, 50–51. Copyright © 1940, 1965 by The Museum of Modern Art. All rights reserved. Reprinted by permission of The Museum of Modern Art. Footnotes have been deleted.

the post-revolutionary school of cinematography, and exercised a pro-found influence on the work of men like Eisenstein and Pudovkin. It is true that Griffith is largely instinctive in his methods where the Russian directors are deliberate and organized; but it was nevertheless in large measure from his example that they derived their characteristic staccato shots, their measured and accelerated rhythms and their skill in joining pictorial images together with a view to the emotional overtones of each, so that two images in conjunction convey more than the sum of their visible content.

The scale and sumptuousness of *Judith of Bethulia* and of *Intolerance* profoundly affected filmmaking everywhere. At home, they undoubtedly influenced Cecil B. De Mille, whose name later became synonymous with glittering spectacles. In France, the effect of Griffith's work at this period can be traced in the later productions of Abel Gance, and in Germany in those of Fritz Lang. He had conferred both magnitude and complexity as well as expressiveness on the motion pictures and, in Europe and America alike, all the most ambitious films of the 1920s reflected his influence and followed his example.

Though *Intolerance* has been revived time and again, especially in Europe, unlike *The Birth of a Nation* it was not a great popular success. Audiences find it bewildering, exhausting. There is so much in it; there is too much of it; the pace increases so relentlessly; its intense hail of images—many of them only five frames long—cruelly hammers the sensibility; its climax is near hysteria. No question but that the film is chaotic, difficult to take in, or that it has many evident faults. The desire to instruct and to reform obtrudes awkwardly at times. The lyricism of the subtitles accords oddly with the footnotes appended to them. The Biblical sequence is weak, though useful dramatically to point up the modern sequence. The French episode seems to get lost, then reappears surprisingly.

Of the Babylonian and the modern episodes little adverse criticism is permissible, and only admiration remains for the last two reels, when the climax of all four stories approaches and history itself seems to pour like a cataract across the screen. In his direction of the immense crowd scenes, Griffith achieves the impossible, for—despite their profusion and breathtaking scale—the eye is not distracted, it is irresistibly drawn to the one significant detail. The handling of the actors in intimate scenes has hardly been equaled either for depth or for humanity, particularly in the modern sequence and most notably—where a last-minute rescue again serves him well—with Miriam Cooper and Mae Marsh racing to the prison as Robert Harron approaches the gallows. This searching realism, this pulsing life comes not only from Griffith's power to mould his players but, in equal measure, from his editorial skill.

The American film industry by now was passing out of the era of small enterprises and quick individual profits into that of high finance and corporate endeavor. Griffith was not a businessman and he was wholly an individualist. For the future he would often be operating under difficulties. But for the moment the United States was preparing to enter the European war. J. Stuart Blackton's pro-war and anti-German *The Battle Cry of Peace* and Thomas Ince's anti-war and anti-German *Civilization* had already indicated the uses to which films might be put and now it was the moment for propaganda for the Allied cause.

The following notes by Eileen Bowser supplement Miss Barry's comments.

A separate company, formed to finance and distribute *Intolerance,* was incorporated in December 1915 with the name of the Wark Producing Corporation. Because the handful of investors in Epoch got rich, many were eager to invest in the new company. Griffith was the largest single investor, but there were nearly fifty others, including Harry and Roy Aitken, Lillian Gish and Mae Marsh. Wark went bankrupt in 1921. Griffith "lent" the company money during 1922–23 to help pay off its debts, enabling him to retain all the rights to *Intolerance.*

In addition to *Intolerance,* Wark distributed the two films that were later cut from it, *The Mother and the Law* and *The Fall of Babylon.* Griffith had thought of this way to recoup money as soon as he realized that *Intolerance* was not a box office success. In August 1917 he cabled instructions from London to "Preserve all *Intolerance* discards perhaps may use in separate stories later." More money had to be poured into Wark to pay for the exploitation of the two films, and little if any profit remained.

The Los Angeles fire department ordered immediate dismantling of the giant *Intolerance* sets in 1916, no doubt because they were not built in accordance with the local building code. Incredibly, these sets had been built without any architectural plans—they just grew from day to day as Griffith had new ideas and told his carpenters what he wanted. Griffith managed to delay the job of dismantling them until the fall of 1917, but they were so solidly built that parts of them survived on back lots of Hollywood many years later.

The problem of finding a complete archival print of *Intolerance* is compounded by the fact that late in 1918 the original negative was cut to make the negatives for two separate films, *The Fall of Babylon* and *The Mother and the Law.* In December 1919, when a print of *Intolerance* was needed to fulfill a contract in Brazil, the studio reported that there were no good copies on hand and that none could be printed because the negative no longer existed in its original form. The negatives for *The Fall of Babylon,* and *The Mother and the Law* were needed to fill other orders. In order to avoid a threatened lawsuit, a patched-up used print of *Intolerance* was supplied to Brazil. Griffith later tried to restore the *Intol-*

erance negative, but it was never as long as the original. It has been estimated from the running time that *Intolerance* was about 13,500 or 13,700 feet at the time it opened, though Lillian Gish remembers seeing an earlier four-hour version. Prints ordered to fill foreign contracts during the 1920s averaged fewer than twelve reels, while prints supplied to London in 1922 only amounted to ten-and-one-half reels. The remaining negatives and prints were acquired by the Film Library in 1938. Using a combination of materials, the Film Library now has a preservation copy, not to be projected but preserved as an archive copy, measuring 11,811 feet, including an introductory title attached to it. We cannot know if in the climax the incredibly swift cutting and rhythmic pace is just as it was in the 1916 version, but it remains a powerful experience.

There never existed a written script for the film; it was all in Griffith's head. He tried to reconstruct good prints for the 1926 and 1933 revivals, but they were also short versions. His mental picture of the film probably changed in seventeen years—just as he had changed. Griffith never stopped trying to improve his films. As Paul Valéry said: "A work of art is never completed, but merely abandoned," and instead of completing his films, Griffith eventually abandoned them.

The hazards of filming on such a large scale were recalled by Griffith in his 1933 radio series. He described the pre-dawn hours of the day scheduled for filming the Fall of Babylon sequence, with some 15,000 people and 250 chariots on call. The sun alone was to be the source of light. The weather bureau had been checked, but in addition a half-dozen men were stationed sixty miles apart to report by telephone on a fog bank that was progressing in the direction of the location. On its fate depended 15,000 salary checks and 15,000 box lunches and a thousand other details. Before daylight Griffith gave the order to proceed to location, and the scene was filmed just before the fog arrived.

Griffith at Work

LILLIAN GISH

Mr. Griffith hurled himself into the making of *Intolerance* with incredible energy and concentration. Again he did all the research himself, although he often discussed the source material with "Daddy" Woods. His encyclopedic mind had always filled me with awe, but the knowledge he called on during the filming of *Intolerance* was simply staggering.

Once again everyone became absorbed in history—Babylonian, French, and, of course, biblical. One of the dancers in *Intolerance* was Carmel Meyers, whose father, Rabbi Meyers, helped with the biblical research. Mr. Griffith knew the Bible well, but it was his habit to use people as a sounding board. He talked to all of us, and we often came up with sound ideas.

As always, Mr. Griffith worked without a script. We all helped compose the subtitles.

. . .

A small village of shacks and tents on a vacant lot across the street from our studio provided housing for construction workers and extras. Railroad tracks were laid to reach the huge main gate to the walled city of Babylon. Freight cars from two railways brought in food and building supplies, as well as horses and elephants. Mr. Griffith raised the pay of extras to $2 a day plus a 60-cent free lunch, which was a new high for the industry.

. . .

A few weeks later, passers-by halted and stared in disbelief. Above them rose a huge network of scaffolding. Gradually in the following days the outline of an immense walled city took shape, reaching skyward until the extraordinary set was visible for miles around.

The immense, opulent Babylonian set was unlike anything that had ever been constructed for movies. The walls enclosing the court of Belshazzar were over 200 feet high. The court, which was approached by numerous steps, was flanked by two colonnades supporting columns fifty feet high, each column in turn supporting a great statue of the elephant god erect on his hind legs. Behind the court were towers and ramparts 200 feet high, their crests planted with flowering shrubs and trees to represent the famed hanging gardens. The set was studded with rows of rosettes, rich entab-

FROM the book *Lillian Gish: The Movies, Mr. Griffith, and Me* by Lillian Gish with Ann Pinchot, pp. 168–77. © 1969 by Lillian Gish and Ann Pinchot. Published by Prentice-Hall, Inc., Englewood Cliffs, New Jersey.

latures, huge torchères, finials, tiled fretwork, and bas-reliefs of winged deities, lions, and bulls.

The east wall of the Babylon set was three-quarters of a mile away from the main camera. The tops of the walls were as wide as roads, enough for two chariots to pass each other at top speed. . . .

As the sets grew in magnitude, Allan Dwan, one of the assistant directors on *Intolerance,* as well as director for many of the other films being made at the studio, said to Mr. Griffith: "You've bitten off one hell of a chunk. How are you going to get actors to dominate all this magnificence?"

"If it's good," Mr. Griffith answered with a wry smile, "you'll be doing it yourself next year."

Mr. Griffith designed and was responsible for many of the costumes. He worked particularly hard on the Babylonian ones. Whenever there was a break in his schedule, he would have the players model the costumes. If he had fifteen minutes after lunch before he was due back on the set or a little time in the evening, he would say to one of his acting company: "Get into that costume. I want to see it."

Then he would call in Billy Bitzer or "Daddy" Woods or whoever happened to be nearby and ask: "What do you think? Do you like this headdress? Is it too high—too dark, perhaps? How will it photograph?"

In the Babylonian period young girls went into the Temple of Sacred Fire, and as their contribution to the love goddess Ishtar each one gave herself to a man who came to the temple to worship. Mr. Griffith wanted to show these young virgins in costumes that would be seductive yet in no way offensive. All the young girls—among them Mildred Harris, who was to be Charlie Chaplin's first wife—were dressed in floating chiffons and photographed in a fountain, not dancing but moving rhythmically and sensually to music. Some of the scenes were shot through veiling or fountain sprays to add to the erotic yet poetic effect.

. . .

To heighten the tragedy of the fall of Babylon, Mr. Griffith created the story of the Mountain Girl, who falls in love with the King and tries to save him. A Brooklyn girl, Constance Talmadge, played the part. A natural comedienne, she was the youngest of the three Talmadge girls— Norma and Natalie were the other two—who, guided by their staunch mother, were to achieve film fame. Constance's carefree, fun-loving nature made her the pet of the studio.

Mr. Griffith wanted Constance's costume to look as if it were made of whatever stuff would be available to her in her mountain lair. The homespun fabric was rough and the weather hot, and during the long delays between shots Constance sometimes took off the pads that made her figure more womanly. Often by the time she was called before the camera, she had forgotten them completely.

"If you please, Miss Constance," Mr. Griffith would say, "half of your figure is missing again. Do you think I want a lopsided heroine?"

She would forget where she had left the pads, and we would all go in search of Constance's figure.

. . .

Two major scenes highlighted the Babylonian episode—the feast of Belshazzar and the fall of the city to Cyrus. For the feast, more than 4,000 extras in costume filled the immense court and its ramparts. Hundreds of dancers, led by Gertrude Bambrick, opened the great feast. Three bands, placed strategically about the quarter-mile set, played for the dancers. Among the Denishawn-trained dancers was Carol Dempster, who was later to appear in films as a Griffith heroine.

Mr. Griffith was no longer satisfied with the technique he had used in directing *The Birth* crowd scenes. As in *The Birth*, he used a megaphone to reach his lieutenants in the field and worked out a set of signals, this time with his megaphone, for the others, who were half a mile away. But for this film he decided against directing from a stationary tower. He wanted the camera to record every detail of the fantastic scene, so he installed Billy in a balloon that could be raised or lowered. But the wind played havoc with Billy's attempts to keep within the limits of the set, so Mr. Griffith came up with another idea. He put the camera on a rope-manipulated elevator—with a platform large enough to hold himself, Billy, and me sitting with feet hanging over to take up less room—and placed the entire contraption on tracks that ran deep into the set.

. . .

Billy was called "Eagle Eye" because his camera could see far beyond the range of the human eye. In a later scene, during which the King drives his chariot on top of the wall surrounding the city, one sees from a mile away the busy life of the city. The distant city, as well as the foreground action of the King in his chariot, is in focus. Yet this vista was not superimposed, as audiences might think; one camera photographed both scenes.

For the siege of Babylon, one of the largest scenes ever staged, Mr. Griffith filled the screen with mass shots of Cyrus' army. During the shooting of this sequence, word went out that Mr. Griffith would pay an additional $5 to any extra who would jump off the wall. There were nets below to catch the jumpers, of course. When the camera began grinding again, all the extras started leaping from the parapets.

"Stop those crazy fools!" Mr. Griffith ordered. "I haven't enough nets—or enough money."

There were always ambulances, a nurse, and a doctor on the set, but apart from minor injuries no mishaps or casualties occurred. Credit for this extraordinary safety record goes to Mr. Griffith, who had everything so well organized that no one became excited or confused about what was expected of him.

During the shooting of the mass scenes, everyone on the lot, including actors from other productions, blended into the mob. After all, this looked like an important "first" by the director who was by then God of Hollywood.

Next in magnitude came the court scenes in the palace of Catherine de Medici. It was there that Mr. Griffith used ceiling shots for the first time. Sets generally do not have ceilings, but Mr. Griffith wanted to show the magnificent ceiling of the throne room and had Billy shoot up at it. This technique later won acclaim for Orson Welles in *Citizen Kane,* long after Mr. Griffith had discarded shooting from the floor.

.   .   .

My role as the Eternal Mother took less than an hour to film. Nevertheless, I was closer to *Intolerance* than anyone else except Billy Bitzer and Jimmy Smith, the cutter. I felt that there was more of me in this picture than in any other I had ever played in. Perhaps because I wasn't acting a long role, Mr. Griffith took me into his confidence as never before, talking over scenes before he filmed them, having me watch all the rushes, even accepting some of my ideas. He sent me to the darkroom to pick the best takes and to help Jimmy with the cutting. At night, as I watched the day's rushes, I saw the film take shape and marveled at what Mr. Griffith was creating.

Every week overwhelming effects poured from the darkroom. Some of the scenes were shot in startling shapes: triangles; diamonds; diagonals; frieze-like panels that blocked out all but a long thin strip of the film; and semicircles that opened like fans. In the shots of the virgins in the Temple of Sacred Fire, the impression of sensual motion was reinforced by having the camera turn from left to right and back again, and also by having the screen frame close in, then move out, then in again. Small iris shots opened to reveal huge panoramas. Other shots contained double and triple exposures. There were huge closeups of only the lower half of Miriam Cooper's face or of only Margery Wilson's eyes.

The lighting effects were equally dramatic. The contrasts extended from Babylon under a brilliant glaring sun to the darkened backstreets of Paris, where moonlight washed the cobblestones. Mr. Griffith used tinted film for parts of each story, to intensify emotional impact. Night scenes were blue; the Babylonian night battle scenes were red; the French court was amber. But the principal source of light was the sun. For the shot of me at the cradle, the set was darkened, and sunlight poured through a hole in the roof. Perhaps his extensive use of sunlight suggested to his mind the subtitle of the film, *A Sun Play of the Ages.*

The intricate interweaving of plots in *Intolerance* and its astounding length, which began to run into hundreds of reels, demanded the concentration and decision making that could have gone into thirty or forty films. Yet Mr. Griffith continued to work without notes or script, and, in the months it took to make that gigantic film, he continued to supervise other films that Triangle produced. With the burden of so many smaller films, Mr. Griffith took more than twenty months to complete *Intolerance*. Left free, he could no doubt have finished it in six.

The true power and magnificence of *Intolerance* came not from its size but from the cutting and editing of the negative. Mr. Griffith worked on every foot of film, slicing each scene to the core of its drama, joining the sequences in amazing harmony. The picture began with the modern story; then, after a transitional shot of me rocking the cradle, the camera moved back through centuries to focus on the massive gate of Babylon, then wandered through the gate into the crowded alleyways. Once the stories were all introduced, time spent on each segment was shorter. The scenes gained momentum, as the camera shifted freely from the modern factory to the wedding at Cana, from the parapets of Babylon to the Medici court. Each story was in itself a miracle of parallel action and cross-cutting. In the swift, overpowering climax, the four stories mingled in "one mighty river of emotion," to use his own words, as short, staccato shots from each story exploded across the screen: the Mountain Girl racing to warn King Belshazzar; the first bloodletting in Paris; the Dear One hurrying to obtain a pardon for her innocent husband; Christ on the road to Calvary. At the breathless climax some of the shots were mere flashes, each hardly perceived, as the succession of pictures pelted the viewer: the fall of Babylon, the Crucifixion, the massacre, the Boy saved from the scaffold seconds before the trap was to be sprung.

Like all Mr. Griffith's films, *Intolerance* was rich in unforgettable moments: the closeup of Mae Marsh's anguished hands as she hears her husband's death sentence; the knives in the hands of the executioners, ready to cut the ropes that will plunge the young husband to his death; the death of the Mountain Girl; Cyrus' warriors galloping toward Babylon; the tiny chariot with its white doves.

Never had Mr. Griffith's technique been so fresh and resourceful. Again and again the film leaves the viewer with an after-image that does not fade but continues to intrigue the mind, keeping alive the emotions he experienced originally in seeing the film. Mr. Griffith could arouse a sense of horror in the viewer and then make him weep with tenderness. In *Intolerance* his genius reached its fullest expression.

When Mr. Griffith finished editing *Intolerance,* it ran approximately eight hours. He planned to exhibit it in two parts, each a four-hour section, on two consecutive nights.

The dimensions of this film have never been equaled. When the exhibitors who were going to show *Intolerance* heard of its length they refused to handle it, and by that time they were in a position to dictate what they would or would not book. Although Mr. Griffith had ignored similar objections when he introduced the two-, four-, five-, and twelve-reel films, this time, unfortunately, he listened.

He was advised to cut the film to one evening's entertainment. He should have ignored the advice. His own instinct was right. Success or failure, *Intolerance* was his monument, the measure of the man himself. But the exhibitors won. The public was never shown *Intolerance* in its entirety.

Technique in *Intolerance*

LEWIS JACOBS

Profound though its theme is, the commanding feature of *Intolerance* is its internal organization. Years ahead of its time (it was to become a major influence on the Soviet school of directors), *Intolerance* surpassed even *The Birth of a Nation*. The comparatively simple editing pattern of the latter film, based on one single event and story related in time and space, was in *Intolerance* expanded into a complex form with four movements, all progressing simultaneously. The film cuts freely from period to period as the theme of intolerance in each is developed. Episode is paralleled with episode. With bold, staccato cutting, Griffith interweaves the motifs of Christ struggling toward Calvary, the Babylonian mountain girl speeding to warn Belshazzar that his priests have betrayed him, the massacre on St. Bartholomew's Day by the French mercenaries, and Dear One rushing frantically to save her husband at the gallows.

These passages are vividly motivated by every means Griffith had at his disposal. A shot is cut before the completion of its action; the moving camera parallels and reinforces a movement; iris and masks are used to

FROM Lewis Jacobs, *The Rise of the American Film: A Critical History with an Essay,* "*Experimental Cinema in America, 1921–1947*" (New York: Teachers College Press, 1968; copyright 1939, 1947, 1967 by Lewis Jacobs), pp. 191–92, 197–99. Reprinted by permission of the publisher. Footnotes have been deleted.

emphasize a significant detail or eloquently effect a transition; large detail close-ups and extreme long shots produce effects of intensity and vastness. All these camera devices are brought into play to create a rich and varied film which flows in unbroken and mounting suspense until the end. Here, as in *The Birth of a Nation,* an underlying movement creates a rhythmic beat, which increases in frequency as the four climaxes approach. There is not a moment, not a shot, that is not controlled, timed, and selected for what it means and adds to the whole.

In the climactic sequences, particularly, is Griffith's artistry supreme. Here all the opulent details of the lavish scenes are subjected to an unceasing movement, action follows action, and none is ever allowed to terminate as the rhythm sweeps along. Christ is seen toiling up Mount Calvary; the Babylonian mountain girl is racing to warn her king of the onrushing enemy; the Huguenot is fighting his way through the streets to rescue his sweetheart from the mercenaries; the wife is speeding in an automobile to the prison, with a pardon for her husband who is about to be hung.

Images whirl across the screen, startling the spectator with their pace and holding him spellbound by their profusion, rhythm, suspense. They are a visual symphony, swelling steadily until the final moment when all the movements are brought together in a grand finale. As Iris Barry wrote of these passages, "History itself seems to pour like a cataract across the screen."

.   .   .

As in its cutting, so in its details *Intolerance* had impressive originality. Huge close-ups of faces, hands, objects, are used imaginatively and eloquently to comment upon, interpret, and deepen the import of the scene, so that dependence upon pantomime is minimized. A celebrated instance is the huge close-up of the clasped hands of Mae Marsh, suggesting her anguish during the trial of her husband. Camera angles are used to intensify the psychological impact: the extreme long shot of the industrialist alone in his office (lord of his domain) characterized him better than any action, incident, or subtitle. The handling of crowds as organized units in movement, as in the firing of the militia or in the notable Babylonian sequences, heightened the dramatic intensity of such scenes. The deliberate use of artificial sky above the onrushing Persian chariots gave the panorama great depth and massiveness, heightening the sense of impending doom as no natural sky could have done, and incidentally introducing to film technique the "process shot."

The singling out of significant action on one part of the screen by lights, irises, or masks—examples of which appeared in almost every sequence—indicated Griffith's sensitive regard for the apt image. With admirable ease, he cuts daringly into the square shape of the screen and blocks out whole sections, sometimes leaving them blocked out for the duration of the scene, sometimes opening the frame to its size. But whether he uses it closed in or opened out, he rarely uses the same shape twice in succession, but contrasts them so that the eye of the spectator is kept moving. For example, if the screen opens in a semi-circle from the lower right-hand corner to the upper-left, as in the opening mass scene of Babylon, the next time, the screen opens in a semi-circle from the upper left-hand corner, then opens out and down diagonally to the lower right.

This dramatic "framing" of the image throughout the film is done with a variety and skill that has rarely been equaled. The screen is sliced down the center revealing only the middle (the great wall of Babylon), then opens out. The screen is cut across diagonally, sometimes from upper left to lower right, sometimes from upper right to lower left. Details are thus brought to our attention and yet kept part of the larger scene itself in a more precise way than the use of close-up insertions could afford. This movement and variety of screen shapes keep the image ever-fresh and vital and heighten the momentum of the whole.

If the "framing" of the screen is remarkable, no less so is the fluid and active participation of the camera. Its physical capacities for movement and dramatic angle—generally conceded to be the original contributions of the post-war German craftsmen—must have strained to the taxing point whatever was known then of camera grace and flexibility. Yet there is never a sense of striving for sheer mechanical wonder, but always a subordination of such capabilities to the subject and the point to be made. The unceasing use of the camera to drain everything that is significant out of the scene, accounts in no small measure for the overwhelming sense of lavishness and opulence that is so impressive to all. For example, we are shown the court of France, 1572, first from an extreme long-shot. The camera is stationary for a few moments as we take in the elaborate scene; then the camera begins slowly to "truck" into the court, moving in on King Charles receiving on his throne; then the camera "pans" to the right around the crowded room to pause on the Prince-Heir, who, incidentally, is portrayed as a decadent fop with a realism worthy of von Stroheim. Later in the film, in the marriage market of ancient Jerusalem, the camera "pans" to the right, showing the painted women framed in a diagonal strip across the screen from lower left to upper right. Again, in the Temple of Sacred Fire in Babylon, the camera plays caressingly over the white nudeness of erotic and sensual women clothed in flimsy chiffons, beflowered and be-jeweled, by "panning" from right to left, then from left to right; then the screen frame closes in, then moves out, and in again with marvelous facility.

More spectacular than any of these devices, however, was the remarkable "trucking" camera shot which traveled, without a pause or a cut, hundreds of feet from an extreme distant view of the entire grandeur of ancient Babylon to a huge close-up of the scene itself. This shot, embracing immense sets, thousands of people and animals, was unprecedented and is still an amazing piece of camera bravura.

The Modern Story in *Intolerance*

PAUL O'DELL

The first story to appear in *Intolerance* is the Modern Story. . . . This was originally planned and filmed as a separate picture called *The Mother and the Law* and Griffith had almost completed it when he decided to incorporate it into a much bigger and expansive plea against intolerance of various kinds. This story, based on true events drawn from two contemporary sources,* deals mainly with social intolerance, the miscarriage of justice and class-hatred.

At first we see a group of ladies who, because of their self-realised inability to share the youthful enjoyment with which they find themselves surrounded, propose to dedicate themselves to the abolition of pleasure and diversion in the community in an attempt to reduce the people to their own idea of respectability. In order to make this effective, they need funds, and they approach Mary Jenkins, unmarried sister of a rich and influential industrialist. We see her at a party she is giving, entertaining young men who continually prefer the company of girls their own age rather than Miss Jenkins herself. Her deeply-felt isolation from "the

FROM *Griffith and the Rise of Hollywood* (1970) by Paul O'Dell. Reprinted by permission of A. S. Barnes & Co., Inc.

* The Federal Industrial Commission, in an official report, cited a chemical factory combine, under the control of a man "fervid in charity and zealous in ecclesiastical activities" whose practice it was to pour his companies' profits into charities while keeping his employees' wages at $1.60 a day. A request, subsequently refused, of a rise to $2.00 a day led to a full scale strike, which was brought to a halt only with the co-operation of "deputy sheriffs" and "constables" and at the cost of the lives of no less than nineteen of the strikers. The Steilow murder case, in which an innocent man was actually brought to the electric chair, provided Griffith with the germ of the second idea in the Modern Story of *Intolerance*. This incredible case includes the gruesome detail of the fact that the innocent man was reprieved only when being placed in the chair, his trouser leg already slit for the electrode.

younger world" is indicative of the fact that she is about to become one of what Griffith calls "The Vestal Virgins of Uplift." Jenkins's Mill is the only source of employment in the small town, and most of the main characters at this stage are introduced through the mill. The Dear One's ageing father is employed there, and so too are the Boy and his father. When we first see the Dear One (Mae Marsh), she is playing among ducks, watching them waddle contentedly about, and recognising the simple attraction to each other that they share. Here again is Griffith's insistence on identifying his leading women with animals in the opening passages of a picture, in order to underline their childish innocence—an innocence which, more often than not, as a result of the following action, gives way to a fuller maturity and realisation of what hardships life can offer.

The "Vestal Virgins of Uplift" succeed in interesting Miss Jenkins in their project, and she approaches her brother for the funds they require. But even Jenkins finds it difficult to raise the amount of money his sister demands, and as a result orders a ten per cent cut in all wages at his mill. From now on we are to witness how the intolerance of a few individuals will spread and expand through the enormous sums supplied by Jenkins from a self-styled group of reformers to the grandiose and powerful "Jenkins Foundation" employing many people; and how this intolerance will lead to the corruption of those it seeks to reform.

As a result of the cut in wages, a strike follows, and the angry workers are subdued by the militia. At one point during this sequence showing the defenceless workers being fired upon by the military, we can discern painted on a fence behind the crowd the words "The Same Today as Yesterday." Film historian Seymour Stern has noted that "It is commonly accepted that Griffith conceived the basic idea for the story of *Intolerance* when he saw a billboard advertisement from a train window, travelling from California to New York for the *première* of *The Birth of a Nation*, bearing the words, 'The Same Today as Yesterday.'"

During the shooting, several men, including the Boy's father, are shot down. Griffith makes his point even more meaningful and poignant by cutting from a shot showing the Boy cradling his dead father in his arms to one of Jenkins sitting alone in his large and empty office. Griffith uses this shot of Jenkins several times during the film to give a scene added dramatic content.

And so the escalation continues. The Committee of seventeen, as the reformers now call themselves, drive many people, jobless as a result of the strike, from the town to a nearby city. The Boy, as a last and desperate resort, turns to theft in order to survive, while the Friendless One (Miriam Cooper), a one-time neighbour of the Boy (Bobby Harron), is taken into the employ of the Musketeer of the Slums. Before very long, the Boy, too, is drawn into the Musketeer's gang. The Dear One and her ailing father are forced to live in a sordid slum, and gradually this brings about his eventual death.

Up to this point we have been presented with a ruthless picture of social intolerance and class-hatred, and it is one that will grow to frightening proportions later on. Griffith is never afraid to push home his point as far as it will go, and it is after this sequence in which we are shown the degradation of human morals and standards that a parallel with one of the other stories underlines the fundamental cause of this degradation. Immediately following the sequence in which the Dear One's father dies, we see first the shot mentioned above of Jenkins alone in his huge office, and then Griffith switches to the Judean Story, equating the reformers of the Modern Story with the Pharisees in the story of Christ. The Pharisees arrive at Cana just as the wedding feast is getting underway. There follows the sequence in which Christ performs the miracle of turning the water into wine, preceded by the title, put into the mouths of the Pharisees, "Meddlers then as now. There is too much pleasure-seeking among the people."

The construction of *Intolerance* is such that each story continually finds parallels with itself in one or more of the other three, is complemented by the other stories, and is made more forceful dramatically by comparison. There are many times when the narrative of one story stops abruptly to give way to another story; but the linking of the factor, either the image of the cradle or a more direct parallel in the action of the two stories, carries on the momentum of the film and the effect is almost never jumpy or irritating. Griffith chooses to make several parallels between the Pharisees and the Committee of seventeen. Apart from the one already mentioned above, he cuts from them to the Woman Taken in Adultery sequence from the Judean Story: "He that is without sin among you, let him first cast a stone at her."

. . .

As a result of the Dear One's attempts to attract attention to herself by imitating women in tight dresses with swaggering walks, the Boy is captivated by her charming innocence. "Say, kid, you're going to be my chicken" reads a sub-title during a scene in which the Dear One experiences the unforeseen results of her experiment. The Boy runs his fingers along her arm, and she registers successively alarm, embarrassment and ecstasy—after which the Boy pulls her towards him and kisses her. Her father arrives, and hustles her upstairs, making her kneel before the statuette of the Virgin and "pray to be forgiven."

The Dear One's father, old and with a weak heart, finally dies through his "inability to meet new conditions." This scene, darkly lit with heavy shadows in the little apartment room, carries with it a great pathos and sense of grief that are due entirely to the forcefulness of Miss Marsh's acting. Mae Marsh wrote of this scene, which is not one that has attracted too much attention in this extraordinary film, at considerable length in her autobiography.

> While we were playing *Intolerance,* one cycle of which is still being released as *The Mother and the Law,* I had to do a scene where, in the big city's slums, my father dies. The night before I did this scene I went to the theater . . . to see Marjorie Rambeau in *Kindling.* To my surprise and gratification she had to do a scene in this play that was somewhat similar to the one that I was scheduled to play in *Intolerance:* it made a deep impression on me.
>
> As a consequence, the next day before the cameras in the scene depicting my sorrow and misery at the death of my father, I began to cry with the memory of Marjorie Rambeau's part uppermost in my mind. I thought, however, that it had been done quite well, and was anxious to see it on the screen.
>
> I was in for very much of a surprise. A few of us gathered in the projection room and the camera began humming. I saw myself enter with a fair semblance of misery. But there was something about it that was not convincing.
>
> Mr. Griffith, who was clearly studying the action, finally turned in his seat and said—"I don't know what you were thinking about when you did that, but it is evident that it was not about the death of your father."
>
> "That is true," I said. I did not admit what I was thinking about!
>
> We began immediately on the scene again. This time I thought of the death of my own father and the big tragedy to our little home in Texas. I could recall the deep sorrow of my mother, my sisters, my brother and myself.*

When the Dear One's father dies, the Boy's genuine tears of sympathy reveal his true character, still retained under a veneer of lawlessness which he wears for the Musketeer of the Slums. Their subsequent courtship is complemented by that of Brown Eyes and Prosper, who, as Griffith explains in a sub-title, are "happily ignorant of the web Intolerance is weaving around them." The Dear One and the Boy are only too aware of their own predicament and the cause of their suffering, but they are as powerless to control the situation as Brown Eyes herself. However, there follows a short interlude of happiness amongst all the misery inflicted by intolerance, with Brown Eyes and Prosper listening to her father reading. "Love's silent mystery" points the scene, which is followed by one showing the Dear One, whose "passing days of youth have healed the wound," and the Boy spending a "Coney Island day."

The Committee of seventeen, now calling itself the Jenkins Foundation, has meanwhile succeeded in purging the city of all drinking and dancing. After a sequence in which they congratulate themselves and we are shown

---

* Mae Marsh, *Screen Acting* (Los Angeles: Photo Star Publishing Co., 1921).

the empty bars and dance halls turned into restaurants or simply deserted, Griffith then shows us where all the "pleasure-seeking" has gone. We see men distilling their own liquor in cellars and people dancing secretively behind buildings—an extraordinarily prophetic anticipation of the prohibition years incidentally. "When women cease to attract men they often turn to reform as a second choice" accompanies close-ups of members of the Foundation watching a raid on a brothel, a series which is followed by one close-up of an old and toothless man.

The Boy proposes to the Dear One, and they eventually marry. Such is the persuasive innocence of the Dear One that he is soon made to realise the folly of his present existence. He tells the Musketeer of the Slums in no uncertain manner that he is giving up his life of crime, and he thrusts his pistol back into the Musketeer's hand. This is an action that is to become more significant than it appears, and the shot is repeated later on in flashback, for it is this gun that will condemn him to death. Ironically, his genuine self-reformation is to become his death sentence.

Frightened that this denial of allegiance is a potential danger to his own security, the Musketeer arranges a "frame-up" of the Boy by planting stolen goods on him after partially beating him up in the street. When the police arrive, the goods are discovered on him, he is arrested, and sent for a short term of imprisonment.

Griffith calls the penitentiary in a sub-title "The, sometimes, House of Intolerance," and people whose judgement is usually very sound and valuable have suggested that Griffith did this simply because he recognised that the Modern Story had in fact little to do with Intolerance. This is clearly not valid, since the central characters' lives are governed by the intolerance of the self-styled reformers. Their intolerance is as present in the Modern Story as in the Catholic hierarchy in the Medieval Story. To suggest that Griffith recognised a need to bolster up the Modern Story with obvious titles shows a remarkable lack of insight. One can find titles such as the one quoted above, or "Intolerants away for a term" in all four stories. In the Medieval Story for example, those who seek to instigate the massacres are called "the Intolerants," and the King despises what he calls "this intolerant measure." Again, in the Babylonian Story, Griffith calls Cyrus's sword of war "the most potent weapon forged in the flames of intolerance." Perhaps these titles may have dated after half a century, but this fact need not necessarily indicate that they replace an element in the film itself.

.   .   .

During the period of the Boy's imprisonment, his wife gives birth to their first child, and there follows a brief sequence typical of Griffith, who depicted similar situations in several other works, in which we see the Dear One playing with the child and finding in her love for the infant a source of considerable solace amid the injustices that have so far befallen her. This sequence is directly preceded by the image of the cradle and the title, "Out of the cradle—endlessly rocking. Baby fingers hopefully lifted."

The now-powerful Jenkins Foundation hear of her case, and, in view of the fact that the husband is already branded a criminal and that she and the child live in a slum district, they decide that the child would be better off in their own clinic. They therefore make a call on the Dear One to verify the reports they have received. Before they arrive, however, we are shown her visiting a neighbour who gives her a bottle of whisky as a remedy for a slight cold. While she is out, the group from the Foundation arrive to find the baby unattended and assume expressions of an "I told you so" or "It's just what you'd expect" nature. The Dear One returns, whisky bottle in hand, and greets them in a friendly manner, not realising their ultimate purpose. The group see the bottle she is holding and before she is able to offer any kind of explanation they once again find their suspicions confirmed. They tell the Dear One that she is no fit mother, and she flies into an uncontrollable rage, chasing the women out of the room with a broomstick. The group go away, but, unknown to the Dear One, only in order to report and to obtain a warrant for the seizure of the child.

When they return some time later, the Dear One is in the middle of a modest meal, with which she is drinking a glass of beer. This naturally only helps to convince the group of the child's "undesirable" environment. The scene that follows is one of shattering dramatic intensity. One of the women tells the Dear One that they have come to seize the child, and picks up the baby from its cot. The Dear One, stupefied, snatches the baby from her and backs away from the women, crying and screaming that no one will ever take her child from her. They fling themselves upon her and knock her to the ground, snatching the child from her arms and disappearing with it from the room, leaving the exhausted girl half-conscious on the floor. Griffith shows us a close-up of the Dear One's head, and then pans slowly along her outstretched arm to reveal her hand lying across one of the child's bootees, perhaps stroking it in her half-conscious state.

The parallel Griffith draws here brings the sequence to a touching and poignant close. He cuts back to the Judean Story—without any linking title or images—and superimposes over a picture of Christ surrounded by children the title: "Suffer little children."

.   .   .

It is at this point that the Musketeer of the Slums makes his reappearance in the development of the Modern Story. He ostensibly offers his help in getting the Dear One's baby back for her (this without the knowledge of the Boy), although in effect being as powerless as the Dear One herself. But his real motives are of a less genuine nature. His designs on the Dear One are suspected by the Friendless One, who follows him to her house, picking up, as she leaves, the gun that the Boy had thrown back at the Musketeer earlier in the film.

As it happens, when the Musketeer arrives, the Boy himself is out playing cards, and after first making sure that the Dear One is alone by looking through the keyhole, he knocks and she lets him in. A passer-by sees him go in, and, suspicious, rushes off to inform the Boy. Meanwhile the Friendless One arrives to overhear the dulcet tones of her unfaithful lover with the Dear One. The close-up of Miriam Cooper—who played this part—shows her biting her lip and drawing blood, trying to conceal the mental pain she suffers by self-inflicted physical pain.

When the passer-by arrives to tell the Boy of his wife's visitor, he can hardly get home quickly enough, suspecting the worst. As he comes up the stairs, the Friendless One, on the landing outside the door, quickly clambers out of a window on a narrow ledge. The Musketeer has by this time taken the Dear One roughly into his arms and is kissing her violently, despite her efforts to struggle free. The Boy bursts in, and a bitter fight follows, in which the Boy's strength is no match for the burly Musketeer. The Friendless One has meanwhile climbed along the ledge across to the window into the Dear One's room. She draws the gun, and at this point Griffith fades the picture out and fades up a flashback, which is a repeat of an earlier scene at the beginning of *Intolerance*, when the Boy, leaving the town after the strike, meets the Friendless One and offers to carry her bag. The scene fades out and Griffith once more returns to the Friendless One perched outside the window on the narrow ledge. She aims the revolver through the window and fires several times, fatally injuring the Musketeer before throwing the gun into the room and jumping from the ledge to the ground and escaping unnoticed.

In the room itself, all is confusion. The Boy picks up the gun without thinking what he is doing, utterly incredulous at what has happened. On the advice of neighbours, the police arrive and discover the Boy standing over the Musketeer's body, the murder weapon in his hand. He is discovered holding his own death-warrant.

This sequence is incredibly short. It is constructed in such a way as to convey each portion of the action, from the moment when the Musketeer leaves his house until the arrival of the police, as quickly and as precisely as possible. The whole passage lasts about five minutes, and contains one hundred and eleven shots averaging about three seconds in length. There is nothing at all to break up the action, which travels at a pace akin to that at which the characters themselves experience it. The effect is such as to create in our minds the bewilderment which is present in the mind of the Boy. And yet each action, the Friendless One leaving, putting the gun into her bag, the passer-by, the Boy playing cards, the Musketeer assaulting the girl, the movements of the Friendless One, all these shots are cut before the action contained within them is wholly completed, a device Griffith understood long before any other director of his era. Each shot is as brief as is possible without making it incomprehensible. For example, when the Musketeer leaves his house, the shot of his closing the door lasts for three-quarters of a second; of his going out into the street, just under a second; when he locks the door of the Dear One's room after being let in, the action of his doing so lasts, again, three-quarters of a second. When the Friendless One fires the revolver, the shot lasts only fourteen frames (and the film travels at sixteen frames per second). When she tosses the gun into the room, the shot of the gun landing on the floor lasts eleven frames; the following shot, of her leaping from the ledge, is exactly one second long. The next shot, of the Boy getting up from the floor, is ten frames long; the next, a continuation of the action of him rising, lasts only half a second. The sequence is over almost before we have realised what has happened, although in fact the whole passage is carefully and completely documented.

From this point onwards, the whole pace of the film quickens, and the events and the method by which they are presented to us on the screen generate, in the words of Iris Barry, "near hysteria."*

From the end of the above sequence, one shot of the Friendless One sitting nervously alone in her room leads straight into the scene of the Boy on trial for his life, facing a charge of murder and a penalty of death if found guilty. Griffith quite conventionally opens this, one of the most powerful sequences in *Intolerance,* by showing us a close-up of the Dear One as she shifts uneasily in her chair, watching the proceedings.

There follows a shot of the Friendless One—the real guilty party—whose actions are just as nervous. Next we see the Jury, and a fourth cut brings us to a shot of the Judge. There remains only one person's appearance to follow. The Boy himself is brought to the witness box, and is sworn in.

He is cross-examined by the council for the prosecution, and his guilt is practically established beyond questionable doubt. It *was* his gun; but his word that he had returned it is naturally discounted. Griffith inserts a flashback scene of the Boy giving the gun back to the Musketeer we saw earlier in the film. The Boy's defence council is totally ineffectual—it is his maiden case and he stutters helplessly in reply to the prosecution. The Jury therefore return a verdict of guilty. A sub-title, re-introducing the phrase "an Eye for an Eye" and developing the concept to "a murder for a murder," leads to a transition to the Judean Story, where Griffith parallels the verdict with the Judgement of Christ: "Let Him be crucified."

The extreme close-up shots of the Dear One during her husband's trial

* Iris Barry, *D. W. Griffith: American Film Master* (New York: Museum of Modern Art, 1965).

are much quoted and illustrated as examples of Griffith's use of this technique in order to obtain dramatic intensity. Much more mention could be made, however, of the performance of Mae Marsh, which in this scene reaches one of its many peaks. Sir Alexander Korda included her performance as one of the most outstanding pieces of acting in the silent film era, and June Barry rated her playing of the Dear One as second only to Falconetti's Joan of Arc. But recalling Miss Marsh's youthful exuberance in the opening passages of *Intolerance,* her maturity to womanhood in these climactic scenes is one of the most natural transitions yet astonishing things Griffith has obtained from any of his actresses. She bears her grief to smile and wave nervously at her husband, suppressing the tears in case her husband should think her moral support is not forthcoming.

Miss Marsh herself, in her autobiography, has little to say about the scene, but there is little that words could add to the emotional force of her mime.

> The hardest dramatic work I ever did was in the courtroom scene in *Intolerance.* We re-took those scenes on four different occasions. Each time I gave to the limit of my vitality and ability. I put everything into my portrayal that was in me. . . . Parts of the four "takes"—some of them done at two weeks' intervals—were assembled to make up those scenes which you finally beheld on the screen."*

And speaking of the shots of her hands which appear in the scene, she goes on:

> I quite unconsciously began to wring my handkerchief and press it to my face. "Good," he (Griffith) said, "Keep it up."†

Perhaps the phrase "Each time I gave to the limit of my vitality and ability," crystallises the intensity that surely no one seeing the film is unable to sense; the intensity that must be attributed above all to the ability of the actress or actor, but also in equal measure to Griffith himself, since, as Miss Marsh's statement implies, it was he who was able to coax from his players their utmost efforts. "He gave us," Miss Marsh has said, "of his genius and personality, and for that there is no return coin." Perhaps she did not altogether realise that in fact she had returned the coin already, in the form of the performance she gave him, and gave the world.

After the trial, when she has returned to her room, all the pent-up grief rises to the surface not, as might be expected, with much weeping and melodramatic gesticulating, but in one shot of Mae Marsh's drawn and

---

* Mae Marsh, *op. cit.*
† *Ibid.*

incredulous face. She enters the room in long shot and walks slowly into full close-up, her face conveying all the deep and violent emotion of a woman's sensibilities in one eloquent portrait so typical of Griffith. No need here for mime or other substitutes for words; the motion picture camera has become, in the hands of D. W. Griffith, the true and unobtrusive mediator between the actress on the screen and the audience themselves, lifting her out of characterisation and into life.

And yet we are not to be spared the full extent of her suffering, because Griffith accentuates it with the cruellest of ironies. He follows this shot with a scene of Jenkins sipping tea with members of the Jenkins Foundation. The caption inserted reads: "The people everywhere are singing your praises."

A shot preceded by the title, "The irresistible impulse," shows the Friendless One returning to the scene of the murder, which in turn precedes a scene in which the Dear One discovers—with the aid of a neighbouring policeman—the method by which the Musketeer was shot—from a ledge outside the window. On her behalf, therefore, the policeman goes to the visiting Governor to make an appeal for the Boy's release. Again Griffith shows us the Friendless One, at home, playing solitaire, her conscience allowing her no respite. He then shows us her thoughts by introducing a shot of the Boy in prison. After a brief sequence showing him among the other prisoners, we learn that the appeal has been rejected, and the execution will go on as planned. . . .

The Dear One and the policeman arrive at the Governor's hotel, as the Friendless One arrives soon afterwards, remaining some distance down the road, hoping she'll not be noticed. The Governor is just leaving for his train, and brushes off the policeman who is acting on the Dear One's behalf. He even ignores the desperate pleas of the Dear One herself. His decision, it seems, is final.

As the Governor's taxi draws away, the policeman and the Dear One stand stunned on the pavement. The policeman happens to look along the pavement and recognises the Friendless One, whom he had seen, presumably, at the Boy's trial. When she sees that she has been recognised, she begins to run for her taxi, but the policeman chases after her and catches her. The Dear One hurries after him and the Friendless One, at her wits' end, confesses that it was she who killed the Musketeer of the Slums.

Now there is no doubt about what to do. The chase, a standard device in silent movies and used extensively by Griffith to provide a thrilling climax to his pictures, is used again here. But it is given three times the emotional charge by virtue of the fact that while we are involved with the fate of the Boy, we are also concerned about the outcome of the other three stories, intermixed with each other. The Boy is to be hanged for a crime of which he is innocent, Christ is condemned to death for proclaiming himself the King of the Jews, the Huguenots are to be massacred because of their religion, and Babylon is to fall unless the Mountain Girl is able to bring the message to Belshazzar in time.

As the Dear One, the policeman and the Friendless One jump into the taxi and chase off to the station in a desperate effort to reach the Governor before he boards the train, The Mountain Girl, having watched the proceedings in Cyrus's camp, at last realises what is happening. Babylon, and "her prince," are being betrayed to the Persians. She jumps onto her chariot and races furiously back towards Babylon, closely followed by the whole Army of Cyrus.

While the Boy is being given the Last Sacrament, the Dear One and the guilty girl arrive at the station only to discover that the train has already left, with the Governor on it. Suddenly all hope seems to have disappeared. Then, the policeman sees a racing car in the station yard, with a driver and his friends talking about the vehicle. The policeman, followed by the two women, rushes over to them and explains his situation. The driver does not hesitate. The policeman and the two women crowd on to the car and the chase after the train begins.

.   .   .

The cradle rocking leads to the train pulling into a station; the Boy's pardon has been signed—all that remains is to reach the gallows before the trapdoor is released. But the Boy is already being led to the gallows, and beside him still is the priest who, unable any longer to stand the strain, stumbles as he walks. Griffith cuts directly to a shot of Calvary Hill, and three crosses in the background, heavy swirling clouds overhead, and people in the foreground waving their arms to and fro.

The Friendly Policeman rushes to the nearest telephone to have the execution stopped. At the prison, a guard receives the call, and runs excitedly to tell the executioner, who is already supervising the preliminaries—the Boy is having a hood placed over his head, and the noose placed around his neck. Meanwhile the party have rushed to the prison in the car. They arrive outside the building as we see the noose being tightened around the Boy's neck, a shot which is followed by a shot of the executioners, holding their knives over the strings which will release the trapdoor.

The Executioner is just about to give the signal when the Dear One, the Friendless One, the Governor and the policeman waving the pardon excitedly in the air rush into the chamber, and the execution is stopped.

The reunion between the Boy and his wife is one of uncontrollable relief; and the woman he sees in his arms ruffles his hair, tears in her eyes, much as she played happily with ducks at the beginning of the film. But then she was a child; and now she is a woman.

WIENE, MAYER, JANOWITZ

the cabinet of
dr. caligari

CREdiTS

The Cabinet of Dr. Caligari (Germany, 1919)
German title: *Das Kabinett des Dr. Caligari*
Directed by Robert Wiene from a scenario by Carl Mayer and Hans Janowitz
Produced by Decla-Bioscop

Photography: Willi Hameister
Design: Hermann Warm, Walter Reimann, Walter Röhrig
Distributors (16mm): Audio-Brandon Films, Film Images (a division of Radim
  Films), United Films, *et al.*

Main performers:

Conrad Veidt (*Cesare*)
Werner Krauss (*Dr. Caligari and the Doctor*)
Lil Dagover (*Jane Olsen*)

Friedrich Feher (*Francis*)
Hans von Twardovski (*Alan*)
Rudolf Lettinger (*Dr. Olsen*)
Rudolf Klein-Roggee (*Criminal*)

Length: 5 reels

The appearance of *The Cabinet of Dr. Caligari* not only heralded "the golden age of the German film" but also firmly established the possibility of an intellectual cinema. Conceived visually in the then-current style of the expressionist stage drama, *Caligari* challenged the supremacy of the theater in the dramatization of modern ideas. The presentation of a psychologically disoriented perspective of reality, which was inherent in the style of expressionist theater, was for the first time transferred effectively to the screen. It was inherent not only in the scenic design, which can be done on the stage, but also in the first-person narrative structure, which is not suitable to stage narrative. At the beginning of the film, one character tells another that he has a mysterious story to relate; the rest of the film, until the final sequence, is a flashback that is clearly intended to convey the personal view of the speaker. The excitingly visual story, a murder mystery with elements of a horror tale, lent itself readily to the fashionable postwar themes of persecution, neurosis, loss of will, and mental domination, as well as to such older motifs as vengeance, pursuit of a criminal, and guilt.

Yet *The Cabinet of Dr. Caligari* was an original example of expressionist art, not a pastiche of styles and concepts borrowed from other art forms. The ending, which reveals the insanity of the narrator and thus reverses the premise of his reliability that we had accepted throughout the film, requires us to rethink the entire esthetic experience. We are able to do this first because the visual imagery has impressed itself so strongly on our minds, and second because the information revealed at the end remains consistent with the disordered perspective—the instability of the environment—that we have observed throughout. The film works on us subconsciously to integrate style, theme, and story into an artistic unity that we are unaware of while watching the film for the first time. On repeated viewings, aware of the secret of the plot, we can concentrate on the filmmakers' artistry in evoking a persistent sense of tension or conflict in both the content and the form of every sequence. The stark tonal contrasts effected by the lighting, the ever-encroaching shadows accentuated by the frequent use of masking shots (in particular the iris shot), and especially the contrasts in volume (the flatness and obvious artificiality of the environment surrounding the three-dimensional characters) reinforce the narrative emphasis on the alienation of the main characters from the places they inhabit and from one another.

The Cabinet of Dr. Caligari is probably the cinema's most distinguished example of art by collaboration. Although an artistic film is always dependent on the efforts of writers, technicians, and performers, as well as of a director, we can usually discern the creative force and the organizing esthetic sensibility as emanating from one person, almost always the director, sometimes the writer, and in rare cases, the star (Lloyd, Fairbanks, Astaire, Laurel and Hardy, and a very few others). Viewing *Caligari,* we encounter a combination of individual achievements in the directing, writing, acting, and scenic design that works superbly in this one instance, perhaps because its stylized depiction of the bizarre permits or even encourages divergent claims on our attention. Even when we are familiar with the film, we are never at ease watching it; its images continue to elicit subconscious responses, scattered impressions, random associations. The individual efforts of each contributor may be examined out of context for the purpose of analysis, but without the total effect, the parts always fall far short of the whole. Robert Wiene, the director, did not become a major name in the cinema; nor did Hans Janowitz, one of the writers, nor Willi Hameister, the photographer. Carl Mayer, the other writer, went on to write other major films, including *The Last Laugh* (1924), and some of the performers became stars, but there is no denying that the enduring appeal of *Caligari* remains totally distinct from the later successes or failures of its separate contributors. A few months after *Caligari,* Wiene, Mayer, and Hameister collaborated on another expressionist film in a similar style, *Genuine,* a work that has been almost completely forgotten—a fact that lends credence to the notion that essentially *Caligari* was a unique and probably somewhat fortuitous association of great talents who joined together at the right time and place.

Aside from *Caligari,* the expressionist cinema was no more than a minor

The Making of *Caligari*

SIEGFRIED KRACAUER

The Hans Janowitz-Carl Mayer screenplay for *The Cabinet of Dr. Caligari* is located in a fictitious North German town near the Dutch border, significantly called Holstenwall. One day a fair moves into the town, with merry-go-rounds and side-shows—among the latter that of Dr. Caligari, a weird, bespectacled man advertising the somnambulist Cesare. To procure a license, Caligari goes to the town hall, where he is treated haughtily by an arrogant official. The following morning this official is found murdered in his room, which does not prevent the townspeople from enjoying the fair's pleasures. Along with numerous onlookers, Francis and Alan—two students in love with Jane, a medical man's daughter, enter the tent of Dr. Caligari, and watch Cesare slowly stepping out of an upright, coffinlike box. Caligari tells the thrilled audience that the somnambulist will answer questions about the future. Alan, in an excited state, asks how long he has to live. Cesare opens his mouth; he seems to be dominated by a terrific, hypnotic power emanating from his master. "Until dawn," he answers. At dawn Francis learns that his friend has been stabbed in exactly the same manner as the official. . . .

Francis continues spying on Caligari, and, after nightfall, secretly peers through a window of the wagon. But while he imagines he sees Cesare lying in his box, Cesare in reality breaks into Jane's bedroom, lifts a dagger to pierce the sleeping girl, gazes at her, puts the dagger away and flees, with the screaming Jane in his arms, over roofs and roads. Chased by her father, he drops the girl, who is then escorted home, whereas the lonely kidnaper dies of exhaustion.

.   .   .

Caligari himself manages to escape. He seeks shelter in a lunatic asylum. The student follows him, calls on the director of the asylum to inquire about the fugitive, and recoils horror-struck: the director and Caligari are one and the same person.

The following night—the director has fallen asleep—Francis and three members of the medical staff whom he has initiated into the case search the director's office and discover material fully establishing the guilt of this authority in psychiatric matters.

.   .   .

FROM *From Caligari to Hitler* (1947) by Siegfried Kracauer. Reprinted by permission of Walter and Conston, P. C., attorneys for the estate of Elizabeth Kracauer.

To make him admit his crimes, Francis confronts the director with the corpse of his tool, the somnambulist. No sooner does the monster realize Cesare is dead than he begins to rave. Trained attendants put him into a strait jacket.

This horror tale in the spirit of E. T. A. Hoffmann was an outspoken revolutionary story. In it, as Janowitz indicates, he and Carl Mayer half-intentionally stigmatized the omnipotence of a state authority manifesting itself in universal conscription and declarations of war. The German war government seemed to the authors the prototype of such voracious authority. Subjects of the Austro-Hungarian monarchy, they were in a better position than most citizens of the Reich to penetrate the fatal tendencies inherent in the German system. The character of Caligari embodies these tendencies; he stands for an unlimited authority that idolizes power as such, and, to satisfy its lust for domination, ruthlessly violates all human rights and values. Functioning as a mere instrument, Cesare is not so much a guilty murderer as Caligari's innocent victim. This is how the authors themselves understood him. According to the pacifist-minded Janowitz, they had created Cesare with the dim design of portraying the common man who, under the pressure of compulsory military service, is drilled to kill and to be killed. The revolutionary meaning of the story reveals itself unmistakably at the end, with the disclosure of the psychiatrist as Caligari: reason overpowers unreasonable power, insane authority is symbolically abolished. Similar ideas were also being expressed on the contemporary stage, but the authors of *Caligari* transferred them to the screen without including any of those eulogies of the authority-freed "New Man" in which many expressionist plays indulged.

A miracle occurred: Erich Pommer, chief executive of Decla-Bioscop, accepted this unusual, if not subversive, script. Was it a miracle? Since in those early postwar days the conviction prevailed that foreign markets could only be conquered by artistic achievements, the German film industry was of course anxious to experiment in the field of aesthetically qualified entertainment.* Art assured export, and export meant salvation. An ardent partisan of this doctrine, Pommer had moreover an incomparable flair for cinematic values and popular demands. Regardless of whether he grasped the significance of the strange story Mayer and Janowitz submitted to him, he certainly sensed its timely atmosphere and interesting scenic potentialities. He was a born promoter who handled screen and business affairs with equal facility, and, above all, excelled in stimulating the creative energies of directors and players. In 1923, Ufa was to make him chief of its entire production.† His behind-the-scenes activities were to leave their imprint on the pre-Hitler screen.

Pommer assigned Fritz Lang to direct *Caligari*, but in the middle of

---

* Vincent, *Histoire de l'Art Cinématographique*, p. 140.
† *Jahrbuch der Filmindustrie*, 1922/3, pp. 35, 46. For an appraisal of Pommer, see Lejeune, *Cinema*, pp. 125–31.

the preliminary discussion Lang was ordered to finish his serial *The Spiders;* the distributors of this film urged its completion.* Lang's successor was Dr. Robert Wiene. Since his father, a once-famous Dresden actor, had become slightly insane towards the end of his life, Wiene was not entirely unprepared to tackle the case of Dr. Caligari. He suggested, in complete harmony with what Lang had planned, an essential change of the original story—a change against which the two authors violently protested. But no one heeded them.†

The original story was an account of real horrors; Wiene's version transforms that account into a chimera concocted and narrated by the mentally deranged Francis. To effect this transformation the body of the original story is put into a framing story which introduces Francis as a madman. The film *Caligari* opens with the first of the two episodes composing the frame. Francis is shown sitting on a bench in the park of the lunatic asylum, listening to the confused babble of a fellow sufferer. Moving slowly, like an apparition, a female inmate of the asylum passes by: it is Jane. Francis says to his companion: "What I have experienced with her is still stranger than what you have encountered. I will tell it to you."‡ Fade-out. Then a view of Holstenwall fades in, and the original story unfolds, ending, as has been seen, with the identification of Caligari. After a new fade-out the second and final episode of the framing story begins. Francis, having finished the narration, follows his companion back to the asylum, where he mingles with a crowd of sad figures—among them Cesare, who absent-mindedly caresses a little flower. The director of the asylum, a mild and understanding-looking person, joins the crowd. Lost in the maze of his hallucinations, Francis takes the director for the nightmarish character he himself has created, and accuses this imaginary fiend of being a dangerous madman. He screams, he fights the attendants in a frenzy. The scene is switched over to a sickroom, with the director putting on horn-rimmed spectacles which immediately change his appearance: it seems to be Caligari who examines the exhausted Francis. After this he removes his spectacles and, all mildness, tells his assistants that Francis believes him to be Caligari. Now that he understands the case of his patient, the director concludes, he will be able to heal him. With this cheerful message the audience is dismissed.

Janowitz and Mayer knew why they raged against the framing story: it perverted, if not reversed, their intrinsic intentions. While the original story exposed the madness inherent in authority, Wiene's *Caligari* glorified authority and convicted its antagonist of madness. A revolutionary film was thus turned into a conformist one—following the much-used pattern

---

* Information offered by Mr. Lang.

† Extracted from Mr. Janowitz's manuscript. See also Vincent, *Histoire de l'Art Cinématographique*, pp. 140, 143–44.

‡ Film license, issued by Board of Censors, Berlin, 1921 and 1925 (Museum of Modern Art Library, clipping files); *Film Society Programme*, March 14, 1926.

of declaring some normal but troublesome individual insane and sending him to a lunatic asylum. This change undoubtedly resulted not so much from Wiene's personal predilections as from his instinctive submission to the necessities of the screen; films, at least commercial films, are forced to answer to mass desires. In its changed form *Caligari* was no longer a product expressing, at best, sentiments characteristic of the intelligentsia, but a film supposed equally to be in harmony with what the less educated felt and liked.

If it holds true that during the postwar years most Germans eagerly tended to withdraw from a harsh outer world into the intangible realm of the soul, Wiene's version was certainly more consistent with their attitude than the original story; for, by putting the original into a box, this version faithfully mirrored the general retreat into a shell. In *Caligari* (and several other films of the time) the device of a framing story was not only an aesthetic form, but also had symbolic content. Significantly, Wiene avoided mutilating the original story itself. Even though *Caligari* had become a comformist film, it preserved and emphasized this revolutionary story—as a madman's fantasy. Caligari's defeat now belonged among psychological experiences. In this way Wiene's film does suggest that during their retreat into themselves the Germans were stirred to reconsider their traditional belief in authority. Down to the bulk of social democratic workers they refrained from revolutionary action; yet at the same time a psychological revolution seems to have prepared itself in the depths of the collective soul. The film reflects this double aspect of German life by coupling a reality in which Caligari's authority triumphs with a hallucination in which the same authority is overthrown. There could be no better configuration of symbols for that uprising against the authoritarian dispositions which apparently occurred under the cover of a behavior-rejecting uprising.

Janowitz suggested that the settings for *Caligari* be designed by the painter and illustrator Alfred Kubin, who, a forerunner of the surrealists, made eerie phantoms invade harmless scenery and visions of torture emerge from the subconscious. Wiene took to the idea of painted canvases, but preferred to Kubin three expressionist artists: Hermann Warm, Walter Röhrig and Walter Reimann. They were affiliated with the Berlin Sturm group, which, through Herwarth Walden's magazine *Sturm,* promoted expressionism in every field of art.*

. . .

"Films must be drawings brought to life": this was Hermann Warm's formula at the time that he and his two fellow designers were contructing

---

* Mr. Janowitz's manuscript; Vincent, *Histoire de l'Art Cinématographique,* p. 144; Rotha, *Film Till Now,* p. 43.

the *Calgari* world.* In accordance with his beliefs, the canvases and draperies of *Caligari* abounded in complexes of jagged, sharp-pointed forms strongly reminiscent of gothic patterns. Products of a style which by then had become almost a mannerism, these complexes suggested houses, walls, landscapes. Except for a few slips or concessions—some backgrounds opposed the pictorial convention in too direct a manner, while others all but preserved them—the settings amounted to a perfect transformation of material objects into emotional ornaments. With its oblique chimneys on pell-mell roofs, its windows in the form of arrows or kites and its treelike arabesques that were threats rather than trees, Holstenwall resembled those visions of unheard-of cities which the painter Lyonel Feininger evoked through his edgy, crystalline compositions. In addition, the ornamental system in *Caligari* expanded through space, annulling its conventional aspect by means of painted shadows in disharmony with the lighting effects, and zigzag delineations designed to efface all rules of perspective. Space now dwindled to a flat plane, now augmented its dimensions to become what one writer called a "stereoscopic universe."

.　　.　　.

If Decla had chosen to leave the original story of Mayer and Janowitz as it was, these "drawings brought to life" would have told it perfectly. As expressionist abstractions they were animated by the same revolutionary spirit that impelled the two scriptwriters to accuse authority—the kind of authority revered in Germany—of inhuman excesses. However, Wiene's version disavowed this revolutionary meaning of expressionist staging, or, at least, put it, like the original story itself, in brackets. In the film *Caligari* expressionism seems to be nothing more than the adequate translation of a madman's fantasy into pictorial terms. This was how many contemporary German reviewers understood, and relished, the settings and gestures. One of the critics stated with self-assured ignorance: "The idea of rendering the notions of sick brains . . . through expressionist pictures is not only well conceived but also well realized. Here this style has a right to exist, proves an outcome of solid logic."†

In their triumph the philistines overlooked one significant fact: even though *Caligari* stigmatized the oblique chimneys as crazy, it never restored the perpendicular ones as the normal. Expressionist ornaments also overrun the film's concluding episode, in which, from the philistines' viewpoint, perpendiculars should have been expected to characterize the revival of conventional reality. In consequence, the *Caligari* style was as far from depicting madness as it was from transmitting revolutionary messages. What function did it really assume?

.　　.　　.

* Quotation from Kurtz, *Expressionismus*, p. 66.
† Review in 8 *Uhr Abendblatt*, cited in *Caligari-Heft*, p. 8.

Wiene, Mayer, Janowitz

. . . The expressionist style of *Caligari* . . . had the function of characterizing the phenomena on the screen as phenomena of the soul—a function which overshadowed its revolutionary meaning. By making the film an outward projection of psychological events, expressionist staging symbolized—much more strikingly than did the device of a framing story—that general retreat into a shell which occurred in postwar Germany. It is not accidental that, as long as this collective process was effective, odd gestures and settings in an expressionist or similar style marked many a conspicuous film. *Variety*, of 1925, showed the final traces of them. Owing to their stereotyped character, these settings and gestures were like some familiar street sign—"Men at Work," for instance. Only here the lettering was different. The sign read: "Soul at Work."

After a thorough propaganda campaign culminating in the puzzling poster "You must become Caligari," Decla released the film in February 1920 in the Berlin Marmorhaus.* Among the press reviews—they were unanimous in praising *Caligari* as the first work of art on the screen—that of *Vorwärts*, the leading Social Democratic Party organ, distinguished itself by utter absurdity. It commented upon the film's final scene, in which the director of the asylum promises to heal Francis, with the words: "This film is also morally invulnerable inasmuch as it evokes sympathy for the mentally diseased, and comprehension for the self-sacrificing activity of the psychiatrists and attendants."† Instead of recognizing that Francis' attack against an odious authority harmonized with the Party's own antiauthoritarian doctrine, *Vorwärts* preferred to pass off authority itself as a paragon of progressive virtues. It was always the same psychological mechanism: the rationalized middle-class propensities of the Social Democrats interfering with their rational socialist designs. While the Germans were too close to *Caligari* to appraise its symptomatic value, the French realized that this film was more than just an exceptional film. They coined the term *"Caligarisme"* and applied it to a postwar world seemingly all upside down; which, at any rate, proves that they sensed the film's bearing on the structure of society. The New York première of *Caligari*, in April 1921, firmly established its world fame. But apart from giving rise to stray imitations and serving as a yardstick for artistic endeavors, this "most widely discussed film of the time" never seriously influenced the course of the American or French cinema.‡ It stood out lonely, like a monolith.

· · ·

Whether intentionally or not, *Caligari* exposes the soul wavering between tyranny and chaos, and facing a desperate situation: any escape from tyranny seems to throw it into a state of utter confusion. Quite

* *Jahrbuch der Filmindustrie*, 1922/3, p. 31.
† Quoted from *Caligari-Heft*, p. 23.
‡ Quotation from Jacobs, *American Film*, p. 303; see also pp. 304–5.

logically, the film spreads an all-pervading atmosphere of horror. Like the Nazi world, that of *Caligari* overflows with sinister portents, acts of terror and outbursts of panic. The equation of horror and hopelessness comes to a climax in the final episode which pretends to re-establish normal life. Except for the ambiguous figure of the director and the shadowy members of his staff, normality realizes itself through the crowd of insane moving in their bizarre surroundings. The normal as a madhouse: frustration could not be pictured more finally. And in this film, as well as in *Homunculus*, is unleashed a strong sadism and an appetite for destruction.[*] The reappearance of these traits on the screen once more testifies to their prominence in the German collective soul.

Technical peculiarities betray peculiarities of meaning. In *Caligari* methods begin to assert themselves which belong among the special properties of German film technique. *Caligari* initiates a long procession of 100 per cent studio-made films. Whereas, for instance, the Swedes at that time went to great pains to capture the actual appearance of a snowstorm or a wood, the German directors, at least until 1924, were so infatuated with indoor effects that they built up whole landscapes within the studio walls. They preferred the command of an artificial universe to dependence upon a haphazard outer world. Their withdrawal into the studio was part of the general retreat into a shell. Once the Germans had determined to seek shelter within the soul, they could not well allow the screen to explore that very reality which they abandoned. This explains the conspicuous role of architecture after *Caligari*—a role that has struck many an observer. "It is of the utmost importance," Paul Rotha remarks in a survey of the postwar period, "to grasp the significant part played by the architect in the development of the German cinema."[†] How could it be otherwise? The architect's façades and rooms were not merely backgrounds, but hieroglyphs. They expressed the structure of the soul in terms of space.

Caligari also mobilizes light. It is a lighting device which enables the spectators to watch the murder of Alan without seeing it; what they see, on the wall of the student's attic, is the shadow of Cesare stabbing that of Alan. Such devices developed into a specialty of the German studios. Jean Cassou credits the Germans with having invented a "laboratory-made fairy illumination,"[‡] and Harry Alan Potamkin considers the handling of the light in the German film its "major contribution to the cinema."[§] This emphasis upon light can be traced to an experiment Max Reinhardt made on the stage shortly before *Caligari*. In his *mise-en-scène* of Sorge's

[*] Rotha, *Film Till Now*, p. 33.
[†] Rotha, *Film Till Now*, p. 180. Cf. Potamkin, "Kino and Lichtspiel," *Close Up*, Nov. 1929, p. 387.
[‡] Cited in Leprohon, "Le Cinéma Allemand," *Le Rouge et le Noir*, July 1928, p. 135.
[§] Potamkin, "The Rise and Fall of the German Film," *Cinema*, April 1930, p. 24.

prewar drama *The Beggar (Der Bettler)*—one of the earliest and most vigorous manifestations of expressionism—he substituted for normal settings imaginary ones created by means of lighting effects.* Reinhardt doubtless introduced these effects to be true to the drama's style. The analogy to the films of the postwar period is obvious: it was their expressionist nature which impelled many a German director of photography to breed shadows as rampant as weeds and associate ethereal phantoms with strangely lit arabesques or faces. These efforts were designed to bathe all scenery in an unearthly illumination marking it as scenery of the soul. "Light has breathed soul into the expressionist films," Rudolph Kurtz states in his book on the expressionist cinema.† Exactly the reverse holds true: in those films the soul was the virtual source of the light. The task of switching on this inner illumination was somewhat facilitated by powerful romantic traditions.

The attempt made in *Caligari* to coordinate settings, players, lighting and action is symptomatic of the sense of structural organization which, from this film on, manifests itself on the German screen. Rotha coins the term "studio constructivism" to characterize "that curious air of completeness, of finality, that surrounds each product of the German studios."‡ But organizational completeness can be achieved only if the material to be organized does not object to it. (The ability of the Germans to organize themselves owes much to their longing for submission.) Since reality is essentially incalculable and therefore demands to be observed rather than commanded, realism on the screen and total organization exclude each other. Through their "studio constructivism" no less than their lighting the German films revealed that they dealt with unreal events displayed in a sphere basically controllable.§

* Kurtz, *Expressionismus*, p. 59.
† *Ibid.*, p. 60.
‡ Rotha, *Film Till Now*, pp. 107–8. Cf. Potamkin, "Kino and Lichtspiel," *Close Up*, Nov. 1929, p. 388, and "The Rise and Fall of the German Film," *Cinema*, April 1930, p. 24.
§ Film connoisseurs have repeatedly criticized *Caligari* for being a stage imitation. This aspect of the film partly results from its genuinely theatrical action. It is action of a well-constructed dramatic conflict in stationary surroundings—action which does not depend upon screen representation for significance. Like *Caligari*, all "indoor" films of the postwar period showed affinity for the stage in that they favored inner-life dramas at the expense of conflicts involving outer reality. However, this did not necessarily prevent them from growing into true films. When, in the wake of *Caligari*, film techniques steadily progressed, the psychological screen dramas increasingly exhibited an imagery that elaborated the significance of their action. *Caligari's* theatrical affinity was also due to technical backwardness. An immovable camera focused upon the painted décor; no cutting device added a meaning of its own to that of the pictures. One should, of course, not forget the reciprocal influence *Caligari* and kindred films exerted, for their part, on the German stage. Stimulated by the use they made of the iris-in, stage lighting took to singling out a lone player, or some important sector of the scene. Cf. Barry, *Program Notes*, Series III, program 1; Gregor, *Zeitalter des Films*, pp. 134, 144–45; Rotha, *Film Till Now*, p. 275; Vincent, *Histoire de l'Art Cinématographique*, p. 189.

The Beginnings of the Expressionist Film

LOTTE H. EISNER

The leaning towards violent contrast—which in Expressionist literature can be seen in the use of staccato sentences—and the inborn German liking for chiaroscuro and shadow, obviously found an ideal artistic outlet in the cinema. Visions nourished by moods of vague and troubled yearning could have found no more apt mode of expression, at once concrete and unreal.

.   .   .

In 1817, in a letter to the archetypal Romantic Rahel Varnhagen, Astolphe de Coustine wrote: 'Behind the lives and writings of the Germans there is always a mysterious world whose light alone seems to pierce the veil of our atmosphere; and the minds disposed to ascend towards that world—which ends with the beginning of this one—will always be alien to France.'

It was in this mysterious world, attractive and repugnant at the same time, that the German cinema found its true nature.

The making of *Caligari* was strewn with incidents, which have been variously reported by the different people responsible for it.

We know from the comments of one of the authors of the scenario— quoted by Kracauer in *From Caligari to Hitler* (1947)—that the prologue and epilogue were added as an afterthought in the face of objections from both authors. The result of these modifications was to falsify the action and ultimately to reduce it to the ravings of a madman. The film's authors, Carl Mayer and Hans Janowitz, had had the very different intention of unmasking the absurdity of asocial authority, represented by Dr. Caligari, the superintendent of a lunatic asylum and proprietor of a fairground side-show.

Erich Pommer, who used to claim to have 'supervised' *Caligari*, alleges that the authors submitted the scenario to him and informed him of their intention of commissioning the sets from Alfred Kubin, a visionary designer and engraver whose obsessed works seem to arise from a chaos of light and shadow. Kubin's *Caligari* would certainly have been full of Goyaesque visions, and the German silent film would have had the gloomy

FROM *The Haunted Screen: Expressionism in the German Cinema and the Influence of Max Reinhardt* (1969) by Lotte H. Eisner, pp. 20–27. Originally published by the University of California Press; reprinted by permission of The Regents of the University of California.

hallucinatory atmosphere which is unmistakably its own without being sidetracked into the snares of abstraction. For Kubin, like Janowitz, came from Prague, a mysterious town whose ghetto, with its tortuous back-alleys, was a survival from the Middle Ages. Like Janowitz, Kubin knew all the horrors of an in-between world. In a half-autobiographical, half-fantastic tale, *Die Andere Seite*, published in 1922, he describes his wanderings through the dark streets, possessed by an obscure force which led him to imagine weird houses and landscapes, terrifying or grotesque situations. When he entered a little tea-shop, everything seemed bizarre. The waitresses were like wax dolls moved by some strange mechanism. He had the feeling that his intrusion had disturbed the few customers sitting at the tables; they were completely unreal, like phantoms hatching satanic plots. The far end of the shop, with its barrel-organ, seemed suspicious, a trap. Behind that barrel-organ there was surely a bloody lair wreathed in gloom . . . It is a pity that so vivid a painter of nightmares was never commissioned for *Caligari*.

The practical Pommer relates that while Mayer and Janowitz were 'talking art' at him, he for his part was considering the scenario from a very different point of view. 'They wanted to experiment,' he wrote in 1947, 'and I wanted to keep the costs down.' Making the sets in painted canvas was a saving from every point of view, and largely facilitated production in days when money and raw materials were scarce. On the other hand, at a time when Germany was still going through the indirect consequences of an abortive revolution and the national economy was as unstable as the national frame of mind, the atmosphere was ripe for experiment. The director of *Caligari*, Robert Wiene, subsequently claimed in London to be responsible for the film's Expressionist conception.

Yet it is difficult to be sure of the true details of these remote events.

Here is Hermann Warm's version of the facts about Caligari.* The producer was not Erich Pommer but Rudolf Meinert, the director of such unknown quantities as *Der Hund von Baskerville*, *Nachtasyl*, *Rosenmontag* and *Marie-Antoinette*. So it was Meinert, not Pommer, who, following the practice current in those days—when the sets were given more importance than everything else—gave the script of *Caligari* to the designer Warm. The latter studied it with two friends employed at the studios as painters, Walter Röhrig and Walter Reimann.†

'We spent a whole day and part of the night reading through this very curious script,' writes Warm. 'We realized that a subject like this needed something out of the ordinary in the way of sets. Reimann, whose painting in those days had Expressionist tendencies, suggested doing the sets Ex-

---

* In a manuscript sent to the editor of *Der Neue Film* following an article by Ernst Jaeger.

† Lang assures me that Pommer did supervise the film, and not Meinert. See, for Pommer and *Caligari*, his comments in 'Carl Mayer's début', *A Tribute to Carl Mayer*, London, 1947.

pressionistically. We immediately set to work roughing up designs in that style.'

Next day Wiene gave his agreement. Rudolf Meinert was more cautious and asked for a day to think about it. Then he told them, 'Do these sets as eccentrically as you can!'

This story illustrates one of the basic principles of the German cinema: the essential role played by the author, the designer, and the technical staff. It also helps to explain why, apart from the abstract film, the German silent cinema never had a proper avant-garde such as that found in France. German industry immediately latched on to anything of an artistic kind in the belief that it was bound to bring in money in the long run.

·   ·   ·

. . . Fritz Lang, who was chosen as the director of *Caligari* before Robert Wiene (he refused because he was still engaged in the filming of *Die Spinnen*), suggested to the production company that a good way of not scaring off the public would be to bring in a kind of *Rahmenhandlung* (framing-treatment), a prologue and epilogue in conventional settings supposed to take place in a lunatic asylum. Thus the main action, related in a conversation between two lunatics sitting in the asylum garden, became the elaborate invention of a fantastic world seen through the eyes of a madman.

When Abel Gance, that eternal pioneer, had made his own attempt at filming a world seen through the eyes of a madman he had gone about it in a quite different way. In *La Folie du Dr Tube,* knowing nothing of anamorphic lenses, he borrowed several concave and convex mirrors from a Hall of Mirrors in a nearby amusement-park and filmed the reflections of people and objects, occasionally obtaining, in addition to 'stretching' effects, mere blobs and wavy lines. This was a fundamentally Impressionistic use of the camera; the distortions of *Dr Caligari* lie in the basic graphic idea, and can therefore be termed *Expressionistic*.

The sets of *Caligari*, which have often been criticized for being too flat, do have some depth nonetheless. As Rudoph Messell says in *This Film Business* (1928), 'the background comes to the fore.' The depth comes from deliberately distorted perspectives and from narrow, slanting streets which cut across each other at unexpected angles. Sometimes also it is enhanced by a back-cloth which extends the streets into sinuous lines. The three-dimensional effect is reinforced by the inclined cubes of dilapidated houses. Oblique, curving, or rectilinear lines converge across an undefined expanse towards the background: a wall skirted by the silhouette of Cesare the somnambulist, the slim ridge of the roof he darts along bearing his prey, and the steep paths he scales in his flight.

In *Expressionismus und Film*, Rudolf Kurtz points out that these curves and slanting lines have a meaning which is decidedly metaphysical. For the psychic reaction caused in the spectator by oblique lines is entirely

Wiene, Mayer, Janowitz

different from that caused in him by straight lines. Similarly, unexpected curves and sudden ups and downs provoke emotions quite different from those induced by harmonious and gentle gradients.

But what matters is to create states of anxiety and terror. The diversity of planes has only secondary importance.

In *Caligari** the Expressionist treatment was unusually successful in evoking the 'latent physiognomy' of a small medieval town, with its dark twisting back-alleys boxed in by crumbling houses whose inclined façades keep out all daylight. Wedge-shaped doors with heavy shadows and oblique windows with distorted frames seem to gnaw into the walls. The bizarre exaltation brooding over the synthetic sets of *Caligari* brings to mind Edschmid's statement that 'Expressionism evolves in a perpetual excitation'. These houses and the well, crudely sketched at an alley-corner, do indeed seem to vibrate with an extraordinary spirituality. 'The ante-diluvian character of utensils awakens,' says Kurtz. This is Worringer's 'spiritual unrest' creating the 'animation of the inorganic'.

The Germans, used as they are to savage legends, have an eerie gift for animating objects. In the normal syntax of the German language objects have a complete active life: they are spoken of with the same adjectives and verbs used to speak of human beings, they are endowed with the same qualities as people, they act and react in the same way. Long before Expressionism this anthropomorphism had already been pushed to the extreme. In 1884 Friedrich Vischer, in his novel *Auch Einer*, talks about 'the perfidy of the object' which gloats upon† our vain efforts to dominate it. The bewitched objects in Hoffmann's obsessed universe appear in the same light.

Animate objects always seem to haunt German narcissism. When couched in Expressionist phraseology the personification is amplified; the metaphor expands and embraces people and objects in similar terms.‡

So we frequently find German-speaking authors attributing diabolical overtones to, for example, the street: in Gustav Meyrink's *Golem*, the houses in the Prague ghetto, which have sprouted like weeds, seem to have an insidious life of their own 'when the autumn evening mists stag-

---

* Modern prints of this film (originally tinted in green, steely-blue and brown) give no idea of the unity of composition afforded in the original by the images and their titles, the latter in strangely distorted 'Expressionistic' lettering. A few traces of this are left today in the hallucination scene, when the doctor, swept along by his obsession, perceives the written phrase 'You must become Caligari' flashing and undulating across the narrow entrance to a garden of flat spiny trees.

† Vischer's term is *Schadenfreude*, hard to translate with its typically German overtones of diabolical persistence and enjoyment of others' misfortunes.

‡ On the one hand the poet becomes 'a field fissured with thirst'; on the other hand, the 'voracious' mouths of windows or the 'avid' darts of shadow pierce 'shivering' walls, while the 'cruel' leaves of 'implacable' doors slash the 'moaning' flanks of 'despairing' houses.

nate in the streets and veil their imperceptible grimace'. In some mysterious way these streets contrive to abjure their life and feelings during the daytime, and lend them instead to their inhabitants, those enigmatic creatures who wander aimlessly around, feebly animated by an invisible magnetic current. But at night the houses reclaim their life with interest from these unreal inhabitants; they stiffen, and their sly faces fill with malevolence. The doors become gaping maws and shrieking gullets.

'The dynamic force of objects howls their desire to be created,' Kurtz declared, and this is the explanation of the overpowering obsessiveness of the *Caligari* sets.

But light, atmosphere, and distance are not the only determinants of the object-distortion which we find in Expressionist art. There is also the power of Abstractionism. Georg Marzynski informs us in his book *Methode des Expressionismus* (1920) that a selective and creative distortion gives the artist a means of representing the complexity of the psyche; by linking this psychical complexity to an optical complexity he can release an object's internal life, the expression of its 'soul'. The Expressionists are concerned solely with images in the mind. Hence oblique walls which have no reality. For, as Marzynski says, it is one of the characteristics of 'imagined images' to represent objects on the slant, seen from above at an acute angle; this viewpoint makes it easier to grasp the whole structure of the image.

The Germans love watching the reflections of distorting mirrors. The Romantics had already observed certain formal distortions. One of Ludwig Tieck's heroes, William Lovell, describes the impression of an unstable, ill-defined universe: 'at such times the streets appear to me to be *rows of counterfeit houses* inhabited by madmen . . .' The streets described by Kubin or Meyrink and those of the *Caligari* sets find their perfect echo in this phrase.

The abstraction and the total distortion of the *Caligari* sets are seen at their most extreme in the vision of the prison-cell, with its verticals narrowing as they rise like arrow-heads. The oppressive effect is heightened by these verticals being extended along the floor and directed at the spot where the chain-laden prisoner squats. In this hell the distorted, rhomboid window is a mockery. The designers succeed in rendering the idea of a gaol-in-the-absolute, in its 'most expressive expression'.

Hermann Warm stated that 'the cinema image must become an engraving'. But the German cinema's use of light and shade did not issue from this affirmation alone. The serial film *Homunculus,* made three years earlier, clearly demonstrates the effect that can be obtained from contrasts between black and white.

A lack of continuity is apparent between the Expressionistic sets and the utterly bourgeois furniture—the chintzy armchairs in Lil Dagover's sitting-room or the leather armchair in the madhouse yard. The break in style is fatal. Similarly, the façade of the asylum is not distorted, yet the end of the film is seen in the same weird décor. It is hard to say which is the more responsible for this: the Expressionist tendencies of the designers, or the parsimony of the producer.

The stylization of the acting is dictated by the sets. Yet Werner Krauss in the part of the satanic Dr Caligari and Conrad Veidt in that of the sinister somnambulist are the only actors who really adapt themselves to it, and—in Kurtz's words—achieve a 'dynamic synthesis of their being', by concentrating their movements and facial expressions. Through a reduction of gesture they attain movements which are almost linear and which—despite a few curves that slip in—remain brusque, like the broken angles of the sets; and their movements from point to point never go beyond the limits of a given geometrical plane. The other actors, on the other hand, remain locked in a naturalistic style, though, owing to the old-fashioned way in which they are dressed (cloaks, top hats, morning-coats), their outlines do achieve an element of the fantastic.

The characters of Caligari and Cesare conform to Expressionist conception; the somnambulist, detached from his everyday ambience, deprived of all individuality, an abstract creature, kills without motive or logic. And his master, the mysterious Dr Caligari, who lacks the merest shadow of human scruple, acts with the criminal insensibility and defiance of conventional morality which the Expressionists exalted.

Caligari as a Film Classic

ARTHUR LENNIG

The Cabinet of Dr. Caligari (1919) has long been cited in film histories as one of the undoubted masterpieces of the cinema and, by far, the best example of expressionism. Its style derived from an artistic movement which had started shortly after the turn of the century, but which did not affect the cinema until the turmoil and malaise of the post-war days. It became, at least for a while, a strong influence on German films.

Expressionism, like most "isms," is difficult to define, but (at least in terms of the cinema) it was a mode of seeing, a means by which random

FROM *The Silent Voice: A Text* by Arthur Lennig. Copyright 1969 by Arthur Lennig. Reprinted by permission of the author.

reality was forced and bent to more stylized forms. Since the story of
Caligari is a neurotic one, filled with shadows, madmen, and murder, the
sets were designed to reinforce (and in a way even create) the film's basic
substance. The expressionistic style was not used merely to form a backdrop for natural action and behavior. This method governed all aspects:
costumes, make-up, characterization, and even plot. Expressionism was
not, then, a gimmick that was added, but rather an organic part of the
very thing being said.

The Cabinet of Dr. Caligari plunges beneath the comforting façade
of order and reason and rips away the dissembling veneer of objects and
people, to reveal a nightmare world, a disintegrating universe buffeted by
unfathomable drives and shrouded by jagged but pervasive shadows.
Here then is a film that depicts *essence* rather than *appearance*. In doing
so, this 1919 film became a curiously prophetic work, for it caught the
alienation, frustration, tension, and horror of existence. What only a very
few European intellectuals of the time perceived has now filtered down
into popular culture, so that *Caligari* is not just a freakish art work but
closer to the Kafka-like reality of our era.

Because *Caligari* consists of obviously painted sets and was photographed in the studio without any use of the "real" world, it has been
considered by some critics to be nothing but photographed theatre and
therefore a non-film or anti-film, a production that would be just as effective on stage. This view is nonsense. Although each setting could be reproduced, a theatrical version of the picture would not even be an approx-
imation, for *Caligari,* in spite of certain shortcomings, is essentially a
film.

What are its shortcomings? The film has been accused of not using some
of the basic devices of the cinema, such as frequent shot breakdowns,
cross-cutting, and the moving camera. Its vision, we are told, is theatrical;
its eye that of a seat in the orchestra, not of a dynamic camera. These
accusations are in a sense true. Certainly the film does not often break
down scenes into closer, more effective shots, nor does it contain involved
cross-cutting, nor shrewd manipulations of shot to shot. The camera,
however, is not quite as stodgy as some critics have asserted. True, it
records a number of scenes in long shot, but it also cuts in closer at times.
There is cross-cutting (simultaneous action showing Alan in his room and
Caligari at the town-clerk's; and later the girl being attacked by Cesare
while Caligari is being watched by Francis); camera movement (an occasional pan); an attempt at camera fluidity by means of the iris (a primitive
way of singling out a particular part of a scene and then opening the iris
to reveal the context of the "close-up"); and an involved, though effective,
use of flashback. All these devices, plus the fact that the film contains over
370 cuts, averaging about one shot every ten seconds, should prove that
the film is more than just photographed theatre.

Wiene, Mayer, Janowitz

Of course the film hardly has the vital rhythms and sense of engage-ment of a Griffith production. In fact, in terms of technique, the film is much less imaginative and progressive than *The Birth of a Nation*, made five years before. But, for that matter, that is also true of sound films by Renoir and Dreyer. *Caligari* may not employ all the rich resources of the medium, and may seem archaic to some critics, but its originality of con-tent and perfection of decor more than compensate for its less dynamic manner.

To discuss whether one motion picture is more filmic than another can prove fruitful up to a point, but just as most literary critics have outgrown the pedantic occupation of examining which novels are more "novelistic" than others (as if that itself were a virtue), so must film scholars not founder over this issue. As the novel is larger than any narrow definition, so, indeed, is the film. To demand that an art work make use of *all* the potentialities of its medium—in short, to condemn a work for not being novelistic or cinematic without taking into account other compensatory and redeeming qualities—is to miss much of the richness and variety of the aesthetic experience.

When *Caligari* first appeared, it was liked by many intellectuals (pseudo and otherwise) because it was more "art" than photographed reality. Many who praised the film did not really appreciate the medium for its own sake, but for how it could preserve or render kindred arts. *Queen Elizabeth* (with Sarah Bernhardt) was a far more tedious experience than a Griffith Biograph film, although the first received greater praise in the newspapers and theatrical columns than the latter. It has taken a long time for film to be accepted for what it is, and not for what it echoes.

But if the theatre lovers approved of the film, other critics (oriented far differently) disapproved. Siegfried Kracauer, in his *Theory of Film*, exam-ines the problem in his somewhat obtuse manner:

> Obviously screen fantasies which rely on staginess and at the same time claim to be valid manifestations of the medium run counter to the basic aesthetic principle; they pass over the specific potentialities of the medium for the sake of objectives which the cinema is not particularly fit to fulfill.*

Kracauer feels that *Caligari* is a "radical negation of camera-realism" and a "retrogression."† Kracauer fits his Procrustian theory to the film and finds it wanting. Perhaps a more pragmatic approach would be that the film is an exciting and stimulating visual experience (admittedly from *what* is shown, rather than *how*), and by far one of the most interesting and

---

* Siegfried Kracauer, *Theory of Film*, p. 84.
† *Ibid.*, p. 85.

individual works in cinematic history. That it is not in the mainstream of the film's development is not quite saying that it is a retrogression. It is, rather, another aspect.

It must be remembered that many of the criticisms and evaluations of *Caligari,* condemning it for being theatrical, were made during the late twenties and thirties when montage was *de rigueur;* but that method, however fascinating it may be, is but one facet of the cinema. Eisenstein, for example, criticized the film for its "silent hysteria . . . unnatural broken gestures and actions of monstrous chimeras." Furthermore, he criticized the German cinema for its "mysticism, decadence, and dismal fantasy."* Yet, ironically, what he had disapproved of, he in many ways emulated in his *Ivan the Terrible.* Its stylized movement, elaborate lighting effects, carefully designed sets, and absence of obvious juxtaposition, are closer to *Caligari* than the great Soviet director would have cared to admit, nor is the shadowy world of *Ivan* much saner than that of *Caligari.*

Caligari is the first film to capture the nightmare quality of the modern world. In its largest context, the film is a representation of this age of anxiety. Even the opening scene, photographed amidst bare, dangling branches of a willow-like tree, suggests the tangled and web-like substance of existence. Throughout the film, dark forms and cutouts appear in the corners of the frame, as if the gloom of the theatre were intruding even onto the dim-lit screen. This use of twisted forms, this play of light and shadow, is more than merely decorative. It suggests, reinforces, substantiates, and, indeed, creates the content. The world is no longer the scientific and rational place that the Age of Enlightenment and the scientific progress of the nineteenth century promised. The film, like a Dostoyevsky novel, provides a psychologically truthful picture of the modern neurosis.

The world of *Caligari* is a bleak one, full of despair. Alan, the student, is first shown rapidly turning the pages of a book in his garret. He is more than nervous. Representing at least an aspect of intellectualism, he is experiencing *Angst.* Overwhelmed with the dark squalor of his room, with the torment of existence, he is undergoing that awful feeling of dread. In despair, he rushes out of his room to see his friend, Francis, and convinces him to go to the fair, that is, to escape to the outer world. But he receives little comfort. Intrigued by the strangely evocative poster outside of the cabinet of Dr. Caligari,† Alan enters. When the doctor asks for questions from the audience, Alan feverishly utters the words, "How long shall I

---

* Sergei Eisenstein, *Film Form,* pp. 202–3.
† English-speaking people tend to think that the cabinet refers solely to the coffin-like box that Cesare is kept in. But *cabinet,* in German, also implies a room or, more specifically, a piece of furniture containing *objets d'art,* or, in a larger sense, a "collection." Thus there is the overtone that Cesare is Caligari's supreme art object, a thing to be exhibited proudly.

live?" This is a question that everyone asks himself, but which few raise in public. But Alan is obsessed with the problem of existence. When Cesare, slowly opening his mouth, replies that the time is short, for "You will die at dawn," Alan is overcome. He seems almost as pleased as appalled at the prediction.

The film also touches upon the difficulty of discerning appearance from reality. Soon after the first murder occurs, a prowler is caught. The audience feels that he may be the murderer, but this murderer is comforting, for his motive is money, something humanly comprehensible. To the contrary, Cesare's killings are particularly horrible, for they are logically indefensible. Their lack of motivation adds to the nightmare quality of the picture.

This theme of appearance versus reality runs throughout the film. While Francis is watching Cesare in his box, the camera shows Jane being attacked by Cesare. Appearance again belies reality, for Francis has been observing a dummy. Later, when Francis pursues Caligari to the institute, the audience's expectations are again shocked, for the insane man is not a patient but the director of the institute. The last important twist comes in the frame story when the tables are turned again and the seemingly villainous Caligari is now benign and Francis the deranged one. Amidst these shifting forms and misleading surfaces, the world becomes even more muddled, more shrouded than ever from the clarifying light of reason and order.

The film, to put aside its O. Henry ending for a moment, is essentially the story of a doctor who, after making a profound study of somnambulism, causes one of his patients who has lost all consciousness of self to become his will-less subject. On this first level alone, the film deserves analysis. The doctor is, in a sense, a man with a quest, a man who wishes to find out how far his will can overcome that of another; in short, he wants, ostensibly, to discover to what criminal lengths the captive mind of his patient, Cesare, can be brought. When, as a flashback indicates, Cesare is brought to the head of the institute, the doctor immediately decides to carry out his plans. He is not akin to the scientist—so familiar to horror film viewers of the thirties—who pursues his thesis so obsessively that he loses all sense of human values. Caligari does not seem to have gone over the brink of sanity, but seems to have been diseased from the beginning. In short, the lust for power and murder was there; only the docile instrument of his evil was missing.

Is this strange doctor to be taken merely as a specific aberration or is he symbolic of something more? Although he is the head of an insane asylum staffed by efficient and knowledgeable men in white coats, the doctor does not seem part of this scientific milieu. His study, for example, hardly in keeping with the clean, white sterility of scientific experiment, is filled with piles of scattered books; a skeleton (more omen or symbol than object of study) hangs in the corner; and the interior, more Gothic than modern, lies shrouded in gloom.

Although the doctor lives in a scientific age, his interests are metaphysical. He does not care about the outer world and its political façade, but rather is obsessed by the inner world, a world of will, power, crime, perhaps even "evil" itself. He is fascinated by the dark forces, by the shadows that lurk and brood in man's mind. Psychological and psychiatric investigation cannot really solve the questions he has raised. He knows in his own crazed brain that reason is but the unwieldy rudder of a phantasmal ship. And so he returns to an age when the forces of evil were accepted and not brushed aside or considered irrelevant or old-fashioned. His guidance comes, then, not from contemporary inquiry but from a medieval manuscript. He decides to repeat the experiments of an eleventh-century monk who traveled throughout the countryside with a somnambulist, Cesare.

The doctor, as a poet would see him, is a symbol of the shadow which does not fade with the light of civilization. He is, in a sense, the *id*, the dark, irrational element that lurks and glides behind the placid expression of man.

Although Caligari is a destructive force, it is his power over others that poses the real threat to civilization. For this reason the relationship between Caligari and Cesare merits examination.

As we meet Caligari in the film, he is anti-social, willful, petulant, and quick to take offense. Because the town clerk makes the doctor wait, he is murdered. And later, when Alan asks how long he will live, Cesare's answer is not a prophesy of what fate had had in store for Alan; instead Caligari orders his death seemingly to carry out the prediction.

Caligari keeps the somnambulist in a coffin-like box (suggestive of dead consciousness) and feeds him like a child. But Caligari has not taken complete control over Cesare, for the somnambulist still has some remnants of his value system and morality. When commanded by his master to kill the girl, he enters the room and stands before her with a dagger in his hand, but pauses, unwilling to carry out his master's orders. Confused, he attempts independent action by carrying her across the rooftops. Finally, in exhaustion, he puts her down and runs off only to die. From a theological point of view, Cesare has gained back a small portion of his soul and so escapes Caligari's evil dominance in death.

But what does this relationship of the Doctor to his somnambulist signify? It is master to slave, will to will-lessness, possessor to the possessed, perhaps even *id* to *ego*. But this situation takes on further meaning in a social context. Siegfried Kracauer has shown in *From Caligari to Hitler* that the authors of the script intended to make a social statement concerning man's relationship to the leaders of government. Thus Cesare (the common man who has been propagandized and brain-washed) is told to

Wiene, Mayer, Janowitz

go out and kill for the whims of his master. Caligari, then, represents the rulers of the state, rulers who spoon-feed the people, who make them act against their basic morality, who sacrifice them to satisfy under the banner of nationalism their own egotistical and insane predilections for violence. In this relationship of populace to ruler, of soldier to general, the film takes on further meanings. Such a sociological approach, however, can easily be vulgarized and debased and the rich meanings of the film be subverted into narrow and partisan channels.

Kracauer errs in his sociological-psychological analysis by forcing Caligari to apply only to a specific situation—to Germany's leaders—and then compounds his errors by seeing Caligari as Hitler, and culminates his fabrication by seeing this same master–slave relationship through a number of subsequent German films. In short, Kracauer has transformed a perfectly valid theme (as presented by the film's authors) and applied it only to Germany rather than to similar social problems everywhere in the world.

.   .   .

The Caligari–Cesare relationship forms the basic plot of the film. But the director, so Kracauer says, chose to add a frame story, much against the objection of the authors. This complication of the film's narrative has various effects upon the central tale. If one accepts the film as an indictment of a social structure which allows evil Caligaris to control it, then the frame story modifies this point. Thus Francis, who says that Caligari (the establishment) is deranged, is himself deranged. This change makes the film conformist, not rebellious; makes it docile, not revolutionary, for whoever complains that the government is insane is himself insane.

This film, like Sophocles' *Antigone,* deals with a universal problem. For a critic to explain the character of Creon by saying that he acts the way he does because he's a Greek, and that's the way the Greeks are, is to miss the whole point of the play. Creon is not merely a native product, but the embodiment of an age-old type. For the critic to conclude that the Greeks are a cruel people—observe the violence in their drama—and to say that that is the reason their civilization collapsed, is, at best, foolish, if not actually vicious. To particularize a universal, to reduce a broad and meaningful theme to specific and, indeed, irrelevant details (such as the accidents of history, assuming that history is not inevitable) is to miss the whole wonder of the process of art.

And this, unfortunately, Kracauer does. Ignoring the film's subtleties and intentions, he comes to the business at hand: to convince his reader that Caligari is "a premonition" of Hitler.

> Caligari is a very specific premonition in the sense that he uses hypnotic power to force his will upon his tool—a technique fore-

shadowing, in content and purpose, that manipulation of the soul which Hitler was the first to practice on a gigantic scale.[*]

. . .

If the film is a parable of the common man and his evil masters, then Cesare's action with the girl can perhaps be examined further. When Cesare sees whom he is supposed to kill, he pauses, gazes at her a moment, and strokes her cheek. It is at this moment that Caligari's evil powers cannot subvert all of Cesare's good impulses. In a larger sense, Cesare sees before him, through the dim veil of his befuddled consciousness, not only a woman, but his fellow man. This situation, if we can return to the social context of the film, has often been paralleled in the war. Soldiers from opposite sides who have found themselves thrown together in the same shell-hole have been faced with a unique problem. If they do not kill each other immediately, the hate quickly disappears; the abstraction of "The Enemy" at whom each has been shooting vanishes before their common humanity. They are both afraid, tired, hungry. If the commands of their leaders do not still echo in their ears, they will show each other crumpled pictures of their wives and children in their wallets and begin to "fraternize."[†]

. . .

Although this refracting frame story transforms a rather strict allegory into a more oblique and ironic work, it does not by any means remove all the punch or sting from the central story. For the frame to have been a negating force to the main ideas of the film, this frame should then have returned the audience to the natural world, a world of supposed order, logic, reason, and sanity. But it does not do this. As can be seen, the sets have not been changed, nor the neurotic ambience purged. Shadows and weird angles still abound. In the real world that concludes the film, whether quite intended or not, still lurks that dark and mysterious something.

. . .

When the film was shown at the Capitol Theatre in New York in April, 1921, Mr. Rothafel (Roxy) added a stage prologue and epilogue. At the conclusion of the film (with Dr. Caligari's comments that he could cure his patient), the curtains at the theatre opened on a stage actor saying:

[*] Siegfried Kracauer, *From Caligari to Hitler,* Princeton University Press (1947), p. 73.
[†] This is a common scene in war films. It has been dramatized in *The Big Parade* (1925), in which an American watches the German soldier whom he has wounded die; *All Quiet on the Western Front* (1930), where a German soldier sees a Frenchman die and removes from the corpse's pocket the pictures of his family; and *The Man I Killed* (1932), in which the surviving soldier expiates his guilt by visiting the family of the boy whom he killed during the war.

> And he did. [*That is, Dr. Caligari, did cure him.*] Francis Purnay is today a prosperous jeweler in Edenwald, happily married, with a couple of healthy, normal children. And the strangest thing about his recovery is the lapse of memory that accompanies it. He is like a man suddenly awakened from a bad dream and unable to remember any detail of its horror. The name "Dr. Caligari" today means no more to him than Smith or Jones. He has completely forgotten his hallucination.

This ridiculous epilogue which, by the way, the American critics liked because they thought it "clarified" the film, does more than to satisfy the public's wish for a happy ending. It says, in effect, forget the whole thing. Francis has forgotten it, he can't "remember any detail of its horror," so why don't you? And, anyhow, he's doing all right with that jewelry shop and those two children of his.

The Cabinet of Dr. Caligari obviously supports analysis on a number of levels. Its suggestiveness is a tribute to both its content and construction. Having weathered the ravages of time, fashion, and technique, the film is, for the most part, as modern and fresh as when it was first made, and well merits its appellation as a masterpiece of the cinema.

EISENSTEIN

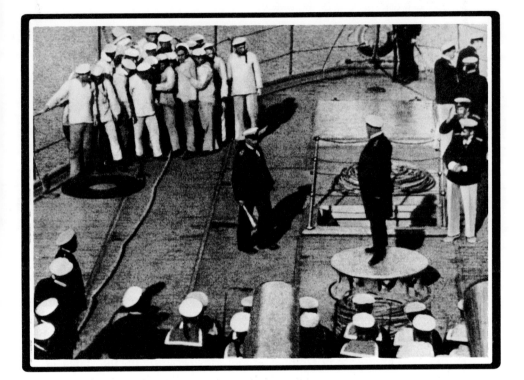

POTEMKIN

CREdiTS

Potemkin (Russia, 1925)
Original title: *Bronenosets Potemkin (Battleship Potemkin)*
Directed by Sergei Eisenstein from his own screenplay based on an original
   story by Nina Agadzhanova-Shutko in collaboration with him
Produced by Jacob Bliokh for First Goskino Production, Moscow

Assistant director: Grigory Alexandrov
Photography: Eduard Tisse
Art director: Vasili Rakhals
Original musical score: Edmund Meisel
Subtitles: Nikolai Asseyev
Distributors (16mm): Audio-Brandon Films, United Films, *et al*

Main performers:
A. Antonov (*Vakulinchuk*)
Vladimir Barsky (*Commander Goli-
   kov*)

Grigory Alexandrov (*Senior Officer
   Gilyarovsky*)
M. Gomorov (*Matyushenko*)

Smirnov, the ship's surgeon, and the Priest are played by anonymous non-
   professionals.

Length: 5 reels

Sergei Eisenstein was the cinema's leading theorist as well as one of its greatest directors. Between the appearance in 1924 of his first feature film, *Strike,* and his death in 1948 at the age of fifty, he was able to complete only six additional films, abandoning a few other projects because of difficulties with producers in Hollywood and Mexico and with the state-controlled industry in Russia. The fact that lack of opportunity to work continually at his art provided him with the time to lecture and write with exceptional penetration about the nature of film partially reconciles us to the loss of other great films that we could have expected from so original a cinematic mind as Eisenstein's.

In both theory and practice Eisenstein epitomizes the school of fragmentation editing that originated with D. W. Griffith, a major influence on Eisenstein. Eisenstein's use of the French term for editing, montage, came to be associated with a certain style characterized by very rapid cutting. The international success of his second film, *Potemkin,* fixed in the public's mind the exaggerated notion that the Russian school of filming specialized exclusively in the highly analytical process of piecing together film

meaning according to rigidly formalistic patterns derived from preconceived ideas of exactly what the finished film would look like. In spite of
the fact that *Potemkin* was an experimental project, the production of
which was characterized by improvisation and frequent changes in plan,
it was virtually the only film that would completely fit Eisenstein's published theories, and it remains the textbook example of the Russian style.
The reason for *Potemkin's* perfection *in practice* of Eisenstein's theories is
obvious: after the success of the film, Eisenstein used it as the model to
illustrate his ideas. It was by no means a film made to the specifications
of theory, but rather a work of art so brilliant in its execution that it later
lent itself readily to the application of theories not previously articulated.

For a number of years after its appearance, many viewers considered
Potemkin the greatest film ever made. After Eisenstein's death, a reaction
gradually set in among critics, and today, even though the film appears
regularly on lists of critics' all-time favorites, its true merit has been somewhat obscured by attempts to view it as a representation of a style or a
theory or a tradition. In fact, it represents nothing but itself, a unique
achievement that has in recent years been more appreciated than seen—
that is, admired more for what it is thought to stand for than for what it is.

First of all, *Potemkin* is an emotionally charged story of a group of sailors
forced to suffer unendurable indignities at the hands of their tyrannical
commanding officers. These officers clearly stand for a government that is
habitually oppressive and contemptuous of its citizens, as we come to understand when we see other representatives of the Czar participating in
the most brutal civilian massacre ever filmed. The reputation of *Potemkin*
mistakenly suggests that it is a highly intellectualized work, photographed
with dispassionate objectivity. Actually, it was aimed at a mass audience
of barely educated people, many of whom could not even read the insert
titles. What everyone could comprehend at the time of the initial distribution of the film was the force of its emotional commitment to ordinary
people, good citizens confronted by brutal symbols of governmental
power. The film's structure utilizes emotional moments of mass recognition of universal brotherhood: the sailors aboard the *Potemkin* discover
their kinship with a group of rebellious sailors about to be executed and
prevent the execution; the citizens of Odessa recognize their relationship
with the mutineers of the *Potemkin* and support them; the seamen of the
Russian fleet sent to intercept the *Potemkin* acknowledge their brotherhood with the mutinous sailors and, disobeying their admirals, allow the
ship to pass safely through the fleet. All the recognitions are intuitive or
emotional: a rational case is not needed for the participants in the film or
for the audience. In every sequence, Eisenstein in a highly subjective
fashion directs the viewer's attention to the condition of the suffering
masses. The film's most memorable sequence, the massacre on the Odessa
steps, is constructed so as to generate the most intense feeling of identity

Theory into Practice

JAY LEYDA

Strike made a great impression not only on Soviet film-makers, but on its own maker. It convinced Eisenstein that his chief interest was cinema. So long as he remained at Proletkult he would have to divide his attention between theatrical and film work. On completion of his first film (but before its general release) Eisenstein resigned from the direction of Proletkult's Central Theatre, and went to work at the Moscow studio of Seyzapkino, where he began the preparation of a film on the First Cavalry Army's role in the Civil War, a project that must have been dear to [Eduard] Tisse, who had filmed and fought with Budyonny's cavalry during the war.

Nineteen hundred and twenty-five was an anniversary year. It was one of the duties of the appointed jubilee committee to assign and supervise the production of films to celebrate the 1905 Revolution. The two most important scripts, *Ninth of January* and *Year 1905*, had been approved as early as June 1924, but the committee found themselves well into 1925 without having decided on a director for the latter, larger, scenario. Nina Agadzhanova-Shutko had sketched a panorama of the events of 1905 that seemed too huge for any of the established directors to tackle. After pre-release screenings of *Strike* in March the jubilee committee and the Commissariat of Education felt that, at last, the director for *Year 1905* had been found. Eisenstein was withdrawn from the Cavalry Army film before shooting was started, and assigned to the *1905* panorama.

We often have occasion to note the extraordinary speed of the Soviet film's development as communication, as art, growing in the power of its propaganda and its aesthetics. This growth seems even more remarkable when we watch it through the leading individuals of this period. As sophisticated as Eisenstein's approach was to the Proletkult staging of Ostrovsky's *Wise Man,* the twenty-five-year-old artist who did that seems many years younger than the twenty-six-year-old artist who directed *Strike.* And the making of *Strike* had speeded up the process of his artistic maturity to an astonishing degree that can be measured only by looking at *Strike* and *Potemkin* on the same day. There have been other instances of such swift growth in young artists, but the leap between those two works is as great as the leap from theory to full realization. The plunge into the new medium brought new light to his whole theoretical approach

FROM *Kino: A History of the Russian and Soviet Film* (1960) by Jay Leyda, pp. 193–99. Reprinted by permission of George Allen & Unwin Ltd.

to the problems of art. The psychological basis of artistic creation, always important to Eisenstein after the profound impression made upon him by Freud's essay on Leonardo da Vinci, now had a new world to be applied to. He later said that Marx and Lenin furnished the philosophical basis for his psychological researches, which were drawn from Pavlov (reflexology) and Freud (psychoanalysis)—and *Strike* had, apparently, come, at just the right time in his theoretical development, as the incentive he needed to transform his next material into a masterpiece. Kuleshov, as he would, explained Eisenstein's swift development in a much simpler way— 'will, persistence, and sharp eyes'.*

As handed to Eisenstein by Goskino, the scenario of *1905* covered the Revolution from the Russo-Japanese War to the armed uprising in Moscow.† Filming began March 31, 1925. The first episodes to be filmed were of a demonstration in St Petersburg and incidents of the general strike—and then film history was changed by the continued concealment of the sun, both in Leningrad and in Moscow. Towards the end of his life Eisenstein wrote a memoir‡ on the making of *Potemkin* that tells of the group's decision to work on episodes that could be filmed in the south, and of their chase after the last rays of summer sun there. Odessa was to be the setting for a strike of dock-workers and the demonstration after the mutiny of the battleship Potemkin. In the script forty-two shots were to cover the Potemkin mutiny and consequent events. But when Eisenstein saw the great flight of marble steps leading down to Odessa's harbour, he knew that this was the stage for the Cossack massacre of the Odessa crowd:

> I believe that nature, circumstances, the setting at the moment of shooting, and the filmed material itself at the moment of montage, can sometimes be wiser than author and director. . . .
>
> The fragments [to precede the battleship's cannonade] had at first been planned to develop the harshness of the Cossack reprisals through various ascending stages (on the street, in a printshop courtyard, on the outskirts of the city, in front of a bakery) into one monumental flight of stairs, the steps of which were to serve as rhythmic and dramatic links for the victims of the tragedy, scattered about the steps.
>
> No scene of shooting on the Odessa steps appeared in any of the preliminary versions or in any of the montage lists that were prepared. It was born in the instant of immediate contact.

* In *Eisenstein: Potemkin* (Moscow, 1926), a brochure containing three essays, by Shklovsky, Kuleshov, and Tisse.
† 1. Russo-Japanese War; 2. January 9th and the following wave of strikes; 3. Peasant risings; 4. General strike and its liquidation; 5. Reaction attacks—Jewish pogroms, Armenian massacres; 6. Krasnaya Presnaya.
‡ Posthumously published in *Iskusstvo Kino*, No. 4, 1950; translated as 'The Birth of a Film' in *The Hudson Review*, Summer, 1951.

The anecdote about the idea for this scene being born as I watched the bouncing from step to step of the cherry pits I spat out while standing at the top, beneath the Duc de Richelieu's monument, is, of course, a myth—very colourful, but a downright myth. It was the very *movement* of the steps that gave birth to the idea of the scene, and with its "flight" roused the fantasy of the director to a new "spiralling". And it would seem that the panicky *rush* of the crowd, "flying" down the steps, is no more than a materialization of those first feelings on seeing this staircase.

And, too, it is possible that this was helped by some looming from the womb of memory, some illustration in a magazine of 1905—a horseman on a staircase veiled in smoke, slashing someone with a sabre. . . .

Out of this decisive idea grew another, as the actual filming began: to make the Potemkin mutiny the central episode of *1905;* in the cutting-room, or even later, it became apparent that this single episode contained all that was typical of the whole revolution. In the final cutting, all material but *Potemkin* was dropped, and thus evolved what has been called the most perfect and concise example of film structure.

Many of the accomplishments in *Potemkin* can be ascribed to the understanding with which Eisenstein and Tisse worked together. Aside from the almost incredible efficiency with which *Potemkin* was filmed (all shots of the funeral procession completed in one morning, the whole drama on the quarter-deck filmed on their last day),[*] Tisse's ingenuity was ideal for Eisenstein's invention. The slaughter on the steps needed filming techniques as original as the new montage principles. A camera-trolley was built the length of the steps—dollyshots were then almost unknown in Russian films. Several cameras were deployed simultaneously. A hand-camera was strapped to the waist of a running, jumping, falling (and circus-trained) assistant. Many realities put on film for the first time, such as the scene in an actual ship's engine-room, have long since been absorbed by documentary techniques; John Grierson's work on the American version of *Potemkin* lends veracity to the story that the British documentary film movement was born from the last reel of *Potemkin*.

Although this is the classic example of a non-documentary film without 'roles,' *Potemkin* was introduced to the United States as 'played by Moscow Art Theatre actors'! There are a few actors in the film, chiefly all of Eisenstein's assistant directors from Proletkult,[†] and Vladimir Barsky, a film director who played the part of Captain Golikov, but the Moscow

[*] The tumult around the steps during the filming led a French traveller, André Beucler, to suppose that Civil War had again broken out (*Les Nouvelles Littéraires,* 15 October 1927).
[†] Levshin plays the first ship's officer whom we see; in a manner almost identical with his characterization in *Strike,* Alexandrov plays Chief Officer Gilyarovsky; Antonov

Art Theatre can hardly claim the Sevastopol gardener who played the role of the priest or the furnace-man who was cast as the ship's doctor,* not to mention the dozens of vivid 'bit' roles, played as much by Eisenstein's compositions and Tisse's camera as by the sailors and citizens whose faces we see.

The importance of cutting and editing as a creative process was perhaps the most widely recognized revelation of *Potemkin*. The sensations of fear on the quarter-deck, panic and machine-like murder on the steps, tension on the waiting ship could only have been communicated by this revolutionary cutting method. What must be remembered is that the total construction and the frame-compositions of *Potemkin*, notwithstanding all spiteful legends about 'happy accidents'† to the contrary, were gauged and carried out with most of the eventual juxtapositions in mind. The shots taken on the steps were filmed looking forward to the cutting-table as much as were the famous shots at the end of the fourth reel—three different marble lions which become one single rearing lion in the editor's hands and the audience's eyes. Heretofore, the movement of a film had depended largely on the 'logical' progression of action within the sequence of shots. Eisenstein now created a new film-rhythm by adding to this content the sharply varying lengths and free associations of the shots, a technique growing directly from his interest in psychological research. Besides the behaviouristic stimulation made possible by this method, a new range of rhythmic patterns and visual dynamics was opened by *Potemkin*.

The story of *Potemkin*'s public release is one that has never been told fully, possibly because it would reflect small credit on the administration of the film industry at that time. On December 21, 1925, *Potemkin* was shown for the first time, at the 1905 jubilee evening held at the Bolshoi Opera Theatre.

> When the day of the solemn jubilee meeting came, we were still editing the film [after eighteen days in the cutting-room].
>
> When the hour for the screening struck, the last reels were not yet ready.
>
> Cameraman Tisse left for the Bolshoi Theatre with the completed first reels, so that the screening could be started. Eisenstein followed him as soon as the next to the last real was ready. I stayed behind to splice the last reel. As soon as I finished I started off with it, but my motor-cycle refused to go beyond the Iberian Gate, and I had to run from there to the Bolshoi.

---

plays Vakulinchuk; Gomorov plays the sailor whom we see oftenest. Matyushenko is played by a former naval officer who was also the technical advisor on the film's period details.

* 'The Birth of a Film' describes the discovery of this 'actor'.

† Agadzhanova-Shutko apparently never forgave the cavalier treatment of her ambitious script, and some stories can be traced to her friends.

As I raced up the stairs to the projection booth, I was overjoyed to hear the noise of applause coming from the theatre. This was the first happy sign of our film's success.°

It is a pity that there is little contemporary evidence on the opinion of that first of many audiences to see it, for this invited audience must have contained all the leading members of the Government and representatives of all the arts. Between this occasion and the date of the film's public release, January 18, 1926, would seem a normal interval to prepare the release prints and distribution apparatus, though it does appear that Goskino might, with a little haste, have released the film within the anniversary year. On December 25th, Goskino released, instead, the other anniversary film, *Ninth of January*, directed by Viskovsky. This delay gives some substance to a story (told after Eisenstein's death) by Waclaw Solski,† then assisting Goskino in foreign sales. His errors may be due to a faulty memory, natural after twenty-five years, or to a less excusable tendency toward 'angling' his story. The most credible portion of his story concerns a private screening that may have taken place between the two public showings:

> Vladimir Mayakovsky, the famous Soviet poet, saw *Potemkin* with me. His friend, the poet Aseyev, had written the titles for it, and he was always loyal to his friends. Immediately after the showing, Mayakovsky and I went to see Sovkino's president, Konstantin Shvedchikov, a party man who once had hidden Lenin in his home before the Revolution. But this was long ago, and in 1925 Shvedchikov was a Soviet bureaucrat with pronounced bourgeois habits. He didn't know anything about movies, but he liked the products Hollywood sent to Moscow in hope of finding a Russian market. Sovkino bought very few American films, but Shvedchikov used to spend hours enjoying them in his private projection room, and the more banal the movie, the better he liked it. He was also slightly anti-Semitic and he didn't like Eisenstein, whom, in private conversation, he used to call "The Nobleman of Jerusalem".
>
> Mayakovsky took the floor first. He talked, as usual, in a thunderous voice, pounding the table with his fists and rapping on the floor with the heavy cane he always carried at that time. He demanded that Shvedchikov immediately export *Potemkin* and told him he would go down in history as a villain if he did not. Several times Shvedchikov tried to get a word in, but in vain. Nobody ever could say anything when Mayakovsky spoke. The climax of his speech was rather dramatic. Having finished, he turned to go.

° Alexandrov, 'From the Memories of a Regisseur-Assistant,' *Iskusstvo Kino*, December 1955.
† Solski, 'The End of Sergei Eisenstein,' *Commentary* (New York), March 1949.

"Are you through?" Shvedchikov asked. "If you are, I would like to say a few words myself."

Mayakovsky paused in the doorway and replied with great dignity: "I'm not through yet and I won't be for at least five hundred years. Shvedchikovs come and go, but art remains. Remember that!"

With that he left. I stayed behind and tried to argue with my boss in more reasonable terms, but in vain. It was only later, under the pressure of an ever-growing group of writers and journalists as well as some influential party men who liked the film, that Sovkino finally did agree to send *Potemkin* to Berlin.

Whatever the story behind it, the fact of *Potemkin*'s triumph in Berlin is indisputable. This was the beginning of a series of shocks and triumphs in every country where the film was shown—a series that shows no sign of yet ending. What is more doubtful is that *Potemkin*'s Berlin success made Soviet critics pay more attention to the film; this seems to strain probability, and is based on the fact that all Soviet critical reactions were published after the later public release rather than after the Bolshoi showing. In a later detailed complaint at Sovkino executives, Mayakovsky said, 'On its first showing *Potemkin* was relegated to second-rate theatres only, and it was only after the enthusiastic reaction of the foreign press that it was put into the best theatres.'* And Lunacharsky also gave evidence on this point:

> . . . we have many examples of Soviet films that do not pay for themselves, and have no success. It is true that some of these deserve such a reception, but there are also facts of an opposite significance. It is commonly hushed up that *Potemkin* had no success with us. I remember the strange impression I had when I entered the First Sovkino Theatre on Arbat Square, decorated with a display representing a ship, and with ushers costumed as sailors. I found the theatre half-empty. And this was the first run of *Potemkin*. Only after the German public enthusiastically greeted *Potemkin* was it properly shown here. Its greatest publicity came from the wish to see a film that had brought us our first victory in the foreign film-market.†

Before *Potemkin*'s foreign acclaim there was a never-disputed concept in the Soviet film industry: that no Soviet film with 'agitational value' could be shown abroad with success. Obviously the revolutionary material saturating *Potemkin* had not interfered with its success abroad; even in those countries, such as France and England, where it was forbidden publicly, the private screenings were to attract enormous interest. This was

---

* Printed in Mayakovsky's *Kino* (Moscow, 1940).
† Lunacharsky's contribution to *The Soviet Film Confronted by Society*, edited by K. Maltsev (Moscow, 1928).

an unpleasant shock to those directors who had defended their 'minimal-agitational' films by this myth of foreign coolness to Bolshevik art.

Potemkin has been the subject of more *post facto* examination than any other film. Eisenstein himself has provided the best of these analyses in his later theoretical writing; in one article he concentrates on the over-all structure and content of his masterpiece:

> *Potemkin* looks like a chronicle (or newsreel) of an event, but it functions as a drama.
>
> The secret of this lies in the fact that the chronicle pace of the event is fitted to a severely tragic composition. And furthermore, to tragic composition in its most canonic form—the five-act tragedy. . . . This was further emphasized by the individual titling of each "act".[*] Here, in condensation, are the contents of the five acts:
>
> *Reel 1—"Men and Maggots"*. Exposition of the action. Milieu of the battleship. Maggotty meat. Discontent ferments among the sailors.
>
> *Reel 2—"Drama on the Quarterdeck"*. "All hands on deck!" Refusal to eat the wormy soup. Scene with tarpaulin. "Brothers!" Refusal to fire. Mutiny. Revenge on the officers.
>
> *Reel 3—"Appeal from the Dead"*. Mist. The body of Vakulinchuk is brought into Odessa port. Mourning over the body. Indignation. Demonstration. Raising the red flag.
>
> *Reel 4—"The Odessa Steps"*. Fraternization of shore and battleship. Yawls with provisions. Shooting on the Odessa steps. The battleship fires on the "generals' staff".
>
> *Reel 5—"Meeting the Squadron"*. Night of suspense. Meeting the squadron. Engines. "Brothers!" The squadron refuses to fire. The battleship passes victoriously through the squadron. . . .
>
> From a tiny cellular organism in the battleship to the organism of the battleship itself; from a tiny cellular organism of the fleet to the organism of the whole fleet—thus flies through the theme the revolutionary feeling of brotherhood. And this is repeated in the structure of the work containing this theme—brotherhood and revolution.
>
> Over the heads of the battleship's commanders, over the heads of the admirals of the Tsar's fleet, and finally over the heads of the foreign censors, rushes the whole film with its fraternal "Hurrah!" just as within the film the feeling of brotherhood flies from the rebellious battleship over the sea to the shore.[†]

[*] From the first years of the Soviet film, with its emphasis on travelling and rural film exhibitions, rarely equipped with more than one projector, the film-makers planned each reel as an independent unit that could be followed by a (hopefully) brief pause. Scenarists and directors exploited the dramatic possibilities of this physical part-structure. In both *Strike* and *Potemkin* Eisenstein went a little further by giving each reel a title.

[†] 'The Structure of Film', *Iskusstvo Kino*, June 1939; translated in *Film Form*.

One of the curious effects of the film has been to replace the facts of the Potemkin mutiny with the film's artistic 'revision' of those events, in all subsequent reference, even by historians, to this episode.* It is partly the history of the film's evolution that explains such a 'revision,' for as the whole material of the *1905* film was gradually replaced by the single episode of the mutiny, that episode had to work as a synthesis of the whole 1905 Revolution. One result has been to transform an episode of the revolution into the symbolic episode of the whole revolution. In the process *Potemkin* often sacrificed the lesser historical facts for the dramatic essence of history. In actual fact, for example, other ships did join the *Potemkin* in mutiny, and the Cossack slaughter occurred quite differently. Eisenstein once received a letter from one of the mutineers, thanking him for the film, and identifying himself as 'one of those under the tarpaulin.' Eisenstein did not have the heart to tell him that the tarpaulin had been a dramatic invention—but he was interested in how even an eye-witness, a participant, after exposure to the power of empathy, could revise his memory of the fact.

Image and Structure in *Potemkin*

SERGEI EISENSTEIN

To return anew to the question of purity of film form, I can easily counter the usual objection that the craft of film diction and film expressiveness is very young as yet, and has no models for a classic tradition. It is even said that I find too much fault with the models of film form at our disposal, and manage with literary analogies alone. Many even consider it dubious that this "half-art" (and you would be surprised to know how many, in and out of films, still refer to the cinema in this way) deserves such a broad frame of reference.

FROM *Film Form* by Sergei Eisenstein, translated by Jay Leyda, pp. 115–20, 163–66, copyright, 1949, by Harcourt Brace Jovanovich, Inc., and reprinted with their permission.

* When a *Potemkin* opera was later composed, it was the film, not the fact, that the librettist followed.

Forgive me. But this is the way things are.

And yet our film language, though lacking its classics, possessed a great severity of form and film diction. On a certain level our cinema has known such a severe responsibility for each shot, admitting it into a montage sequence with as much care as a line of poetry is admitted into a poem, or each musical atom is admitted into the movement of a fugue.

There are plenty of examples that may be brought in from the practice of our silent cinematography. Not having the time to analyze other specimens for this present purpose, I may be allowed to bring here a sample analysis from one of my own works. It is taken from material for the conclusion of my book *Direction* (Part II—*Mise-en-cadre*) and concerns *Potemkin.* In order to show the compositional dependence between the plastic side of each of the shots, an example has been intentionally chosen not from a climax, but from an almost accidentally hit-upon place: fourteen successive pieces from the scene that precedes the fusillade on the Odessa steps. The scene where the "good people of Odessa" (so the sailors of the *Potemkin* addressed the population of Odessa) send yawls with provisions to the side of the mutinous battleship.

This sending of greetings is constructed on a distinct cross-cutting of two themes.

1. The yawls speeding towards the battleship.

2. The people of Odessa watching and waving.

At the end the two themes are merged. The composition is basically in two planes: depth and foreground. Alternately, the themes take a dominant position, advancing to the foreground, and thrusting each other by turns to the background.

The composition is built (1) on a plastic interaction of both these planes (within the frame) and (2) on a shifting of line and form in each of these planes from frame to frame (by montage). In the second case the compositional play is formed from the interaction of plastic impressions of the preceding shot in collision or interaction with the following shot. (Here the analysis is of the purely spatial and linear directions: the rhythmic and temporal relations will be discussed elsewhere.)

The movement of the composition takes the following course:

I. The yawls in movement. A smooth, even movement, parallel with the horizontals of the frame. The whole field of vision is filled with theme 1. There is a play of small vertical sails.

II. An intensified movement of the yawls of theme 1 (the entrance of theme 2 contributes to this). Theme 2 comes to the foreground with the severe rhythm of the vertical motionless columns. The vertical lines foreshadow the plastic distribution of the coming figures (in IV, V, etc.). Interplay of the horizontal wakes and the vertical lines of both sails and columns. The yawl theme is thrust back in depth. At the bottom of the frame appears the plastic theme of the arch.

III. The plastic theme of the arch expands into the entire frame. The play is effected by the shift in the frame's content—from vertical lines to the structure of the arch. The theme of verticals is maintained in the movement of the people—small figures moving away from the camera. The yawl theme is thrust completely into the background.

IV. The plastic theme of the arch finally moves into the foreground. The arc-formation is transposed to a contrary solution: the contours of a group are sketched, forming a circle (the parasol emphasizes the composition). This same transition in a contrary direction also takes place within a vertical construction: the backs of the small figures moving towards the depth are replaced by large standing figures, photographed frontally. The theme of the yawls in movement is maintained by reflection, in the expression of their eyes and in their movement in a horizontal direction.

V. In the foreground is a common compositional variant: an even number of persons is replaced by an uneven number. Two replaced by three. This "golden rule" in shifting the *mise-en-scène* is supported by a tradition that can be traced back to the principles of Chinese painting as well as to the practice of the *Commedia dell'arte*. (The directions of the glances also cross.) The arch motive is again bent, this time in a contrary curve. Repeating and supporting it is a new parallel arch-motif in the background: a balustrade—the yawl theme in movement. The eyes gaze across the whole width of the frame in a horizontal direction.

VI. Pieces I to V give a transition from the yawl theme to the watcher's theme, developed in five montage pieces. The interval from V to VI gives a sharp returning transition from the watchers to the yawls. Strictly following the content, the composition sharply transforms each of the elements in an opposite direction. The line of the balustrade is brought swiftly into the foreground, now as the line of the boat's gunwale. This is doubled by the adjacent line of the water's surface. The basic compositional elements are the same, but counterposed in treatment. V is static; VI is drawn by the dynamics of the boat in motion. The vertical division into "three" is maintained in both frames. The central element is texturally similar (the woman's blouse, and the canvas of the sail). The elements at the sides are in sharp contrast: the dark shapes of the men beside the woman, and the white spaces beside the central sail. The vertical distribution is also contrasted: three figures cut by the bottom horizontal are transformed into a vertical sail, cut by the upper horizontal of the frame. A new theme appears *in the background*—the side of the battleship, cut *at the top* (in preparation for piece VII).

VII. A sharply new thematic turn. A background theme—the battleship —is brought forward into the foreground (the thematic jump from V to VI serves somewhat as an anticipation of the jump from VI to VII). The viewpoint is turned 180°: shooting from the battleship towards the sea— reversing VI. This time the side of the battleship in the *foreground* is also cut—but by the *lower* horizontal of the frame. In the depth is the sail theme, developed in verticals. The verticals of the sailors. The static gun-barrel continues the line of the boat's movement in the preceding shot. The side of the battleship would seem to be an arch, bent into an almost straight line.

VIII. A repetition of IV with heightened intensity. The horizontal play of eyes is transformed into vertically waving hands. The vertical theme has moved from the depth into the foreground, repeating the thematic transfer to the watchers.

IX. Two faces, closer. Speaking generally, this is an unfortunate com-bination with the preceding shot. It would have been better to have brought between VIII and IX a shot of three faces, to have repeated V with a heightened intensity. This would have produced a 2:3:2 structure. Moreover, the repetition of the familiar groups of IV and V, ending with the new IX, would have sharpened the impression of the last shot. This error is somewhat remedied by the slight change in plane, coming closer to the figures.

X. The two faces change to a single, closer face. The arm is thrown very energetically up and out of the frame. A correct alternation of faces (if the suggested correction were made between VIII and IX)—2:3:2:1. A second pair of shots with a correct enlargement of the dimensions in relation to the first pair (a proper repetition with a qualitative variation). The line of odd numbers differs both in quantity and quality (differing in the dimen-sions of the faces and differing in their quantities, while retaining the common direction of the odd numbers).

XI. A new sharp thematic turn. A jump, repeating that of V–VI, with new intensity. The vertical *up-throw* of the arm in the preceding shot is echoed by the vertical *sail*. In this the vertical of this sail rushes past in a horizontal line. A repetition of the theme of VI in greater intensity. And a repetition of the composition of II with this difference, that the horizontal theme of the moving yawls and the verticals of the motionless columns are here molded into a single horizontal movement of the *vertical* sail. The composition repeats the *sequence's theme* of an identity between the yawls and the people on the shore (before moving on to the concluding theme of this reel, the fusion of the yawls and the battleship).

XII. The sail of XI is broken up into a multitude of vertical sails, scudding along horizontally (a repetition of piece I with increased in-tensity). The little sails move in a direction opposite to that of the large single sail.

XIII. Having been broken up into small sails, the large sail is newly re-assembled, but now not as a sail, but as the flag flying over the *Potemkin*. There is a new quality in this shot, for it is both static and mobile,—the mast being vertical and motionless, while the flag flutters in the wind. Formally, piece XIII repeats XI. But the change from sail to banner trans-

lates a principle of plastic unification to an ideological-thematic unification. This is no longer a vertical, a plastic union of separate elements of
composition,—*this is a revolutionary banner, uniting battleship, yawls and
shore.*

XIV. From here we have a natural return from the flag to the battleship. XIV repeats VII, with a lift in intensity. This shot introduces a new
compositional group of *interrelationships between the yawls and the battleship,* distinguished from the first group, *yawls and shore.* The first group
expressed the theme: "the yawls carry greetings and gifts from the shore
to the battleship." This second group will express *the fraternization of
yawls and battleship.*

The compositional dividing-point, and simultaneously the ideological
uniter of both compositional groups, is the mast with the revolutionary
banner.

Piece VII, repeated by the first piece of the second group, XIV, appears
as a sort of foreshadowing of the second group and as an element linking
the two groups together, as though the latter group had sent out a "patrol"
into the territory of the first group. In the second group this role will be
played by shots of waving figures, cut into scenes of the fraternization between yawls and battleship.

It should not be thought that the filming and montage of these pieces
were done according to these calculations, drawn up *a priori.* Of course
not. But the assembly and distribution of these pieces on the cutting table
was already clearly dictated by the compositional demands of the film
form. These demands dictated the selection of these particular pieces from
all those available. These demands also established the regularity of the
alternation of these pieces. Actually, these pieces, regarded only for their
plot and story aspects, could be re-arranged in any combination. But the
compositional movement through them would hardly prove in that case
quite so regular in construction.

One cannot therefore complain of the complexity of this analysis. In
comparison with analyses of literary and musical forms my analysis is
still quite descriptive and easy.

.   .   .

From a tiny cellular organism of the battleship to the organism of the
entire battleship; from a tiny cellular organism of the fleet to the organism
of the whole fleet—thus flies through the theme the revolutionary feeling
of brotherhood. And this is repeated in the structure of the work containing this theme—brotherhood and revolution.

Over the heads of the battleship's commanders, over the heads of the
admirals of the tzar's fleet, and finally over the heads of the foreign
censors, rushes the whole film with its fraternal "Hurrah!" just as within
the film the feeling of brotherhood flies from the rebellious battleship over

the sea to the shore. The organic-ness of the film, born in the cell within the film, not only moves and expands throughout the film as a whole, but appears far beyond its physical limits—in the public and historical fate of the same film.

Thematically and emotionally this would, perhaps, be sufficient in speaking of organic-ness, but let us be formally more severe.

Look intently into the structure of the work.

In its five acts, tied with the general thematic line of revolutionary brotherhood, there is otherwise little that is similar externally. But in one respect they are absolutely *alike:* each part is distinctly broken into two almost equal halves. This can be seen with particular clarity from the second act on:

II. Scene with the tarpaulin   → mutiny
III. Mourning for Vakulinchuk → angry demonstration
IV. Lyrical fraternization   → shooting
V. Anxiously awaiting the fleet → triumph

Moreover, at the "transition" point of each part, the halt has its own peculiar kind of *caesura.*

In one part (III), this is a few shots of clenched fists, through which the theme of mourning the dead leaps into the theme of fury.

In another part (IV), this is a sub-title—"*SUDDENLY*"—cutting off the scene of fraternization, and projecting it into the scene of the shooting.

The motionless muzzles of the rifles (in Part II). The gaping mouths of the guns (in Part V). And the cry of "Brothers," upsetting the awful pause of waiting, in an explosion of brotherly feeling—in both moments.

And it should be further noted that the transition within each part is not merely a transition to a merely *different* mood, to a merely *different* rhythm, to a merely *different* event, but each time the transition is to a sharply opposite quality. Not merely contrasting, but *opposite,* for each time it *images exactly that theme from the opposite point of view,* along with the theme that *inevitably grows from it.*

The explosion of mutiny after the breaking point of oppression has been reached, under the pointed rifles (Part II).

Or the explosion of wrath, organically breaking from the theme of mass mourning for the murdered (Part III).

The shooting on the steps as an organic "deduction" of the reaction to the fraternal embrace between the *Potemkin's* rebels and the people of Odessa (Part IV), and so on.

The unity of such a canon, recurring in *each act* of the drama, is already self-evident.

But when we look at the work as a whole, we shall see that such is the whole structure of *Potemkin.*

Actually, near the middle, the film as a whole is cut by the dead halt of a *caesura;* the stormy action of the beginning is completely halted in order to take a fresh start for the second half of the film. This similar *caesura*, within the film as a whole, is made by the episode of the dead Vakulinchuk and the harbor mists.

For the entire film this episode is a halt before the same sort of transfer that occurs in those moments cited above within the separate parts. And with this moment the theme, breaking the ring forged by the sides of one rebellious battleship, bursts into the embrace of a whole city which is topographically *opposed to the ship*, but is in feeling fused into a unity with it; a unity that is, however, broken away from it by the soldiers' boots descending the steps at that moment when the theme once more returns to the drama at sea.

We see how organic is the progressive development of the theme, and at the same time we also see how the structure of *Potemkin*, as a whole, flows from this movement of the theme, which operates *for the whole* exactly as it does *for its fractional members*.

Montage in *Potemkin*

A. R. FULTON

The greatest of Eisenstein's films is *The Battleship Potemkin*. Eisenstein had been commissioned to make a film about that earlier, though not successful, Russian revolution of 1905. It was in fact to have been called *1905*. But after shooting scenes in Moscow and St. Petersburg, he was not satisfied with the results. Part of the trouble is said to have been that the weather in the north of Russia was unfavorable for photography. Then Eisenstein's cameraman, Edward Tisse, came back from Odessa with reports of sunshine and the beauty of that city on the Black Sea. He was particularly enthusiastic over the great marble steps leading down to the shore and the curving quay. So Eisenstein changed his base of operations to Odessa. One of the incidents in the 1905 revolution had taken place off Odessa anyway—the mutiny aboard the armored cruiser *Potemkin* during the last days of the Russo-Japanese War. When Eisenstein arrived in Odessa and saw for the first time the great steps leading down to the beach where the Tsarist troops had massacred the citizens, the scene so

FROM *Motion Pictures: The Development of an Art from Silent Films to the Age of Television,* by A. R. Fulton. Copyright 1960 by the University of Oklahoma Press.

appealed to his imagination that he decided to discard the work he had already done on *1905* and limit the subject to the mutiny aboard ship and the immediately related events in the city. The original cruiser *Potemkin* had been scrapped, but for the scene of the meeting Eisenstein obtained the use of a ship of the same class—the *Twelve Apostles*. Since the superstructure of the *Twelve Apostles* had been dismantled, Eisenstein had it replaced by a replica of lath and plywood. The other shipboard scenes he shot on the cruiser *Komintern*. Most of the actors in the film were residents of Odessa and sailors of the Russian Navy. Before he began shooting, Eisenstein reconstructed the Odessa incident of twenty years before. He talked to survivors of the massacre. "The only thing I need is contact with the people," Marie Seton quotes him. "How many times I have gone out with a preconceived plan of execution, all thought out, with sketches and drawings, and then, on feeling their nearness, I have changed the idea completely. It is they, in their spontaneity, who actually imprint on the film the great tone of reality." The shooting of the scenes at Odessa and on shipboard in the harbor at Sevastopol took only twenty-three days. . . .

Typical of Eisenstein, *Potemkin* presents a theme more than a story. The theme, symbolized by the ship, is resistance to oppression. The theme is inherent from the beginning of the film. The first few shots are of water flowing over a jetty and of water breaking over rocks, after which appears the first subtitle, a quotation from Lenin: "Revolution is the only lawful, equal, effectual war. It was in Russia that this war was declared and begun." There is, of course, the story of the mutiny, and the mutiny is led at first by an individual, the sailor Vakulinchuk. But Vakulinchuk is killed, and he too becomes a symbol, round which the people gather and which makes the sailors only the more determined to throw off their oppressors. The hero is no longer Vakulinchuk, except as a symbol. The hero is the masses.

Thus the characters in *Potemkin* are not individualized. Here, in another way, Eisenstein's work is documentary-like. Eisenstein deliberately selected his actors to represent types. He used the word *typage* to describe his selection of a non-actor to play a particular role because the person seemed to him to represent the characteristics the role calls for. Eisenstein's typage is comparable to what in the theatre is called type casting. Eisenstein once explained to Marie Seton how he applied his theory:

> When he wanted to create a character, a street cleaner, for example, he went out into the streets and there observed the characteristics of people who were engaged in cleaning the streets. From the general characteristics he observed, he formed a composite image of a typical street cleaner. Then he searched for the individual who possessed the greatest number of traits

observed in the many street cleaners, though he might in fact
not be a street cleaner. When he found that person, he considered
him as the best and the truest image of the "type."

When he was filming *Potemkin*, he could not find anyone in Odessa
who seemed to him to be the type of Smirnov, the ship's surgeon. But
when he was in Sevastopol, where he had gone to shoot the shipboard
scenes, he recognized . . . the type he had in mind. The actor is nameless,
but having seen *Potemkin*, one remembers the perky little doctor. When
the doctor is tossed overboard, his glasses catch on one of the ship's lines
and hang dangling there. Eisenstein had Tisse make a close shot of the
dangling glasses, all the more effective because in an earlier scene the
doctor takes his glasses off and uses them as a magnifying lens to examine
the controversial meat. Eisenstein said: "The doctor with his sharp beard,
nearsighted eyes, and nearsighted mind is perfectly epitomized by the
pince-nez in the 1905 style which is held in place, like a fox terrier, by
a thin metal chain attached to the ear."

Another unforgettable character is the priest, the ship's chaplain. Eisenstein again had decided exactly what the priest should be like, and he
found a gardener who fitted the type. He did not even need make-up.
Eisenstein said: "A thirty-year-old actor may be called upon to play an
old man of sixty. He may have a few days' or a few hours' rehearsal. But
an old man will have had sixty years' rehearsal." When it came to the
scene in which the priest is knocked down the companionway, the old
gardener demurred. So Eisenstein made himself up as the priest for this
scene. The scene was shot by Tisse as the gardener watched and, thus
reassured, the old man acted the scene himself. It is possible that when
Potemkin was edited, the footage of Eisenstein was incorporated in the
film. As the priest lies at the foot of the companionway pretending to be
dead, he opens one eye and immediately closes it, in an expression said
to have been characteristic of Eisenstein. If Eisenstein had not intended
to be in the film, it is odd that he should have made himself up just to
show the gardener how to fall down stairs.

The documentary quality in *Potemkin* is not in the characters alone.
The staging is documentary-like for its background of Odessa and the
Black Sea coast. In the scenes at sea, however, there is a lack of reality.
Although the film is about a ship, the sea is slighted. The oncoming
squadron, for example, is ridiculously close when it is first sighted by the
crew of the *Potemkin*. Eisenstein does not have the feeling for the sea
that Robert Flaherty does. On the other hand, the harbor scenes are
effective—the tender bringing Vakulinchuk's body ashore, the fog, the
ships at anchor, and the gulls. Particularly documentary-like are the
scenes aboard ship—the sequence of shots, at the beginning of the film,
of the crew's quarters, shots of shipboard routine in the sequence before

the mutiny and, in the last part of the film, the variety of shots as the *Potemkin* is got under way—the engines beginning to turn, the signal light flashing, the bugler sounding the alarm, and sailors manning the ammunition hoist, handling shells, and loading guns. Interspersed with these are other shots—of the water rushing past the side, of the ship's wake, and of smoke pouring from the funnels.

There is a great variety in the temporal and spatial length of shots and in angles. There are distance shots of the harbor, the Odessa shore, and the quay. There are close shots of a ship's dial, a candelabrum, a life preserver. It is a tendency of the Russian directors not to move the camera, and Eisenstein is no exception. In the scenes on the Odessa steps, however, Eisenstein had a trolley built large enough to hold himself, Tisse, the assistants, and the camera and carry them up and down the side of the steps to photograph the massacre. In making this sequence Eisenstein had a camera attached to a man's waist to photograph the scene as the man falls. There are tracking shots of the tender moving through the harbor and a tilting and panning of the camera to show the people marching on the quay. But otherwise the camera is stationary. Eisenstein had Tisse change lenses instead of moving the camera, saying he did not want to disconcert his inexperienced actors.

Documentary-like as *Potemkin* is, there is hardly a shot in the film that is not studiedly composed. The sailors' hammocks form a variety of geometric patterns. A ship's grating casts a checkered shadow on a sailor's face, emphasized by a close-up. The little boats on their way out to the *Potemkin* are photographed through a colonnade on the shore. The masts of the sailboats tied up at the curving quay fill a scene from foreground to background, suggestive of the composition in the line of the hooded horsemen in *The Birth of a Nation* and anticipating that shot in *Henry V* in which a pattern is formed by the longbows in the hands of the English archers at the Battle of Agincourt. The opening of a tent, through which the camera photographs the harbor, masks the shot triangularly. Two of the *Potemkin's* guns symmetrically frame the deck. The film is brought to a close as the great bow of the ship comes directly head-on until it blacks out the screen.

Eisenstein is a master not only in directing crowd scenes but in moving groups of people in studied composition. For example, he had Tisse set up his camera aboard ship to catch sailors simultaneously running in opposite directions at different levels, a ship's rail forming a dividing line from lower left to upper right in the manner of a split screen. Taking advantage of the steep slope from Odessa down to the shore and of bridges, walls, steps, and other architectural features of the city, Eisenstein moves crowds in more than one direction in individual shots. A line of people moves down an incline from upper right to lower left while another line is crossing the scene from left to right at the bottom. In another shot the pattern of movement represents a line moving from right to left at the top while a second line comes in from center to left at the bottom. One of the lines may represent a curve, or two curves, or three. A crowd moves from lower left toward upper right through the arch of a bridge; joining this line, another group comes in from the left and moves toward lower center; at the same time, a line marches across the bridge from right to left at the top.

But *Potemkin* is important most of all for its montage. Few films depend less on movement of the camera. Few depend as little even on movement within the scene. No other film depends so much on the arrangement of shots. It is said that Eisenstein was converted to the motion pictures by *Intolerance*. Indeed all of *Potemkin* is built up in a way suggestive of the last sequence in *Intolerance*, in which Griffith cuts back and forth not only within each of the four stories but among them. But whereas in *Intolerance* the cutting becomes a tour de force, in *Potemkin* it is effected so smoothly that the story is told without calling attention to the cutting. In *Intolerance*, Griffith does not, as Eisenstein says, "try through the juxtaposition of shots to shape import and image." In *Potemkin*, Eisenstein does try to do just that. As a result he succeeds in effecting montage.

On examination one can see how he does it. Consider, for example, the Prologue. Its two scenes—water flowing over a smooth jetty and splashing up in sheets and water dashing roughly over rocks—are separated into five shots, arranged alternately. They symbolize Lenin's words, quoted as the first subtitle. The scene in the sailors' quarters is built up by thirty-nine separate shots, on the screen an average of four seconds each. . . . The action in this sequence depends almost entirely, except for five brief titles, on the arrangement of the shots.

One of the famous sequences in *Potemkin* is that in which the shots of the marble lions are interpolated. It occurred to Tisse, who had noticed the statues of the lions decorating the imperial gardens at Alupka, that shots of three of the lions, each in a different position—asleep, awake, and rising—could be made to represent a single lion springing to action. Although at first Eisenstein was not impressed by Tisse's suggestion that they photograph the lions for this purpose, he later acquiesced; he and Tisse went back to Alupka and made the shots. Eisenstein then interpolated them in the sequence of the massacre. He says in *Film Form*, "In the thunder of the *Potemkin's* guns a marble lion leaps up in protest against the bloodshed on the Odessa steps." There is no better example of movement obtained entirely by editing. The shots of the stone lions, arranged in rapid succession—ten frames for the first lion, fourteen for the second, and seventeen for the third—are as motionless as stills.

Montage effects another kind of relationship in the sequence of the mutiny. To show that the Church supports the Tsarist oppression of the common people, Eisenstein cuts from a shot of the officer tapping the hilt of his sword with his finger tips to a shot of the priest tapping his crucifix against the palm of his hand. And to make the implication obvious Eisenstein has the camera brought up close to each of these objects, the sword hilt and the crucifix, in succession.

The shots of the priest and the officer, the crucifix and the sword, interrupt the action at a crucial moment. The marines, lined up on deck, have been given the command to fire on the sailors massed under the tarpaulin in the bow. Eisenstein then, as it were, makes time stand still while he digresses to call attention to the affinity of the Church with the Military. He expands time even further by other digressions here. The incident, beginning with the officer's command "Attention!" and continuing until the marines lower their rifles, would in actuality be a matter of but a few seconds, but it lasts on the screen for nearly three minutes. The time is expanded by the interpolation of a series of shots, varying in spatial as well as in temporal length: a medium-close shot of two officers; a close shot of the executive officer; a long shot of the deck, the sea in the background; a medium-close shot of the marines; a long shot of the deck, the turret in the background; a distance shot of the ship on the water; a full shot of the tarpaulin over the sailors; a two-shot of Vakulinchuk and another sailor; a close shot of a life preserver; a long shot of the ship's bow head-on; a close shot of a bugle; etc. The incident is edited in fifty-seven shots. Editing similarly expands time in other parts of the film, particularly in the scene of the massacre on the Odessa steps.

Although Eisenstein seldom resorts to the dissolve, there are several dissolves in *Potemkin*. When Captain Golikov threatens the sailors with hanging, he points up. Then follows a shot of the yardarm as seen from the deck. After several shots of men and officers turning their heads to look—here again time is expanded—the shot of the yardarm is repeated. This then dissolves to a similar shot of the arm, except that now six men are hanging there. Here, of course, Eisenstein is effecting what Griffith meant when he said that "you can photograph thought." Two other dissolves in *Potemkin* are also reminiscent of Griffith. In the sequence in which citizens come to pay their respects to the dead sailor, a long flight of steps extends down the center of the screen, masked on both sides to emphasize height. This scene dissolves to that of the same steps crowded with people descending them. The coming of night aboard ship is implied by a dissolve from a shot of the deck massed with sailors to that of the deck empty. One is reminded of the photograph of the interior of Masters Hall in *The Birth of a Nation* dissolving to the shot of Griffith's replica of the hall occupied by the Negro legislature or of the shot of the empty office in the modern story of *Intolerance* dissolving to that of the office bustling with uplifters.

Potemkin is so cinematic that, watching it, one forgets that it is a silent film. It is, of course, enhanced by musical accompaniment. The original musical score for *Potemkin* was composed by Edmund Meisel, a pioneer in film music. Kurt London records that several European countries which permitted the showing of *Potemkin* forbade Meisel's music to be played with it because the provocative rhythm was liable to incite revolutionary instincts. "The rhythms which mark the departure of the mutinous ship, as the engines begin to move," London observes, "have become famous and have since been imitated countless times." Although the Meisel score for *Potemkin* has been lost,* the music can be approximated, for Arthur Kleiner has composed a score for piano accompaniment based on his recollection of the original. In 1950, the Film Studio of Moscow produced a "sound version" of *Potemkin,* consisting, not of spoken dialogue, but of sound effects and background music by N. Kryukov. Except for a few changes in titles, this version presents Eisenstein's original film intact.

Potemkin is the opposite of *A Trip to the Moon* because of montage. Whereas in Méliès' film the values are primarily in the photographed objects, in Eisenstein's they are primarily in the way the photographs are arranged. Arrangement is the province of the artist. Willa Cather says in "The Novel Démeublé":

> Whatever is felt upon the page without being specifically named there—that, it seems to me, is created. It is the inexplicable presence of the thing not named, of the overtone divined by the ear but not heard by it, the verbal mood, the emotional aura of the fact or the thing or the deed, that gives high quality to the novel or the drama, as well as to poetry itself.

For "page" may be substituted "screen." In *Potemkin,* as in any truly cinematic film, "the inexplicable presence of the thing not named" is effected by arrangement. Griffith established the principle of arrangement in the motion pictures as *editing*. Eisenstein extended it as *montage*.

---

* The music has recently been recovered.—S.J.S.

CHAPLIN

THE GOLD RUSH

CREDITS

The Gold Rush (United States, 1925)
Directed, written, and produced by Charles Chaplin for United Artists

Associate directors: Charles Riesner and H. d'Abbadie d'Arrast
Photography: Rollie Totheroh and Jack Wilson
Distributors (16mm): Audio-Brandon Films, United Films, Film Images, *et al.*

Main performers:
Charles Chaplin (*The lone prospector*)
Mack Swain (*Big Jim*)
Georgia Hale (*Georgia*)
Tom Murray (*Black Larsen*)
Henry Bergman (*Hank*)
Malcolm White (*Jack Cameron*)

Length: 9 reels (reissued by Chaplin in 1942 with a sound track: 72 minutes)

Charles Chaplin's universal popularity as the cinema's greatest performer has frequently obscured his reputation as a great filmmaker. Yet the nature of his performance is related so intimately to the conception of the films he both wrote and directed that we can hardly distinguish the execution of the idea from its intellectual derivation in Chaplin's mind. We know this much: the editing is always unobtrusive, though at any particular moment the image in front of us seems exactly right—the right angle, the right distance, and above all, the right duration. In his undisputed masterpieces—*The Gold Rush* (1925), *City Lights* (1931), and *Modern Times* (1936)—and in the other major films about which some critics have expressed reservations—*The Circus* (1928), *The Great Dictator* (1940), *Monsieur Verdoux* (1947), and *Limelight* (1952)—Chaplin combines a classically formal approach to the satirist's craft with a romantic sensibility for the plight of the lonely individual in an absurd world.

Born into poverty in England in 1889, Chaplin became a successful vaudeville star. He entered the cinema in 1914 under contract to the Keystone Film Company, which specialized in short comedies, all of them supervised or directed by Mack Sennett. Sennett, a student of D. W. Griffith's and a man of peculiar genius in his own right, edited his slapstick films on the model of Griffith's one-reel Biograph melodramas. Thus, Chaplin learned the art of filmmaking in the Griffith tradition, but since Griffith himself was not present and since the great spectaculars, *The Birth of a Nation* and *Intolerance*, had not yet appeared, Chaplin was better able to avoid the domination of Griffith's influence than anyone else of importance in the American cinema of that period. Departing from Griffith's editing method of depicting pieces of an idea so that it was intelligible only in terms of each shot's interactions with other shots in a sequence, Chaplin worked out a way of synthesizing ideas by means of the developing action within the frame. His films thus required less cutting than those of Sennett, Griffith, William Hart, Thomas Ince, and other major filmmakers of this early and highly creative era of motion pictures. Chaplin went from Keystone to Essanay in 1915 and to Mutual Films in 1916 and 1917 (where in a series of twelve two-reel films he perfected his artistry, needing only an opportunity to broaden and deepen the characterization and ideas already apparent in his work). He went next to First National and made his superb first full-length film, *The Kid* (1920). Finally, he joined forces with Douglas Fairbanks, Mary Pickford, and D. W. Griffith to form United Artists.

The Gold Rush is probably the finest product of this joint venture. Chaplin exercised even more control over *The Gold Rush* than Orson Welles did over *Citizen Kane* years later, and also had a much bigger budget than did Welles. A variation on Chaplin's already fully developed tramp character, the hero was his most subtle characterization up to that time. Vulnerable to the crude manipulations of a callous woman, susceptible to the most sensitive kinds of emotional pain, the hero demonstrates an indomitable will to survive with dignity and spirit. For all its memorable comic episodes, *The Gold Rush* veers constantly toward the edge of despair. Its visual imagery presents or suggests various forms of death, by murder, avalanche, starvation, and cannibalism. In fact, according to Chaplin, a major inspiration for the film was a contemporary expedition that actually ended in cannibalism, an unusual source for a classic screen comedy. Chaplin shaped his tragicomic vision so as to unify the themes of greed, indifference to human suffering, and perseverance with the setting, a harsh environment that challenges the humanity and ingenuity of man. As a result, the triumph of Charlie the tramp, which emerges from his own inner resources, is externalized so clearly that the film provokes similar profound responses from the most sophisticated film critics and from children. *The Gold Rush* is truly one of the classic art works of American culture.

The Frozen Hills

ROBERT PAYNE

When *The Gold Rush* was completed after fourteen months of work, Chaplin declared: "This is the film I want to be remembered by." There is no reason why we should take this statement too seriously, for he had said the same about *The Kid* and he was to say it again when he completed *Monsieur Verdoux;* and less than any other producer is he in danger of being forgotten.

The Gold Rush is mistitled, perhaps deliberately. There is very little about rushing after gold. The gold-diggers in their long weary march through the snows, the heavy clouds brushing low over the earth, the eternal wastes, all these are things which belong to the natural habitat of the clown. He must go where danger is. On the edge of a precipice he is in his element. Before he had fought cops; now he must set himself against the elements, and in the frozen hills of an imaginary Alaska he creates his own setting. And where *The Circus* is cold, shining like the cold fire which is employed to cut through steel below the surface of the sea, *The Gold Rush* is all warmth, blazing like the hearth-logs of our remembered winters. So we see him first in the freezing wastes, appearing belatedly after a long line of prospectors has passed before the camera, a small defiant ink-stain among the hills, twirling his cane a little to keep his spirits up.

An announcement says the scene is the snowy Chilkoot Pass in the Klondike gold rush of 1898, but we know better. He has entered the mysterious world of snows, which children know: it is his own home, one of his many homes, and he is perfectly at ease there. He wanders along a narrow ledge. An enormous black bear follows him. He is not in the least discountenanced, pays no attention to the bear, smiles happily, whistles a tune, and twirls his cane. When the bear disappears in a cave and is no longer dangerous, Charlie hears a noise of stones falling somewhere— then he jumps with fear, and falls the whole way down the mountain. At the bottom he leans on his cane, and he is a little surprised when it sinks to the handle. Thereupon, like any child journeying in any fairyland, he takes out a map and follows the arrow pointing North.

We shall not understand the clown unless we remember that he is an adventurer. Unhappily, no one has yet been able to draw that absolute map of the mind where the real adventures take place. There are places

FROM *The Great God Pan* (1952) by Robert Payne, pp. 196–203. Reprinted by permission of Bertha Klausner International Literary Agency, Inc.

on the map marked "Here are tigers" and other places marked "icy wastes." "The mind has mountains, cliffs of fall," as Gerard Manley Hopkins has reminded us; it also has pleasant cottages and meadows flowing with milk and honey and odd-shaped rabbit-holes, and Mount Olympus has its place there, and somewhere in the east upon the sunset is Kafka's gilded castle. It is the function of the clown to hurl himself at the most dangerous places, if only to show that there is no danger there. So he will dither on the highest trapezes and cock snooks at the most muscular cops. As for his method of journeying, Giles Earle has expressed it well enough in an Elizabethan song called *Tom o' Bedlam:*

> With a heart of furious fancies
> Whereof I am commander,
>   With a burning spear
>   And a horse of air
> To the wilderness I wander.
>
> By a knight of ghosts and shadows
> I summoned am to tourney
>   Ten leagues beyond
>   The wild world's end:
> Methinks it is no journey.

Charlie is of the same opinion. Having come "ten leagues beyond the wild world's end," he is in territory he knows well, and clearly he thinks it is no journey. Why, then, should he fear such little things as bears?

The journey up the pass is the curtain-raiser. There follows the real terror, the terror at the heart of terror. Charlie makes no bones about it. It is ridiculous to fear bears; as for men—fear them always when they are freezing cold, when they are miserable, whenever they are not laughing. The scene in the hut, where Charlie, Big Jim McKay and Black Larsen huddle against the storm is terrifying. It is the world of delirium and nausea, the lurid dreams of men in doss-houses, the evil in the heart and the knife gleaming in the unsteady hand, exhaustion and near-murder on the edge of nowhere, storms and the creeping cold and no escape anywhere, and this world of pure delirium is transformed into one which is lit with a magical tenderness. The terror, however, remains. It is there in the background, always ready to spring out. The hut belongs to Black Larsen. Charlie is blown in, and then Big Jim is blown in, and Larsen wants nothing more than to be rid of the two interlopers, and since Larsen has a gun the two together must put an end to him. When Larsen is subdued, Big Jim goes mad. Charlie treats him gently, throws an arm round him, offers him a bone and gazes at him with all the sweetness of a child, or like a puppy prepared to play with the first stranger who comes along though its master lies dead.

Charlie's behavior during the storm is something to wonder at. The worse the storm, the more terrible the consequences, the gayer he becomes. Charlie attempts to make them laugh, smiles eagerly, salts a candle and offers it to them as though it were a celery-stalk, and shrugs his shoulders against the storm. A dog has wandered in and taken up its place in the next room. They are all hungry, nervously eyeing one another, and when Big Jim goes to the room where the dog is and then returns picking his teeth, Charlie has good reasons for thinking the worst has happened. They decide to cut cards and decide who shall go out foraging. The choice falls on Larsen, who ambushes two mounted police and wanders out into the wilds on their sled. Larsen has no part in the story. He is a *deus ex machina,* and not a very convincing one. But Big Jim, a huge bear of a man, resembling a cross between a bear and Jupiter Tonans, is the perfect foil for Charlie, shaggy where Charlie is still the dandy, blustering where Charlie is rapier-sharp; one is an elemental force, and the other is the human comedy.

While the storm increases in violence, so does their hunger. They are so hungry that Charlie decides to cook one of his shoes, those enormous shoes which have always resembled sausages. He cooks it expertly, places it on a dish, pours some of the gravy over it, holds his finger to his nose, sharpens a knife, separates the uppers from the sole, and then with a fleeting smile of satisfaction offers Big Jim the sole, only to have his offer rejected. Big Jim settles for the uppers. Charlie is perfectly content with the sole, sucks the nails and the laces, and finding a nail shaped like a wishbone offers to break it with Big Jim. When we see Charlie again he is out on a foraging expedition and both his feet are wrapped in rags. Another shoe is cooking. Empty-handed, Charlie returns to the hut and prepares dinner. In the middle of the dinner Big Jim goes hideously mad, and imagines that Charlie is a plump chicken.

Then the nightmare begins. Nothing like this nightmare was ever to occur to Charlie again; nothing like it had ever happened before. Big Jim is out to murder. He will take the neck of the chicken, lay it on the table and cut off the protesting head, and Charlie looks at him with immense sadness and pity, almost prepared to offer himself as a sacrifice. They chase each other round the room, and suddenly Charlie becomes the chicken, and the frightened chicken is standing on the table: all Mack Swain has to do is to wring its neck. But Charlie escapes his fate by the use of a transformation scene: he changes from a chicken back to a man again, and Mack Swain is sufficiently aware of the change to pause for a moment—no more than a moment. When he looks for the chicken again, it is fluttering in panic round the room. Mack Swain chases it round the room and out into the snowfields, seizes a gun, fires at it, and we see the flapping wings, but suddenly they are Charlie's arms. The scene is played with an unrelenting effect of tragedy, Mack Swain becoming Mephistopheles with a spurt of powder and a column of blue flame. The sense of real panic emerges, and it is still there the next morning when we see them in bed, shuddering against the storm. Charlie has taken the inevitable precaution: his hands, not his feet, are inside his shoes—a trick he had played successfully in *Triple Trouble*. He hopes Mack Swain will not see that he is prepared to run. Unfortunately Mack Swain resembles nothing so much as Dickens' Mr. Bunsby, who appeared over the bulkhead of the cabin "with one stationary eye on the mahogany face, and one revolving one, on the principle of some light-houses." Mack Swain sees everything. There is another fight, as tense and malevolent as the fights the previous night, and Charlie would have been smothered under blankets if a bear had not taken it into its head to enter the cabin at that moment. The bear is not altogether convincing. It has an extraordinary resemblance to Mack Swain, just as the plump chicken bore an extraordinary resemblance to Charlie in his padded clothes. But Charlie is not plucked and dressed for a giant's dinner. Mack Swain shoots the bear, and we see Charlie sharpening the knives.

The subplot concerns Larsen, and it is wholly mismanaged and unconvincing. We have odd glimpses of Larsen working his claim, and Big Jim goes to join him. They fight together, and we are not quite sure what has happened to them, for they are left casually in the snow. It does not matter. We are concerned with Charlie, who wanders off to the boom town and falls in love with Georgia Hale, a cabaret singer who has only to smile for Charlie to be lifted up to the highest heaven, but in fact she is not smiling at Charlie, she is smiling at someone behind him, and though this trick has been used before, notably in *The Cure*, the use of it in *The Gold Rush* has a sharpness which was not apparent before; and Charlie's pain when he discovers she is not smiling at him is unbearably painful to watch. Charlie wanders off to the bar and drinks disconsolately by himself, and never had he appeared so lonely as in the obscure shack in Alaska. The loneliness vanishes only when, gazing out from his little cabin, he sees Georgia playing with snowballs, and by good fortune one of her snowballs hits him smack in the face. He invites her into his cabin with her companions, two other girls of a weird dowdiness. While Charlie goes in search of firewood, Georgia sees that a discarded photograph lies under Charlie's pillow. It is her own photograph, one that had been torn and later patched together after a barroom brawl. For the first time she becomes aware of Charlie as a person, and when he invites her to enjoy a New Year's dinner with her companions in his own shack, she smiles winningly, and Charlie is convinced that she will come.

The preparations for her coming are among those handsome gifts which Charlie has given to the world. There is not a moment of those delighted preparations which is not memorable. He tears a newspaper cunningly into a resemblance of a lace tablecloth. He carefully arranges the knives and forks, touching them gently and with love as he places them on the table which is forever in danger of collapsing. He writes out place-cards, sweeps the dust from the chairs, studies with mounting excitement the cooking of the chicken on the stove, but once more the chicken is himself, and there are no guests except a nanny goat which comes to munch the paper favors. What then? He will pretend they are late or unavoidably detained elsewhere. He is sure they will come. Have they not promised to come? He smiles wearily, heartbroken, but breaks out into smiles as he imagines them actually present, and suddenly to his intense joy they are present, and Charlie is bowing to them, and they sit beside the table as they would sit at the table of a king. To amuse them Charlie dances his wonderful breadroll dance, which is no more than the cavortings of two breadrolls on a pair of forks; but just as the chicken represented only too clearly Charlie himself, so the breadrolls exactly resemble two bleeding hearts dancing to keep their courage up. The breadrolls dance the cancan, hop sideways, pause magnificently before continuing the dance to the applause of the girls, and at the end they take their bows. It was the first time that bleeding hearts had ever bowed to an audience, and Charlie celebrated the occasion by performing with astonishing verve and brilliance. But at last the hearts lie dead upon the table, and Charlie wanders away, leaving the uninhabited room where the girls were present only in his dreams. He wanders among the dark huts, sick with loss and misery, and very timidly he approaches the lighted window where the girls are dancing and there is a furious air of festivity.

As he gazes through the window, Charlie is like someone looking at an unattainable paradise in a dream. Inside the dancehall an unearthly mystery is being performed. He is like a child watching a gas-illuminated pantomime. There are shadowy grottoes and mermaids' crowns, and strange distorted shapes like fishes, and everywhere there is the sound of joy. The mysteriously diffused light in which he sees the celebrants, the sudden appearance of Georgia dancing there, the memory of the dancing breadrolls, all these fuse together to make a picture of misery seen in the light of an unbearable tenderness. His misery now is a child's misery, the misery of rejection. He wanders abroad in the dark, and while he is wandering Georgia remembers her promise to come to him, and when she comes to his shack, he is gone. This is the end for the time being of Charlie's hopeless love for Georgia. The bloody hearts had been torn out of the living flesh, and in the abandonment of sorrow he goes on his way—to the shack where he had fought so menacingly with Big Jim.

. . .

The Gold Rush has only one imperfection, and that is its ending. For the rest, the world which Chaplin conjured out of the snows is terrifyingly real. The very simplicity of the snow scenes gives dimension to Charlie.

Charlie, that thin black isosceles triangle hopping across the snows, partakes of geometry; the pattern he forms against the snow has the inevitability of Euclidian theory. There is the round face of Georgia, the square of the shack, the immense black V-shaped wedge of Mack Swain—out of these simplicities the film is constructed. It is comedy reduced to its geometric essentials, and the breadrolls can be interpreted as bleeding hearts or zeros as we please. To have placed the wildest comedy against the snowfields was a mark of genius, for in the field of the cinema this was the equivalent of playing out a comedy on the stage without props, and with only a single white sheet as a back-cloth. This is comedy naked, and set in the white fields of eternity.

Classics Revisited: *The Gold Rush*

ERNEST CALLENBACH

The Gold Rush certainly is one of Chaplin's achieved masterpieces of silent comedy, the work of a great artist of sentiment and pathos.* But it is worth looking at rather more closely. The year Chaplin made it, 1924, was also the year of *The Navigator, Sherlock Jr., The Freshman*—a year of fantastic burgeoning of talents in that great uprush when American comedy threw off the technical domination of vaudeville and stage to become an art form with its own perfections. Like those other films, *The Gold Rush* can remind us of much about comedy that we badly need to know.

The picture opens with an iris-in revealing a thin line of aspiring miners crawling across a snowy mountain landscape; the narration hits us with travelogue melodrama. In a moment, though, we notice the tramp ("the little fellow," the narration calls him) wandering along an icy ledge. He

FROM Ernest Callenbach, "Classics Revisited: *The Gold Rush*," © 1959 by the Regents of the University of California. Reprinted from *Film Quarterly*, Volume XIII, Number 1, pp. 31–37 (with deletions), by permission of The Regents.

* Theodore Huff in *Charlie Chaplin* (New York: Henry Schuman, 1951, p. 187) says that "Chaplin himself characterized *The Gold Rush* as 'the picture I want to be remembered by.'" In his book Huff gives a very detailed post-hoc scenario for the film, conforming to the version now being shown except in minute details that are probably the result of slight lapses in Huff's reconstruction of his notes; the action of the film is recorded fully, and something of its flavor—though this is a more or less hopeless enterprise for silent comedy.

slips but recovers his balance; he is followed momentarily by a gigantic bear; he slides down a snow slope. He is the full-blown tramp figure, complete with cane (which sinks to the handle in the snow when he leans on it): urban and possibly Londoner, a little picturesquely Dickensian in the derogatory sense; perky, naïve, no longer mischievous or vengeful. (There is in *The Gold Rush* virtually none of the earlier kicking-in-the-pants that makes even high school kids cringe.) The gestures are those of the tramp-dandy, made excruciatingly un-apropos (like his costume) when he finds himself amid fur-coated sourdoughs in the arctic wilderness.

The story-line (*The Gold Rush* was made after *A Woman of Paris*) has become firm and rich. And if the film has none of the flabbergasting imagination of a Keaton (is it in *The Frozen North*—1922—that Keaton emerged deadpan from an IRT subway exit into an icy waste?) it nonetheless creates a comic world as viable as any, and with a great deal of genuine poetry to it.

.   .   .

[The latter part of the film contains] one of the most neatly constructed passages in all of film comedy, and it bears a great deal of study since silent structure has literally become a forgotten art. In it we can see Chaplin working according to the accepted tenets of silent method; the waves of gags grow and break, grow and break, with the ground swell of the story-line pushing them in and over us.

The tramp and Big Jim find the cabin with no trouble. They go in; the tramp drinks from Jim's immense flask as he lugs in provisions—staggering more and more as he does so, until he finally curls up on a bunk. Big Jim shakes the empty flask in amazement, and sacks out himself. In the night a blizzard blows the cabin, in a series of unconvincing model shots, to the edge of an abyss, where it comes to rest with about half of it hanging over the edge.

The little fellow awakes with a frightful hangover. He crawls out of bed and goes to the window to look out. The frost, however, is too thick to rub off, and he gets no inkling of the cabin's new location. He walks toward the side of the cabin that is over the precipice, and his weight makes it begin to tilt; he walks back, and it returns to horizontal. This basic scene sets up in the audience's mind a rough series of expectations, and the film proceeds to exploit them with horrifying precision. The little fellow moves the table out for breakfast; as the cabin tilts he pushes it back just in time, and the cabin falls back again. When Big Jim wakes up and he again tilts the cabin, he explains it as a "liver attack," pointing to his stomach. Big Jim rises, and his bulk now seems agonizingly large. However, in a delightful variation on the underlying situation, each time Chaplin crosses to the abyss side of the cabin, Big Jim goes the other way, so their weights counterbalance each other. Chaplin picks icicles from the roof to melt for breakfast. As the cabin tips again, the men conclude that it can't really be their livers: "There's something missing underneath!" And, of course, the next gag follows with the inevitability that in silent comedy functions like fate in Greek tragedy: Chaplin must open the door to see what is missing. First, however, he jumps up and down on one side of the cabin—that deliciously rapid jump involving only his legs, a kind of hop. And Big Jim jumps heavily up and down on his side, with of course no result. The tramp then goes to the door opening on the abyss side of the cabin. We know, from the establishing long shot of the cabin in its new location (crisp morning after snow), that outside the door is nothing at all. The door sticks. The tramp bumps it with his shoulder. It still sticks; he bumps it harder still. We watch in medium shot as his efforts become stronger; it is all admirably economical—no cuts back to the outside. With a great push he succeeds; the door opens; we cut to the outside long shot in time to see his tiny figure swing out clutching the door, wriggle in terror, and swing back abruptly and aghast into the cabin; cut to an interior shot (a little closer now) of Big Jim dragging him firmly back in, and then of him fainting away and slumping to the floor.

The initial set of tensions is now resolved; the predicament is clear, and one would expect the two simply to get out of the cabin onto terra firma as promptly as possible. This, however, they are immediately prevented from doing by an ominous creaking and additional tilting of the cabin, which lurches sickeningly and seems about to plunge over the precipice, but is caught by a rope somehow tied to it, which catches in a rock crevice. Inside, Big Jim and the tramp find themselves lying on the floor, which has assumed about a 45-degree angle. A new set of gags thus begins as they attempt to get out of this new predicament.

First the tramp hiccups (as he does at several other points in the film), shaking the cabin and bringing down an angry caution from Big Jim. As the cabin lurches again, the tramp scrabbles desperately up onto Big Jim and tries to climb up to the door and safety; but in spite of treading ruthlessly on Big Jim's head he doesn't make it, and takes a sickening slide back down and out the abyss-side door, only to be caught by the scruff of the neck by Big Jim, and hauled back in again. Now Big Jim insists that he be given a hoist up on cupped hands and on shoulders; as he gropes for the door, it swings in, hits him on the head, and *he* takes the long slide—but the tramp is somehow able to drag him back. (At this point, the audience is limp.)

On his next attempt Big Jim makes it. Leaping to the ground, he discovers his claim marker by the cabin, and in his delight forgets about the little fellow, who calls out to him. Finally, Big Jim lowers a rope; the tramp grabs it, walks up the steeply sloping floor, and jumps. As he does so, the cabin tips over the edge and crashes downward out of sight;

the tramp staggers on the brink, almost faints again, and collapses beside Big Jim and the claim marker. Fade-out.

Whatever Chaplin's possible debt to Harold Lloyd's *High and Dizzy* and *Safety Last*, he has here carried the device of near-escapes from falling to a quite agonizing perfection, and with a complexity and subtlety beyond those shorter films. And if, as experimental psychologists maintain, fear of falling and fear of loud noises are our only inborn fears, the appeal of such sequences goes very deep indeed—and by skillful titillation of such a basic anxiety the comedian may obtain rather more than belly-laughs from his audience . . . .

The third and remaining sections of the film is anticlimactic. Big Jim and the tramp sail for the States, rich men. While dressed in his tramp costume for a photographer, the little fellow falls backwards down a ladder into the steerage, and lands next to Georgia, who is also on board. He is apprehended as a wanted stowaway, and it seems inevitable that the impending happy ending will be destroyed. Georgia offers to buy his passage; but this gesture proving her feelings turns out to be unnecessary as his new status is reëstablished by the ship's officers. All ends happily, we are told, with a marriage. Yet we have seen often before the smug smile leading to the prat fall, the happy dream giving way to grim reality; and we half-see the tramp soon again walking away in the snow "to resume his bleak lonely existence," as the narration at one point put it.

For the emotional center of gravity of the film is the sequence in which the tramp is deceived by Georgia and her friends, as its comic center is the cabin scene; and the triumphs of true love cannot long keep the world at bay.

The key elements in the vision?—The search for love, above all; this time found in the person of a girl harder and less "good" than the usual Chaplin heroine. But the pattern is basically the same: the tramp, we are asked to assume, is a very lovable little fellow indeed in spite of his superficially unprepossessing appearance; he is good in the way a child is good, and the girls are made to love him with a stylized love that might be thought somewhat maternal—at any rate, they finally recognize his affectionateness, his true worth and dignity, and in those films where the tramp is saved from his "bleak lonely existence" it is through this sort of grace. —The existence of good and evil, too; the Big Jims and the Black Larsens of the world exterior to the tramp's person, who struggle violently, often for objectives the tramp has no hope of reaching through struggle, and can only attain through luck or guile. Sometimes, as in the case of Big Jim when he is delirious from hunger, or the millionaire of *City Lights*, these merge in an ambiguous power figure who must be cajoled, placated, or even fought; more often still the good figure is not there at all, so that the tramp wanders through a hostile universe ruled by street bullies, tyrannical headwaiters, and the like. It is worth noting that in Chaplin films as a whole evil is portrayed rather convincingly and in detail: greed and poverty, guile and deception; but the goodness of the tramp rests upon charm and pathos much of the time, or, as in *City Lights,* is dramatized mawkishly.—Most of all, the vision shows the world as a series of traps and dangers: physical peril, hunger, trickery that will not always be reversed as Georgia's is here. It is a world, like those of all great artists, having the power to haunt us afterwards, physically: we *see* that world in our mind's eye, more real than the supposedly real world of most "realistic" films, with a timelessness that every "serious" film maker, beset with problems of costume, slang, and manners, must sometimes wildly envy. The wonderful shabbiness of dress and settings in *The Gold Rush* seems beyond our art directors today. The grime and disrepair seen now in the beautiful soft grays of a good print have disappeared from the screens but not from our minds; they still remind us of poverty, sadness, and the essential human condition—the last because, no matter how materially fat and sassy we become, we sense all too well on other levels that moths still corrupt and thieves break in and steal—and villains wield sticks and what is old must be made to serve. At the end of *The Gold Rush* the luxuries of Big Jim and the tramp are precarious indeed—only an accidental fall away from the miseries of *The Immigrant.*

It is because of the intensity of this vision, of course, that films like *The Gold Rush* will last and last, when today's bloated extravaganzas have crumbled to dust in the vaults. Even in the heartless and mechanical world of the cinema, art tells. . . .

It is an art of charm or sympathy of character, ingenuity, timing, grace: an athletic and kinesthetic kind of beauty that can be very moving. (In silent comedy no one can forget that the cinema is an art which involves bodily responses—from the acute and delicious agony of the comic ecstasy to the imperceptible delights in even the least movements of a Chaplin or a Keaton.)

. . . I would maintain that Keaton surpassed Chaplin with *The Navigator* and *The General,* both works of astonishing virtuosity and purity of aesthetic motive, and moreover of great technical brilliance.

But Chaplin's work as a whole clearly stands out far and above Keaton's as it stands out above everyone else's: he is the undeniable Hero of the cinema, who has shown beyond doubt what can be done with this new medium . . .

. . .

Of *The Gold Rush* we may say, I think, that it is Chaplin near or at the peak of his powers. He had mastered feature-length construction; he had peeled away from the tramp almost all of the mere silliness inherited from the music halls. (When Jack twice trips the little fellow in *The Gold Rush*, it is in a complex dramatic context; nobody laughs.) In Georgia he created a somewhat lifelike portrait, though basically in the good-bad, heart-of-gold tradition; the other figures have the oversize effect that people have in our emotional life if not ocularly. *The Gold Rush* has the simple, lasting appeals of a well-defined constellation of characters, an overwhelmingly sympathetic hero, a satisfying pattern of frustrations followed by surprising and deserved success. It is a remarkable film, though it is not "life," any more than is *Br'er Rabbit*, really—except that, as Freud once remarked, there is no such thing as an adult unconscious . . .

Premise and Progression in *The Gold Rush*

JOHN HOWARD LAWSON

Chaplin presents a wonderful accumulation of violent incidents in the opening of *The Gold Rush*. The first scene shows a procession of prospectors struggling through Chilkoot Pass in the Gold Rush of 1898. Thus the real background is established. Then we see a lone prospector, flourishing his cane, walking along a narrow ledge amidst Arctic scenery, unaware that a bear is following him. He takes refuge from a storm in the cabin of a desperado, Black Larsen. When Big Jim enters, he and Larsen start a furious fight over a gun, while Charlie endeavors to keep out of range. Soon, the three men are snowbound in the cabin without food. This establishes the conditions for the progression, which begins when the three cut cards to see which of them shall go in search of provisions.

Chaplin is unmerciful in his mockery of all the situations that clutter the usual adventure film. But his virtuosity consists in making these situations flow with clarity and varying tempo around the central figure. The element of plot is removed with surgical skill, so that each event is freshly conceived as an original experience of the tramp. The events that crowd the beginning of *The Gold Rush* would suffice for a complete film. But Chaplin orchestrates the material as preliminary variations on the theme— snow, isolation, storms, gun-play. A mood has been created; the tramp's

FROM *Film: The Creative Process*, 2nd ed. (1967) by John Howard Lawson, pp. 332–35. Copyright © 1964, 1967 by John Howard Lawson. Reprinted by permission of Hill and Wang, a division of Farrar, Straus & Giroux.

place in this novel environment has been made so clear and natural that we are ready for all that follows.

Suppose the film faded in on Charlie cooking the shoes for a Thanksgiving feast, or on Charlie turning into a chicken while Big Jim pursues him in a delirium induced by hunger. We could understand the physical fact that the two men are marooned in a cabin, for a single shot of the exterior would explain their situation. But we would be unprepared emotionally to participate in the experience, and to laugh at its comic possibilities. The premise has prepared us for the progression.

·　　·　　·

Chaplin makes a valuable comment on his method: "I do not strive for surprise in the general composition of a film, but I force myself to make my personal gestures come in some surprising form."* In other words, he does not make suspense the main factor in the structure of the work. Yet there is progression in his films to a definite climax.

No other films offer such rich materials for the study of cinematic structure as Chaplin's works. Let us return to *The Gold Rush* for a more detailed analysis of its over-all construction. The picture is divided into five parts, the first being the premise and the last the climax. The second movement is the Thanksgiving Day incident—the cooking and eating of the shoes and the pursuit of the imaginary chicken. The third movement is the dance-hall sequence in which he meets Georgia and defends her in a fight, which he accidentally wins when he hits a post and jars a balcony clock so that it falls on his opponent for a knockout. The fourth sequence takes place on New Year's Eve; he prepares a party for Georgia in his cabin and while he is waiting for her he goes to sleep and dreams of a gay scene with Georgia and her friends. She kisses him in the dream. But in reality, he is alone and asleep while Georgia is enjoying the celebration at the dance hall. The climax shows Charlie going with Big Jim to find his claim; after a long journey, they reach a lonely cabin; while they are asleep a storm rises and the cabin teeters on the edge of a precipice. They escape just as it is about to fall, and we find them as millionaires on the ship returning to the United States. He discovers Georgia in the steerage and they plan to be married.

These movements can be regarded as a series of "gags," but they are much more than that. Each is a situation in which suspense is a factor. But Chaplin does not "strive for surprise" in the construction; there is no attempt to create mounting suspense building to the final crisis. There is a story connection between Parts 2 and 5, because both deal with Charlie and Big Jim, and with their adventures as prospectors. There is a close continuity between Parts 3 and 4, since both deal with Georgia and the dance hall. There are two stories, one of men facing hunger and the ele-

* R. J. Minney, *Chaplin, The Immortal Clown* (London, 1954), p. 81.

ments, linking the beginning of the progression with the climax, and a love story developing in the middle of the film.

But the design of the film is not solely determined by the interwoven stories. Having established the Arctic background, with its conventional danger and violence, the film begins to explore the way in which Chaplin would respond, with his illusions, his dreams of friendship and love, to this environment. The progression starts with gay fantasy: Charlie endures hunger and makes the best of it with comic gravity. A new emotional tone is added when he meets the girl. His feeling about her forces him to face social reality in the person of the dance-hall ruffian. He wins, but this leads to a deeper conflict between illusion and reality—his dream in the lonely cabin while the girl enjoys the New Year's Eve celebration with his rival. Since his love cannot be realized, there is nothing for Charlie to do but go on the apparently hopeless prospecting journey with Big Jim, which ends, literally, on the edge of an abyss. Then his fate is suddenly, magically, transformed in the ironic happy ending.

Each section has a distinctive mood and tempo that suggest a musical pattern: Part 2 (beginning the progression)—*scherzo;* Part 3—*allegro;* Part 4—*adagio;* Part 5 begins slowly and develops to a furious *presto.* This design has a dynamic development which does not depend on suspense, and which has more scope and imagination than the plot. We can look at *The Gold Rush* in two ways, as a plot, and as variations on a theme. These two aspects can be examined separately. They develop in different ways yet they are fused together as the sum total of the tramp's experience. The dialectical conflict and unity between them creates the form of the film. We cannot identify the story with the plot. On the contrary, the thematic pattern gives the story its full scope and meaning.

Chaplin's Comedy of Character

GERALD MAST

Chaplin and Keaton are the two poles of silent comics. Chaplin's great strength is his development of character and the exhausting of a particular

FROM *A Short History of the Movies* by Gerald Mast, pp. 153–56, 160. Copyright © 1971 by The Bobbs-Merrill Company, Inc., and reprinted by permission of the publisher.

comic and social situation; Keaton's strength is the tightness of his narrative structures and his contrast between the numbers one and infinity.
Chaplin is sentimental; his gentle, smiling women become idols to be revered. Keaton is not sentimental; he stuffs his females into bags and hauls
them around like sacks of potatoes; he satirizes their finicky incompetence
and even raises his fist to the silly lady in *The General* who feeds their
racing locomotive only the teensiest shavings of wood. It was especially
appropriate and touching to see the two opposites, Chaplin and Keaton,
united in *Limelight* (1952), both playing great clowns who were losing
their audiences and their touch. It may be no accident that one of the
most significant works of our era, *Waiting for Godot,* was produced in
the same year as *Limelight* and used the same metaphor of two old
vaudeville tramps whose act (in *Godot* their act is their life) had become
a bomb. If the Godot of Beckett's title suggests Charlot, it should also be
remembered that Beckett wrote a film script especially for Buster Keaton,
Film. The influence of the pair of comics continues to be felt.

No two films more clearly reveal the contrasting strengths and interests
of the two clowns than *The Gold Rush* and *The General,* both of which
were made at about the same time (1925–26). Like the short comedies,
The Gold Rush is an episodic series of highly developed, individual situations. The mortar that keeps these bricks together is a mixture of the film's
locale (the white, frozen wastes), the strivings and disappointments of
Charlie, and the particular thematic view the film takes of those strivings
(the quest for gold and for love, those two familiar goals, in an icy, can-
nibalistic jungle). All the Chaplin features, including those he made with
synchronized sound, would share this common episodic structure. *The
Gold Rush* also benefits from the circular patterns of the sequence of
episodes: Prologue (the journey to Alaska), the Cabin, the Dance Hall,
New Year's Eve, the Dance Hall, the Cabin, Epilogue (the journey home).

The individual sequences of *The Gold Rush* are rich both in Chaplin's
comic ingenuity and his ability to render the pathos of the tramp's disappointment, his cruel rejection by the woman he loves. Several of the
comic sequences have become justifiably famous. In the first cabin scene,
a hungry Charlie cooks his shoe, carves it like a prime rib of beef, salts
it to taste, and then eats it like a gourmet, twirling the shoelaces around
his fork like spaghetti, sucking the nails in the soles like chicken bones,
offering his friend one of the nails as a wishbone. This is the Chaplin who
treats one kind of object (a shoe) as if it were another kind of object (a
feast), the same minute observation he used in dissecting the clock in
The Pawnshop. In the dance hall, Charlie hastily ties a rope around his
middle to keep his sagging trousers up. He does not know that the other
end of the rope is attached to a dog, who then trots around the dance
floor following his dancing master. Charlie, however, must follow the
leader when the dog takes off after a cat.

But the comic business is matched by the pathos that Charlie can generate, often itself growing out of the comic business. Charlie's saddest moment is when Georgia, the woman he loves, whose picture and flower he preserves beneath his pillow, callously stands him up on New Year's Eve. When Charlie realizes that it is midnight and that she is not coming, he opens his door and listens to the happy townspeople singing "Auld Lang Syne." The film cuts back and forth between Charlie, the outsider, standing silently and alone in a doorway, and the throng of revelers in the dance hall, clasping hands in a large circle and singing exuberantly together (excellent use of Griffith cross-cutting here). But this pathetic moment would have been impossible without the previous comic one in which Charlie falls asleep and dreams he is entertaining Georgia with his "Oceana Roll." Charlie's joy, his naive sincerity, his charm, his gentleness, all show on his face as he coyly makes the two rolls kick, step, and twirl over the table on the ends of two forks. The happiness of the comic dream sequence creates the pathos of the subsequently painful reality.

If the reality proves painful for Charlie, it is because the lust for gold makes it so. The film's theme is its consistent indictment of what the pursuit of the material does to the human animal; as in *Greed*, it makes him an inhuman animal. Charlie, the least materialistic of men, has come to the most materialistic of places—a place where life is hard, dangerous, brutal, uncomfortable and unkind. Unlike the life of Nanook (might Chaplin have been influenced by Flaherty?), in which hardness becomes a virtue in itself, the men who have rushed for gold want to endure hardship only temporarily, just long enough to snatch up enough nuggets to go home and live easy. The quest for gold perverts all human relationships in the film. It creates a Black Larsen who casually murders and purposely fails to help his starving fellows. It creates a Jack, Georgia's handsome boyfriend, who treats his fellow men and women like furniture. Just as Charlie's genuine compassion reveals the emptiness of Jack's protestations of love, Chaplin's film technique makes an unsympathetic villian out of the conventional Hollywood leading man.

The rush toward gold perverts both love and friendship. Georgia herself, though Charlie perceives her inner beauty, has become hardened and callous from her strictly cash relationships with people in the isolated dance hall. And Charlie's friend, Big Jim McKay, is one of those fairweather friends whose feelings are the functions of expediency. When Big Jim gets hungry, he literally tries to eat Charlie; although Jim's seeing his buddy as a big chicken is comic, the implied cannibalism of the sequence is not. Later, Big Jim needs Charlie to direct him to his claim; once again Charlie becomes a friend because he is needed. But when Jim and Charlie get stuck in the cabin that teeters precariously on the edge of a cliff, the two men turn into dogs again, each trying to scramble out of the cabin by himself, stepping on each other to do so.

Whereas *The Gold Rush* combines a thematic unity with the episodic structure of exhausting the individual situations, the thematic coherency of *The General* is itself the product of the film's tight narrative unity. *The General* is the first, probably the greatest comic epic in film form. Like every comic epic, *The General* is the story of a journey, of the road (albeit a railroad). As in every comic epic, the protagonist suffers a series of hardships and dangerous adventures before achieving the rewards and comforts of returning home. As in every comic epic, the protagonist's opponents are both men and nature (particularly those two natural enemies, fire and water). As in every comic epic, there is a comic insufficiency in the protagonist and a disparity between his powers and the task he is asked to accomplish; but like every protagonist in the comic epic, Buster triumphs despite his insufficiencies. Everything in the Chaplin film, every gag, every piece of business, every thematic contrast, is subordinate to the delineation of the lonely tramp's character and the qualities that make him both lonely and superior to the men who have betrayed their humanity to keep from being lonely. Everything in *The General*, every gag, every piece of business, is subordinate to the film's driving narrative, its story of Johnny Gray trying to save his three loves—his girl, his country, and, most important of all, his locomotive. *The Gold Rush* is a comedy of character, *The General* a comedy of narrative.

.   .   .

The power of the Chaplin film comes from the expressiveness of his pantomime. Mime is mute. To reveal the significant gestures and facial flickers, Chaplin, as is his wont, uses the range of shots from full to close. Only expository shots—the opening shots of the men trekking north, the establishing shots of the dance hall, etc.—pull away from the characters. Chaplin's unobtrusive editing consistently allows the pantomime to play itself out without a cut—for example, the roll dance.

The power of the Keaton film comes from the contrast between his simple efforts and the immense problems surrounding him. Keaton, the character, is as tight-lipped as he is expressionless. His character is essentially mute. His blank stare says everything that can be said about the chaos he sees. To reveal the contrast of man and chaos, Keaton, as is his wont, uses the range of shots between full and extreme long. His camera works further away from the characters than Chaplin's, consistently comparing them with their surroundings. His cutting is slightly quicker than Chaplin's—to increase the pace and to reveal the different perspectives of man and environment—but never so quick or obtrusive as to make the stunts seem faked.

With such control of physical business, of thematic consistency, of appropriate structure, of placement of the camera, and of functional editing, neither *The Gold Rush* nor *The General* requires speech to speak.

DREYER

THE PASSION OF JOAN OF ARC

CREDITS

The Passion of Joan of Arc (France, 1928)
French title: *La Passion de Jeanne d'Arc*
Directed by Carl Dreyer from a script by Dreyer and Joseph Delteil
Produced by Société Générale de Films, Paris

Photography: Rudolph Maté
Art directors: Hermann Warm and Jean Hugo
Costumes: Valentine Hugo
Music: Victor Alix and Léo Pouget
Distributor (16mm): Audio-Brandon Films

Main performers:

Marie Falconetti (*Joan of Arc*)	Antonin Artaud (*Massieu*)
Eugène Silvain (*Pierre Cauchon*)	Ravet (*Jean Beaupère*)
Maurice Schutz (*Nicholas Loyseleur*)	André Berley (*Jean d'Estivet*)
Michel Simon (*Jean Lemaitre*)	Jean d'Yd (*Guillaume Evrard*)

Length: 8 reels

Carl Theodor Dreyer, the great Danish filmmaker, produced only fourteen feature films and a few documentaries in his forty-six years as a director. A lack of financial backing prevented him from working on feature films for two separate ten-year periods, even though *The Passion of Joan of Arc* (1928), the culmination of nine films made during the 1920's, brought him international renown among a knowledgeable segment of the public. This and his other best-known films—*Vampyr* (1932), *Day of Wrath* (1943), *Ordet* (1955), and *Gertrud* (1964)—are characteristically slow-paced and intellectually demanding. They convey the mood of gloom that is often associated with Scandinavian films (Dreyer made films in Norway, Sweden, and Denmark, as well as in France and Germany), particularly with those of Ingmar Bergman, who may very well have been influenced by Dreyer. In any case, Dreyer's following, devoted as it was, seems never to have been extensive enough to guarantee him the same opportunity to work continually in the cinema that was enjoyed by most of his great contemporaries such as Griffith and Chaplin.

Dreyer is more memorable for the power and consistency of his style than for his individual images, though a sense of visual beauty along with the austerity and somberness of the pictorial elements is always part of our general impression of his work. The composition of his frames is tightly controlled; all nonessential aspects are removed. Viewers have always felt the depth of Dreyer's images and wondered how the faces in his films manage to suggest so much more of the inner life of the characters than do similar shots by other major directors. In *Joan of Arc*, for example, a close-up of a face is sometimes depicted against a plain, light or dark background with no walls or subordinate elements to distract from the point of interest. This simplification of visual forms within the frame and the resulting clarity of emphasis mark the classicist's approach. Thus, the choice is often made for profundity and against complexity.

Yet it would be a mistake to suggest that technical mastery alone accounts for Dreyer's extraordinary power to evoke the fundamental reality of his characters. He always evinced a gift for understanding people beyond the verbal delineation of personality; that is, although dialogue may reveal characterization, in a Dreyer film it is not more important than gesture or detail carefully selected for its implications. Therefore, it has sometimes been argued that, more than other directors, Dreyer is dependent on his performers. Marie Falconetti, in *The Passion of Joan of Arc*, is a case in point: her superb performance seems largely responsible for the film's emotional impact. But, not to denigrate her major achievement, what we really see in this film is a series of marvelously photographed expressions, reactions, glances—portraits and visual designs, in fact—brilliantly displayed and arranged by an extremely conscientious and highly imaginative filmmaker who carefully determines his artistic effects. Nothing is left to chance in Dreyer's *Joan of Arc*.

The career and martyrdom in 1431 of Joan of Arc have interested writers for a long time. In Shakespeare's *Henry VI, Part I*, Joan is portrayed in an unfavorable light, but with her canonization in 1920 she became more than the historical freedom fighter, national liberator, and Christian saint; in George Bernard Shaw's play *St. Joan*, for example, she became the tragic symbol of the individual crushed by social forces that demanded a compromise of her integrity. Dreyer and others who later used the trial as the focus of their narrative tended to retain Shaw's perception of Joan's tragic predicament and her courageous decision to accept death rather than spiritual and physical imprisonment. But whereas Shaw's version widens the scope of the materials in order to emphasize the tragedy inherent for society in her situation, Dreyer deliberately narrows the grounds for his film: the Shavian theological and intellectual issues are played down in order to focus on an essentially innocent nineteen-year-old girl facing a fate that is virtually inevitable, as a result of her beliefs and the ruthlessness of her antagonists. Dreyer's film provides us with a unique visual experience of the final private moments of one of the most fully realized characters ever presented on the screen.

Psychological Intensity in *The Passion of Joan of Arc*

ROGER MANVELL

The first impression one gains from seeing this film is its silent cry for sound. Most of the time is occupied by five gruelling cross-examinations of Joan. The great ecclesiastical heads with their gesticulating mouths seem to require some corresponding cataclysmic uproar of the human voice. Dreyer himself says that he would prefer to have made the film with sound. But the treatment of the film as it stands is purely visual, and very often involves a carefully contrived interplay between the written dialogue and the visual action, which does not duplicate it so much as follow it through. The film, therefore, operates on two planes at once, first the hard, factual plane of the terms of the examinations, with its succession of wearying questions directed at Joan and given to the audience in the form of printed words, and, second, the stylized visual interpretation of what the trial meant emotionally and psychologically to Joan and to her persecutors, the French ecclesiastics led by Bishop Cauchon and the English occupation authorities led by the gross, overbearing military figure of the Earl of Warwick.

The process of the trial itself, which is conducted in the brutal manner of a third degree investigation, has its twentieth-century parallels, for it is essentially an ideological trial in which Joan for reasons of state must be led to condemn herself for the sake of power politics. The stylized presentation of the trial gives it a universality which goes beyond its immediate historical setting. Joan is the victim of an earthly authority which cannot allow itself to be put to question by a future saint whose integrity of vision is never deluded by its complex diplomacy. The significance of the trial of Joan of Arc will always appeal to poets who celebrate our human liberties, and the film remains almost unbearably poignant.

Falconetti, who never made another remarkable appearance in films, relives Dreyer's interpretation of Joan so intensely that one becomes completely oblivious of her as an actress. This *is* Joan of Arc, or, at any rate, *a* Joan of Arc, her face sunk and wasting, her body near collapse, her short hair matted with sweat and eventually shaved from her head before our eyes, her cheeks streaked with the teardrops of real suffering. Her lips move, but she seldom seems to speak more than a word or a phrase. Her head, photographed in almost continuous close-up, mostly against a plain white background, turns now this way, now that. She peers round over a

FROM *The Film and the Public* (1955) by Roger Manvell, pp. 119–23. Reprinted by permission of Roger Manvell.

shoulder raised in fear; now her head sinks in profile, or lifts full face as her eyes light with the emotion of her belief that she is fulfilling the will of God. She is not Joan the warrior, but Joan the sexless maid dressed in a poor jerkin and surrounded by towering male enemies she cannot understand but whose trickeries she evades through the great integrity of her faith. Dreyer's relentless presentation of Joan's situation is without any romantic relief. There is no way out for her except the way of recantation closed to her by her own convictions, and even that way, which she seems at one stage to be prepared to take, would undoubtedly be denied to her by the English authorities. The situation gives full play to Dreyer's passionate desire to portray on the screen the very roots of human persecution and suffering.

For the purposes of the film's dramatic structure, Joan's long trial is contracted to one day. We see her called before the ecclesiastical court which is gathered in the prison, examined later in her cell when she is presented with a forged letter seeming to come from the King of France urging her to recant, mocked by the English soldiers and given, like Christ, a mock crown and a mock sceptre, faced with instruments of torture which make her faint, bled in her cell and then taken out on a stretcher to be examined in a graveyard where, in her weakness, she signs the recantation which angers the Earl of Warwick. While the common people who side with her celebrate the recantation (shots of jugglers and contortionists give a macabre touch to this misplaced joy), her head is shaved and she realizes that the birds and the flowers, symbols of life and liberty, possess the freedom denied to her, now that she finds herself condemned to perpetual imprisonment. She renounces her recantation, receives the last sacrament and is handed over to the English military to be burnt as a witch. The film ends with the horribly violent measures used by the English soldiers to quell the riots which break out round the pyre where Joan coughs and twists in agony and finally droops to death in the smoke and flames.

The film proceeds with an unrelieved intensity, and is a great strain as well as a great experience to watch. The fact that no real change in Joan's situation is possible in the successive examinations to which she is subjected (there are five of them, all abortive, except for the last which results in her temporary recantation) means that there can be no element of dramatic development in the film. The result is that the film, considered purely as drama, sometimes seems tedious. There is no story to tell, only a situation to present in various successive phases. The beauty of the images provides a certain measure of relief, though this, of course, is insufficient in itself. The stylization often goes to extremes, when, for example, three monkish heads are arranged in the perspective of a receding pyramid, or when the instruments of torture are seen by Joan in a montage of moving wheels, spiked rollers and saw-toothed silhouettes, or when, in the final scenes of the film, soldiers and people are shot from unnecessarily impressionistic angles immediately overhead and even underfoot. But for the most part the stylization of treatment and the theatrical austerity of the settings suit the film exactly, and give it the right sense of universality, lifting it out of a particular period of the past and making it belong to all and every time. The camera, when it is not concentrating on the succession of cruel monkish heads, foxy, narrow, cadaverous, pitted, warted, gross, be-sweated and brutal, or, in the case of the young priest who helps Joan, idealistically handsome, tracks about a great deal to emphasize the patterned groupings of priests and soldiers. The acting itself is an interesting mixture of stylization and naturalism; Dreyer obviously wanted to intensify and emphasize the psychological realism of his film, and the acting as a result becomes slightly slower and slightly larger than life. He used panchromatic film to photograph his carefully chosen cast, none of whom wore make-up. The contours and markings of their faces, therefore, appear as in relief.

Critics in the past have insisted that Dreyer sacrifices true film technique in order to emphasize the separate values of individual shots. There are, however, many sections of the film which use, sometimes almost over-use, the dynamic methods of film technique implied by the word montage—some moments in the cross-examinations, for example, when the hostile faces seem to surround and even to punch forward at Joan, or the interchanges in the cell between the half-trusting girl and the foxy monk who organizes the forgery of the King's letter, or the terrible scenes in the torture-chamber and graveyard, and especially the long burning and rioting sequence which ends the film. But it is true to say that very frequently a consciously posed image which is, in effect, a single static composition is put on the screen in a manner unrelated to the continuity of the images which precede and follow it. That is why still photographs from this film appeal so strongly to collectors and to publishers of illustrated books on the cinema.

But the compelling power of this film remains unaltered by age or criticism. Dreyer rehearsed and photographed it in the exact order of the script, treating his cast with a strict discipline, above all in the case of Falconetti. The deep suffering which marks her portrayal of Joan bears all the signs of a profound personal experience in carrying out an exacting part under the relentless direction of an uncompromising artist.*

---

* [Dr. Manvell is now of the opinion that Falconetti was working at least to some extent under hypnosis. This hypothesis seems plausible in light of the intensity both of her performance and of Dreyer's method of directing.—S.J.S.]

The World Beyond

TOM MILNE

La Passion De Jeanne d'Arc is probably the Dreyer film that separates the sheep from the goats where his admirers are concerned. Or, to
put it another way, the film that divides those who believe that Dreyer
was a Christian for churchgoers, from those who, like myself, see him as a
pagan or a pantheist, living, like Gertrud, by one credo alone: *Amor
Omnia*. Perhaps this is simply another way of saying that since Dreyer
spent fourteen films denouncing the cruelties, prejudices, superstitions,
hypocrisies and dogmatic assertions that make up so great a part of the
history of so many established churches, it is difficult to imagine him being
seriously involved in any debate as to whether Joan of Arc was or was not
a witch, was or was not a saint. This, of course, is the stumbling block in
any film or play about Joan: it is virtually impossible to engage the mind
in any discussion about the whys and wherefores, rights or wrongs, of her
trial, since the dice are so completely loaded from the very start. All one
can do is wait for the outcome, harrowed to a greater or lesser degree by
the portrayal of her suffering. Even Bernard Shaw, the great debater,
couldn't find much to say of any conviction, though he said it wittily
enough and padded out the gaps with petty squabblings and much byplay
between Joan and her male friends and enemies. Even Bresson couldn't
really engage one's passions, except pity for the sufferings and terror at
the bleak final image of the charred, empty stake. Ultimately, Joan is an
impossible heroine, at least for Dreyer's kind of cinema, since she stands
alone, her fears and hopes communicated by and to those mysterious invisible voices, which even he couldn't quite seize through her eyes, her
expressions, her gestures.

After the enormous success in France of *Master of the House,* Dreyer
was approached by a French company, the Société Générale de Films, to
make a film for them. Dreyer proposed three historical heroines—Catherine
de Médicis, Marie-Antoinette and Joan of Arc—and the last was selected,
with a script to be based partly on a novel by Joseph Delteil and partly
(rather more than partly, as it would seem to have turned out) on the
original transcripts of the trial. As usual, Dreyer approached the project
by making extensive preparations, so that the film took a year and a half
to complete from conception to final cut: the costumes were exhaustively
researched, details of everyday life in the Middle Ages were copied from

FROM *The Cinema of Carl Dreyer* (1970) by Tom Milne, pp. 92–107. Reprinted by
permission of A. S. Barnes & Company, Inc.

.

Dreyer

the illuminations in a medieval manuscript, as were the vast, incredibly solid sets:

> The sets were all built into one complete construction: a great septagonal or octagonal castle with a very tall tower in each of the corners and a high wall running between the towers. Inside there were little houses built very simply, but with crooked angles and windows set out of line, like those in the miniatures. In the centre of the coutryard, opposite the drawbridge, was the church or chapel, and at the side the entrance to the churchyard where the burning took place. The walls consisted of a cement shell ten centimetres thick, enough to carry the weight of the actors and technicians during the shooting. The whole construction was painted pink to give it a grey effect against the sky, which stood out white in the film.*

The whole set was never seen, of course, only small segments of it, since the action was very fragmented and shot largely in close-up, but it helped Dreyer not only to inspire a sense of authenticity in his actors, but to reduce the story of Joan of Arc's trial (which in reality dragged out over some eighteen months) to *Kammerspiel* proportions. To this end, the twenty-nine examinations she underwent are telescoped into one, and the film starts with Joan at the end of her drama, so that the action takes place in a single day; all pre-history and picturesque detail, such as one finds in Shaw's *Saint Joan* or Anouilh's *L'Alouette,* is ruthlessly expunged so that the entire action takes place within the Palais de Justice at Rouen and its surrounds; and the action itself is reduced to what is virtually a symphony of faces. The last essential ingredient was a Joan *pre-existing* enough not to have to build a performance:

> I went to see her [Falconetti] one afternoon and we talked for an hour or two. I had seen her in a play in a little boulevard theatre whose name I have forgotten. She was playing a light modern comedy and she was very elegant in it, a little flighty, but charming. She didn't win me over right away, and I didn't have immediate confidence in her. I simply asked if I could come to see her the following day, and during that visit we talked. It was then I felt that there was something in her which could be brought out; something she could give, and something, therefore, that I could take. For behind the make-up, behind the pose and that ravishing modern appearance, there was something. There was a soul behind that façade. So I told her I would like to do some tests with her the next day. "But without make-up," I added, "with your face completely naked." The next day she came, ready and willing. She had removed her make-up, we did the tests, and

* Ebbe Neergaard, *Carl Dreyer: A Film Director's Work* (London: British Film Institute, 1950).

> I found in her face exactly what I wanted for Joan: a country
> girl, very sincere, but also a woman of suffering.*

Falconetti's performance is unarguably superb, no matter how it was
achieved (rumour said that Dreyer made her kneel on stone floors until
she was suffering enough, or played rushes back over and over again in an
exhausting attempt to refine the tiniest detail of an expression, and she
certainly submitted to having her head shaved for the cause), and the rest
of the cast is beautifully chosen, even if inclined to resort to the heavy
grimacing which disfigured *The President, Leaves from Satan's Book* and
Love One Another. Yet somehow the style Dreyer found for the film seems
irremediably false. Instead of flowing naturally from his chosen materials,
as it does in *The Parson's Widow, Mikaël* and *Master of the House*, here
it seems imposed upon them. The opening track, for instance, which takes
one slowly right through the court, past soldiers and ecclesiastics, to
close-ups first of Cauchon, then of Joan and Massieu, irresistibly recalls
the long, slow pans in *Day of Wrath* which become a terrible sign of
doom attending the victims of justice; here, although the slow track (or
pan) becomes associated with Joan's movements, dogging her footsteps as
she is led from place to place, this opening shot seems simply an introductory flourish in a film that is to be articulated so precisely on a balanced exchange of close-ups. Throughout the film there is a constant
stylistic uncertainty, an impurity, which jars heavily today: in the zoom
effects, for instance, when the camera darts in to over-stress a cruel or
sardonic point made by one of Joan's persecutors; in the overhead shots
of the crowds rushing about which seem totally arbitrary; in the irritating
cross-cutting which ruins the beautiful scene where Joan smiles at seeing
a cross on the floor of her cell made by the shadow of her barred window,
fragmenting it unnecessarily in order to show the preparation of a supposed letter from the King of France. One might even query the validity
of the mannerism whereby the camera is almost invariably looking up at
the characters, giving them a sense of dominating majesty. Ebbe Neergaard justifies this *motif* by suggesting that it implies Dreyer's "humility
in the presence of great human emotion."† This may be true, but it still
feels like an attempt to impose reverence.

Again, it is difficult to avoid making comparisons between the judges in
La Passion de Jeanne d'Arc and those of *Day of Wrath*. In the later film,
the camera moves slowly over serene, impassive faces with all the calm,
withdrawn dignity of impartial justice. The outcome is the same—a summary condemnation of the witch—yet somehow their presence, reasoned
and almost indifferent, is twice as effective as the vindictiveness etched in

---

* Michel Delahaye, "Entre terre et ciel: entretien avec Carl T. Dreyer," *Cahiers du
Cinéma*, September 1965.
† Neergaard, *Carl Dreyer*.

every nook, pock-mark and cranny of Cauchon and his colleagues. Of course Dreyer was right to want to get down to the truth in the naked human face; but with Joan exuding simple grace and Massieu (Antonin Artaud at his most handsome) glowing like an angel, all the wrinkles and the warts, the gross pouches of fat and the sadistic sneers, begin to look like an attempt to have one's cake and eat it. One thinks of Godard's remark that there isn't much point in making a film about concentration camps nowadays because the emotion is too automatic—unless one changed perspective to make a film about a typist working at Auschwitz, the day-to-day problems, the calculations necessary for the disposal of bodies, the inventories she was required to make, and so on.* In *Day of Wrath* Dreyer does change those perspectives, making ordinary human beings of his judges, and giving an edge of real malevolence to both the poor helpless women accused of witchcraft.

Finally, there is the problem of the "dynamic" editing style of the film, which goes back via Eisenstein to Griffith and Dreyer's own clumsy beginnings in the cinema. Without getting into aesthetic deep waters about the validity of the montage principle which underlies the (over-rated) excitements of the ice-floe sequence in *Way Down East* or the Odessa Steps sequence in *Battleship Potemkin,* one can say that it is inimical to Dreyer's nature as a director who loves to savour the feel and texture of people, places, objects. In theory, since the central *motif* of the film is the rhythm of question and answer, the alternation or parallel editing of very brief shots is right; in practice, the constant cutting away to take in a sneering face, a baby at its mother's breast, the shots of the doves that punctuate the march to the stake and the burning, is not only distracting, but tends to dissipate the film's emotional charge.

And yet . . . and yet. Like Gance's *Napoléon,* like *Intolerance,* like *Battleship Potemkin* even, *La Passion de Jeanne d'Arc* has a majestic power which steamrollers its way through all its faults and excesses, a power mostly stemming from Falconetti's performance, but partly at least created by the sheer weight of Dreyer's conception. Many critics have claimed that, with its constant stream of titles quoting question and answer as Joan's agony proceeds to its remorseless conclusion, *La Passion de Jeanne d'Arc* was a silent film crying out for sound. Comparison with Bresson's *Procès de Jeanne d'Arc,* made in 1962, suggests that they are wrong on purely aesthetic grounds, since Bresson's film proceeds like an actual trial, Dreyer's like an agonised commentary on it, with the divorcement between words and image acting as the equivalent of a Brechtian distantiation device. Sound would have been absolutely incompatible with Dreyer's conception, in which the titles and the huge close-ups of Joan and her judges are intercut as the two separate dramas—the farce of a trial which is being manipulated to a desired end, and the tragedy of

* Jean-Luc Godard, "Feu sur les Carabiniers," *Cahiers du Cinéma,* August 1963.

Joan alone with herself and her fear—evolve only tangentially to each other. Ultimately, in other words, it is perfectly possible to forget all the mannerisms which remind one that the film was made in France in 1927–28 at the height of the *avant-garde* movement and its technical excesses—or at least relegate them to the background of one's mind—and concentrate on Joan's interior, rather than exterior, experience.

So one comes back to Falconetti's performance, and the almost Brechtian manner in which Dreyer used artifice to strip it of artifice. Ebbe Neergaard has described the way in which he insisted on absolute truth from his actress:

> When Dreyer was about to shoot an important scene with Falconetti, everyone not directly concerned was banished from the set, and absolute silence was demanded. . . . When he was describing what he wanted, he would stammer and go red in the face, not from shyness or any hesitation as to what he meant, but simply from eagerness to make his feelings and intentions completely understood. The blotchy red face and the disjointed speech were evidence of his unswerving belief that there is only one expression that is right, that can and must be found. But just because it seemed so difficult for him to express himself clearly, the actress was fired to work in with him with all her power. She was, as it were, activated into expressing what Dryer could not show her, for it was something that could only be expressed in action, not speech, and she alone could do it, so she had to help him. And she realised that this could only be done if she dropped all intellectual inhibitions and let her feelings have free access from her subconscious to her facial expression. "When a child," says Dreyer, "suddenly sees an onrushing train in front of him, the expression on his face is spontaneous. By this I don't mean the feeling in it (which in this case is sudden fear), but the fact that the face is completely uninhibited." In a big scene the face must be relaxed to the point of emptiness, then the expression will appear of itself.[*]

All this is good Stanislavsky system[†] or Actors' Studio Method, and unlike the rest of the cast, Falconetti's feelings never seem manufactured: her agony simply exists, naked, unromantic and real in its ugly, sweat-soaked torment. But of course Dreyer's *use* of this emotion is artificial in the extreme. One notices, for instance, that while Joan's lips move during the trial scenes, they rarely frame more than a word or at most a phrase, so that she seems to be suffering her judges rather than answering them.

---

[*] In his lecture to the Danish Students League, delivered in Copenhagen on December 1, 1943, Dreyer stated that he was an adherent of the Stanislavsky system, adding: "No actor is able to create real and true feelings to order, because you cannot *extort* feelings, they must appear from within."

[†] Neergaard, *Carl Dreyer.*

Similarly, his use of panchromatic film to photograph the faces in close-up against white walls or backgrounds gives them an extraordinary quality of etched relief, in which the lighting ensures that high contrasts shadow Joan's tormentors with lines of malice while she herself is seen in the neutral tones of passive despair. Inexorably, Dreyer highlights his heroine's isolation, her helplessness to counter the weight massed against her, so that the dry, chapped lips, the face streaked with sweat and tears, the eyes shadowed with intolerable pain, the head thrown back in supplication, can still move an audience to tears today as they do Nana in *Vivre sa Vie* with their marvellous soundings of the well-springs of the human will.

Yet there is something more to the film than Joan's suffering, something that Dreyer would probably have described as that abstract spiritual quality he never tired of defining:

> Where is the possibility of artistic renewal in the cinema? I can only answer for myself, and I can see only one way: *abstraction.* In order not to be misunderstood, I must at once define abstraction as something that demands of the artist to abstract himself from reality in order to strengthen the spiritual content of his work. More concisely: the artist must describe inner, not outer life. The capacity to abstract is essential to all artistic creation. Abstraction allows the director to get outside the fence with which naturalism has surrounded his medium. It allows his films to be not merely visual, but spiritual. The director must share his own artistic and spiritual experiences with the audience. Abstraction will give him a chance of doing it, of replacing objective reality with his own subjective interpretation.[*]

There are, however, abstractions and abstractions, and although Dreyer and Bresson both approached Joan from the same orthodox view of her sanctity, their interpretations of her spirituality, as Robert Vas has pointed out very neatly, are very different as seen through the texture of the films. Noting that Joan's tragedy lies in her agony between faith and doubt, Vas observes:

> With a peasant stubbornness, Dreyer's Joan wanted to live; Bresson's Joan doesn't mind dying. When Joan sees the pigeons in Dreyer's film, you feel that she *must* leave something behind, something that would have been worth living for. But Bresson's pigeons flutter their wings above a world not worthy of such a sacrifice. Dreyer's heroine is left painfully alone; Bresson's is made lonely by Bresson.[†]

[*] Carl Dreyer, "Thoughts on My Craft," *Sight and Sound* (Winter 1955/56).
[†] Robert Vas, "The Trial of Joan of Arc," *Sight and Sound* (Winter 1962/63).

Dreyer's film, in other words, is not so much concerned with the eternity of peace and salvation that awaits Joan after her brief martyrdom, as with the life she is losing for ever, and so she is constantly surrounded by intimations of mortality, by the presence of the natural world, by the purely material malice of her trial. Not merely the fluttering pigeons which accompany her to the stake, the sunlight filtering through to the floor of her cell, or the child at its mother's breast; there is also the sudden spurt of blood as Joan is bled, the skull thrown up by a gravedigger in the cemetery where she is taken to be questioned, the pathetic remnants of hair being swept up after her head has been shaved. Appropriately enough, her journey to the stake is accompanied by a *danse macabre* of contortionists and jugglers, since this is a film in which life is made a mockery of by a travestied spiritual ideal which can only impose itself through pain and torture. And as inescapably present as anything in the film are the weapons with which life is threatened: the fire and the stake, of course, and the monstrous instruments of torture, but also the spears between which Joan walks to her martyrdom, the huge clubs thrown down from a tower to waiting soldiers as the crowd begins to murmur, the chains knobbed with whirling iron balls with which the soldiers quell the impending riot.

In a curious way, therefore, one can see the whole film as a primordial struggle between life and death, in which the opposing forces are personified almost as literally as those in a medieval mystery play, with Joan and Massieu as the angels of light, and the gross, sneering judges as the demons of darkness. Antonin Artaud was perhaps thinking along these lines when he said, in the course of an interview about his work in the cinema, that Dreyer's purpose was to "reveal Joan as the victim of one of the most terrible of all perversions: the perversion of a divine principle in its passage through the minds of men, whether they be Church, Government or what you will."* Ultimately, the conception does not quite come off, since the material is too intractably rooted in its historical and religious contexts; but it was a theme—the dissolution of life by death as humanity struggles to keep its tenuous foothold on earth—to which Dreyer was to return and realise to perfection three years later in *Vampyr*.

---

* Antonin Artaud, *Oeuvres Complètes,* Vol. III (Paris: Gallimard, 1961). Interview originally published in 1929.

Carl Dreyer's World

RICHARD ROWLAND

To visit Carl Dreyer's *Passion of Joan of Arc,* filmed in France in 1928, after seeing his more recent Danish production, *Day of Wrath,* is an extraordinarily exciting experience. These two films, produced at an interval of nearly twenty years, scarcely reveal the difference in their ages. The motion picture is always more likely to date itself than any other art, partly because it relies as no other art ever has upon technology. But these two films, remembered together, seem to be of the same moment; their passionate directness is of no specific day. Such agelessness in any art is usually the result of a highly personalized style. The artist who is branded as of his age dates within his lifetime; the individualist who goes his own way—Blake, El Greco, Berlioz, at their most original—is as fresh today as ever. A style that represents a coherent and considered judgment of life, even in the flickering light of the cinema, transcends fashion or technical development.

Dreyer's style is wholly pictorial. One of these films is a sound film, the other silent, but in both it is visual images that we remember. There are some striking effects on the sound track of *Day of Wrath,* but we remember the faces, lights, and shadows more vividly than the sounds. Even the use of the hymn from which *Day of Wrath* draws its title is impressed upon us pictorially; we cut from the agonized face of the ancient witch as she falls forward upon the bonfire to the witnessing choirboys as they sing the austere hymn whose song is so discordant with its angry words. But it is the blank innocence of their angelic faces that jars our hearts more than the sound of the high, unrepentant voices.

Carl Dreyer's style seems an extraordinarily simple one, and at first glance an anticinematic one. It consists largely of reliance upon the close-up. At times one almost feels that one is back at the beginning of Griffith's great period, when the close-up had just been discovered and the screen was constantly filled with swollen gigantic shadows of human faces. But Dreyer's use of the close-up and the photographic detail is by no means so naïve.

Reliance on such a limiting device might be expected to make the film static; some critics have so described these films. But they are not truly static; there is constant development. The spectator must learn to watch

FROM *Hollywood Quarterly,* Volume V, Number 1, pp. 53–60. © 1950 by The Regents of the University of California. Reprinted by permission of The Regents.

for slighter gestures; the droop of an eye may carry the weight of tragedy; the quiver of a lip will be a clue to unspoken paragraphs. Here each fragment of a gesture is meaningful and revealing.

The Passion of Joan of Arc reveals this in its purest form. The film is devoted entirely to the trial and execution of its heroine; Joan is first seen as she appears before the ecclesiastical court. We see her at full length as she strides into the room with a boy's gait, but never again in the entire film do we see more than her head and shoulders. The long first episode alternates close-ups of Joan's face, crop-headed, boyish, unbeautiful, with close-ups of her inquisitors, a fascinating gallery of individual portraits. Such a scene seems scarcely possible without the words of the inquisition, yet here we scarcely miss them. In a few minutes we have forgotten that this is that absurdly archaic art form the silent film. The concentration upon the faces is unrelenting, one's first impulse is to say cruel. One of the clerics has a large wart; another's face is splashed with freckles which we contemplate until we find ourselves counting them. Falconetti's face as Joan becomes the most familiar face in the world; every crevice, every pore, is familiar after the unblinking study Dreyer has made of it. A fly lights upon her eyelid, and with the back of her rough soldier's hand she brushes it away before she replies stubbornly to the harrowing questions which she cannot comprehend; it is a gesture so rude that there can be no art in it, one tells oneself, and yet it scrapes the nerves with an unforgettable poignancy. One of the inquisitors, a bland fat man, suddenly spits at Joan and the camera watches passionlessly the confused hurt in her eyes as the spittle splashes on her cheek. Later she is blasphemously crowned, humiliated, and mocked by two gross soldiers, one an obese hairy brute whose unheard laughter needs no sound track to reveal its vulgarity; as she submits to their leering gibes, saliva trickles from the corner of her mouth.

Obviously, it is a film that has a physicality quite unfamiliar to the average filmgoer. Its incessant magnification of the coarse physical basis of life might understandably suggest an attempt to satirize and deflate humanity, or at least to disgust the spectator. Certainly this is a method and aim familiar to anyone who has read the second book of *Gulliver's Travels*. Magnify the human body twelve times, Swift says, and no one can fail to be disgusted by his own beastliness.

But the Brobdingnagian effect is clearly not the aim of this film. The aim is much closer to that of the early Flemish painters whose painstaking realism is as full of compassion as it is unrelenting in its mirroring of nature. One thinks of Breughel's stubble-chinned "Old Shepherd," or the brutally unmistakable humanity of Bosch's "Crowning with Thorns" in the National Gallery in London; like theirs, Dreyer's art stems from a conviction, both disillusioned and confident, that whatever coarseness or cruelty may characterize them, men are what matter in this world; now you, the spectator, are the dead center of that world, involved in mankind with a painful, inescapable, and somehow ennobling intensity.

One scene in *Joan of Arc* underlines this with curious power. The court has decided that Joan is ill (else how could she defy the Church and claim to have seen naked angels?) and may possibly be cured if she is bled. No detail of the bleeding is spared us; the audience writhes as the cut is made and the black vital stream spurts into the bowl. But, curiously, in the end the effect is neither unpleasant nor clinical. One feels the river pulsing in one's own veins; one remembers mortality, and immediately, as its corollary, vitality. This is the sort of physicality that Dreyer's films have, but it springs not at all from Swiftian disgust. He never lets us forget the shell of flesh which we inhabit, but he never forgets the mystery of the personality that fills the shell—the quality to which Swift's outrage at natural functions never let him penetrate. The love scenes in *Day of Wrath* are brilliant in their ability to suggest, without representing, the tumult of lust. The dappled sunlight agitating the faces of the lovers suggests overpoweringly what is made more specific by the image of the plunging horses later. The lovers' experience is general and universal, but it is also individual, and it is the individuality that is ultimately of interest to Dreyer. The physicality serves, as it were, to draw us into the film, but the real subject is the ceaseless struggle that individuality wages against the enclosing world.

The close-up is necessary for all this; this is realism in one sense, though the films are highly poetic, highly symbolic, highly selective. This is how the world looks from the center. We feel the trial much as Joan feels it; the series of close-ups looks at us with the eyes of the inquisitors, some of them merciless, some of them compassionate, some of them shifty, some of them as hurt and confused as Joan herself. We feel these eyes as we feel the delicate feet of the fly that weighs on Joan's eyelid.

But Joan is at the center. We feel her physically from within at the same time that we watch her from without. There is no attempt specifically to penetrate her mind; the camera watches, it rarely interprets. Yet we become aware of a complexity and depth in Joan that are rare in any heroine, entirely through watching her face—for here there is almost no help from words.

There have been two more or less recent attempts by directors of genius to tell stories through a revived emphasis upon the close-up, both more or less disastrous. In *The Paradine Case* Alfred Hitchcock, that master of movement, reduced his story to a series of close-ups; we saw little more than the furrowed brow of Ann Todd, the noncommittal, passionless beauty of Valli, the sulky, sleepy beauty of Louis Jourdan, all varnished and frozen into blank meaningless perfection. This was static, as Dreyer's films are not. Eisenstein, in his *Ivan the Terrible*, kept our eyes focused for long periods upon the icon-like images of his primitivized actors.

There was beauty and splendor in the film, but the close-ups were inter-
ruptions, and meaningless ones, for there was no interest in individual
human beings in the film at all, as there has rarely been in his work.

Eisenstein is interested in human masses in motion, but not in the individual; when the armies clash on the ice in *Alexander Nevsky,* when
the fluttering crowd tumbles down the steps of Odessa before the Czarist
forces in *Potemkin,* when the statue-like symbol of a king stands beneath
the rain of gold in *Ivan the Terrible,* the film leaps into breathtaking life.
But when we close in on an individual there is nothing there—a pseudo-
man marked Czarist (Bad) or Revolutionary (Good) in whom no one can
feel any interest. Even the haunting face of the mourning wife in
Thunder Over Mexico is a dehumanized idealization of all grief, a face
without a name. These pictures are huge spectacles where ignorant armies
clash incessantly but no individual creature lives or breathes. Nothing new
is revealed in his close-ups; they merely reiterate monotonously what was
stated at the start.

But Dreyer is precisely opposed to this. The individual is *all* that matters to him; as a result the background and environment recede completely. In *The Passion of Joan of Arc* we often do not even know where
the scene takes place. We see a head and are left to guess whether this is
outdoors or in; when pageantry becomes necessary to the narration the
mob is broken into individuals. There is a street fair in *Joan of Arc* that
is filled with life and excitement, but we see each tumbler individually
and the delighted faces of the audience are single and living. The crowd
at Joan's martyrdom is symbolized in a close-up of a large peasant woman's
breast as she suckles her child—the most Brobdingnagian effect of all, yet
it gives no offense for it speaks not of nauseous brutality but of the persistence of life.

In some ways, *Day of Wrath* exemplifies more strikingly the nakedness
of Dreyer's drama. It is a historical film in the best sense, for it is a minutely
faithful reproduction of a historical situation. But we never think of it as
a historical film; we are enclosed in these people whose selves lead
them on to their own doom. History, environment, the *Zeitgeist* have had
their effect; this is so obvious that Dreyer does not bother to say it; but
they have had their effect upon *these* people and not other people, and
that is the great wonder and mystery which makes it worth making a film
about them.

The story is extremely simple. A widowed pastor marries a young girl,
the daughter of a woman who has been burned as a witch. The pastor's
mother resents her intrusion. When the pastor's grown son returns from
abroad, the young wife and he fall in love. She wishes the pastor dead,
and he dies with his finger flung out in accusation. She is burned as a
witch. *Day of Wrath* is a study in witchcraft, and yet there is no historical
analysis of the cause and effect of the phenomenon. Here is a witch; what

does that mean? Dreyer tells us. It means, specifically, to be a lonely and frightened girl longing for tenderness and companionship, uncertain of her own worth and strength, a quiet girl with sly slant eyes which suggest her lusting after the flesh and an external repose which is her only strength against the jealousy of her mother-in-law and the frozen righteousness of her pastor husband. Was she a witch? It is a question that is almost impertinent. Dreyer on the whole avoids the supernatural although the subjects of both films invite supernatural treatment. Only when the pastor hurries home in the storm does the extravagance with which nature conforms to humanity, in the storm-swept skies and the black threatening trees, suggest a decisively supernatural element in the story. And in fact the scene seems in many ways a mistake. For the girl has discovered that she is a witch, and the audience is not interested in supernatural corroboration.

The Passion of Joan of Arc, in the same way, avoids the question of Joan's voices. Was she a saint? This, too, is an irrelevancy. She was Joan; she heard these voices; she was *such* a person. And in the end we know her as a girl strong chiefly in her simplicity, confused and frightened and uncomprehending of what has happened to her but determined to abide by what she believes in. And the face which seemed so plain as we first saw her has grown to have a beauty quite beyond expression or convention.

In these pictures no judgment is expressed. The ugly churchmen who doom Joan are mixed and muddled in their motives; they are not wrong; we can spare pity from Joan for them. The bored and silly witch, the cruelly possessive mother, the troubled ineffectual pastor, are all seen with the same detached compassion as is Joan of Arc. One subject of *Day of Wrath* is the inarticulate isolation of all souls. Partly we feel this because the dialogue is so sparse, not only because the central characters are taciturn, but because each of the characters finds himself cut off by private desires and ambitions; we see these people as we see the pastor's young wife through the web she has spun, a tapestry of the temptation, where a stiff and formal Eve offers the apple to Adam, and behind which the wife's eyes burn in witchery.

The effect depends almost entirely upon the close-ups which magnify and isolate the personalities. Joan, for all her humility, her plainness, her obvious ignorance, has an almost Homeric stature. The characters in *Day of Wrath* are in no possible sense "larger than life," yet they crowd the imagination because we have seen them in their terrible isolation and with an appalling completeness, in the flesh and in the spirit. And this is what such loving cinema techniques were designed for; the humanist (and Dreyer is one) can use them to reveal the darks and lights of humanity with unrelenting art; the antihumanist (as Eisenstein proves to be, at heart) can use them only to oversimplify men into the cogs of a vast and mindless machine. Dreyer's humans are independent, and are frightened and frightening because of that independence. Even the unrelieved grimness of *Day of Wrath* has a certain lift because it is such a tangled web of responsibilities. And *The Passion of Joan of Arc*, twenty years old now, remains an exalted portrait of the splendid solitude of a pure and determined woman; we do not know whether she is a saint, but we know what it is like to burn at the stake and why it could be thought worth doing. By so much has our experience been enlarged. There are few films of which we could say more.

LANG

M

CREdiTS

M (Germany, 1931)
Directed by Fritz Lang from a screenplay by Thea von Harbou after an article
   by Egon Jacobson
Produced by Nero Films

Photography: Fritz Arno Wagner
Art directors: Karl Vollbrecht, Emil Hasler
Distributors (16 mm): Audio-Brandon Films, Janus Films

Main performers:

Peter Lorre (*Hans Beckert*)   Fritz Gnass (*The burglar*)
Otto Wernicke (*Inspector Lohmann*)   Fritz Odemar (*The safe-breaker*)
Gustaf Gründgens (*Shränker*)   Georg John (*The blind beggar*)
Ellen Widmann (*Mrs. Beckmann*)   Rudolf Blümner (*The lawyer*)
Inge Landgut (*Elsie Beckmann*)   Theodor Loos (*Inspector Groeber*)

Length: 99 minutes (other released prints: 90, 92, 114 minutes)

Before making his first sound film, *M*, Fritz Lang worked for more than a decade in silent films during that notable period of the German cinema that began with *The Cabinet of Dr. Caligari* in 1919 (a film Lang was originally supposed to direct) and culminated with *M* in 1931. He was one of the few filmmakers of an international repute to make the changeover to sound with no apparent difficulty. *M* stands out as both a classic film and a great technical achievement in its relating of the soundtrack to the visuals, a feat that has rarely been equaled to this day, even though innumerable filmmakers have attempted to deal with some of the esthetic problems created by the two distinctive visual and verbal modes of communication. Lang's economy of dialogue, counterpoint of sound and picture, and occasional use of silence influenced filmmaking on an international scale.

In the silent era Lang perfected a visual style noteworthy for its imposition of architectural design on rather spectacular subject matter. Some of these huge films required fantastic studio sets. The great German studio Ufa prided itself on the construction of monumental sets for both realistic and nonrealistic scenes. A few of Lang's longer films are actually two films that can be viewed separately (for example, the Wagnerian *Die Nibelungen* [1924] consists of Part One, *Siegfried's Death*, and Part Two, *Kriemhild's Revenge*). To his large-scale films with unusual scenic locations, such as *Metropolis* (1926) and *The Woman in the Moon* (1929), Lang brought a highly objective point of view, an almost clinical interest in the study of man's relationship to the lines and shapes of the materials in his environment. Combining visual austerity with a feeling for linear rhythm, Lang typically examines the way in which the structural designs of an environment seem to frustrate the efforts of an individual to preserve an element of his human dignity. It is not some abstract notion of society that becomes the antagonist, but rather the specifically delineated patterns of organization (the institutions, the social codes), symbolized by the magnificent but cold architecture of the scenery.

Lang's interest in crime and the criminal mentality persisted throughout his career in Germany and the United States. It is curious to note that many years after dealing with the adventures of the master criminal Mabuse (*Dr. Mabuse, the Gambler*, 1922; *The Testament of Dr. Mabuse*, 1933), Lang returned to that subject matter with *The Thousand Eyes of Dr. Mabuse* (1960). In handling crime stories, Lang sometimes seems to work toward allegory in that his characters surmount the sordid substance of their world and tend to assume broad representative implications: ambition, greed, power, and so on. At other times, Lang's work is characterized by overt melodrama, though even then, as in *The Big Heat* (1953) and *Scarlet Street* (1945), the technical brilliance and sense of moral purpose always elevate his films above those of almost any other filmmaker working in the same genres. Lang's genius remains distinctive even when his subject matter is commonplace.

In *M*, Lang's divergent tendencies merge under the influence of the extraordinary subject matter: a psychotic child-murderer presented in an almost sympathetic light. The killer, pursued by the symbolic forces of established order (the police and the citizenry) and anti-order (the criminal underworld), achieves allegorical stature as the outsider, the individual branded with the mark of Cain, hunted and dehumanized, finally appealing to our sympathy merely by exhibiting the basic level of "humanness." We can never ignore the horror of the man's maniacal existence—his persecutors despise him and confront him with the brutality of his crimes—but we watch him cornered and helpless within the rigid frame of Lang's camera, terrified by society's power, and we are actually relieved to see him rescued from execution, presumably to be confined in an institution, considered a destroyed victim of mental derangement and allowed to retain some measure of childlike ignorance of his divided self.

Lang's remarkable accomplishment of making a classic film from such material includes the presentation of many vivid, even beautiful, images, dreadful as their implications may be. One of the murders is indicated by the camera's focusing on the little girl's abandoned balloon floating away and entangling briefly in some telegraph wires—letting us know that offscreen she has been slain. The utter desolation of the underlying idea and

Murderer Among Us

SIEGFRIED KRACAUER

Fritz Lang told me that in 1930, before *M* went into production, a short notice appeared in the press, announcing the tentative title of his new film, *Mörder unter uns* (*Murderer Among Us*). Soon he received numerous threatening letters and, still worse, was bluntly refused permission to use the Staaken studio for his film. "But why this incomprehensible conspiracy against a film about the Düsseldorf child-murderer Kürten?" he asked the studio manager in despair. "*Ach,* I see," the manager said. He beamed with relief and immediately surrendered the keys of Staaken. Lang, too, understood; while arguing with the man, he had seized his lapel and caught a glimpse of the Nazi insignia on its reverse. "Murderer among us": the Party feared to be compromised. On that day, Lang added, he came of age politically.

M opens with the case of Elsie, a schoolgirl who disappears and after a while is found slain in the woods. Since her murder is preceded and followed by similar crimes, the city lives through a veritable nightmare. The police work feverishly to track down the child-murderer, but succeed only in disturbing the underworld. The city's leading criminals therefore decide to ferret out the monster themselves. For once, their interests coincide with those of the law. Here Thea von Harbou borrows a motif from Brecht's *Dreigroschen oper:* the gang of criminals enlists the help of a beggars' union, converting its membership into a network of unobtrusive scouts. Even though the police meanwhile identify the murderer as a former inmate of a lunatic asylum, the criminals with the aid of a blind beggar steal a march on the detectives. At night, they break into the office building in which the fugitive has taken refuge, pull him out of a lumber room beneath the roof, and then drag him to a deserted factory, where they improvise a "kangaroo court," which eventually pronounces his death sentence. The police appear in time to hand him over to the authorities.

Released in 1931, this Nero production found enthusiastic response everywhere. It was not only Lang's first talkie, but his first important film after the pretentious duds he had made during the stabilized period. *M* again reaches the level of his earlier films, *Destiny* and *Nibelungen,* and moreover surpasses them in virtuosity. To increase the film's documentary value, pictorial reports on current police procedures are inserted in such a

FROM *From Caligari to Hitler* (1947) by Siegfried Kracauer, pp. 218–22. Reprinted by permission of Walter and Conston, P. C., attorneys for the estate of Elizabeth Kracauer.

skillful way that they appear to be part of the action. Ingenious cutting interweaves the milieus of the police and the underworld: while the gang leaders discuss their plans, police experts, too, sit in conference, and these two meetings are paralleled by constant shifts of scene which hinge on subtle association. The comic touch inherent in the cooperation between the lawless and the law materializes on various occasions. Witnesses refuse to agree upon the simplest facts; innocent citizens indict each other fiercely. Set against these gay interludes, the episodes concentrating upon the murders seem even more horrifying.

Lang's imaginative use of sound to intensify dread and terror is unparalleled in the history of the talkies. Elsie's mother, after having waited for hours, steps out of her flat and desperately shouts the child's name. While her "Elsie!" sounds, the following pictures pass across the screen: the empty stairwell; the empty attic; Elsie's unused plate on the kitchen table; a remote patch of grass with her ball lying on it; a balloon catching in telegraph wires—the very balloon which the murderer had bought from the blind beggar to win her confidence. Like a pedal point, the cry "Elsie!" underlies these otherwise unconnected shots, fusing them into a sinister narrative. Whenever the murderer is possessed by the lust for killing, he whistles a few bars of a melody by Grieg. His whistling threads the film, an ominous foreboding of his appearance. A little girl is seen walking along: as she stops in front of a shop window, the weird Grieg melody approaches her, and suddenly the bright afternoon street seems clouded by threatening shadows. Later on, the whistling reaches the ears of the blind beggar for a second time and thus brings about the murderer's own doom. Another fatal sound is produced by his vain effort to remove, with his jackknife, the lock of the door which has slammed behind him after his flight into the lumber room. When the criminals pass along the top floor of the office building, this jarring noise, reminiscent of the prolonged gnawing of a rat, betrays his presence.*

The film's true center is the murderer himself. Peter Lorre portrays him incomparably as a somewhat infantile petty bourgeois who eats apples on the street and could not possibly be suspected of killing a fly. His landlady, when questioned by the police, describes this tenant of hers as a quiet and proper person. He is fat and looks effeminate rather than resolute. A brilliant pictorial device serves to characterize his morbid propensities. On three different occasions, scores of inanimate objects, much more obtrusive than in *The Blue Angel*,† surround the murderer; they seem on the point of engulfing him. Standing before a cutlery shop, he is photographed in such a way that his face appears within a rhomboid

---

* Arnheim, *Film als Kunst*, pp. 230, 252, 300, comments on several devices in *M*. Cf. Hamilton, "M," *National Board of Review Magazine*, March 1933, pp. 8–11.
† [A famous German film, made by Josef von Sternberg (1930), starring Marlene Dietrich and Emil Jannings.—S.J.S.]

reflection of sparkling knives. Sitting on a café terrace behind an ivy-covered trellis, with only his cheeks gleaming through the foliage, he suggests a beast of prey lurking in the jungle. Finally, trapped in the lumber room, he is hardly distinguishable from the tangled debris in which he tries to evade his captors. Since in many German films the predominance of mute objects symbolizes the ascendancy of irrational powers, these three shots can be assumed to define the murderer as a prisoner of uncontrollable instincts. Evil urges overwhelm him in exactly the same manner in which multiple objects close in on his screen image.

This is corroborated by his own testimony before the "kangaroo court," an episode opening with a couple of shots which render perfectly the shock he experiences at that moment. Three criminals, insensitive to the murderer's frantic protests, push, drag and kick him forward. He lands on the floor. As he begins to look about, the close-up of his face—a face distorted with rage and fear—abruptly gives way to a long shot surveying the group of criminals, beggars and street women in front of him. The impression of shock results from the terrifying contrast between the wretched creature on the floor and this immovable group which, arranged in Lang's best monumental style, watches him in stony silence. It is as if the murderer has unexpectedly collided with a human wall. Then, in an attempt to justify himself, he accounts for his crimes in this way: I am always forced to move along the streets, and always someone is behind me. It is I. I sometimes feel I am myself behind me, and yet I cannot escape. . . . I want to run away—I must run away. The specters are always pursuing me—unless I do it. And afterwards, standing before a poster, I read what I have done. Have I done this? But I don't know anything about it. I loathe it—I must—loathe it—must—I can no longer . . . .

Along with the implications of the pictorial texture, this confession makes it clear that the murderer belongs to an old family of German screen characters. He resembles Baldwin in *The Student of Prague*, who also succumbs to the spell of his devilish other self; and he is a direct offspring of the somnambulist Cesare. Like Cesare, he lives under the compulsion to kill. But while the somnambulist unconsciously surrenders to Dr. Caligari's superior will power, the child-murderer submits to his own pathological impulses and in addition is fully aware of this enforced submission. The way he acknowledges it reveals his affinity with all those characters whose ancestor is the philistine in *The Street*. The murderer is the link between two screen families; in him, the tendencies embodied by the philistine and the somnambulist finally fuse with each other. He is not simply a fortuitous compound of the habitual killer and the submissive petty bourgeois; according to his confession, this modernized Cesare is a killer because of his submission to the imaginary Caligari within him. His physical appearance sustains the impression of his complete immaturity—an immaturity which also accounts for the rampant growth of his murderous instincts.

In its exploration of this character, who is not so much a retrogressive rebel as a product of retrogression, *M* confirms the moral of *The Blue Angel:* that in the wake of retrogression terrible outbursts of sadism are inevitable. Both films bear upon the psychological situation of those crucial years and both anticipate what was to happen on a large scale unless people could free themselves from the specters pursuing them. The pattern had not yet become set. In the street scenes of *M*, such familiar symbols as the rotating spiral in an optician's shop and the policeman guiding a child across the street are resuscitated. The combination of these motifs with that of a puppet incessantly hopping up and down reveals the film's wavering between the notions of anarchy and authority.

Encounters with Sound

PAUL JENSEN

The picture was shot in six weeks in a makeshift studio at the Staaken Zeppelinhalle, outside Berlin. Peter Lorre, who played the killer, performed for Lang by day while appearing on the stage in *Squaring the Circle* (a farce by Valentin Katayev) in the evenings. The original title was shortened to the single letter *M*, though the film has also been referred to as *Eine Stadt sucht einen Mörder* (*A City Searches for a Murderer*) and *Dein Mörder sicht dich An* (*Your Killer Looks at You*). Made for Nero Films, instead of UFA or Lang's own company, it opened at the UFA-Palast am Zoo, Berlin, in June 1931. Its running time was then 114 minutes, but *Variety's* review of the première noted that this was "a little too long. Without spoiling the effect—even bettering it—cutting could be done. There are a few repetitions and a few slow scenes."* This advice was followed two years later when Foremco Pictures released *M* in the U.S.A.; this version was only ninety-two minutes long. The first print shown in New York City was in German, with English subtitles, but after two weeks it was replaced with a dubbed version. Supposedly, Lang had planned for this situation by avoiding close-ups of people talking and by

FROM *The Cinema of Fritz Lang* (1969) by Paul Jensen, pp. 93–103. Reprinted by permission of A. S. Barnes & Company, Inc.

* Magnus, "M," *Variety* (June 2, 1931).

covering lip movements with a prop, such as Lohmann's cigar, or a turn of the head. The dubbing was done in England, by Eric Hakim, and except for Lorre most of the actors involved were not the original performers. New York's Museum of Modern Art now circulates a slightly longer, ninety-seven minute copy to which is added the Museum's own prologue of printed information. (The Museum states on the film and in its catalogue that the original print was thirty minutes longer, but this is simply an exaggeration.)

Seymour Nebenzal, head of Nero Films, produced several quite original films in the early Thirties, including *M* and Lang's *Das Testament des Dr. Mabuse.* In 1950, he and Harold Nebenzal also produced an American version of *M* for Columbia Pictures. "People ask why I do not re-make *M* in English," said Lang some years earlier. "I have no reason to do that. I said all I had to say about that subject in the picture. Now I have other things to say."* Instead, Joseph Losey directed the re-make, which the production code authorities agreed to pass only if it bore clear similarities to an accepted classic. "I'd seen *M* in the early Thirties," says Losey. "I saw it again, once, in a very bad copy, just before I made it. I never referred to it. I only consciously repeated one shot. There may have been unconscious repetitions, in terms of the atmosphere of certain sequences."†

As field research for *M*, Lang spent eight days in a mental institution; he had also known and studied several murderers, supposedly including Peter Kürten, who alone had killed about ten people in the period around 1925. Real criminals were used in certain scenes, resulting in a high turnover rate among the extras; a total of twenty-four cast members were arrested during the filming.

This was Lang's first use of sound, which may have hastened the transition into a realistic mode hinted at in *Die Frau im Mond.* At any rate, though a concern for mob psychology still exists, the crowd is no longer the anonymous mass of *Metropolis.* Instead, all of its members are sharply delineated. Some of Lang's coldness is replaced with pity and a concern for individuals, but though he examines his subjects and characters more closely than before, his observation is still highly objective. There are really no main characters, though Lorre's is the central and most famous role, and no one with whom the viewer is allowed to identify. This gives the film a cool, documentary quality.

Lang's style now emphasises realism, but he still uses people and objects expressively, and his highly calculated structure ties many scenes together with aural and visual transitions. Though his themes remain, they have been translated into a realistic context. Duality has become

* Eileen Creelman, "Picture Plays and Players," *New York Sun* (Oct. 6, 1944).
† James Leahy, *The Cinema of Joseph Losey* (New York: A. S. Barnes and Co., 1967), page 47.

homicidal schizophrenia, with an innocent, unassuming façade hiding a murderer; the line between justice and revenge is again blurred, and mob violence is associated with both; the master villain still exists, but in the slightly more down-to-earth figure of Shränker, the criminal organiser.

This is Lang's favourite of all his own films because of the social criticism it contains. In *M*, the individual who is trapped and menaced is not an idealised Nordic hero (*Die Nibelungen*) or an innocent, hardworking young man (*Fury*); he is a fat psychopath who murders involuntarily. This important difference allows the film to make a statement, denied to Lang's other pictures, by serving a "preaching function." It only lectures overtly at the very end, but throughout it pleads the cause of the mentally ill by showing the "hero" treated as a criminal and a disease, not as a sick man who cannot help himself. This adds a new dimension to the story.

The director himself once stated that he made *M* "to warn mothers about neglecting their children."* He said this, however, in 1937, after *Fury* and *You Only Live Once* had given him a reputation for the courageous handling of social themes. Actually, the questions of mental illness and child watching are only small portions of the film's substantial content. Through the opposition of the criminals and the police (with an individual caught between), *M* really embodies the more general contrasts of disorganisation (the police in one sense, the mob in another) and order (the criminals and beggars), justice and revenge, Democracy and Fascism, and perhaps even the Weimar Republic and the Nazi Third Reich. All of this, however, is subordinate to the film's quality as a semi-documentary crime melodrama.

M is concerned with two types of murder and murderers. The first is that committed by Hans Beckert (Peter Lorre), a disturbed child killer. The pivotal character, he is cut off from the law by his deeds and from the underworld because he is independent and compulsive. The separate worlds of the criminals and the police had previously operated in a kind of balance, but Becker, a psychotic outsider, disrupts this by causing the police to bear down heavily on all aspects of crime. When this happens, the criminals themselves organise and try to locate the killer. Beckert's capture is now inevitable, since both factions are against him. The only uncertainty is about which group will discover him first, and when that will happen. This leads to the second kind of murder: that which is almost committed by the citizens and criminals who hunt him down and give him a "trial." This action begins as simple self-concern; then, convinced it is enacting justice but in reality seeking revenge for the children's deaths, the group attempts to murder the murderer before the

---

* Marguerite Tazeler, "Fritz Lang Likes Hollywood, America and Social Themes," *New York Herald-Tribune* (Feb. 7, 1937).

agents of true justice take charge. As this occurs, its methods change from the precise planning of an organisation to the emotional impulsiveness of a mob.

An equally important contrast is between the methods used by the police and those of the criminals. A police conference is inter-cut with a similar meeting in the underworld, and Superintendent Lohmann's character here, and throughout the film, parallels and opposes that of Shränker. Lohmann's inefficiency typifies the organisation he serves, just as Shränker represents the more efficient criminals. The Superintendent states at the meeting that the public won't co-operate; it refuses to see anything and doesn't care, anyhow. While he talks, however, a substantial portion of this public is gathering for the same purpose as the police. Later, at the "trial," the criminals have been joined by other citizens, including mothers of the dead girls, and so the group even more fully represents the Public. It now cares about Beckert's crimes, having forgotten its original, selfish motive of removing police pressure. This unity throughout the entire underworld appears to have had precedent in the Germany of 1931, but today it appears to be an unlikely and impractical bit of romanticism supported by a slight attempt to present the criminals as magicians, or at least sleight-of-hand experts. One man does card tricks, while another produces an impressive number of watches from his pockets; such talents are echoed by the efficiency with which they take the office building apart in their search for Beckert. This "magic" corresponds to the similar powers of Mabuse's men, and Shränker, the accepted and respected head of this group, is a new version of the old master criminal. With his bowler hat, cane, gloves, and leather coat, he has a distinctive air of authority. Like Joh Fredersen,* he inhabits an ivory tower: he makes the decisions, and leaves others to answer the phone and do the talking (except at the concluding trial). His past is vague, and he maintains this anonymity in the present by avoiding contact with others, symbolised by the gloves he constantly wears. But while for the moment he is completely in power (an idea represented by a shot of his hand placed on a map of the city), this is only for the duration of the search, and the temporary, emergency nature of his position helps to keep the character from slipping off into the fantasy world of a Mabuse.

The methods of the police depend mainly on chance, but this is due less to ineptitude than to a lack of information, manpower, and opportunity. Because an empty candy bag is found near one murder site, all candy stores within the radius of a mile are checked; when this proves fruitless, the circle is gradually enlarged. Such clues lead nowhere, so the police resort to indiscriminate raiding in the hope of discovering the killer or an informant. Though this hit-or-miss method brings about the arrest of

---

* [The industrialist-ruler in Lang's *Metropolis.*—S.J.S.]

several other criminals, it also causes Lohmann to waste time sitting at a table, checking identity papers. It is decided to obtain from prisons, sanatoriums, and mental institutions the names of those recently released as harmless, yet capable of murder (a seemingly contradictory phrase). The result is a giant list of the mentally ill who have been freed, during the past five years, from private and state institutions. Obviously, the murderer might have been released more than five years before or he might never have been committed at all.

Paralleling the police conference is another meeting, at which all branches of criminal activity are represented: Together, these men divide the city into sections and assign one to each member of the Organisation of Beggars, who can secretly observe any children abroad on the streets without arousing suspicion. If and when the murderer reveals himself, he would be readily identified and apprehended. The planning is detailed, with each beggar's name, assignment, and membership card number recorded in a ledger, and everything is so well arranged that chance is theoretically (and practically) eliminated; the entire town is under observation and Beckert has no hope at all. This is where the tension created by Lang differs from the suspense built up by a director like Alfred Hitchcock. The latter uses cutting and close-ups to create uncertainty about what will happen, while Lang forces the viewer to remain in one spot and watch the hero squirm in the net that has trapped him.

With the police doggedly checking each name on the long list of possible suspects, it is little wonder that the criminals spot and capture Beckert first. Lohmann's men do succeed in identifying the murderer, since his name happened to be on the list, but they haven't seen him yet and don't know where he is. While they wait for him to return to his rented room, he is already being followed by the criminals; it is only the lucky arrest of a man who had helped break into the building where Beckert was hiding that allows the police to re-locate him. In fact, Lohmann is so dumbfounded when told of the underworld's search that his cigar drops from his mouth and he has to douse his head with cold water. This same man also tells Lohmann where Beckert was taken for "trial," so the prevention of his murder-execution occurs through chance rather than ingenuity.

The idea that organised justice, while better, is the longer, less efficient method recurs often in Lang's works. The police, slow but in the long run fair, are here contrasted with the violent and vengeful mob; the police are consistent, but the criminals are not. At the start of the film they are a mob, hooting and whistling at Lohmann and talking back to the police. Later, when organised and regimented by Shränker for a goal that is to their advantage, they lose this evil quality of violence and impulsiveness. When Beckert is captured they revert once more to a mob, and the "trial" is a mere formality, a prelude to the enactment of their vengeance. "There is only one just thing for you—kill you," says the mother of one of the murdered children. They have come full circle from a mob, to an efficient organisation, and once more to a mob. Parallel to this, they have gone from being ruled by emotion, to logic and order, and back again to emotion and irrationality. By the time Beckert is given an official trial, the people have been freed from the grip of such violence. They have returned to "normal," and one of the victims' mothers now declares that sentencing the killer would not bring back her little girl.

When Beckert is put on trial by the criminals, he pleads that he cannot keep himself from killing. It is as though there is a second Hans Beckert who takes over his body; "I am always forced to move along the streets, and always someone is behind me. It is I. I sometimes feel I am myself behind me, and yet I cannot escape." Afterwards, standing before a poster, he reads what he has done and remembers nothing about the incident. Though he is haunted and tortured by his deeds, they seem to have been committed by someone else within him. To Beckert, the world is a frightening place, with everyone working against him, from the police to the underworld, and even including a blind, helpless beggar selling balloons. But the greatest threat to him comes from the underworld of his own mind, and the other part of his personality that lurks there waiting to destroy the everyday Hans Beckert. This part consists of the emotional desires generally held in check by logic and reason. Occasionally, at times of great stress or temptation, they are freed while the individual is briefly off guard; mental illness and schizophrenia allow this other self more regular control, but in all cases a lowering of his guard can destroy the person. He himself is his own worst enemy.

In *M*, this idea is given a psychological context which it had previously lacked, with the defence attorney arguing that the uncontrollable compulsion to kill relieves Beckert of responsibility, since he is ill and should be turned over to a doctor. Even the state, he says, does not have the right to kill this sick man; no one has such a right. This is the film's only didactic moment, and the "trial" setting provides a natural motive for the speechmaking. The specific reference is to the misunderstood mentally ill, just as *Fury* deals with the social problem of lynching, but both pictures are just different embodiments of the general themes common to so many of Lang's films: the individual trapped, and menaced from all sides; the danger of allowing the emotions to gain control; the ambiguity of responsibility.

M marks a transition in Lang's directorial style, and contains elements of the pictorial combined with a generally naturalistic presentation. Expressionism—the use and manipulation of objective reality to reflect the inner emotions and responses of the artist—appears in certain stylised visual arrangements which sometimes, but not always, have symbolic reference beyond their factual content and artistic form. The film's opening, an overhead shot of children grouped in a circle with one standing in the center, presents a geometric pattern which is pleasing in itself and also creates a feeling of inescapability like that eventually developed for Beckert. He is trapped between the two outside forces and within the maze of his own mental illness, and his capture is inevitable. Other arrangements, such as the overhead view of a policeman checking Beckert's round table for clues, do not contribute to this idea of being caught (though this case repeats the circle motif), but the majority of *M*'s expressionistic shots do. Most of these are taken from above to bring out geometric qualities that would otherwise go unnoticed. One such is the "X" of an intersection across which Beckert is pursued, with its squares and angles reducing the human figures to pawns on a large chess or checker board. A display of knives, reflected in a store window, seems to circle Beckert's head; he is trapped again, this time by his own implement of death. Some views of high stairways, looking directly down from several flights above, resemble rectangular mazes from which there is no escape; others, taken from the side, allow Lang to compose within his frame an intricate pattern of diagonals. A remnant of the anonymous masses of *Metropolis,* and the force they represent, can be seen during the raid on an underworld hangout. As the rows of policemen march in unison down the steps, the camera is placed so that their heads and shoulders are out of the frame.

This expressionistic art contains an unexpected humanism, a concern for man and his welfare. Lang's earlier films were often peopled with cardboard figures existing merely to advance the plot. They lacked depth and dimension. This is much less true in *M,* though a feeling of calculated characterisation still exists and a natural spontaneity is something quite foreign to Lang. Still, his killer, though a villain of sorts, is sympathetic in his illness. Beckert and several other characters have a new sense of individuality, but Lang remains typically objective in his observation, and approaches realism not through feeling and emotion, but through the objectivity of a documentary. Many scenes are content to describe the workings of the police department, without any thematic "comment" by the director-author. Shots of fingerprints are accompanied by a lecture-like voice explaining their characteristics. Policemen are shown questioning the owners of candy stores, while a narrator reports their negative results. When a guard at the building where Beckert is trapped pulls a warning switch, the camera follows the results, as machines click on and off and the source of the impulse is identified at headquarters. The voice of a handwriting analyst speaks of the killer's "histrionic tendencies," as we see Beckert making faces before the mirror in his room. These are not exactly examples of narration, since the voice used each time is never the same, belongs to a character (albeit an anonymous one), and speaks to others in the film instead of directly to the audience. Still, the principle is the same, and it allows for concise exposition by juxtaposing voice and image from different places and different times.

The film's structure is often admirable. Intercutting is used to contrast two concurrent incidents; one such juxtaposition compares an electric drill, used by the criminals to enter the buildings, with the broken pocket-knife that Beckert uses in trying to escape. His comparative helplessness and the inevitability of his capture are again effectively set forth. Some scenes are linked together by sound bridges, as when Lohmann asks the prisoner where Beckert has been taken. "To the old distillery," he answers, and his voice on the soundtrack describes the place as the screen shows the building's interior. When the talking stops, the image remains; Beckert and his captors enter, and the sounds heard are now of their arrival. The scene has been imaginatively, gradually changed. Another transition made smooth by the use of sound involves the music of a street organ. A shot of an instrument being played indoors is followed by one of a man listening. This is succeeded, with no break in the song, by a shot of an instrument being played, at a later time, on a street corner.

M has been carefully thought out to make good use of sound, as in the narration and transitions already mentioned. Beckert is seen whistling "In the Hall of the Mountain King" early in the film, and once he is solidly associated with this tune it is used by itself to establish Beckert's presence, while the camera remains fixed on a girl gazing into a store window. Such subtlety through suggestion is also applied to Beckert's with a balloon caught among telephone wires and a rolling rubber ball establishing a murder.

Towards the end, we see Beckert crouching in the cluttered darkness of the building, a ray of light reflected in his sweating face. In the background, we hear the gradual approach of his pursuers. As the sound grows louder, the reaction of fear in the hunted man's face increases until a shout of "There's the swine!" ends the sequence. If *M* had been a silent film, Lang would have been required to cut away from Beckert to show the searchers, but now he can establish their approach on the soundtrack and keep his camera unswervingly focused on the quarry's expression. This example epitomises Lang's approach to the thriller form: he creates tension in the viewer by forcing him, almost sadistically, to observe the writhings of a helplessly trapped victim. The development of sound made it possible for the director to avoid an emphasis on editing, which interfered with his individual style, and to make active use of silence (the utter quiet before a police raid is broken by a whistle, and then a low noise swells to the thunder of a crowd rushing to escape). Lang's style is based on fearful anticipation, hence the long takes and lack of action scenes.

M is constructed like a machine, with tightly interlocking parts, and once it is set in motion it proceeds with an inevitable logic. It is a very versatile invention: it entertains, it preaches, it creates tension, it even evokes sympathy to a degree, but nonetheless it does not live. *M* is important to any consideration of Fritz Lang's career and themes. It is also one of those significant pictures from the early Thirties which make use of sound rather than allow it to control them. Some of its techniques, especially that of the narrator, have since become more familiar, but the ingenuity which Lang brings to his subject is something still rare among film-makers.

Fritz Lang (The German Period, 1919–1935)

ERIC RHODE

'Mythopoeia is a far more common characteristic of the human race (and especially of the German race) than veracity.'

H. Trevor-Roper—*The Last Days of Hitler*

Professor Trevor-Roper rightly mocks at Nazi superstition and at its paranoid attempt to dissolve the world into a lurid delusion: yet mythopoeia and veracity are not necessarily opposed. One of the reasons why Fritz Lang's German films have been so long undervalued, I would suggest, is that they are held to be myths of this type—Nazi lies, rather than disturbed reflections of their time.

There are at least three ways in which a myth can reveal truth: by the vividness of its central image—and this vividness depends on the extent to which the image gathers up some aspect of common experience; by such formal qualities as harmony and complexity; and by its conveyed sense of moral discovery. At his best Lang (aided by his script-writing wife, Thea von Harbou) creates myths that fulfil all these requirements. No one has evolved a more telling image of the modern city. Few German artists have conveyed the difficulties of the post-war era so honestly, so naively, so undogmatically—though Lang would understandably disclaim the title of 'artist'; it was one Hitler liked to use of himself. At the beginning, his films trace the confusion and anxieties of the Weimar Republic. Later they dally with an easy persuasive solution to these problems. And yet Lang's flirtation with National Socialism is no more than a

FROM *Tower of Babel: Speculations on the Cinema* by Eric Rhode, pp. 85–86, 97–102, 104–05. Copyright © 1966 by the author. Reprinted by permission of the publisher, Chilton Book Company, Philadelphia.

flirtation. In 1931 he made *M* (working title, *Murderer Among Us*), and in 1932 *The Testament of Dr Mabuse:* both films explicitly reject the Nazi solution.

.　　.　　.

Metropolis remains one of the most vivid of Lang's films, a continuous source of inspiration; it is also one of his least attractive. In *Siegfried* he could get away with his blond beast, epitome of German youth; the myth made no claims to veracity. But *Metropolis* purports to be close to the actual—and on such a level the best I can say for it is that it successfully disproves the cruder forms of the commitment theory: as it shows, the aesthetic quality of a film need not be entirely judged by the value of its political judgements.

Shortly after *Metropolis* came the turning point, for in 1931 Lang made *M*, his first film to call fully on our response as adults, and which uses the boys' own brilliance of the earlier work to stir our deepest feelings. Its plot is based on the case of the Düsseldorf child murderer, Peter Kürsten, and is devised to show how one frightened little man is able, unsuspectingly, to disrupt the entire mechanism of a city. To some extent, then, it is a grotesque comedy—but this comedy is held in check, and not allowed to diminish the tragic element. The first shot is of children playing in a courtyard: the camera pans to mothers on tenement landings talking to each other and to their children below; at the end we see three mothers in mourning at the Murderer's trial. . . . The comedy of the city, its confusions and violence, is measured against this pain of loss.

You could see *M* as a graph of Lang's own development, since many of its ironies play round the conflict between the infantile and the adult. The death of children, made all the more poignant by their remaining toys, or the toys used to seduce them, is contrasted with the Murderer, doomed to remain emotionally like a child. Lang develops his usual theme of fatality without, happily, his usual relish: the Murderer's great confession to the criminals, in which he pleads to being unlike them in the sense that he has no choice but must murder, and of how he is always afraid of the unknown inner forces that can possess him, is in substance commonplace now. But in 1931 it must have been electrifying—and the film still conveys this excitement. Also, the speech is played by Peter Lorre, whose Murderer, ever gobbling or rolling his eyes like a plump and pimply toad, remains a classic amongst screen performances. *M* anticipates such American films as Lang's *Fury* or *Scarlet Street* in so far as much of the time we see the action through the eyes of the exploited rather than the exploiter—as much through the eyes of Count Told as of Mabuse.

'I am always afraid of myself': such is the principal theme. The murders stir up a murderous element in most of the inhabitants of the city. We enter a time of panic, almost insanity, in which good and bad are hopelessly intertwined. Everyone suspects everybody else. A timid elderly man needs merely talk to a girl by a tram-stop and a threatening mob arises round him. Witnesses quarrel. No one observes, no one remembers —and, anyway, it all happened so long ago. Perceptions are doubted; evidence is ambiguous; things are seen through mirrors and windows. Officials fulminate, phone each other and write letters to little effect. The blind lead the blind, so that, not unexpectedly, the first useful clue as to the nature of the murderer is given by a blind balloon-seller.

Above all, this grotesque comedy conditions the sub-plot. The police, under pressure to discover the murderer, round up criminals and raid their dens; the underworld is disrupted, ordinary business is out of the question. So the criminals gang together in a determination to take justice into their own hands and to hunt down the killer themselves—a parody of Justice in the manner of Brecht's *The Threepenny Opera* (1928). The criminals organize themselves with a bourgeois propriety, and their leader echoes bourgeois sentiments: 'This beast has no right to exist'. At times, as they sit round a table smoking furiously, they unknowingly resemble a police conference. Smoking people create their own fog. The more they smoke and think and speculate, the more cloudy things become. But in fact criminals remain criminals, and when they do track down the Murderer and round him up they remind us less of the traditional bourgeoisie than of the Nazis; instead of the cruelty (or smugness) of indifference, we have a realized sadism.

At first this sadism throbs beneath the surface, as the criminals (disguised as beggars) patrol the city. Relationships are, it seems, poisoned by their gaze; a 'blind' man's scrutiny appears to contaminate the spontaneous chat of a mother and child. But this sadism becomes painfully obvious as soon as the Murderer becomes a marked man; that is, when one of the beggars presses a chalk mark *M* on the back of his jacket. Gradually the Murderer realizes he is being watched. There is an extraordinary cat-and-mouse scene, reminiscent of Kirilov's suicide in *The Possessed*, when, finding himself trapped at a crossroad, he comes face to face with one of his persecutors. They stare at each other for a long moment; then the Murderer starts running and the chase begins. The criminals hound him down to a furniture depository, where he locks himself into a room loaded with junk. Finally, when caught, he is taken to a mock-trial in a ruined brewery, and is virtually lynched by the mob.

Lang once said that he lives through his eyes; and it is true that in *Dr Mabuse* his images of hierarchy, of the heights and depths, is principally confined to the spatial: to buildings, to the various levels of the city, to the play of light and dark. In *Metropolis* these images are extended to take in the conflict between the adult and infantile parts of the mind. In *M* the stress on the irrational is even more marked and frequent. Terror is palpable, yet its source is unknown. There is a disparity between act and motive (hence the grotesque comedy). The criminals are more systematic in their violence than the workers in *Metropolis*, yet they act on a slender, almost whimical pretext. Irrationality reigns, and the lord of misrule is the Murderer. Though his function in the film's structure is similar to Mabuse's, he is more real as a person and so more convincing. He is far from being a superior intellect, far from giving the impression of controlling the action—is merely a lodger in a dismal bedsitter.

But the reign of irrationality doesn't last. Indeed no film disproves Kracauer's thesis more trenchantly. To all appearances, certainly, the city turns into a panic-ridden place, hit by inflation as well as the murder scare (again, the disparity of motive and action). Its accumulation of objects—the criminals' loot, the paraphernalia of dossiers and finger-prints, the stacks of food—arouse despair in us since they are so unending. But, we also despair at its state of being a continual prison—a place of locked doors and barred windows. The junk room in the depository where the Murderer is trapped admirably brings together this contrast between meaningless disorder and confinement.

Seemingly, panic brings on a general loss of identity. Individuals are submerged into groups—into being criminals, the police or the mob. Not to ally yourself with a group is to risk becoming a scapegoat. As panic first grips the city, the police raid a thieves' den and hold an identity-card check. One man, having no card, tries to make an unsuccessful escape through a barred window. But there is another man who never needs to escape and who never loses his identity—Lohmann, the police inspector.

According to Kracauer, Lohmann is a 'colourless official'. Nothing is further from the truth. Though under extreme pressure from public opinion and his superiors, this formidable hero never loses his nerve; nor does he waver in his knowledge of what is right or wrong. He may seem paternal and tolerant to the criminals, but in fact he misses nothing and makes no concessions. Under his command the police work diligently; even without the criminals' inside knowledge they are virtually as quick as them in tracing down the Murderer and bringing him to a just trial. At the end, whatever Kracauer may claim, the city's order is restored.

Lohmann's ebullience, you could say, is reflected in Lang's brisk style of narrative. There is no gloating over chaos (as in *Dr Mabuse*), no pleasure in the murders or the hunt. The thematic editing through newspapers, letters and dossiers, or the juxtaposition of such incongruities as an ordinary finger print followed by one blown up to screen size, or the vivid contrast between kinds of lighting, anticipate the bravura shorthand style of *Citizen Kane*. The urgency of this pace underlines the tragedy of loss. . . . Lohmann is like a beacon that brings comfort and yet makes the surrounding night seem darker.

In this sense, I cannot overstress his importance; he is more than a link-man between *M* and *The Testament of Dr Mabuse*. W. H. Auden (amongst others) has described the thriller as a form of debased theology. Lang, like Chesterton in *The Man Who Was Thursday*, tries to polish this tarnished pedigree by turning the thriller into a metaphysical allegory. Tired of his satanic doctor, Lang was only interested in making a sequel on the off-chance of being able (he claims) to subvert Nazi propaganda. In fact, his criticism of the Nazis is veiled, but as much by other interests creeping in as by caution. *The Testament* is a continuation of *Dr Mabuse —the Gambler*, with the insane Mabuse now confined to an asylum, scribbling out his plans and covering the cell floor with sheets upon sheets of paper. But Mabuse soon dies; and his soul transmigrates into the body of his superintendent, the psychiatrist Professor Baum, and forces him to organize plots which, in theory, should allow Mabuse's gang to disrupt the country and come to power. Lang's image of the city is extended: to the familiar ironies of criminals becoming judges, of psychologists becoming lunatics, of lunatics becoming despots, and of the hunter being hunted, is added a further concourse as the world of the dead begins to interfuse with the world of the living.

.   .   .

. . . Lang's criticism of the Nazis was not, it appears, veiled enough; and Goebbels banned the film. This ban might not have taken place if Lohmann had been a less forceful creation. Anyhow, Lang had made up his mind about National Socialism; and, on the evidence of *The Testament*, it is hardly surprising that shortly after the ban he should have separated from his wife (who had joined the Nazi Party) and left Germany, first for France, then for America.

Few directors have had so wide an influence as he has. The historical importance of his lighting innovations and his sense of set design and frame composition have all been acknowledged; but not, I think, the power of his visual ideas. Few other directors have been so influential; one can trace the effect of his ideas in the work of such diverse people as Cocteau and Hitchcock, Kubrick and Carol Reed (*The Third Man*), Godard and Frankenheimer, Losey and Wajda.

RENOIR

rules of the game

CREdiTs

Rules of the Game (France, 1939)
French title: *La Règle du jeu*
Directed by Jean Renoir from a screenplay by Renoir, Karl Koch, and Camille
   François, derived from Alfred de Musset's *Les Caprices de Marianne*
Produced by Jean Renoir for Nouvelle Edition française
Distributer (16mm): Janus Films

Assistant directors: André Zwobada and Henri Cartier-Bresson
Production director: Claude Renoir
Photography: Jean Bachelet
Décor: Eugène Lourié
Costumes: Gabrielle Chanel
Music arranged by: R. Desormières
Editor: Marguerite Renoir

Main performers:
Marcel Dalio (*Marquis, Robert de la Chesnaye*)
Nora Grégor (*Christine, his wife*)
Roland Toutain (*André Jurieu*)
Jean Renoir (*Octave*)

Mila Parely (*Geneviève*)
Paulette Dubost (*Lisette*)
Gaston Modot (*Schumacher*)
Julien Carette (*Marceau*)

Length: 113 minutes (restored print of 1965)

The cinema of Jean Renoir is intelligent, humane, and witty. It is characterized by an unexcelled feeling for camera placement and fluidity, especially in the cinematography of natural surroundings, and features a wide variety of subjects and themes. It is difficult to generalize about Renoir's four decades of directing, not only because his interests and style have ranged so widely—from fantasy to historical re-creations to naturalism—but also because his films often reveal many aspects of the particular civilization under scrutiny. His two greatest works, *Grand Illusion* (1937) and *Rules of the Game* (1939), depict microcosms of societies in transition—or at least in confusion. The richness of these and most other Renoir films, the more we watch them, provides us with increasingly complex notions about the way society functions. The mixture of the comic and the tragic gives to the Renoir universe an almost Shakespearean perspective—at once satiric and distant as well as sympathetic and personally involved. The pathos of one sequence is deliberately dispersed by the mirth or conviviality of another; even the intrusion of an unexpected violent moment, as in *The Crime of Monsieur Lange* (1936) or *The Elusive Corporal* (1962), does not dispel Renoir's general aura of benevolent good humor.

Although *Rules of the Game* is essentially more complicated in its outlook than Renoir's other films, it shares with many of them a range of tones from farce to tragedy as it dissects a dying aristocracy on the eve of a world war. The shortcomings of the Marquis de la Chesnaye, his wife Christine, and the guests at their chateau are often excusable, since their life style has a great attraction for Renoir despite his complete awareness that it is deservedly dying out. Thus, the thematic texture of *Rules of the Game* remains persistently ambiguous: the decaying threads inextricably woven with the remnants of an urbane and attractive world, held in a perpetual state of tension, ripped apart by internal pressures, and finally pieced together again, but only by means of a tacit agreement among those involved to ignore the transparently thin fibers used to repair the social fabric. One lover mistaken for another is killed by a jealous husband; this crime of passion, a momentary violation of the rules of the game, is covered up by the guests at the chateau, who intuitively accept the "accident" in order to preserve the façade of their own jeopardized social class.

Although cynical about the society he is analyzing in this film, Renoir carefully orders our perceptions of its reality so that we willingly suspend our instinctive condemnation of the hypocrisy and triviality and instead extend to the characters a broad sympathy for their weaknesses and illusions. To reinforce our dual perception of the discrepancies within this society, Renoir himself plays one of the leading roles, that of Octave, an unsuccessful musician who sponges off the wealthy as a somewhat awkward but lovable friend and typifies the attractiveness and destructiveness of this life-style. Like everyone else in this society, Octave harbors illusions that make his life pleasant enough, except for the moments when reality intrudes and forces him to glimpse the truth of his situation. Although no more than a hanger-on, Octave belongs among those who gather at the chateau because his dreams complement theirs: in this world of formal codes and social pretenses, everyone is essentially a romantic.

When they conflict with reality romantic ideals can produce tragedy, as when the outsider, the aviator-hero Jurieu, becomes too insistent in pressing his claims to Christine while a guest at her husband's chateau. More often, however, the romantic ideals collide with other ideals to produce comedy, occasionally on an almost farcical level. Renoir constructed *Rules of the Game* so that the extra-marital love relationships of the upper classes would parallel the ludicrous relationships of the servants. During an evening party, while the guests are being entertained by such trifling amusements as the marquis's mechanical organ, the gamekeeper chases his wife's admirer through the rooms while firing a rifle at him; for the startled guests, it is difficult to tell whether the chase is another staged amusement or an actual life-and-death struggle. The real danger, the absurdity of the situation, and the confusion create a satirical parody of the proprieties normally observed by the characters.

A game requires that all players abide by the same rules, but when the game is that of romantic passion and its rules demand antiromantic restraints on conduct, the result is certain to be disastrous disarray; and in fact, the game breaks up after one player is killed. Yet there is no final implication that this new experience will change the nature of the players, but rather, that they will again engage in other implausible games and assume other roles. Unsuccessful attempts will again be made to subject passion to the unworkable rules of conventional society. Renoir amusingly notes the paradox implicit in this upper-class world by introducing, just before the film begins, a title card with a quotation from Beaumarchais's *The Marriage of Figaro*, which concludes:

> If love has wings,
> Are they not to flutter?
> Are they not to flutter?
> Are they not to flutter?

The contradictions that underlie this society are presented with great vitality and humor in *Rules of the Game*. Probably nowhere else in the cinema has so complex a structure revealed so clearly the illusions of a society, but Renoir leads us beyond both laughter and pathos to sympathy and awareness.

from Three Masterworks

PIERRE LEPROHON

In the years immediately before World War II, Renoir directed three masterpieces. The first, *La Grande Illusion* [*Grand Illusion*], won fifth place on the "Best Films of All Time" list (established, not without controversy, however, in 1958 by 117 film historians who met in Brussels). The second film, *La Bête humaine,* is really still underrated, while the third, *La Règle du jeu,* is surely his greatest achievement.

From the vantage point of more than thirty years later, it is clear that the three films share one major unifying quality: their classicism. By this I mean their perfection, not only in terms of the film art of the time but also in terms of Renoir's own art. Today they seem completely finished works, but they were in fact produced under the usual difficult circumstances that included Renoir's own taste for or need to improvise, as well as problems of production and editing. Their classicism also derives from the fact that Renoir achieves a fruitful balance between his characteristic free, improvisational style and the more formal, structured techniques that were current then: the practice of giving first place to dialogue writers and actors, stressing well-constructed and well-acted scenes, and fine lines. Then too, these films are classical because they are so diverse in character, the first being dramatic, the second symphonic, and the third symbolic. Finally, they are classic because they reveal, each in its own way, an equal mastery in their design, a quality that became apparent in the first and last films only after they had been re-edited to correct some initial distortions suffered in the cutting room. Each of the films, especially *La Grande Illusion,* makes good use of the arts of dialogue writing and acting, while at the same time essentially conforming to Renoir's ideas of dramatic construction, especially in the fact that they tell the story of a group. In these works, Renoir deals with diverse social groups whose stories interweave with and confront one another under conditions that are themselves dramatic themes: war, work, the lives of the worldly. These confrontations and relationships constitute the essence and real meaning of the films, while the threads of the plots (escape, crime, or love) are simply the structure through which the real themes work themselves out.

It is little wonder that their profound originality of concept and style caused these movies to be received with less than enthusiasm by critics and public. Today this originality is the main reason why they are classics.

FROM "Three Masterworks," Chapter 5 of *Jean Renoir* by Pierre Leprohon, translated by Brigid Elson, pp. 105–06, 119–25. Translation © 1971 by Crown Publishers, Inc. Used by permission of Crown Publishers, Inc.

All three films, even *La Règle du jeu,* are, beneath their superficial burlesques, among the most realistic of films in their acting styles and plastic expression. This underlying realism or sense of truth gives enormous power to certain unforgettable sequences, like the beginning of *La Bête humaine* or the hunting party in *La Règle du jeu.* Despite Renoir's tendency to transform life into a kind of show, to stylize reality by way of the acting and photography, in these three films he expresses the truth in the most direct way possible. In so doing he attains a remarkable beauty of style and symbolism.

.   .   .

[The history of *Rules of the Game*] began with the producers' problems in raising capital, and with Renoir's trips to Marlotte and then to Sologne to seek inspiration from his friends and colleagues. The end of the story came thirty years later, in 1965, when the complete version Renoir had made in 1939 was finally reconstituted and publicly released once again. In between there were problems, problems: editing difficulties, failure, legal suspension, and, indeed, physical destruction of the film. *La Règle du jeu* was cursed from the beginning, and, worst of all, it was cut from an original 113 minutes to a truncated 85 minutes. This explains at least partly its initial failure. Cuts made many things obscure and broke the rhythm of its perfect development. But with the excellent restoration by Jean Gaborit, Jacques Durand, and J. Maréchal, this masterwork was restored to its fullness of meaning.*

> With *La Règle du jeu* I began to really understand the idea of an ensemble, and to recognize that the world is divided into little circles and squares in the midst of which men act, tied together by ideas and conventions and common interests. I began to be interested in a cinema of "groups."†

To say this is to forget *Toni, M. Lange,* and *La Nuit du carrefour,* among others! In fact, Renoir made use of his freedom to do away completely with dramatic conventions, and to construct, in *La Règle du jeu,* a completely original, disconcerting, and ultimately enchanting film. Within the context of his total production it stands as a link between the social and satiric aspects of the films preceding it and what might be called the "spectacular" character of the films that followed. *La Règle du jeu* is related to *Boudu* and *La Chienne,* but it has ties as well to *Le Carrosse d'or;* that is to say, it is a most Renoir-like film, and thus of immense value.

---

* André-G. Brunelin's remarkable article "Histoire d'une malédiction" (*Cinéma 60,* No. 43, February 1960) tells the story of the problems involved in making and releasing the film.
† *Cinéma 67,* No. 116/117.

When the film was first released, it was generally received as simply a social satire, but to see it just this way is to limit its meaning. Renoir warns about this in the prologue: "This divertissement does not pretend to be a study of social mores . . . ." Although we ought to be a little wary of this statement, the use of the word "divertissement" should be noted. It is applicable to the film in the eighteenth-century sense of the word, as witness the very structure of the work, the parallelism of its double plot, and even the use of Mozart's music which periodically underscores this tragicomic ballet. *Le Carrosse d'or* also confirms Renoir's attraction for this wise and witty artistic form that has been so little used in films.

Jean Prat has written:

> What sort of game have we here [in *La Règle du jeu*]? It is the game of life, the life of a totally corrupt society that knows only how to prolong its boring, useless existence at the price of an absolute rule, a discipline that governs every minute, i.e., the lie. They lie in their words, in their feelings, and their deeds; they stifle all spontaneity under the mask of frivolity and *politesse*. It is a fragile mask though, always at the mercy of an explosion of sincerity: the movie is about just such an accident.*

The explosion of sincerity erupts in the midst of a house party in the country château of the Marquis de la Chesnaye. The guests become carried away by their little weekend amusements; they stop feinting with one another, and yield to their impulses. Their yielding makes them ridiculous, because Renoir, entirely faithful to the principle of "divertissement," never lets us share the feelings of his heroes. Like the spectators at the party, we are strangers to the action. That is why the scurryings of the participants become as ridiculous to us as the antics of a colony of insects.

By dehumanizing the characters, Renoir throws into relief the fragility of that which endows man's life with its emotion and greatness. These people love and struggle and suffer, and appear ridiculous in the process because their feelings are dissected by a pitiless ironist. Renoir's cruelty, which was often masked by his hearty good fellowship or warm tenderness (for example, the railwaymen's ball in *La Bête humaine*), breaks out here into a pulverizing humor that barely spares the pure and the clumsy ones: Jurieu the lover and Octave the dreamer. Everyone else is laughable with their puerile ambitions, their hypocrisies, and their emotional demands, but they are pitiable too. The double-level chase that threads through the whole party, mingling the intrigues of the masters with those of the servants, is prefigured in the famous hunting episode—an admirable

---

* Film analysis published by the Institut des Hautes Études Cinématographiques.

bit of film shot in the pale light of Sologne, which brings into relief the absurdity of a massacre that is played by the rules of that particular game. The final misunderstanding, where fate again strikes the best man, is another play on the same theme; Jurieu is the expiatory victim, the traditional scapegoat, who allows the others to continue their vanity fair.

So this divertissement is, in fact, a moralist's parable, and on the basis of what Renoir shows us, its participants deserved to be condemned. This world is futile, false, and cruel, and Renoir limned it with irony, rather than ferocity, in a form so new that its novelty, on first viewing, is disconcerting. The film's construction is underpinned quite solidly by the main lines of action, but Renoir does not pretend to a classical dramatic form. The film develops by a kind of convergence of characters and episodes toward a conclusion that allows for a coming together of all these elements. The two worlds finally cease to parallel each other, and come together in a clash at the denouement. On first sight one gets a totally invalid impression of incoherence because of the number of actively involved characters and the use of a twofold dramatic movement with masters and servants. Eventually the logic of the work becomes clear, but only, it must be said, in the complete version shown today. And finally, underlying the director's divertissement and the characters' game, there is a bitterness, a kind of desperate anguish that is perhaps less the condemnation of a society than a sort of premonition of the coming world conflict.

La Règle du jeu is essentially a work of cinema in the sense that it was conceived from the start in cinematic terms, rather than to illustrate an already existing story. Hence the freedom of style, the vivacity of rhythm, and the close union of the audiovisual elements. Never had Renoir handled with such mastery the organization of an action that juggles themes and moves forward by leaps and bounds and symbols, all with a rightness of tone that is nearly without peer. The dialogue has no explicative or dramatic function. It is both realistic, in its truthful triviality, and symbolic, because it reveals the characters who speak it. Renoir wisely avoids using close-ups and counter reverse shots, exploiting depth of field instead. The intelligence of the direct sound and the music underline, with a kind of knowing ambiguity, the double aspect of the film: fantasy and realism, humor and deadly seriousness. This novel technique and the subtle development—essential if the originality of the theme were to be carried off—account in large part for the confusion of the public, and indeed of a number of critics, in 1939. Today these same qualities force us to acknowledge that such a complex work cannot be judged with a single yardstick. The film was, of course, well ahead of its time, and it was a turning point both in Renoir's work and in the history of film. Contemporary filmmaking might have turned out quite differently except for the doors opened by *La Règle du jeu.*

Between Theater and Life: Jean Renoir and *Rules of the Game*

JACQUES JOLY

There are two ways of approaching *Rules of the Game*. One can apply oneself to the *structure* of the film, analyze its dramatic scheme, note its resemblances to the comedies of Marivaux, Beaumarchais's *Marriage of Figaro* and Musset's *Marianne*. Thus the film appears tied to an artistic tradition, which is why Jean de Baroncelli insists on its "French" character, and Michel Cournot finds in it "a far more beautiful Marivaux, a living Marivaux." Critics on the left, however, have chiefly emphasized the social and historical *content* of the film. For Georges Sadoul, *Rules of the Game* "was the film of an era"; for Samuel Lachize, "the prelude to the death of a world." It seems to me that the film is original precisely for the connection it makes between a traditional theatrical structure and a new content, and for the way it articulates their relation. For *Rules of the Game* is the one film in a thousand where the study of a given milieu is inseparable from a particular dramatic scheme: in it, artistic reflection is on a par with historical analysis.

Renoir's project was clear: to perform the "autopsy" of the bourgeoisie in crisis, to record the proof positive of a class overwhelmed by the events in Europe. "When I made *Rules of the Game*," Renoir writes, "I knew where I had to go. I knew the disease that was eating my contemporaries. That doesn't mean that I knew how I could give a clear idea of this disease in my film. But my instinct guided me." Thus Renoir's film was intended, in his own words, as "an exact description of the bourgeois of the time." Directly, then, *Rules of the Game* is given as a totality; each of its characters becomes part of a whole and thereby acquires his significance. Thus, the secondary figures in the film form a survey of the bourgeois society of the time: through M. and Mme. de la Bruyère, the aristocrats of La Colinière are connected with the new industrialists from Turcoing; the homosexual, the South American diplomat, the retired general give us a rapid view of a certain society. Some remarks by the servants recall the antisemitism of the time; the crowd's enthusiasm for André Jurieu's exploit appears as a compensation for the humiliation of Munich. One thing is striking in Renoir's description: the allusive character of the references to contemporary history, together with the schema-

FROM *Film Quarterly*, Volume XXI, Number 2, pp. 2–9. © 1967 by The Regents of the University of California. Reprinted by permission of The Regents. Translated by Randall Conrad from *La Nouvelle Critique*, No. 168 (July–August 1965).

tization of the secondary characters, who recall the puppet-figures of conventional social criticism. The industrialists, Saint-Aubain, and the general could appear as they are in the satirical comedies of Jean Anouilh, *Ardèle* for example; and points as important as antisemitism or Munich are entrusted to a simple remark or an indirect allusion. Renoir's intention is, then, not to analyze the society of the time objectively, from outside, but to put together stroke by stroke—by reducing each character to his essential significance within the whole—an image of the bourgeois class which is capable of revealing its contradictions.

Locating his film in a History, Renoir at the same time proceeds to define the essential characteristics of that History: the world of *Rules of the Game* is a world of falsehood. "Everybody lies," Octave tells Christine, "medical products, governments, the radio. . . ." The theme of the film is that of a collective lie: the ruling class's lie to the masses, the bourgeoisie's lie to itself. La Chesnaye lies to his wife, who lies to herself; Lisette lies to Schumacher and Geneviève to Christine. Individual duplicity here symbolizes the elevation of the lie to the status of an institution. Sincerity is impossible; it would challenge the foundations of an order. In the scene of the evening party at the château, Renoir casts over this world a shadow of what awaits it. When the guests of the château, in Tyrolese costumes, sing an old patriotic army song, their derision of the army brutally reveals the willful blindness and frantic need for diversion that characterize a disillusioned and skeptical bourgeoisie. And over this gathering, who are dancing on a powder-keg, passes, for an instant, the wing of death. Saint-Saëns's *Danse Macabre* leads the guests into a dance of death they have prepared with their own hand.

This world, which is pushing France to catastrophe, still holds together only because it has turned in upon itself; it endures only on its own momentum. The structure of Renoir's film was thus dictated by its intentions. Renoir had to find a dramatic scheme that would serve at once as the symbol of this closed universe and the translation of its desire for diversion. He found it in a parallel development of the plot, at the level of the masters and at that of the servants. The film is given as an organic whole, whose different elements acquire their meaning only in reciprocal relation. The schematic and sometimes mechanical aspect of the plot, the "lie" of its structure, translate exactly the "lie" upheld by the characters, in a world itself founded on falsehood. The film is a game that ends in death, just as the bourgeoisie of France was playing with what was to be the ruin of the country. We now understand why the social and historical references remain allusive in character: Renoir enters into the game of the propertied class in order to expose its contradictions *from within*. *Rules of the Game* is above all a "critical" film, which recomposes a class reality using a dramatic scheme capable of appealing to the viewer's intelligence.

The structure of *Rules of the Game* recalls that of Marivaux's comedies, *The Game of Love* and *Chance* for example, with the exception that in Renoir there is no substitution of servants for masters and vice versa: only Schumacher's final error recalls the disguised identities in Marivaux. Moreover, Marivaux's play is directly referred to in the maid's name, Lisette, and in the film's title. On the other hand, the "mad evening" at La Colinière is treated like the "mad night" in the last act of *The Marriage of Figaro,* and the film opens with a quotation ironically recalling the psychological and sentimental imbroglio of Beaumarchais's comedy. And finally, the name Octave, and the exchange between Christine de la Chesnaye and Octave in the greenhouse refer clearly to Musset's *Marianne.* Yet Renoir's film is radically different from the works of these three authors, and the explicit recall of Beaumarchais, supposedly the prelude to a sentimental comedy (*"Si l'amour a des ailes, n'est-ce pas pour voltiger?"*), actually constitutes an ironic invitation not to look for sentimental variations in the film, not to be fooled by the appearances Renoir has momentarily adopted the better to make us see. The similarity to Beaumarchais then concerns, not the particular meaning of the film, but the lucidity of Renoir, the intellectual faced with a world in crisis. Indeed, whereas Marivaux, Beaumarchais and Musset present their plays basically as a "geography of the heart" and a poetics of sentiment, Renoir's point of departure is on the contrary a reflection on the notion of class, so that the film in a way "historicizes" the conventional scheme of these comedies.

In *Rules of the Game,* each character is in strict solidarity with the class he belongs to. What is more, each social category contains in its margins a certain number of satellites—declassed individuals or parasites—opposed to those individuals who are perfectly integrated in the system. This is the case of Jurieu, who is seldom allowed to forget that he lacks wealth, or of Octave, who amuses the bourgeois to live on their charity. But here we must further distinguish between Octave, the failed artist, definitively deprived of a social status and altogether "alienated" from the propertied bourgeoisie, and Jurieu, the pilot, whose personal merit may give him access to a class he doesn't belong to by origin. If we now analyze the relationship of the different groups within the whole, we find that each group is opposed to a sub-group: the bourgeois to the servants, and the servants to Marceau, the poacher, the type of the outlaw (of the sub-proletarian, as it were), who himself dreams of finding his place in a system that rejects him—of becoming a servant, "on account of their costume." Within the world of the servants, moreover, we find the counterpart of Jurieu and Octave in the character of Schumacher, who is only a subordinate in relation to Lisette, the lady's maid, or Corneille, the house steward. So the relationship of the different social categories is clear: Renoir shows us a closed world where each group is totally alienated from the one next above it. Marceau dreams of a "costume"; Lisette is above all "Madame's personal maid" and consents to her marital status only so long as her position is guaranteed: "Leave Madame's service? I'd rather divorce!"

Indeed, in *Rules of the Game*, each character would rather "divorce" than cease to be what he is. The lesson of the film will be that one doesn't gain entry to a class if one is outside it. Jurieu's death, the departure of Octave, and the dismissal of Marceau are necessary, from the moment they set eyes on what is beyond their reach. The film is a closed circuit; no real story appears in it, because it is really the film of a non-story. The more the plot unfolds, the closer we come to the starting point—a characteristic regression in a film in which rigid class structure permits no narrative development outside its closed system. The principal characters in *Rules of the Game* therefore cannot be human and are entitled to a personal story only *up to a certain point*. Not the least of the film's merits is the balance between individual elements and class traits in la Chesnaye or Christine, this way of dialectically constructing a character at once as a type and as an individual.

The Marquis de la Chesnaye is presented from the first as a psychological case. A certain awkwardness, inseparable from his aristocratic polish, suggests the presence of a secret beneath his façade of good breeding. His unexpected timidity with his wife, his inability to refuse anything to anyone (whether Geneviève, de Marrast, Lisette, or Marceau), the repressed sensitivity which only finds expression in his passion for music-boxes, betray a fundamental inadaptation, a sort of guilt complex. The servants' dinner conversation gives us the key to his character: the Marquis is a "foreigner." The Semitic origins of this character, the sense that they constitute a social blemish, account in part for the sensitivity of the Marquis, which culminates with the presentation of the music-boxes* to his guests, and in the scene in which he dismisses Marceau and Schumacher. Similarly, Christine de la Chesnaye is distant kin to the countess in *The Marriage of Figaro*. She is a stranger to the world in which she belongs at once by birth and by her Austrian origin, and has remained nostalgic for her "bohemian" childhood. The character of Christine perhaps recalls certain stage heroines from the 1930's, for example Anouilh's "wild woman." Renoir's skill consists in interesting the viewer in his characters, appealing to sentiment if need be, without ever abolishing a critical distance, a parallel reflection which gives the work its sense. We are introduced into this bourgeois world in order that we may discover its vanity and falsehood. Renoir's attitude toward the protagonists of his

---

* Renoir is even clever enough to give la Chesnaye a hobby which is strictly dependent on his social position. The music-boxes are an image of the harmoniously ordered universe which is the ideal of the propertied class. Thus, even when la Chesnaye seems to touch our sentiments most closely, critical reflection should lead us back to the film's real subject.

drama recalls Brecht's toward his character Puntila, although it is more flexible: la Chesnaye and Christine may be human but they are no less bound to their class interest. Their humanity has been merely apparent; it has never endangered their class logic.

Thus Renoir lends his bourgeois protagonists an individual story only to dissolve it in the collective analysis of a class. In a certain sense, Christine and la Chesnaye have no right to a story; their adventure can unfold only in a false temporality, outside of real history. *Rules of the Game* is a "game of love and history" in which the former term is gradually engulfed by the latter—a privileged moment of diversion outside of a history which is soon to destroy it. For this reason, viewers who laugh when Christine changes her feelings for the fourth time and confesses her love to Octave in the very words of Musset's Marianne are wrong to have expected a psychological coherency which is not among the film's intentions. The only logic of this work is a social one: Christine hesitates because, like Musset's heroine, but for different reasons, she is not really engaged in her feelings as she is in her social function. *Rules of the Game* is, then, not the story of a few characters, but more profoundly, through their lack of a story, the story of a class in crisis. At the end of the film, la Chesnaye and Christine have taken their proper place in their world in spite of their individual characteristics. *Rules of the Game* is the story of a class which discovers its solidarity.

Of course, this story Renoir tells us is not the "real" story of the French ruling class. As in *Grand Illusion* and *La Marseillaise*. Renoir's viewpoint remains that of a moralist. Where one might have expected an analysis of the reasons (and, no doubt, the limits) of the confused French reaction to Hitler, Renoir gives us only a portrait of this confusion. Besides, the characters in *Rules of the Game* are never presented as representative of the ruling class. They simply belong to the propertied class; and la Chesnaye and Saint-Aubain are aristocrats, who do not represent the properly active segment of the class in power. Therefore we must not extend the film's historical scope into regions it never risks entering. It is far from certain that the bourgeoisie had everything to lose in the war of 1940; it may be that Renoir's film sidesteps determinant factors in the policies of the French government. The film should be considered in its true dimension: the critique of certain more or less hypocritical values which have been swept away by the war. The crisis Renoir depicts is, then, a crisis of moral values, which does not prejudge the real destiny of the French bourgeoisie during and after the war. The character of la Chesnaye is merely an extreme case, enabling Renoir to strike the balance of the moral state of the French at the end of the Popular Front. Consequently, to call *Rules of the Game* the story of a class is simply to infer the lesson of the film on the moral level, and from Renoir's own point of view. Renoir has written: "I want to show that every game has its rules. If you play it differently, you lose your match." Thus Jurieu pays with his life for having tried to upset a rigorous order. The class, momentarily threatened, reestablishes its unity.

Renoir has discovered, beneath a complex of moral values endangered by the war, the profound cohesion of a class for which "appearance" is founded in a "reality," which continues to live (and perhaps to threaten) beneath the apparent crisis of moral values which concealed it. Here we reach the threshold which Renoir, for obvious reasons, could not dare to cross. Nevertheless, Renoir's film is not solely that trial of a closed world, that autopsy of a class in crisis which we mentioned at the outset: the bourgeois rules obeyed by the guests at La Colinière are not depicted as a vain and hollow style of life. Renoir has made us sensitive to the latent violence contained in this social structure, at both the individual and the collective level. After his scufflle with Jurieu, la Chesnaye affirms: "Whenever I'd read that a Spanish bricklayer had killed a Polish miner, I thought that such things weren't possible in our world. Well, they are, my friend! They are possible! . . ." But Renoir's film is not limited to satirically exposing the apparent "polish" of a social category which has sought to impose its own order; it also translates, into direct language, the potential for violence belonging to a class threatened in its very existence. In the hunting scene, the hard faces, a certain "family" resemblance, made up of seriousness and cruelty, unites all the hunters, beyond particularities and individual dissensions, in a sort of collective rite, a class's propitiating sacrifice. This clearly symbolic hunt illustrates the deeply rooted solidarity of the propertied class, its ability to sustain its "sacred union" to the point of crime as soon as a foreign element threatens to shake it. Only Octave, by virtue of his origin, remains on the margin of the collective rite, while Christine, though she admits her disgust at hunting, doesn't dare to rebel completely against a world which will eventually absorb her for good. Ultimately, Renoir's lesson is that deep beneath the ridiculous surface of bourgeois proprieties lies a logic, a vital necessity. At the end of the film, it is the general (the most amusing, apparently the least dangerous of the guests at the château, and hence the most suited to express the common opinion of a class) who has the last word. The last resort of this world is to safeguard its unity, its rules. "This la Chesnaye has class, and that's getting rare, my friend, that's getting rare."

A study of *Rules of the Game* would not be complete if we did not situate this work in the history of Jean Renoir himself; we are especially invited to do so by the problematics of this film, above all by the complex character of Octave. In a certain sense—leaving aside *La Bête humaine*, in which Renoir turns again to the work of Zola and the problem of a popular cinema—one can consider *Rules of the Game* as the last part of a trilogy begun by *Grand Illusion* and *La Marseillaise*. Each of these films is closely connected with its contemporary historical problems; together they constitute, beyond the diversity of themes and times, a reflection upon the continuity of a history, which illuminates, and is illuminated by, the atmosphere of 1935–39. In *Grand Illusion,* Renoir, faced with the menace of Nazism, affirms his faith in certain human values, which become so many calls to reason addressed to the German people. The end of the film calls for a collaboration of all classes and all nations to safeguard peace. In *La Marseillaise,* Renoir exalts the union of all Frenchmen in the name of the values proposed by the Popular Front. Even the Coblenz émigrés are entitled to the director's sympathy: even in error, they are still patriots who believed they were serving their country. *Grand Illusion* and *La Marseillaise* thus participate, to different extents, in a political optimism whose idealistic character history would soon expose. When Renoir began making *Rules of the Game,* the Nazi menace had become a reality, the Popular Front had crumbled, and the Munich agreements had consecrated the bankruptcy of the Third Republic: France, "relieved," breathed again, but for how long? It is therefore not surprising that the positive perspective, the optimistic vision of the first two films gave way, in the third, to an internal critique of the class in power: without abandoning the moralist viewpoint of his first two films, Renoir now analyzed the bankruptcy of certain moral values, the "lie" of a world gasping for breath. We have seen that this pessimistic viewpoint is what dictated Renoir's choice of a closed structure and his references to *The Marriage of Figaro,* also the product of a contradictory period and a menaced world. Political reflection is thus necessarily doubled by a reflection upon the French theatrical tradition, on the significance of a cultural and literary heritage, on the role of the artist in a society in crisis.

Already in his first films, Renoir had shown his taste for the *commedia dell' arte,* his wish to think over the significance of traditional theatrical structures and the role of the actor within a work. In *Rules of the Game,* artistic reflection and critical satire are combined: the study of past art is particularly appropriate to the description of a world incapable of reflecting upon present history. Art then takes constant refuge in a complex of rules inherited from the past and recollects its former grandeur. The character of Octave "polarizes" the elements of this reflection, and at the same time poses the problem of the artist in society, and perhaps even (in terms less immediate but still present in the film) the problem of the relationship of the creator to his work.

What does Octave represent in *Rules of the Game?* We have remarked his position as an outsider to the bourgeois world, analogous to Marceau's exclusion from the world of the servants. Is Octave then merely the latest avatar of the character (traditional in French cinema of the period: consider the sailor in *L'Atalante*) of the likeable vagabond, the anarchist opposed to the fossilized world of the bourgeoisie? This character exists in Renoir films previous to *Rules of the Game:* he is most fully personified, and virtually theorized, in the tramp hero of *Boudu Saved from Drowning.*

Yet Renoir did not choose to entrust the role of Octave to Michel Simon, the unifying figure of Vigo's *L'Atalante* and the hero of Renoir's own *Boudu* and *La Chienne*. The figure of Octave, which at first has certain traits in common with that of Boudu (minus the grotesque), acquired an original significance once Renoir decided to play the part himself. Critics, to the present day, have often said that Renoir acts the part badly. This judgment implies a relative understanding, to a certain extent, of the significance of Renoir's rendition of Octave. Octave's part is played, not badly, but *differently* from the other parts. Renoir's acting, free from all constraint in its gestures, from the bourgeois proprieties, partakes of an immediate humanity and brings life into the cinematic fiction. Octave's character is thus enriched with a freedom of expression, including even redundancy and exaggeration, which belongs to him alone, whereas the other characters in the film remain the tributaries, even in expressing their personal feelings, of a certain "language" appropriate to their social position. The conventions which determine their physical and verbal expression objectively reveal their social conditioning, and prepare the conclusion of the film. Octave, on the contrary, is constantly inventing, repeating himself and correcting himself. Renoir improvises each scene from a succinct basic idea, in the manner of the *commedia dell' arte*, but using a real inventiveness, far removed from the characteristic conventions of the eighteenth century's "comedy of art." Renoir's reflection upon the work of the actor, already present in *Nana* and *Boudu*, here ends in the ultimate opposition between life and social convention, between the unexpected and the predetermined.

Such a freedom of expression is altogether appropriate to Octave's status as outsider in *Rules of the Game*. His lack of class affiliation enables him to serve as connecting link between the different social categories: "Monsieur Octave" can embrace Lisette as well as Christine, and trigger the dramatic mechanism by introducing Jurieu into this closed world. Octave thus will lead the game; without him, the film would not exist. In reference to our earlier analysis, we can say that Octave brings the semblance of a story into a world which has no individual right to one. Yet this apparent leader will be the dupe of the others in many respects: because Octave is free, the other characters in the film, conscious of their social conditions, will make use of his freedom to give themselves a story they cannot have. Octave's apparent freedom is thus illusory: he is the slave of the others even while he seems to be leading the game. In fact Octave is merely an idealist, who wrongly insists on seeing the bourgeois around him as individuals. The film's job will be to force him to see the true face of his "friends" and the limits of his own freedom. At the end of the film, Octave discovers he has been the dupe of the others and of himself. He is the only character in the film to evolve (indeed the only one able to evolve); he is the only one really to have a story.

The viewer must not therefore become the dupe of Octave. He must be sensitive to this character's complexity; he must tell when Octave is the persona of the author and when he has himself fallen into the trap of a certain society. On several occasions, Octave invites us to adopt a critical distance from the story we are watching; sometimes he even explains the author's intentions, particularly in his monologue on lies. But Octave is not Renoir: his lucidity is not without blind spots; he lets himself be trapped for a while by his feelings for Christine, even thinks of taking her away. In the long balcony scene before the conclusion of the film, Octave reveals his secret to Christine: he is a failed artist; his "bohemian" air actually conceals an artistic inadequacy. In the figure of this musician who could not confront his responsibility to a public, Renoir thus gives us the portrait of the creator who has miscarried. Octave could never gain his independence as an artist; he is, in a sense, "alienated" from the class that keeps him alive. Far from being a Figaro, from being Musset's Octave, "Monsieur" Octave on the contrary represents everything that Jean Renoir, as an artist, has avoided becoming: a man of the ruling class, the clown who, beneath a satiric exterior, remains in fact the lackey of capitalism. Here Octave's role in the structure of the film takes on another meaning. Octave, we thought, brought an individual story into the game as long as he seemed to be leading it: now that story proves a lie, and turns against the two pariahs. His "story" betrays in fact the pseudo-artist's nostalgia for creation: he "stages scenes" in life to make up for those he cannot realize as a creator. Through the character of Octave, Renoir in a sense exercises the temptation to let the man precede the artist; the true freedom of Renoir consists in the distance he constantly adopts toward the established order in order to criticize it or, at the very least, to satirize it.

The fact that Renoir, the director, has entrusted the role of Octave to Renoir, the man, anticipates the problems of the author's relation to his work as it is currently represented by certain tendencies of contemporary criticism and prose fiction. By focusing the problems of the creative artist in the character of Octave, and by deciding to play the film's essential part himself, Renoir attempts to find the cinematic equivalent of those types of fictional narrative in which the problem of the creator is closely bound to the ideological content and the formal elements of the work: the viewer is invited to the performance of a work (the "game") whose author (Octave) is himself challenged by the director, who constantly establishes a distance between the film as spectacle and the film as reflection.

To conclude this study, it remains to be noted that the perfect fusion of critical and dramatic elements which we have tried to analyze in *Rules of the Game,* and which can also be found in *Grand Illusion, La Marseillaise,* or *Toni,* is characteristic of the films of Renoir before his period of exile in America. The years he spent in the United States accentuated his taste for plastic creation and reflection upon artistic tradition. In *The Diary of a Chambermaid, The Golden Coach, French Cancan,* and *Elena et les hommes,* we find a structure, a direction of actors, a taste for the "theater" which recall those of *Rules of the Game,* but the director has moved gradually towards a cinema of "diversion" (in the most generous sense of the word), towards a universe of form, color, and *brio,* in which the "game" element has decisively prevailed over critical reflection. In Renoir's earlier films, moreover, in *Nana, Madame Bovary, Boudu,* and as far as *La Chienne* or *The Lower Depths,* the appeal of the theater as diversion lent to the acting and direction a freedom, an inventiveness, a refusal of cinematic convention which we have come to associate with Renoir's name. But to this "baroque" Renoir, one may prefer those works in which the director has rooted the formal elements in a concrete reality and has thought out this reality in terms of spectacle, rather than giving the appearance of life to essentially theatrical material.

External Appearances in *Rules of the Game*

R. J. GARLICK

Jean Renoir is a paradoxical figure. Like Eisenstein he has emphatically proclaimed the cinema as a mass art, yet like the Russian his films appeal only to a relatively sophisticated audience. The differing audience reactions to *La Règle du Jeu* at the Melbourne Festival two years ago proved this point.

Even before the recent reconstruction Gavin Lambert called *La Règle du Jeu* a masterpiece, and he has since been supported by critics all over the Continent.

Features said to be common to all Renoir films are the general looseness of his screenplays and the lack of an all-embracing attitude to the problems raised in the films. These points are often stressed by his opponents. But against them it must be said that the looseness is only superficial, for his films have a subjective unity. And this same unity is evidence of Renoir's real attitude or engagement. I hope to clarify the Renoir spirit.

The framework of the action is a week-end spent in a country chateau by a party of aristocrats and their friends. They occupy themselves with a shoot, a fancy dress ball, petty intrigues and adultery. Their surface world

FROM "Renoir: One" by R. J. Garlick, *Film Journal* (July 1964), pp. 35–37. Reprinted by permission of James Merralls.

is elegant, social grace is essential: here they play according to the rules. Beneath this façade the substance of their action has no rule or value. In this world André Jurieu is a foreigner. He is gauche, and even rude. But he is appalled when he finds Christine in the arms of another guest.

André is not alone. Schumacher, the game warden, is rought in manner but desperately faithful to his wife. Renoir's apparent criticism of the faithful is that they are dull. The servants are a mute background working for their employers' pleasure.

The action takes place on the eve of the Second World War, and Renoir's statement that the film is not social criticism is typical of the ingenuous irony of the man. In the same statement he says the film is entertainment. He is right. It is also social criticism, and art.

Like his other films *La Règle du Jeu* is not bound together by a developing narrative. People are shown as they behave in certain situations. "I feel about this as I do about most general ideas: they take on value only when they move to the particular." He considers that all general ideas have some truth but it is only "the application of them which gives them value or not in particular circumstances." But his rational weakness is exposed by his human nature when he contradicts his previous statements: "I do believe in absolute human qualities—generosity, for instance."

His films illustrate these statements. There are heroes and villains, but no character is unsympathetic. Nor is any hero completely right. We might agree with Renoir that no person is ever completely right or completely wrong, but some at least are unsympathetic. Renoir's generosity is not expressed with such great artistry that he can "sympathise" with a really nasty character. It is much easier to be generous to all, to express a buoyant, nostalgic joy in life when you simply remove from consideration the most objectionable people.

The exclusions made by Renoir, his own generosity, the search for generosity in his character, his *joie-de-vivre*, in combination form a tight subjective framework for his films. This framework if analysed as dramatic method would show only disorder. Renoir's dramatic unity is the unity of a flowing river, the continuity of life: an apparently spontaneous series of events, actions and feelings. The shoot sequence in *La Règle du Jeu* is much longer than necessary for showing the attitudes and feelings of the people involved. The cool autumn landscape is delicately presented in depth of focus, enhancing the beauty of the bare trees. The fluid camera moves nervously in close-up among the frightened rabbits. Low-angle lateral tracking shots of the beaters moving steadily through the trees are rhythmically intercut with shots of rabbits and shots of the waiting shooters. The beaters move with military precision; scores of rabbits flee before them; the shooters prepare to fire. The first rabbit enters the clearing and is shot off its feet. A fusillade of shots and the slaughter begins. Rabbits somersault, birds drop in fluttering heaps. The shooting continues, then dies away. A cut away to a long panning shot of a bird which flies through the trees, over the heads of the shooters to safety is followed by a speeding close-up pan of a rabbit. The rabbit is shot and the camera lingers as its legs stretch, the tail quivers, and the body stiffens. Cut to a long shot of beaters picking up the game, a murmur of distant voices and a barking dog.

This scene goes far beyond its dramatic requirements as a part of the whole film. It is almost a self-sufficient poem on man, his culture, and natural life. The formal beauty is simple but breathtaking. The shooters are observed as people; then the shooters and beaters are observed as members of a ritual; then the rabbits are seen hiding in the undergrowth. As the hunt progresses we see beaters, shooters and rabbits, each with greater frequency, by faster cutting and faster panning shots. The natural rise in tension is climaxed by the shooting.

It has been called a textbook example of traditional editing and camera movement, and it is, until the stage where the killing has begun. If the scene were to end there it would be as rounded, competent and dead as an example from Karel Reisz. What lifts it from craftsmanship to art are the three final shots: the long-distance rising pan of the bird which flies over the shooters to safety; the close-up of the last fleeing rabbit and its death; the long shot of the beaters collecting the game. Each of these shots is beautiful, but their powerful effect is due as much to their editing. The long pan of the bird comes after a quick succession of shootings, and as a sustained, quiet shot acts as a musical pause for the final blow, the killing of the rabbit. And this electrifying shot is followed by a receding chord, the long shot of the beaters.

La Règle du Jeu does show more dramatic unity than other Renoir films. Even though the shoot scene is longer than strictly necessary, the scene is necessary. In some other of Renoir's films there are whole sequences which seem wholly unnecessary. The films hang together because of the consistent way he looks at life and because of his highly personal style. Any scene bears his signature. His generosity to people: the sympathetic presentation of the Marquis in spite of the shoot. Easy, limpid technique: Octave puts a fast, trumpeting song on the gramophone and chases Lisette. The camera swings with him to the left of the room where he catches the laughing maid, then sweeps grandly back to the right as the Marquis enters the room and calls Octave a dangerous poet, the gramophone screaming a delirious, happy lunacy in the foreground. Complex *mise-en-scène* with people set in depth: Octave and the Marquis argue in a corridor. They stand in the foreground to the left of the frame. Two servants pass behind them and, moving further into depth, go to the right of the frame. The servants turn right, and just as they move out of the frame a large wall-mirror causes their reflections to march back into the centre of the frame. Painterly sensuousness: Marceau walks into an orchard to check his rabbit traps. A lateral tracking shot catches him slouching through the trees in a sadly drooping hat. The dark, charcoal greys of the landscape and the lonely figure create a beauty and atmosphere made for a tale from the Brothers Grimm. The sensuousness is supported by the capture of the quivering of light: Robert speaks to Geneviève in her apartment. She is aware of the coming break. She rests her arm on the head of a plump, smug Buddha, and says, "I want to be happy." Her face and Buddha's glow in a diffuse, soft light. Refined nostalgia: the hunting calls of a distant horn as Octave and André prepare for bed. Or the nostalgic pain of unhappy love: Geneviève and Robert wander in the marshes after the shoot. Their affair is whimpering to a close. Geneviève faces the camera, in a square cap with a long curving feather. Her expression is frosted misery. Robert, behind her, gazes sideways and speaks indifferently. In deep focus the bare trees form a brushwork background. Manneristic graces: Octave describes to Christine how her father, a musician, once conducted. Octave swaggers to a rostrum, taps with his bow and throws up his arms. There is no orchestra for Octave.

These qualities are present in any of Renoir's films, but *La Règle du Jeu* possesses them in more complex combination. The master scene of all is during the fancy dress party. The guests are assembled in a large hall facing a small stage. A dance performance accompanied by a fat, crude pianist has just concluded. Lights dim and the opening bars of Saint-Saëns' *Danse Macabre* is heard on the piano. The camera moves to the vacant vibrating keyboard, then to the fat pianist who stares at the keys with stupid incomprehension. The curtains part on the darkened stage. Ghosts appear, who quiver and shake to the music. They brandish umbrella frames, and are clad in white sheets and hoods with large black eye-pits. A gangling skeleton joins their dance. The half-intoxicated audience laughs. A sudden cut to a position behind the stage, looking through the ghosts to the audience. In one superb moment the Saint-Saëns changes to a lower key, the ghosts swoop out among the audience, lights play rapidly over the assembled faces, women scream; there is still some laughter. Christine throws herself into Saint-Aubin's arms. Lisette and Marceau try to avoid the furious Schumacher. The camera then moves to André, an enraged, despairing witness to Christine's conduct. Christine leaves the hall with Saint-Aubin.

This scene is delivered with astounding finesse: gliding camera, rhythmic cutting, electrifying changes of camera viewpoint, the growing hysteria of the audience, the flickering lights, action timed to the mood of the music, inter-woven themes of personal emotion and group emotion, and veiled social criticism.

La Règle du Jeu is understandably a popular film with critics, for it combines many virtues. It epitomises the work of Renoir, showing all his qualities which have affected subsequent developments in cinema. It has the pungent social criticism and sense of immediacy practised by the neo-realists; it has the limpid flow of imagery now seen in the work of Satyajit Ray; it has the *joie-de-vivre* now seen in de Broca. Many artists have *joie-de-vivre*, of course, but Renoir's has a peculiar quality of occasionally changing to nostalgia. The transition occurs with such ease that both qualities seem different aspects of the one feeling. There is a definite continuity of style and atmosphere. There is no darkness to this feeling, or we might think of Mahler. It is rather the fine, erratic fervour of Berlioz.

La Règle de Jeu has been acclaimed by the writers of "Les Cahiers du Cinéma." Renoir is one of the few older French directors who attracts the enthusiasm of the younger men. Cocteau is another, and Bresson. It is important to compare Renoir and Bresson, for they are sources of opposing trends in the French cinema. Renoir has always been an artist who *looks* at life and has been satisfied with that. Occasionally he makes statements such as "if I have some slight contact with external appearances, this helps me to penetrate more deeply to the interior of the characters." But his films are not studies of the interior. I do not mean that they have nothing of the interior, but when compared to Bresson the statement is generally correct. Bresson, on the other hand, is not satisfied with the look of life.

Film is a visual medium and by its nature, looks at things. A film artist who wishes to penetrate appearances must concentrate on the relevant thing at length in an effort to bore beneath it. Alternatively, he must move continually around the subject until he expresses it by suggestion: he avoids a direct approach. This approach to film-making has some obvious effects. The audience cannot "sleep." It must be consciously receptive all the time. I do not mean that the audience to an "appearance" film may always be passive, but that this state of mind is possible with some "appearance" films, and impossible with all those of the other kind. The latter we might call Bressonian for convenience. Other effects follow from the Bressonian approach. As the audience cannot simply accept all that it sees initially, it requires more time to become aware of other things, other meanings. This means that as a matter of practice (not principle) such films are slower than "appearance" films. It is a contemplative cinema. The young directors who follow from Bresson are Godard (*Vivre Sa Vie*) and perhaps Rivette (*Paris nous appartient*). A list of Bressonian directors would naturally include Dreyer and Ozu, who took their approach long ahead of Bresson. Truffaut has elements of Bresson but is basically more akin to Renoir. De Broca is the clearest follower of Renoir among the younger men.

Contemporary French and Italian art films are a culminating point of the development of cinema towards a personal medium. The *auteur* speaks directly to an audience through camera, cutting, acting, script and sound, all to varying degrees controlled by him. Penelope Houston has gone further and stated that this cinema speaks not to an audience as a group but to the individuals. This needs further clarification. The Bressonians always speak to the individuals. The Renoirs tend to speak to the group. A film with the subtle complexity of *La Règle du Jeu* speaks to both.

WELLES

CITIZEN KANE

CREdiTS

Citizen Kane (United States, 1941)
Directed by Orson Welles from a screenplay by Welles and Herman Mankiewicz
Produced by Welles for R.K.O. Pictures
Distributors (16mm): Audio-Brandon Films, Janus Films

Photography: Gregg Toland
Art director: Van Nest Polgase
Editor: Robert Wise
Music: Bernard Herrman

Main performers:
Orson Welles (*Charles Foster Kane*)　Ray Collins (*James W. Gettys*)
Joseph Cotton (*Jedediah Leland*)　Erskine Sanford (*Mr. Carter*)
Everett Sloane (*Mr. Bernstein*)　William Alland (*Thompson*)
Dorothy Comingore (*Susan Alexander*　Paul Stewart (*Raymond, the butler*)
　Kane)　George Coulouris (*Walter Parks*
Agnes Moorehead (*Kane's mother*)　　*Thatcher*)
Ruth Warrick (*Emily Norton Kane*)　Buddy Swan (*Kane as a boy*)

Length: 119 minutes

When Orson Welles went to Hollywood at the age of twenty-five in 1940 to make his first professional film his reputation as a prodigy and a theatrical genius created an atmosphere of expectation, with all its accompanying pressures, that would certainly have ruined the artistic sensibility of a lesser man. Never had so much been anticipated of an artistic début, and as we see now, never had so much been fulfilled. *Citizen Kane* by no means represents the only time a filmmaker produced a great work with his initial directorial assignment (John Huston, for example, did so in the same year with *The Maltese Falcon*). But Welles's film presented itself so blatantly as a work of the highest artistic aspirations that it was a challenge to critics to assimilate its resources and to assess its technical achievement. The furor that attended its release, when the Hearst newspaper empire sought successfully to undermine its commercial prospects because Kane's life resembled William Randolph Hearst's, now seems just another episode in Welles's flamboyant career. What really counted—as any twenty-five-year-old would attest—was not an immediate financial windfall, but the glory of artistic achievement and the esteem of a significant number of critics.

In fact, though *Citizen Kane* fell somewhat short of being received unanimously as an "instant classic," its status over the last three decades has increased steadily. For one thing, Welles's performance in the title role established him as a superb film actor. In regard to his filmmaking career, *Citizen Kane* overshadowed Welles's future directorial assignments, which include some other notable films, a few of them marred by studio heads who distrusted his commercial sense and prevented him from exercising total artistic control over such a work as *The Magnificent Ambersons* (1942). Nevertheless, if Welles has not directed as frequently as his admirers would wish, at least he has had more opportunities than some other renowed filmmakers who were considered suspect by various film industries—and this list includes Erich von Stroheim, Sergei Eisenstein, and Carl Dreyer. Welles, like Stroheim, is a talented actor and has often performed in the films of other directors. His presence on a set, even in a small role, can be overwhelming; sometimes the basic style of a lesser director seems to shift to accommodate Welles the performer in the manner of Welles the surrogate-filmmaker. It is as though many directors who come in contact with him as an actor end up paying homage to him as a master filmmaker.

Probably more has been written about *Citizen Kane* than any other film, which is in itself a tribute to its power to engage our interest. To explain that power, many writers have emphasized the film's innovations or its striking cinematic techniques. Yet such an approach is perhaps misleading, for craftsmanship cannot possibly be mastered during a first film assignment, whereas his experimental techniques and extraordinarily bold methods were useful and youthful substitutes for tried but timid conventions. Welles had previously acquired a real knowledge of dramatic effects and significant skills in handling performers in theater and radio, and so in no sense did he have to start from scratch. He approached filming as his creation, Charles Foster Kane, approached journalism: his gusto, drive, and innate grasp of the art of mass communication made up for his lack of experience, and there is no arguing with his results.

What makes *Citizen Kane* a classic has to do with the vitality of its hero and the truly interesting situations conceived for him. Films had been told in flashbacks before (for example, *The Cabinet of Dr. Caligari*), but Welles's inspiration was to focus on several narratives that offered partial insights into the deceased Kane so that when they were combined in the viewer's imagination, they would present a biographical portrait of greater depth than that presented by any one of the film's sections. The search for the true Kane reminds us of those novels of Joseph Conrad, particularly *Lord Jim*, which entail a search through a multitude of ambiguities for an ultimate, but perhaps evasive, truth about a man's character. (Welles, incidentally, went to Hollywood to make Conrad's *Heart*

Composition, Imagery, and Music in *Citizen Kane*

CHARLES HIGHAM

The opening sequence, even after innumerable viewings, still retains its power to haunt and disturb. A close-up of the "No Trespassing" sign dissolves to a slow exploration of the meshes of the iron fence secluding Xanadu from the world. This oppressive image changes to great flowers of iron; and then, in a very gradual, almost Sternbergian dissolve, to the massive single initial "K" framed in wrought iron, the crest of the gate. At the right, Xanadu's towers distantly loom out of the mists in the faintly moonlit night.

Two spider monkeys sit watchfully in a cage to the left of the frame, a gate to the right balances the composition; gondolas gleam against the background of a pier, and the castle shimmers palely, reflected in the water of an imitation Venetian canal, precursor of a similar one in *Touch of Evil*. The figure of Bakst, an Egyptian cat god, stands before a bridge with a raised portcullis, and another gate is seen to the right. A golf marker (365 yards) for a mistily glimpsed course emerges. Almost subliminally we are made aware that a single window of the castle is lit up, casting a sliver of illumination in a bleak and towering tomb of stone.

The effect is brilliantly sinister, mysterious, and magical, pulling us forward in a series of hypnotic dissolves as though in a dream, each successive shot containing glimpses of the castle, a succession of gateways leading us on in our exploration of this secret and fabled world, Kane's strange legacy.* Now we get a closer shot of a crumbling gate, with palm trees around it, shabby and unmoving, a medium shot of the castle, and the lighted Scottish window. The light snaps off, and we cut to a reverse angle shot of the interior of the window, with a figure lying stiffly on a bed like a medieval knight on a tomb: Kane. This image dissolves into a dazzling effect: the entire screen is filled with whirling snowflakes, blotting out everything. We draw back to see a little wooden house, and the camera retreats further to disclose that we are peering into the depths of a circular glass snowstorm paperweight; it is at that precise moment that the word "Rosebud" is spoken, and the lips, repeating the word, fill the screen. The

FROM *The Films of Orson Welles* (1970) by Charles Higham, pp. 34–36, 38–39, 42, 43–45. Originally published by the University of California Press; reprinted by permission of The Regents of the University of California.

* There is an intriguing parallel in Hitchcock's *Rebecca*, made the same year and in the same studio, and originally adapted by Welles for his "First Person Singular" radio series. *Rebecca* was also a precursor of *Ambersons* in its use of narrative.

globe bounces down steps, its tiny flakes whirling in water, a nurse comes
in aslant the image; the little house lies sideways on the left of the frame
and the screen is filled laterally by a piece of shattered globe, the nurse
refracted through it. She folds the dead man's hands and pulls the sheet
over his head, observed entirely in silhouette. Another dissolve leads to
the lighted window and the figure, almost exactly paralleling the shot
introducing the death chamber. Cut to a row of flags painted on a credit
card: "News on the March."

This is apparently meant to be only a portion of a news magazine; the
panel heading is "Obituary: Xanadu's Landlord." In rapid succession we
see the words of Coleridge's poem; a series of shots of San Simeon, partly
from the air, of people disporting themselves in the grounds; the construction of the building; a figure on a horse, vertical wipes removing a series
of images of toil; four horses, two giraffes, birds, an octopus, an elephant,
a huge aviary of glass, a cupid firing a bow and arrow. The funeral of
Kane, his rise and downfall, and excerpts from his career, faultlessly blend
deliberately scratched stock, artificially staged scenes shot by Gregg
Toland, and newsreel photographs.

As the newsreel flickers off with a dying fall on the sound track, the
figures in the screening room strike up matches in the dark. When Thompson receives his orders to track down the facts about Kane, his editor
looms in the arc beam, the light streaming from his body in a series of
fans, splitting the image into fragments. Thompson's first interview with
Susan Kane is introduced with the camera probing through a violent
electric storm to a huge illuminated sign announcing her at the El Rancho
Nightclub, then moving up "through" the rain-swept skylight, followed by
a shot of Susan drunk at a table. . . .

At the Thatcher Memorial Library in Chicago—Thompson's diminutive
entering figure is dwarfed by a huge gray echoing cathedral of stone
pierced by dusty sunbeams; ahead of him a table stretches to infinity, like
a gigantic coffin marking the resting place of the dead banker. A subjective camera representing Thompson explores the pages of the book, reflecting the audience's desire to peer into the secrets of the character. The
tall, slanting, perfectly molded banker's handwriting is followed in a very
gradual left to right pan, and we pick out the words slowly, as though
groping in the dark: here is Bernard Herrmann's figure for woodwind,
moving from faintly sepulchral bars into a gay childlike theme, innocent
and tripping: "I first encountered Mr. Kane in 1871. . . ." The flutes and
piccolos trip still more lightly, blending into a delicate passage for strings
as the page fades away to a mass of snowflakes, as mind-filling as those
which blotted out the image upon Kane's death: an eight-year-old boy is
playing with a sled, coming down a hill; he throws a snowball at the sign
on top of the crude wooden building to the right of frame: the snowball
smashes against letters that read BOARDING HOUSE. Thus in a moment

we have seen that Kane is obstreperous, rebellious: the setting of loneliness and shabby gentility has been permanently fixed in our minds.

The composition of the scene that follows, with Thatcher, the Kanes, and the boy, is very simple: while the sound track is complex with argument, the camera remains stationary at a table, Charles glimpsed through the window in a long-held take. A slow dolly shot introduces and closes the interior scene of the discussion, and at the end we are able to look lingeringly into the house: cheap vases, mats, pictures, an image of rural simplicity. Outside in the snow the grouping of the characters is again observed in a long take, with the camera absolutely fixed. Welles cuts to Mrs. Kane, the camera coming down to take in Charlie, followed by a dissolve to the sled, tossed away on a snowbank; then the sled more thickly covered in driving snow, a symbol of vanished innocence and purity, while a mournful train whistle beyond it brilliantly conveys Charlie's unhappy transference to Chicago.

.   .   .

[We] meet Jedediah Leland at the Huntington Memorial Hospital on 180th Street. We see Thompson below and looking up at a gigantically imposing bridge; dissolve to the hospital, two figures in a blown-up still in wheelchairs, silent, behind Leland, who looks thin and shriveled in his patterned dressing gown, hidden behind dark glasses, his head encased by an old tennis cap-cum-eyeshade. He has become tragically senile; his incarceration in the hospital, the feeling of paralysis that comes with old age, and the terrible isolation of the sick are all conveyed with great economy by the use of an apparently stationary, but in fact almost imperceptibly moving, camera, the dolly pushed forward inch by inch as we get infinitesimally closer to the old man's face. (This effect is repeated in the sequence when Bannister and his wife talk outside the courtroom in *The Lady from Shanghai*.) The grey lighting echoes feebly the mood of the projection-room scene. The composition is divided into sections by diagonal beams of sunlight which move during the conversation, the background sad, drab, tomb-like: a wall to the left, windows at the back beyond the two huddled patients in their heavy rugged wheelchairs, and the figure of Leland nodding on like a scarcely animated mummy. The effect of using a still to freeze the background, instead of living people and a set, is to emphasize the approaching stillness of Leland's end. After this unusually prolonged and subtle take, we see Leland's face retained over the first shot as he describes Kane's marriage: the breakfast table dissolves in, and the old man's head nods, slowly disappearing.

The celebrated sequence of the Kanes' declining marriage is figured in rapid cuts from face to face, seen across a bowl of flowers, with "swish pans" giving a curious effect like a moving train at night or a succession of windows flashing between each successive scene as we see the room grow more elaborately furnished and filled with more lavish displays of tropical plants; finally, the couple is left reading the antagonistic newspapers; the camera draws away to show husband and wife posed at the table, utterly silent. As the sequence ends, we dissolve back to Leland in the hospital; he is observed with an entirely still camera as he begins to talk about Kane's first meeting with Susan Alexander. Now we are in a very "studio" New York street wet with rain, with Kane's shadow on the pavement and Susan giggling off-screen; reflections of the lights of a clothing shop glitter in the puddles. A long shot through the door of her room-in house frames the couple as they enter. Kane closes the door, and we are in Susan's cluttered room: she sits at a mirror, Kane wiggling his ears as she laughs in the reflection, and next to the dressing-table mirror and a portrait of Susan as a child the director has significantly placed the snowstorm glass paperweight that later turns up in Susan's room at Xanadu—it is not only a reminder of his youth, but of her innocence that he destroys.

.　　.　　.

At the wedding of Kane and Susan, she is seen giggling helplessly, carrying a rather large and bedraggled bunch of roses caught in a bright new ribbon. KANE BUILDS NEW OPERA HOUSE, a front page headline shrieks as the singing teacher Matiste shouts "No, No, No, No!" A close-up of Susan has her made up—rather oddly—as Salammbô in a Brunhilde-ish hairstyle, with seventeenth-century Turkish turban. Clouds of incense float around her litter; we are on the stage of the Chicago Opera House. A cue light bobs up: the maid fixes the star's hair: Susan sprays her face with perfume. The camera seems to rise up past a curtain to a little house rather like the one in the paperweight, stored above the stage, then past a gondola, recalling the film's opening images, while Salammbô's voice echoes more and more distantly, until we see two men leaning over, high in the flies, one of them significantly holding his nose.

After the uninteresting scene in which Leland fails to write the review of Susan's performance and Kane completes it—the technique here, as in all the newspaper sequences, is much too labored—we return to the hospital. The transition is achieved with a very curious effect in which we see Kane typing to the right of the screen, illuminated with a kind of spotlight; a dissolve discloses Leland sitting in his wheelchair on the left of the frame, but for a moment the two images are retained together in a notably bizarre composition, followed by one equally strange as two nurses, their heads cut off by the top of the frame, come to wheel Leland away from the interview, back into the silence that precedes death. Here the still of the two patients behind Leland is replaced by a set from which the still was photographed, to admit his retreating form.

.   .   .

Xanadu is introduced, all its lights aglow, with Herrmann's leitmotif figure on the brass. We dissolve to a gigantic jigsaw puzzle, representing what appears to be a huge, shapeless landscape. Two Egyptian figures are on our left, a baronial staircase on the right, Susan sitting by the fireplace (a continuity lapse here: in the introductory shot of Susan, the puzzle was three parts completed; in the new shot of her, it is scarcely begun). The shots are long, and we are given a series of dissolves over successive puzzles, illustrating lapses of time, an increase of boredom: a camel, a (significant) snowscape, a turreted house, a country scene, a river with boats and weeping willows, a ship at sea. Later, as the Kanes talk, a figure of a mounted medieval knight and a Gothic window tower over the conversation: in some shots Kane himself looks as stony and formal as any of his statues—an effect repeated in *Chimes at Midnight* in the scenes involving Henry IV.

The picnic scene is a masterpiece of cinematic strategy: Herrmann's Xanadu figure changes to a ragtime variant as Kane and Susan, dressed in costumes of the early thirties (he in striped blazer, she in white pleated skirt) are observed head-on in the back seat of a Düsenberg. From overhead we see a procession of cars making their way along a "Florida" beach, like a funeral cortège. There is a close-up of a sweating Negro singer, people dancing (from stock footage), and shots of the butler Raymond moving discreetly in the background. A pig turns on a spit as husband and wife quarrel (Kane, mysteriously, looks several years older here than in the preceding sequence of the car drive). As the quarrel reaches its peak, Kane looms enormously, threateningly over Susan, the band becomes more frantic, people slap their hands together in time to the tune, and to a background of flitting animated bats and jungle trees girls scream as they frolic with the male guests, their cries heard off-screen, symbolic of Susan's anguish as well as the sexual abandonment of the picnic.

As Susan packs to leave Xanadu, we are shown her bedroom, which is decorated like a child's nursery, with painted animals. (Now Kane looks far younger than in the picnic scene: can RKO have forbidden more retakes?) Back at the nightclub, chairs and tables are covered, and Susan's story is over. In half-darkness, against a stippled wall, she puffs despairingly at a cigarette lit for her by Thompson.

At Xanadu for the butler's version of Kane's life, the camera moves down the stairs in a very evenly managed long take as the butler pronounces the words: "I knew how to handle him; like the time his wife left him." A screaming cockatoo flaps off a balcony, indicating metaphorically the shock of Susan's departure and her virago-like character. As she moves off to the left of the frame, we see Kane in a long shot in a vaguely "Indian" corridor, framed in the door of Susan's bedroom, which he now almost ritualistically smashes to pieces, looming above our eye level. Phonograph, table, curtains, chests of drawers, chairs and bookshelves—one shelf concealing a bottle of alcohol—all are smashed. But as Kane lurches exhaustedly to the door he finds, next to a bottle of perfume, the snow scene paperweight Susan had owned when he first met her. He picks it up and looks at it in complete silence, the snowflakes whirling. Tears start in his eyes as he breathes the single word "Rosebud." The tears seem to be frozen on his cheeks. The butler comes up; a long dolly shot shows Kane walking past the guests and servants and along a mirrored corridor, his image reflected to infinity. The camera moves forward to take in the multiple image; there is a dissolve back to the butler and Thompson.

As the reporters talk,* the camera moves back into a crane shot, taking in their figures moving through the statues and myriad crates, figures in the background in deep focus climbing up ladders, the camera tracking along-side a Donatello *Nativity*, a fourth-century Venus, across all the knick-knacks, the cup ("value two dollars") given as a welcome present by the staff of *The Inquirer*, its message read out by a woman reporter. A long traveling shot follows the explorers of this monumental material; and as Thompson admits he has not solved the secret of "Rosebud," he puts down the box with a jigsaw puzzle—an obvious but legitimate symbol of Kane's unexplored reality. The whole of this scene takes place in a magnificent single take, the camera rising up again until all the boxes seem like the shattered ruins of a skyscraper city, a vanished empire: a fantastic effect, and the film's greatest single stroke of genius. Finally, after its pitiless inventory of the worldly goods of Charles Foster Kane, the camera comes to the incinerator where trash is being burned.

Somber, eerie chords; a fluffy blonde doll lies sideways, like the broken life of Susan Kane; a violin case lies next to the Rosebud sled in the furnace; gradually the heat warps the paint, which looks almost as though ice and snow are melting on its surfaces. Finally the lettering and the ornamental rose above it are completely blistered away; the camera moves forward very slowly in to the sled; we dissolve to the chimney with its smoke writhing into the night sky; the smoke dissolves slowly over the wire fence, returning us to the "No Trespassing" sign. We have in fact trespassed, and we have been locked out, holding in our grasp only the last shot of the film: the huge initial "K" in its metal scrollwork, the castle, remote as a romantic legend, and the smoke wreathing out, carrying with it like a shadow, like Kane's spirit, everything that he sacrificed for, everything that he struggled to gain.

---

* Among them Alan Ladd and Richard Wilson.

The Dual Cinematic Tradition in *Citizen Kane*

DAVID BORDWELL

The best way to understand *Citizen Kane* is to stop worshiping it as a triumph of technique. Too many people have pretended that Orson Welles was the first to use deep-focus, long takes, films-within-films, sound montage, and even ceilings on sets when these techniques were child's play for Griffith, Murnau, Renoir, Berkeley, Keaton, Hitchcock, Lang, and Clair. To locate *Kane's* essential originality in its gimmicks cheapens it; once we know how the magician does his tricks, the show becomes a charade. *Kane* is a masterpiece not because of its tours de force, brilliant as they are, but because of the way those tours de force are controlled for larger artistic ends. The glitter of the film's style reflects a dark and serious theme; *Kane's* vision is as rich as its virtuosity.

The breadth of that vision remains as impressive today as thirty years ago. *Citizen Kane* straddles great opposites. It is at once a triumph of social comment and a landmark in cinematic surrealism. It treats subjects like love, power, class, money, friendship, and honesty with the seriousness of a European film; yet it never topples into pretentiousness, is at every instant as zestful, intelligent, and entertaining as the finest Hollywood pictures. It is both a pointed comedy of manners and a tragedy on a Renaissance scale. It has a Flaubertian finesse of detail and an Elizabethan grandeur of design. Extroverted and introspective, exuberant and solemn, *Kane* has become an archetypal film as boldly as Kane's career makes him an archetypal figure. "I am, always have been, and always will be only one thing—an American," he declares, and the contradictions in *Citizen Kane* echo those of an entire country. No wonder the film's original title was *American:* like the nation, the film and its protagonist hold contraries in fluid, fascinating suspension.

To unify such opposites, *Kane* draws together the two main strands of cinematic tradition. As both a mechanical recorder of events and a biased interpreter of the same events, cinema oscillates between the poles of objective realism and subjective vision. This tension, implicit in every film (and, as Pasolini points out, in every image), is at the heart of *Citizen Kane.* Faithful to the integrity of the external world, the film is simultaneously expressive of the processes of the imagination. As the ancestor of the works of Godard, Bergman, Fellini, Bresson, and Antonioni, *Kane* is a monument in the modern cinema, the cinema of consciousness.

FROM *Film Comment*, Vol. VII (Summer 1971), pp. 39–46. Reprinted by permission of *Film Comment* and the author.

Since Lumière, motion pictures have been attracted to the detailed reproduction of external reality. Still photography, the literary school of Naturalism, and the elaborate theatrical apparatus of the nineteenth century gave impetus to the documentary side of film. Thus most of the films made before 1940 reflect this sort of objective realism in their *mise-en-scène*. But running parallel to this documentary trend is a subjectivity that uses film to transform reality to suit the creator's imagination. From Méliès' theatrical stylization and cinematic sleight-of-hand come the distorted décor of *Caligari* and the camera experimentation of the European avant-garde.

.   .   .

This tandem line of development highlights the significance of Eisenstein in film aesthetics. He demonstrated that montage could assemble the raw data of the Lumière method in patterns which expressed the poetic imagination. Dialectical montage was an admission of the presence of artistic consciousness in a way that Griffith's "invisible" cutting was not. The audience was made aware of a creator's sensibility juxtaposing images to make a specific emotional or intellectual point. Eisenstein claimed to control montage of attractions "scientifically" (sometimes to the point of reducing metaphor to rebus), but after Eisenstein, a less didactic, more associational montage became a dominant poetic style of the avant-garde.

In its own way, *Citizen Kane* also recapitulates and extends film tradition. On a primary level, it makes sophisticated allusions to several genres: the detective thriller, the romance, the musical, the horror fantasy, the hard-boiled newspaper film, the big-business story, the newsreel, and the social-comment film. But *Kane* is more than an anthology. Testing the Lumière-Méliès tension, Welles, like Eisenstein, gives the cinema a new contemplative density by structuring his material on the nature of consciousness. What Eisenstein does between individual shots, Welles does in the film's total organization. *Kane's* great achievement, then, is not its stylistic heel-clicking, but its rich fusion of an objective realism of texture with a subjective realism of structure. Welles opens a new area to the cinema because, like Eisenstein, he not only shows what we see, but he symbolizes the way we see it.

Kane explores the nature of consciousness chiefly by presenting various points of view on a shifting, multiplaned world. We enter Kane's consciousness as he dies, before we have even met him; he is less a character than a stylized image. Immediately, we view him as a public figure—fascinating but remote. Next we scrutinize him as a man, seen through the eyes of his wife and his associates, as a reporter traces his life story. Finally, these various perspectives are capped by a detached, omniscient one. In all, Kane emerges as a man—pathetic, grand, contradictory, ultimately enigmatic. The film expresses an ambiguous reality through formal devices that stress both the objectivity of fact and the subjectivity of point of view. It is because the best contemporary cinema has turned to the exploration of such a reality that Kane is, in a sense, the first modern American film.

The opening twelve minutes of *Citizen Kane* capsulize its approach and scope. At the very start, Welles uses a basic property of film to establish *Kane's* method and pays homage to the two founts of cinema—the fantasy of Méliès and the reportage of Lumière.

The camera glides slowly up a fence. "No Trespassing," warns a sign. Immediately, the camera proceeds to trespass. It is a tingling moment, because the driving force of cinema is to trespass, to relentlessly investigate, to peel back what conceals and confront what reveals. "The camera," writes Pudovkin, "as it were, forces itself, ever striving, into the profoundest deeps of life; it strives thither to penetrate, whither the average spectator never reaches as he glances casually around him. The camera goes deeper." Cinema is a perfecting of vision because the eye of the camera, unlike that of the spectator, cannot be held back by fences or walls or signs; if anything interferes with the steady progress into the heart of a scene, we know it is an artificial and temporary obstacle. Thus it is this forward-cleaving movement, begun in *Kane's* first scene, that is completed at the climactic track-in to the Rosebud sled.

Immediately, the imagery becomes dreamlike: a castle, a light snapped out and mysteriously glowing back to life, a man's lips, eerily sifting snow, a shattered crystal, a tiny cottage. Dissolves languidly link huge close-ups; space is obliterated; the paperweight smashes but makes no sound; a nurse enters, distorted in the reflection. We then see the deathbed dark against an arched window, and the shot fades out. The sequence is a reprise of the dream-structure of the European avant-garde films, especially *Caligari, Un Chien Andalou,* and *Blood of a Poet.* Welles celebrates the magic of Méliès and stresses, in both the content and the juxtaposition of the images, the subjective side of cinema.

But suddenly, in one of the most brilliant strokes in film, the "News on the March" sequence bursts on our eyes, history fills the screen, and we are confronted with the Lumière side of cinema, reality apparently unmanipulated. The stentorian announcer, the corny sensationalism, the *Time* style, and the histrionic music announce the newsreel's affinity with the popular "March of Time" shorts. (It is still the funniest parody of mass-media vulgarity ever filmed.) Furthermore, since each shot looks like period footage, "News on the March" virtually recapitulates the technical development of cinema from 1890 to 1941. Scratches on the emulsion, jerky movement, jump cuts, overexposures, handheld camerawork, insertion of authentic newsreel clips, the use of different filmstocks and cameras —each frame is historically persuasive. Glimpses of Chamberlain, Teddy

Roosevelt, and Hitler are immediately and indelibly convincing. Thus as the first sequence had given us a private, poetic image of Kane, so this sequence supplies the public, documentary side of him. In clashing the two together, Welles immediately establishes the basic tension of *Kane* (and cinema itself): objective fact versus subjective vision, clearness and superficiality versus obscurity and profundity, newsreel versus dream. By making us question the very nature of experience, this clash of forms and styles produces the tension between reality and imagination that is the film's theme.

"News on the March" does more, though. Jumping, skittery, grainy, the sequence is the narrative hub of the film, the Argument of the story, simultaneously running through Kane's life and outlining the story we are about to see. It builds our curiosity, plants a handful of clues, establishes the film's leaping, elliptical form, and, anticipating a major tendency of contemporary films, reminds the audience *à la* Brecht's "A-effect" that it is an audience and that it is watching a film.

· · ·

Two parts of *Kane's* structure act as summations. The first, the "News on the March" sequence, maps out the course the film will take. But by the end of the film, the personality depicted in the newsreel has been reduced to mere objects. The second summation, the final scene in Xanadu, balances "News on the March." We already know Kane's life story, but Welles gives us a reprise—the piano Susan played, the "Welcome Home" loving cup, the statuary, the bed from the *Inquirer* office, the stove in Mrs. Kane's boarding house. The camera tracks ominously over these from the most recent to the most remote, backwards through Kane's life, to settle on the symbol of his childhood: the Rosebud sled. The uninterrupted flow of this extravagant sequence reassembles the life that has been presented in so fragmented a fashion.

Between these two summations the film rests. Told from the viewpoints of five different people, the movie uses the thread of the reporter Thompson's search for the meaning of "Rosebud" to stitch the stories together. The sections are for the most part chronological and overlapping; with the exception of Thatcher, each narrator begins his story a little before his predecessor ended and carries it past the point from which the next narrator will begin. Some events, then—such as Susan's rise and fall as an opera singer—are shown twice, but from different perspectives.

· · ·

But *Kane* should not be seen as a *Rashomon*-like exploration of the relativity of fact. At no point does Welles suggest that Kane's story is being distorted, wilfully or unconsciously, by any narrator. In fact, we are sometimes made to feel quite differently from the narrator (as in Thatcher's and Leland's narratives) and the narrator's presence is so little stressed during each segment that sometimes scenes are included which the narrators were not present to witness. There is thus no doubt about the *facts* which are revealed.

The film's complexity arises from the narrators' conflicting *judgments*, their summing-ups of Kane. Each one sees a different side of him at a different stage of his life, yet each takes his estimate of Kane as definitive. To Thatcher, Kane is an arrogant smart aleck who became "nothing more nor less than a Communist." Bernstein's Kane is a man of high principles, with a sharp business sense and a love of the common man. Leland's Kane, only "in love with himself," is a man of no convictions, a betrayer of the masses. Susan sees Kane (in imagery that recalls Caligari and Svengali) as a selfish but piteous old man. And Raymond's story of Kane as a lonely hermit betrays the cold detachment of his own nature. Each narrator judges Kane differently, and each judgment leaves out something essential. As T. S. Eliot puts it in *The Confidential Clerk:* "There's always something one's ignorant of/About anyone, however well one knows him;/And that may be something of the greatest importance."

The effect of seeing so many conflicting assessments is to restrain us from forming any opinions of Kane we might take as definitive. As each character tells his story, the reporter's search for an accurate judgment is taken up by the audience as well. Thompson, whose face we never see, is a surrogate for us; his job—voyeuristic and prying, yet ultimately disinterested and detached—is the perfect vehicle for the curiosity without consequences that film uniquely gratifies. The more we see of Kane, the harder it becomes to judge him; understanding passes beyond praise or condemnation. This complex frame of mind in the audience is central to much of contemporary cinema, from *Vertigo* to *La Chinoise,* and is a major source of *Kane's* originality. Its multiple-narration structure warns us not to look for conventional signals of recognition and resolution. A film that opens and closes with "No Trespassing" and that completes its dialogue with "I don't think that any word can explain a man's life" suggests that the authors mean no simple judgment can be final. The portrait of Kane that has emerged is contradictory and ambiguous. "The point of the picture," Welles has remarked, "is not so much the solution of the problem as its presentation."

The problem may have no solution but it does have a meaning. The structure of the film, while discouraging easy judgments, leads us down a path of widening insight. The newsreel surveys Kane's public career but does not penetrate to his soul. Thatcher's narrative offers us our first clue, hinting at matters of love, childhood, and innocence. Bernstein's story renders Kane sympathetically, suggesting that "Rosebud" may be "something he lost." Leland's narrative prickles with his urge to puncture Kane's reputation, but his invective doesn't obscure a further clue: "All he ever wanted was love." Finally, Susan's narrative demonstrates that Kane bought love from others because he had no love of his own to give. Thus we are led, step by step, to confront an ego bent on domination; like Elizabethan tragedy, the film proposes that action becomes an egotistical drive for power when not informed by love.

. . .

Part of Kane's love problem is bound up with his mother. Hinted at throughout, this is made explicit in the scene in which Kane, having just met Susan, talks with her in her room. Here, for the first time in a character's narrative, the snowstorm paperweight is seen—on Susan's dressing table, among faded childhood snapshots. Kane tells her he had been on his way to a warehouse "in search of my youth," intending to go through his dead mother's belongings: "You know, sort of a sentimental journey." But now, with Susan's reflection behind the paperweight, he decides to remain here; all the elements are present for a symbolic transfer of Kane's love to this new mother-figure. And when Susan tells him that her desire to sing was really her mother's idea, the transfer is complete: Kane quietly agrees that he knows how mothers are.

Kane seeks love from anyone—Leland, Bernstein, Emily, Susan, "the people of this state"—but the film traces a growing-apart, through imagery of separation, as Kane's life, from the moment he leaves home, becomes haunted by lovelessness. His relations with his wives typify this: the intimacy of the honeymoon supper yields to the distance of the long breakfast table and, eventually, to husband and wife shouting across the halls of Xanadu. The movement is from crowdedness (the busy *Inquirer* office) to emptiness (the hollow vaults of Xanadu); from cheerfulness (Kane as a young editor) to despair (after Susan has left); from true friendship (Bernstein and Leland) through gradually materialistic relationships (Emily and Susan) to sheerly mercenary companionship (Raymond); from a quick tempo (the liveliness of the *Inquirer's* crusades) to a funereal one (the picnic cortege and Kane's final, deadened walk); from self-sacrifice to selfishness; from the brash openness of youth to the cancerous privacy of "No Trespassing"; from intimate joking with Leland to shouts in a mausoleum and long silences before a huge fireplace. Kane's degeneration parallels these shifts in relationships: his contacts with people slough off in proportion to the accumulation of his material goods until, solitary and friendless, only cherishing a cheap snowstorm paperweight, he is engulfed by infinite extensions of his ego.

In the central portion of *Citizen Kane*, then, the various points-of-view balance the stream-of-consciousness of the opening and the detachment of "News on the March." Charles Foster Kane is observed from various angles, making the film more kaleidoscopic portrait than straightforward plot. But the matter is complicated because Kane's character changes with time, as does that of each narrator. Thus the clash of fact and bias, objectivity and prejudice, interweaving through the history of a personality, creates a world that is nearly as complex as reality and yet as unified as great art.

. . .

By now it should be clear that *Kane's* stylistic pyrotechnics are not just meaningless virtuosity, but rather aural and pictorial expressions of the tension between reality and imagination at the heart of the film. Objectively, the wide-angle lens renders every plane of a shot, from the nearest to the most distant, in sharp focus. Thus there is no stressing of one image by throwing its context out of focus; ambiguity increases when all characters and objects are equal in definition. As André Bazin puts it, "The uncertainty in which we find ourselves as to the spiritual key or interpretation we should put on the film is built into the very design of the image." There are scarcely a dozen true close-ups in the film, and most appear at the very beginning, as an abstract procession of images which contrasts with the spatial authenticity of the rest of the film. Montage, which stresses the juxtaposition of images more than the images themselves, always implies the shaping hand of a creator, but the compression of multiple meanings into one shot can seem to efface the director, giving the illusion of unarranged reality. Thus the compositional detachment of each shot corroborates the film's pull toward realism.

Keeping all the action in the frame may suggest a kind of objectivity, but camera angle belies the detachment by expressing attitudes toward the action. For instance, when Kane is a child, the viewpoint is usually that of the adult looking down. But as Kane's career progresses, he is often shot from an increasingly low angle, not only to indicate his growing power but also to isolate him against his background as he becomes more and more lonely. In Xanadu, though, Kane is again seen from a high angle which points out his smallness within the cavernous crypt he has erected. Within the objectivity of the single frame, Welles' angles (unlike, say, Hawks') suggest subjective bias and point-of-view.

Welles' *mise-en-scène* modulates the drama's flow with great subtlety, using angle to indicate patterns of domination. Recall the climactic scene when Kane confronts Boss Jim Gettys in Susan's apartment. Gettys' entrance is as thunderous as a kettledrum roll: Kane, Emily, and Susan are on the staircase, light is pouring out of the doorway, and quietly Gettys' silhouette steps into the shot; for once someone has the upper hand over Kane; Nemesis has caught up with the hero. (In Welles' Macbeth, Macduff storms out of a smoking beam of light on a similar mission.) Inside Susan's bedroom, the angles crisply build the tension. First, a shot frames Emily in the foreground, Susan in the middle ground, and Gettys and Kane facing each other deep in the shot. But as Gettys explains the power he has over Kane, he advances to the foreground, dwarfing his rival; Emily says that apparently Kane's decision has been made for him; Kane, in the distance, seems overpowered by circumstance. But when Kane decides to assert his will, the shot cuts to an opposite angle: he dominates the foreground, and Gettys, Susan, and Emily taper off into the background. Then, a head-on shot, with Kane in the center, Susan on the left and Gettys on the right, capsulizes his choice: he can save his mistress or fight his opponent. Welles' arrangement of actors in the frame and his timing of the cuts brilliantly articulate the drama of the scene. The material seems to be objectively observed (no close-ups or first-person points-of-view), but the structure of each shot and the pacing of the editing inject subjective attitudes.

Welles can also use the moving camera to efface the director's controlling hand by choreographing the material in fluid, unobtrusive patterns. Take, for instance, the scene in which the boy Charles is sent from home. (1) In long-shot we see the boy playing in the snow. (2) A snowball hits the sign over the porch. (3) The camera travels back from the boy in the snow, through the window as his mother closes it, and back from her, Thatcher, and Mr. Kane as they advance to the desk, where the papers are read and signed; the camera then follows them back to the window. (4) We are now outside the window, and after the camera travels back to the snowman and Charles, the scuffle between the boy and Thatcher takes place in the same shot. (5) A close-up of Charles and his mother closes the scene. In a sequence of several minutes, we have five shots, two of negligible length. Yet the shots seem realistically observed because Welles has intricately moved his actors and his camera; despite the complexity of the set-ups, we gain a sense of a reality—actual, unmanipulated, all of a piece.

Yet the moving camera can suggest the drift of subjective interest too, because it is also a tool of discovery. Again and again the camera probes like an inquisitive reporter, nosing relentlessly to the center of a scene, gradually stripping away extraneous dramatic matter. Welles' tracking shots imitate the process of investigation itself—a gradual narrowing of the field of inquiry—so that the progress *inward*, toward the heart of a mystery, becomes the characteristic camera movement. The opening dissolves which draw us deeper into Xanadu; the slow dolly up to the flashing "El Rancho" roof sign and then between the letters to the skylight; the imperceptible closing in on Bernstein as he begins his narrative; the diagonal descent to Susan and Kane meeting on the street; the sudden, curious rush to Susan's door when Kane shuts it; the traveling shot over the heads of the audience at Kane's speech; the implacable track to Kane and Emily standing at the door of Susan's house—all these are preparations for the portentous tracking shots through the costly rubbish of Xanadu, coasting slowly over Kane's belongings to settle on the Rosebud sled—the answer to the quest.

Welles' use of sound is indebted, intentionally or not, to Lang's *M* and Clair's *À Nous la Liberté*. In the latter film, a policeman outdoors saying, "We must all—" cuts to a teacher in a classroom saying, "—work." Welles called these "lightning mixes," in which the sound continues (although from a different source) while the scene cuts or dissolves to a new locale and time. A shot of Susan at the piano in her shabby rooming house dissolves to a shot of her, much better dressed, at a finer piano in a more elegant house, while she continues to play the same piece. Kane's applause immediately dissolves to a crowd's applause of Leland's harangue. Thatcher says to the child Kane, "Merry Christmas, Charles," the boy answers, "Merry Christmas—" and the story leaps ahead seventeen years to Thatcher saying, "And a Happy New Year." Leland's promise to a street crowd that "Charles Foster Kane . . . entered upon this campaign —" cuts to Kane himself in a huge auditorium bellowing, "—with one purpose only. . . ." Scenes Eisenstein would have linked by visual metaphor Welles links by the soundtrack; Eisenstein would have announced the presence of a manipulating directorial intelligence, while Welles suggests the interlocked imagery of mental-association processes.

We should not overlook Welles' celebrated *tours de force,* those moments of sheer cinematic pluck that everyone cherishes in *Kane*. When Kane, Leland, and Bernstein peer in the *Chronicle* window, the camera moves up to the picture of the *Chronicle* staff until it fills the screen; Kane's voice says, "Six years ago I looked at a picture of the world's greatest newspaper staff . . ." and he strides out in front of the same men, posed for an identical picture, a flashbulb explodes, and we are at the *Inquirer* party. Another famous set-piece is the breakfast-table sequence, in which the deterioration of Kane's marriage is traced in a number of brief scenes linked by a whirling effect (swish pans over the windows of the *Inquirer* building). The music pulsates in the background, rising in tension, and the mounting pace of the cutting gives impetus to the final surprises: Mrs. Kane reading the *Chronicle* and the length of the breakfast table.

These, then, are the techniques Welles drew on in *Kane*. Exciting in themselves, they coalesce into a unified style by expressing the film's juxtaposition of reality and imagination. The spatial and temporal unity of the deep-focus, the simultaneous dialogue, the reflections and chiaroscuro, the detached use of the moving camera, the intrusion of sounds from outside the frame—all increase the objectively realistic effect. These are correlatives for the way we seem to see and hear in life. The inquisitive camera movements, the angled compositions, the "lightning mixes" of sound and image—these suggest subjective attitudes and the workings of narrators' memories. They are stylistic equivalents for the way we seem to channel our thoughts in life. The cinematic traditions of Lumière and Méliès become surrogates for an epistemological tension. Here are the facts; here are subjective interpretations. Alone, neither has value. Can we then ever know "the" truth? Thompson's final remark " I don't think any word can explain a man's life," the enigma of the Rosebud sled, "No Trespassing," the black smoke drifting into a gray sky—these, finally, unmistakably, convey the film's answer.

At bottom, the film's reality/imagination tension radiates from the hero's own nature. *Citizen Kane* is a tragedy on Marlovian lines, the story of the rise and fall of an overreacher. Like Tamburlaine and Faustus, Kane dares to test the limits of mortal power; like them, he fabricates endless *personae* which he takes as identical with his true self; and, like them, he is a victim of the egotism of his own imagination.

Up to a point, Kane's career rises steadily. He is a rich, successful publisher, he has married well, he has a chance to become governor. But his flaw is that he sees love solely in terms of power. His friends, Leland and Bernstein, are also his employees; his wife Emily is the President's niece. He expands his idea of love to include "the people," his aspiration to public office is a confirmation of his confusion of love with power. Thus his liaison with Susan (whom he calls "a cross-section of the American public") represents the pathetic side of his desire, the need for affection which his mother aroused and which Emily could not gratify. Ironically, it is this weakness which undoes him, for in the end, Kane's immense vision of love as power falls tragically short of basic humanity.

The turning point of Kane's life is the confrontation with Gettys in Susan's room. It is the climax of his personal life (Emily or Susan, which will he choose?) and of his political career (the love of "the people" of the love of his family and mistress?). Surprisingly, Gettys turns out to be more sensitive and humane than Kane. He was led to blackmail Kane by the newspaper cartoons Kane printed of him, which humiliated him before his children and, significantly, his mother. Unlike Kane, Gettys distinguishes between attacking a man personally and attacking him politically; thus he gives Kane a chance ("more of a chance than he'd give me") to avoid personal embarrassment. Gettys assumes that Kane places the same value on personal relations that he does.

He is wrong. Up till now Kane has always defined himself by telling others what to do, by bossing Mr. Carter, Leland, Bernstein, Emily, and Susan. Now morality demands that Kane give in and for once define himself by placing others' welfare above his own. But Kane cannot relinquish the role of an autonomous power: "There's only one person who's going to decide what I'm going to do, and that's me." It is the voice of the bully, but also that of the tragic hero. By sacrificing others to his delusion of moral omnipotence, Kane commits his energy to an idea of himself that has become divorced from human values. How can he accept "the love of the people of this state" when he will not show love for his family and mistress? This refusal of imagination to recognize reality constitutes tragic recklessness, but Kane's punishment brings no recognition. Gettys is prophetic: "You're gonna need more than one lesson, and you're gonna get more than one lesson."

After his defeat at the polls, Kane's career declines. His image shattered, he constructs a new one: Susan's singing career. He announces, *"We're going to be a great opera star"*; as his alter ego, she may find the public acclaim in art that he couldn't find in politics. At the opera, Kane in the balcony dwarfs the tiny Susan onstage like a harsh god overseeing his creation. From singing lesson to opera rehearsal, Susan is not an identity in her own right, only an extension of himself. But again Kane fails to win the love of "the people"; the public's response to Susan's première is symbolized by the judicious grimace of the stagehand high in the flies. So, when Susan attempts suicide, Kane must change his *persona* again.

The next image Kane constructs is on a mammoth scale. He builds Xanadu, a miniature world, which he stocks with every kind of animal. This parody of God's act of creation gives a blasphemous dimension to Faustus-Kane's galactic vision of power. Yet in the end this god is swallowed up by his own universe. Since he can breathe no life into his creations, he gradually becomes an object like them. Appropriately, the last time we see Kane is as an *image:* a zombie moving stiffly against an endlessly receding tunnel of mirrors, mocking duplications of his own self-absorption. Dying, he can only clutch the icon of love and innocence: his last moment becomes a final assertion of imagination in the face of the ultimate reality of death.

from Raising *Kane*

PAULINE KAEL

Seeing the movie again recently, I liked the way it looked; now that the style no longer boded a return to the aestheticism of sets and the rigidly arranged figures of the German silents, I could enjoy it without misgivings. In the thirties, Jean Renoir had been using deep focus (that is, keeping

FROM "Raising *Kane*" by Pauline Kael. Copyright © 1971 by Pauline Kael. This material appeared originally in *The New Yorker* (February 27, 1971), pp. 47–48, 57, 58–60, and is now part of *The Citizen Kane Book*, which also includes the shooting script by Herman J. Mankiewicz and Orson Welles, published by Atlantic-Little, Brown Books. Copyright © 1971 by Bantam Books, Inc.

the middle range and the background as clear as the foreground) in a naturalistic way. The light seemed (and often was) "natural." You looked at a scene, and the drama that you saw going on in it was just part of that scene, and so you had the sense of discovering it for yourself, of seeing drama in the midst of life. This was a tremendous relief from the usual studio lighting, which forced your attention to the dramatic action in the frame, blurred the rest, and rarely gave you a chance to feel that the action was part of anything larger or anything continuous. In Welles' far more extreme use of deep focus, and in his arrangement of the actors in the compositions, he swung back to the most coercive use of artificial, theatrical lighting. He used light like a spotlight on the stage, darkening or blacking out the irrelevant. He used deep focus not for a naturalistic effect but for the startling dramatic effect of having crucial action going on in the background (as when Kane appears in a distant doorway). The difference between Renoir's style and Welles' style seems almost literally the difference between day and night. Welles didn't have (nor did he, at that time, need) the kind of freedom Renoir needed and couldn't get in Hollywood—the freedom to shoot outside the studio and to depart from the script and improvise. *Kane* is a studio-made film—much of it was shot in that large room at R.K.O. where, a few years earlier, Ginger Rogers and Fred Astaire had danced their big numbers. However, Welles had the freedom to try out new solutions to technical problems, and he made his theatrical technique work spectacularly. Probably it was the first time in American movies that Expressionism had ever worked for comic and satiric effects (except in bits of some of the early spoof horror films), and probably it would have been impossible to tell the *Kane* story another way without spending a fortune on crowds and set construction. Welles' method is a triumph of ingenuity in that the pinpoints of light in the darkness conceal the absence of detailed sets (a chair or two and a huge fire-place, and one thinks one is seeing a great room), and the almost treach-erously brilliant use of sound conceals the absence of crowds. We see Susan at the *deserted* cabaret; we see her from the back on the opera-house stage and we imagine that she is facing an audience; we get a sense of crowds at the political rally without seeing them. It was Welles' experi-ence both in the theatre and in radio that enabled him to produce a huge historical film on a shoestring; he produced the *illusion* of a huge historical film.

But, seeing *Kane* now, I winced, as I did the first time, at the empty virtuosity of the shot near the beginning when Kane, dying, drops the glass ball and we see the nurse's entrance reflected in the glass. I noticed once again, though without being bothered by it this time, either, that there was no one in the room to hear the dying Kane say "Rosebud." I was much more disturbed by little picky defects, like the pointless shot up to the bridge before the reporter goes into the hospital. What is strange about reseeing a movie that one reacted to fairly intensely many years ago is that one may respond exactly the same way to so many details and *be aware* each time of having responded that way before. I was disappointed once again by the clumsily staged "cute" meeting of Kane and Susan, which seemed to belong to a routine comedy, and I thought the early scenes with Susan were weak not just because while listening to her dull, sentimental singing Welles is in a passive position and so can't animate the scenes but—and mainly—because the man of simple pleasures who would find a dumb girl deeply appealing does not tie in with the personality projected by Orson Welles. (And as Welles doesn't project any sexual interest in either Kane's first wife, Emily, or in Susan, his second wife, we don't know how to interpret Susan's claim that he just likes her voice.) Most of the newspaper-office scenes looked as clumsily staged as ever, and the first appearance of Bernstein, Kane's business manager, arriving with a load of furniture, was still confusing. (He seems to be a junk dealer—probably because an earlier scene in *American* introducing him was eliminated.) I disliked again the attempt to wring humor out of the sputtering confusion of Carter, the old Dickensian editor. It's a scene like the ones Mankiewicz helped prepare for the Marx Brothers, but what was probably intended to make fun of a stuffed shirt turned into making fun of a helpless old man trying to keep his dignity, which is mean and barbarous. I still thought Susan became too thin a conception, and more shrill and shrewish than necessary, and, as Emily, Ruth Warrick was all pursed lips—a stereotype of refinement. I was still uncomfortable during the visit to Jed Leland in the hospital; Leland's character throughout is dependent on Joseph Cotten's obvious charm, and the sentimental-old-codger bit in this sequence is really a disgrace. The sequence plays all too well at a low conventional level—pulling out easy stops. I still didn't see the function of the sequence about Kane's being broke and losing control of his empire, since nothing followed from it. (I subsequently discovered that things weren't going well on the set at one point, and Welles decided to go back to this scene, which had been in an earlier draft and had then been eliminated. What it coördinated with was, unfortunately, not restored.) This sequence also has the most grating bad line in the movie, when Kane says, "You know, Mr. Bernstein, if I hadn't been very rich, I might have been a really great man."

What's still surprising is how well a novice movie director handled so many of the standard thirties tricks and caricatures—the device of the alternative newspaper headlines, for example, and the stock explosive, hand-waving Italian opera coach (well played by Fortunio Bonanova). The engineering—the way the sequences are prepared for and commented on by preceding sequences, the way the five accounts tie together to tell the story—seems as ingenious as ever; though one is aware that the narrators are telling things they couldn't have witnessed, one accepts this as part of the convention. The cutting (which a reading of the script reveals to have been carried out almost exactly as it was planned) is elegantly precise, and some sequences have a good, sophomoric musical-comedy buoyancy.

What had changed for me—what I had once enjoyed but now found almost mysteriously *beautiful*—was Orson Welles' performance. An additional quality that old movies acquire is that people can be seen as they once were. It is a pleasure we can't get in theatre; we can only hear and read descriptions of past fabulous performances. But here in *Kane* is the young Welles, and he seems almost embarrassed to be exposed as so young. Perhaps he *was* embarrassed, and that's why he so often hid in extravagant roles and behind those old-man false faces. He seems unsure of himself as the young Kane, and there's something very engaging (and surprisingly *human*) about Welles unsure of himself; he's a big, overgrown, heavy boy, and rather sheepish, one suspects, at being seen as he is. Many years later, Welles remarked, "Like most performers, I naturally prefer a live audience to that lie-detector full of celluloid." Maybe his spoiled-baby face was just too nearly perfect for the role, and he knew it, and knew the hostile humor that lay behind Mankiewicz's putting so much of him in the role of Hearst the braggart self-publicist and making Kane so infantile. That statement of principles that Jed sends back to Kane and that Kane then tears up must surely refer to the principles behind the co-founding of the Mercury Theatre by Welles and Houseman. Lines like Susan's "You're not a professional magician, are you?" may have made Welles flinch. And it wasn't just the writer who played games on him. There's the scene of Welles eating in the newspaper office, which was obviously caught by the camera crew, and which, to be "a good sport," he had to use. Welles is one of the most self-conscious of actors—it's part of his rapport with the audience—and this is what is so nakedly revealed in this role, in which he's playing a young man his own age and he's insecure (and with some reason) about what's coming through. Something of the young, unmasked man is revealed in these scenes—to be closed off forever after.

Welles picks up assurance and flair as Kane in his thirties, and he's also good when Kane is just a little older and jowly. I think there's no doubt that he's more sure of himself when he's playing this somewhat older Kane, and this is the Kane we remember best from the first viewing—the brash, confident Kane of the pre-election-disaster period. He's so fully—classically—American a showoff one almost regrets the change of title. But when I saw the movie again it was the younger Kane who stayed with me—as if I had been looking through a photograph album and had come upon a group of pictures of an old friend, long dead, as he had been when

I first met him. I had almost forgotten Welles in his youth, and here he is, smiling, eager, looking forward to the magnificent career that everyone expected him to have.

.   .   .

Welles is right, of course, about Rosebud—it *is* dollar-book Freud. But it is such a primitive kind of Freudianism that, like some of the movie derivations from Freud later in the forties—in *The Seventh Veil,* for instance—it hardly seems Freudian at all now. Looking for "the secret" of a famous man's last words is about as phony as the blind-beggar-for-luck bit, yet it does "work" for some people; they go for the idea that Rosebud represents lost maternal bliss and somehow symbolizes Kane's loss of the power to love or be loved. The one significant change from Hearst's life— Kane's separation from his parents—seems to be used to explain Kane, though there is an explicit disavowal of any such intention toward the end. Someone says to Thompson, "If you could have found out what Rose-bud meant, I bet that would've explained everything." Thompson replies, "No, I don't think so. No. Mr. Kane was a man who got everything he wanted, and then lost it. Maybe Rosebud was something he couldn't get or something he lost. Anyway, it wouldn't have explained anything. I don't think any word can explain a man's life. No. I guess Rosebud is just a piece in a jigsaw puzzle, a missing piece."

Nevertheless, the structure of the picture—searching for the solution to a mystery—and the exaggerated style make it appear that Rosebud *is* the key to Kane's life, and the public responds to what is presented dramatically, not to the reservations of the moviemakers. Rosebud has become part of popular culture, and people remember it who have forgotten just about everything else in *Citizen Kane;* the jokes started a week before the movie opened, with a child's sled marked "Rosebud" dragged onstage in the first act of *Native Son,* and a couple of years ago, in *"Peanuts,* Lucy walked in the snow with a sled and Snoopy said "Rosebud ? ? ? " The Rosebud of Rosebud is as banal as Rosebud itself. It seems that as a child Herman Mankiewicz had had a sled, which may or may not have carried the label "Rosebud" (his family doesn't remember); he wasn't dramatically parted from the sled, but he once had a bicycle that was stolen, and he mourned that all his life. He simply put the emotion of the one onto the other.

.   .   .

As the newspaper business and the political maneuvering were pared away, the personal material took on the weight and the shape of the solution to a mystery. Even so, if the movie had been directed in a more matter-of-fact, naturalistic style, Thompson's explanation that Rosebud was just a piece in a jigsaw puzzle would have seemed quite sensible. Instead,

Welles' heavily theatrical style overemphasized the psychological explanation to such a point that when we finally glimpse the name on the sled we in the audience are made to feel that we're in on a big secret—a revelation that the world missed out on. However, Rosebud is so cleverly worked into the structure that . . . it is enjoyable as beautiful tomfoolery even while we are conscious of it as "commercial" mechanics. I think what makes Welles' directorial style so satisfying in this movie is that we are constantly aware of the mechanics—that the pleasure *Kane* gives doesn't come from illusion but comes from our enjoyment of the dexterity of the illusionists and the working of the machinery. *Kane,* too, is a clock that laughs. *Citizen Kane* is a film made by a very young man of enormous spirit; he took the Mankiewicz material and he played with it, he turned it into a magic show. It is Welles' distinctive quality as a movie director— I think it is his genius—that he never hides his cleverness, that he makes it possible for us not only to enjoy what he does but to share his enjoyment in doing it. Welles's showmanship is right there on the surface, just as it was when, as a stage director, he set *Julius Caesar* among the Nazis, and set *Macbeth* in Haiti with a black cast and, during the banquet scene, blasted the audience with a recording of the "Blue Danube Waltz"—an effect that Kubrick was to echo (perhaps unknowingly?) in *2001.* There is something childlike—and great, too—about his pleasure in the magic of theatre and movies. No other director in the history of movies has been so open in his delight, so eager to share with us the game of pretending, and Welles' silly pretense of having done everything himself is just another part of the game.

Welles' magic as a director (at this time) was that he could put his finger right on the dramatic fun of each scene. Mankiewicz had built the scenes to end at ironic, dramatic high points, and Welles probably had a more innocently brazen sense of melodramatic timing than any other movie director. Welles also had a special magic beyond this: he could give *élan* to scenes that were confused in intention, so that the movie seems to go from dramatic highlight to highlight without lagging in between. There doesn't appear to be any waste material in *Kane,* because he charges right through the weak spots as if they were bright, and he almost convinces you (or *does* convince you) that they're shining jewels. Perhaps these different kinds of magic can be suggested by two examples. There's the famous sequence in which Kane's first marriage is summarized by a series of breakfasts, with overlapping dialogue. The method was not new, and it's used here on a standard marriage joke, but the joke is a basic good joke, and the method is honestly used to sum up as speedily as possible the banality of what goes wrong with the marriage. This sequence is adroit, and Welles brings out the fun in the material, but there's no *special* Wellesian magic in it—except, perhaps, in his own acting. But in the cutting from the sequence of Kane's first meeting with Susan (where the writing supplies almost no clue to why he's drawn to this particular twerp of a girl beyond his finding her relaxing) to the political rally, Welles' special talent comes into play. Welles directs the individual scenes with such flourish and such *enjoyment of flourish* that the audience reacts as if the leap into the rally were clever and funny and logical, too, although the connection between the scenes isn't established until later, when Boss Jim Gettys uses Susan to wreck Kane's political career. As a director, Welles is so ebullient that we go along with the way he wants us to feel; we're happy to let him "put it over on us." Given the subject of Hearst and the witty script, the effect is of complicity, of a shared knowingness between Welles and the audience about what the movie is about. Kane's big smile at the rally seals the pact between him and us.

Until Kane's later years, Welles, as Kane, has an almost total empathy with the audience. It's the same kind of empathy we're likely to feel for smart kids who grin at us when they're showing off in the school play. It's a beautiful kind of emotional nakedness—ingenuously exposing the sheer love of play-acting—that most actors lose long before they become "professional." If an older actor—even a very good one—had played the role, faking youth for the young Kane the way Edward Arnold, say, sometimes faked it, I think the picture might have been routine. Some people used to say that Welles might be a great director but he was a bad actor, and his performances wrecked his pictures. I think just the opposite—that his directing style is such an emanation of his adolescent love of theatre that his films lack a vital unifying element when he's not in them or when he plays only a small part in them. He needs to be at the center. *The Magnificent Ambersons* is a work of feeling and imagination and of obvious effort—and the milieu is much closer to Welles' own background than the milieu of *Kane* is—but Welles isn't in it, and it's too bland. It feels empty, uninhabited. Without Orson Welles' physical presence—the pudgy, big prodigy, who incarnates egotism—*Citizen Kane* might (as Otis Ferguson suggested) have disintegrated into vignettes. We feel that he's making it all happen. Like the actor-managers of the old theatre, he's the man onstage running the show, pulling it all together.

DE SICA

the bicycle thief

Although Vittorio De Sica has had a long distinguished career as both an actor and a director, his reputation among critics and many filmgoers declined in the 1960's. He was virtually ignored as a subject of serious criticism for that decade—in which, ironically, he was entrusted by commercial interests with some rather large-scale productions. *The Garden of the Finzi-Continis* (1971), however, served as a reminder of how powerful a filmmaker De Sica can be. The Chaplinesque ability to capture the essence of a character in a few gestures or a revealing glance is an elusive art in the era of sound, but De Sica probably exhibits this skill to a greater degree than any other contemporary filmmaker.

The Bicycle Thief is the best-known example of the most important movement in the post-World War II cinema: neorealism. Neorealism is usually said to have begun even before the end of the war, with Luchino Visconti's *Ossessione* (1943); the movement attracted international attention with Roberto Rossellini's *Open City* (1945) and *Paisan* (1946), De Sica's *Shoeshine* (1946), and Visconti's *La Terra Trema* (1948); and with *The Bicycle Thief* it became fashionable and was imitated everywhere. The chief characteristic of neorealist cinema is its attempt to depict simply, accurately, and without romantic illusions, the lives of ordinary people who are representative of great masses of people who engage in similar activities. Cesare Zavattini, who collaborated on the scripts of many De Sica films, including *The Bicycle Thief*, claimed that the ideal neorealist film would consist of ninety consecutive minutes in the routine of some worker. This extreme idea seems ludicrous within the framework of the conventional story-film, but it emphasizes the political commitment of neorealism to the plight of the anonymous man in an industrialized world.

Ricci, the protagonist of *The Bicycle Thief*, is a worker who is obviously typical of the masses in search of work at a time of high unemployment; but in the process of presenting a *typical* case, De Sica and other neorealist directors elevated the stature of the individual by concentrating on his capacity for suffering and on his sensitivity to the situations that he encounters. The audience is swept up in Ricci's problem of finding his stolen bicycle so that he can keep his new job. If this is no more than a typical predicament that might have been shared by a million Italians in 1948, why should the audience of today still care deeply about it? We care because De Sica has made his hero, Ricci, not merely the average man—but a symbol of the capacity for heroism within all men who find themselves in a tragic predicament. Also, in typical neorealist fashion, De Sica used non-actors in the major roles. One result of this is the memorable performance of Lamberto Maggiorani as Antonio Ricci, an accomplishment that the best theater director could never achieve using a non-actor in a stage role. If the neorealist ideal of capturing truth on film were pursued literally, the consecutive filming of a non-actor in any situation would result in a non-film. De Sica avoided this and, instead, extracted a great performance by skillfully constructing highly dramatic sequences and by photographing a naturally expressive face at just the right moment in relation to the dramatic tensions generated within the environment. The impact of the film is, in fact, a matter of editing— the same sort of editing that enabled early directors like Pudovkin and Eisenstein to use non-actors in their films. Since editing is the artificial arrangement of selected images of reality, neorealism, as it approaches great art and yet retains the basic impulses of its original spirit, sacrifices absolute factual fidelity for the higher truth involved in the artistic portrayal of human behavior.

Because the basis of neorealism is the depiction of an individual experiencing life in ordinary surroundings, the movement gave great impetus to on-location filming. The use of city environments not only served to fix the characters in direct visual relationship with one main source of their problems, but sometimes provided a means for structuring the experience into an artistic unity. *The Bicycle Thief* takes us on a journey through Rome, not the "Eternal City" of the tourists' guidebooks but the universal city of workers, people struggling for survival or preoccupied with their private interests. As Ricci and his son Bruno move around the city, the discrepancy between their preoccupation with finding the bicycle and the indifference of other people, who have their own problems, creates a compelling sense of pathos and alienation. At the same time, the city reveals similar cases of hardship, and the apprehended thief, who is even worse off than Ricci, is not arrested. Viewers have often remarked that De Sica's films typically make us sympathetic toward all the characters, even the outwardly villainous ones. This results from his emphasis on environment as the basic source of man's inhumanity to his fellow man. The overcrowding and poverty of city living provoke men to acts that they would ordinarily not commit. *The Bicycle Thief* ends with a desperate and unsuccessful attempt by Ricci to recover his loss by stealing someone else's bicycle; but here, De Sica leads us to a point of understanding: compassion replaces condemnation and Ricci is not prosecuted. The journey through the inner city illuminates the fundamental tenets of brotherhood.

Father and Son in De Sica's The Bicycle Thief

BARBARA H. SOLOMON

One of the most sensitively rendered relationships ever depicted in film is that between Antonio Ricci and his son Bruno in *The Bicycle Thief*. Throughout their painful and disappointing search for the stolen bicycle, their reactions to each other frequently become the focus of the scenes and the source of the film's emotional intensity.

In terms of plot, De Sica dramatizes Ricci's struggle to earn a living for his family and his desperate search for the all-important bicycle, which has been stolen from him on his first day at work. Without the bicycle he will lose his new job as a plasterer of posters, for which he has waited two years. The search takes place, for the most part, against the background of an indifferent and even hostile environment. But in addition to this outer world, Ricci and Bruno constitute their own sensitive inner world, in which they fulfill each other's needs. Occasionally, there is even a subtle exchanging of the roles of father and son, as the boy often comes to the aid of the man.

The boy is both the bewildered child gazing up at the adults and in need of his father's protection, as well as the knowing "old man" who is bitter about the ways of the world and who tries to teach some of them to his innocent, childlike father. Twice during the film Bruno actually saves Ricci from the serious consequences of a crowd's hostility.

Their relationship is depicted as clearly in the visual composition as it is in the dialogue. Significantly, our first glimpse of Bruno is through the spokes of the bicycle wheel he has been polishing. He points furiously to a dent in the bicycle, insisting that it was not there when the bicycle was pawned. Although he is angered by the carelessness of those at the pawn-shop, his anger is directed even more at the easygoing attitude of his father, who failed to notice the dent or to complain about it. Then Ricci, the man of the family and Bruno, his small imitator, prepare to leave home for the day. The father puts the packet containing his lunch in the front pocket of his overalls; Bruno does the same with his smaller packet. In another demonstration of his responsible nature, Bruno closes the shutters as he leaves the room.

In the extended lyrical scene that follows, Ricci rides through the streets of Rome in the early dawn with the boy perched on the bar of the bicycle. Around them are other people also going to work: many on buses and trolleys, some on bicycles. The visual images of this sequence convey a joyous sense of freedom and motion as father and son travel together on their bicycle. Ricci leaves Bruno at a gas station, where the boy immediately sets up some cans next to the gas pump. It is Saturday, and the boy, who is only about ten, has gone to his job. Later, when Ricci returns to pick up his son, we see how reluctant he is to admit that the bicycle has been stolen: Bruno is not merely a child who will be disappointed; he is a little man to whom Ricci is accountable.

That evening, when Ricci goes back to get Bruno, we see Ricci standing in a long line waiting for the bus. The others in the line are resentful and rude to one another, and there is much shoving as those outside attempt to push onto the already overcrowded bus. There are just too many people everywhere—in this sequence as well as in earlier sequences at the employment agency where Ricci got his job and at the pawnshop where he and his wife Maria pawned their linen in order to redeem the bicycle. Even at the workers' meeting where Ricci goes to look for Biaocco for help in his search for the bicycle, he is hushed by the crowd, which is annoyed at his interruption of a speech about the impossibility of finding jobs. It is against this backdrop of Ricci's need and the world's indifference that father and son make their way throughout the film.

Bruno, who accompanies the four adults as they go to look for the bicycle in a bicycle market, is frequently filmed looking up at the men, watching what they do, and imitating them. He gains their approval when, in a discussion of the make and serial number of the bicycle, he immediately tells them that it is a Fides and reels off the number; for this he receives an affectionate pat on the head from Biaocco and his father's promise of a celebration if the bicycle is found. As the men separate so that they can scrutinize the individual parts that are being offered for sale, Bruno is assigned to look at the bells and bicycle pumps on display. While the adults can browse without interference, Bruno is chased away at one point and returns to his father's side. Then, as he continues to look, a close-up reveals the concentration and determination with which he carries out his part of the search. In this sequence, De Sica stresses the fact that Bruno is very much the small boy who depends upon his father. While separated from the others, who are all occupied with the search, Bruno attracts the attention of a homosexual, who offers to buy him a bell. Although he ignores a repeated offer, he does not seem able to cope with the man's overtures. A few moments later, Ricci effectively dispels the danger by casually taking his son's hand and reminding him to stay close.

Although Ricci has been aided during this early Sunday morning by several concerned and sympathetic men, he and Bruno are soon entirely on their own once again as they arrive at another marketplace in the city displaying bicycles and parts. Here, their bad luck is made obvious as a downpour scatters the bicycle vendors and drenches them both. Bruno, with his somewhat large jacket pulled over his head for protection, now seems more like a bent old man than a child. As he follows his father to seek shelter on the sidewalk, he falls on the wet pavement, and he is once again the pitiable child in short pants. His father, who had not seen him fall, asks what is the matter and gives him a handkerchief to wipe his legs. Here, in the image of a bruised or scraped knee, De Sica symbolizes the vulnerability of childhood. Yet shortly after this, Bruno fiercely asserts himself by pushing one of a group of priests waiting for the rain to let up, who is crowding him because of his small size.

The next scenes, in which Ricci and Bruno chase the old man who is their only link to the bicycle thief, once again emphasize the boy's attempt to fulfill a man's role. Ricci stops pulling Bruno along with him in order to run faster; behind him, Bruno runs as fast as his short legs will carry him. When it seems that the old man has successfully evaded them, father and son split up in order to check the nearby streets. Bruno stops to urinate, but when he is called by Ricci, who has again caught sight of the old man, Bruno jumps at the sound of his father's summons and begins to run while still rebuttoning his pants: he is needed. When they catch up with the old man, Ricci collars him. Imitating his father, Bruno grabs hold of the old man's coat, but the boy is scolded by the man, who tells him that he ought to be ashamed of his behavior. Throughout this sequence Bruno and his father have operated as a team, sharing the task of racing down the side streets until they caught up with the old man. Bruno's action indicates his approval of his father's method of dealing with this accomplice of thieves.

After they track the old man to a church, where he eludes them, Bruno becomes the object of our sympathy as a child who twice suffers the blows of exasperated adults. In the first instance, Bruno, acting immediately on his suspicion that the old man may be hiding in the confessional, pulls the curtain aside and finds himself facing an angry priest, who strikes him on the head. He does not react to the blow, and he and Ricci continue their frantic search for a few minutes longer. Then, as they walk away from the church, dejected at having lost the one man who might have led them to the thief, Bruno implies that his father was at fault for losing sight of the old man and that he, Bruno, would not have let him get away. Depressed and irritated, Ricci strikes him. This time Bruno's reaction is more typical of a child and is extremely touching: he cries, tells his father to go on without him, and threatens to tell his mother.

By this point, De Sica has subtly shifted the emphasis of *The Bicycle Thief* from the search for the bicycle to the delicate and complex relationship between father and son. Ricci, now truly sorry for having lost his temper because of his frustration, still continues to assert his parental authority. Eager to end this confrontation about the unjust blow, he orders Bruno to wait for him on the bridge while he looks for the old man. Bruno, once more the dependent child, is shown in a medium shot, still tearful but sitting obediently on the bridge. At some distance from the bridge, Ricci hears cries about someone drowning. Overwhelmed by fear and guilt, he races toward the river calling Bruno's name. Realizing that the figure being carried from the water is not his son, Ricci catches sight of Bruno on the bridge at the top of a long flight of stairs. De Sica handles their reunion with a brilliant shot of the father breathlessly climbing the stairs as he rushes toward the boy. Throughout the film the boy has either followed his father or has been called to come to him, but here the adult rushes to the child, who is never aware of his father's anguish or relief.

The tenderness Ricci feels is expressed by his concern that Bruno will catch a cold because he has taken his jacket off. He attempts to help the boy put it back on, but is rejected. In the next few minutes, the father makes a concerted effort to win back his son's affection and trust. First, he notices how tired Bruno is and suggests that he sit down. Then, as a truckload of soccer fans passes by, he asks Bruno whether he thinks Modena is a good team. Bruno replies, shaking his head negatively, but he is still very withdrawn. Finally, Ricci asks the boy whether he is hungry and whether he could eat a pizza. The first question is answered with a positive nod and the second with an enthusiastic expression. Although there is some pathos in the sight of Ricci counting his money before they go off to eat, the overriding impression is one of relief from tension. The search for the bicycle is over for the time being, and father and son are about to share a pleasurable experience.

In a poignant scene in the restaurant, we see Ricci's discomfort upon learning that it is a more expensive place than he expected and that it does not serve pizza. De Sica here captures two views of Ricci simultaneously: the waiter's obvious disdain for this poorly dressed man who is so gauche as to order pizza and Bruno's pleased and excited admiration for his father. Ricci chooses this occasion to pour some of the wine he had ordered into Bruno's glass. The boy is both happy and surprised to be given his first glass of wine, and considering the manly concern and sense of responsibility that he has shown, it seems quite fitting. The bond between father and son that is here being celebrated is reinforced by Ricci's reference to Maria's not knowing about her son's having this drink and reminds us of Bruno's earlier threat to tell her that his father had struck him.

Bruno's joy during the meal in the restaurant, however, is not quite complete. He is made self-conscious as he watches a well-to-do family at a nearby table enjoying numerous delicacies with no concern for the cost. Bruno and the child at this table exchange glances, and finally even Ricci notices the family's extravagance as the waiter serves them champagne and cakes. He speculates on the amount of money one would have to earn to eat in that style, and the sum he mentions startles Bruno.

In this sequence Bruno is again both boy and man. Many of his gestures, especially his difficulty in cutting and eating his meal, remind us that he is a child. He struggles with his food while his father casually cuts and consumes his own portion, oblivious to the boy's problem. Then Ricci begins to compute the salary he would have received in his new job, and as Ricci pushes the pencil and paper over and tells his son to add the figures, Bruno becomes his father's confidant and partner.

Resuming their search, they eventually catch sight of the thief who had ridden away on the bicycle; his guilty behavior makes it clear that he has recognized Ricci too. The chase begins once more, but only Ricci manages to gain entrance to the brothel into which the thief has disappeared. Bruno appears forlorn, perhaps even bewildered, at having been kept outside the gate of the house. As soon as Ricci returns, Bruno rushes up to him and they move along the street with the thief firmly in Ricci's custody now. When they stop, close to the thief's house, a crowd begins to gather. Bitter and angry, Ricci loudly accuses the thief while holding and shaking him. Ricci is too busy questioning his long-sought quarry to notice his surroundings, but Bruno is not. The camera records the boy's worried expression as a hostile crowd gathers around them. Complicating matters, and making the onlookers who seem to be friends and neighbors of the thief even more aggressive toward Ricci, is the epileptic seizure suffered by the thief. The crowd, now extremely belligerent, turns on Ricci, who with his back to the wall has grabbed a piece of wood to defend himself. Only Bruno's timely appearance with a policeman prevents the mob from continuing the attack on Ricci.

The policeman, accompanied by Ricci and Bruno, searches the single room inhabited by the thief and his family, but finds no evidence. As in the scene when Ricci first reported the theft of the bicycle, his encounter with the police is discouraging rather than helpful. This time, the policeman indicates that in order for any action to be taken, Ricci would have to catch the thief in the act of stealing or catch him in possession of the bicycle. Ricci, who now well knows that he will never be able to do either of those things, walks despairingly down the street to the jeers and threats of the crowd.

As Bruno watches his father with concern, De Sica breaks the pattern of numerous scenes in which the two have walked together—now Ricci seems to have forgotten all about the boy. While they walk toward the stadium, Bruno tries to keep up, but he has trouble getting safely across the street, and he must run in order to match his father's longer strides. When Ricci finally stops, Bruno, panting, sits on the curb to rest. Ricci sits beside him. In a typical shot of Bruno, he looks up at his father, studying his face and waiting for instructions.

Ricci's desperate decision to steal a bicycle himself in order to keep his job is clearly communicated by his actions in the next few minutes. He gives Bruno some money and orders him to take the trolley to a certain spot and wait for him there. Bruno runs toward the car, but he reaches it a moment too late and the car pulls away without him. The audience realizes immediately that Bruno will be present when his father becomes a thief. He sees Ricci being pulled from the stolen bicycle and reviled by the crowd that has gathered. The boy recovers Ricci's hat and wipes it off. He struggles to reach his father at the center of this angry crowd. Throughout this scene, tears have been running down Bruno's face and he has been calling one word: "Papa."

When he finally reaches Ricci, Bruno holds onto his father's legs as the camera details his misery in a medium-close shot seen from Ricci's perspective. Once again, as in the sequence outside the thief's house, Bruno's presence saves his father. The owner of the bicycle, along with several witnesses to the theft, had been making plans to take Ricci to a nearby police station, but after watching the father and son, the owner loses all enthusiasm for the task. In spite of the resentment and desire for revenge expressed by members of the crowd, he decides to allow Ricci to go. Bruno dries his face with a handkerchief, using a gesture similar to that used earlier by Ricci when he had wiped his face in the rain.

This scene of Ricci's despair and degradation is intensified by Bruno's presence. The father has attempted to commit the same despicable crime that had victimized him. Only Bruno knows of the hardship and the inevitable loss of the wonderful job that led Ricci to make this desperate attempt to steal, but at the same time, the boy's presence is the final humiliation for the father. He has failed to find the bicycle and he has failed to retain the dignity of his manhood.

The closing shots of *The Bicycle Thief* record Ricci's loss and Bruno's sorrow for his father's suffering. Again the boy looks up at his father's face, watching him fight to gain control over his emotions. There is a single note of hope as the defeated man walks away with the boy beside him. Bruno is shown in a close-up as he reaches out and takes his father's hand. Ricci responds with his hand, and in a long shot, we see the two of them move down the street. Much has been lost, but much remains.

Neorealism and Pure Cinema: *The Bicycle Thief*

ANDRÉ BAZIN

What seems to me most astonishing about the Italian cinema is that it appears to feel it should escape from the aesthetic impasse to which neorealism is said to have led. The dazzling effects of 1946 and 1947 having

FROM *What Is Cinema?* Vol. II by André Bazin. Essays selected and translated by Hugh Gray. Originally published by the University of California Press; reprinted by permission of The Regents of the University of California.

faded away, one could reasonably fear that this useful and intelligent re-action against the Italian aesthetic of the superspectacle and, for that matter, more generally, against the technical aestheticism from which cinema suffered all over the world, would never get beyond an interest in a kind of superdocumentary, or romanticized reportage. One began to realize that the success of *Roma Città Aperta, Paisà,* or *Sciuscià* was in-separable from a special conjunction of historical circumstances that took its meaning from the Liberation, and that the technique of the films was in some way magnified by the revolutionary value of the subject. Just as some books by Malraux or Hemingway find in a crystallization of journal-istic style the best narrative form for a tragedy of current events, so the films of Rossellini or De Sica owed the fact that they were major works, masterpieces, simply to a fortuitous combination of form and subject mat-ter. But when the novelty and above all the flavor of their technical crudity have exhausted their surprise effect, what remains of Italian "neorealism" when by force of circumstances it must revert to traditional subjects: crime stories, psychological dramas, social customs? The camera in the street we can still accept, but doesn't that admirable nonprofessional act-ing stand self-condemned in proportion as its discoveries swell the ranks of international stars? And, by way of generalizing about this aesthetic pessimism: "realism" can only occupy in art a dialectical position—it is more a reaction than a truth. It remains then to make it part of the aesthe-tic it came into existence to verify. In any case, the Italians were not the last to downgrade their "neorealism." I think there is not a single Italian director, including the most neorealist, who does not insist that they must get away from it.

.   .   .

With *Ladri di Biciclette* [*The Bicycle Thief*] De Sica has managed to escape from the impasse, to reaffirm anew the entire aesthetic of neo-realism.

Ladri di Biciclette certainly *is* neorealist, by all the principles one can deduce from the best Italian films since 1946. The story is from the lower classes, almost populist: an incident in the daily life of a worker. But the film shows no extraordinary events such as those which befall the fated workers in Gabin films. There are no crimes of passion, none of those grandiose coincidences common in detective stories which simply transfer to a realm of proletarian exoticism the great tragic debates once reserved for the dwellers on Olympus. Truly an insignificant, even a banal incident: a workman spends a whole day looking in vain in the streets of Rome for the bicycle someone has stolen from him. This bicycle has been the tool of his trade, and if he doesn't find it he will again be unemployed. Late in the day, after hours of fruitless wandering, he too tries to steal a bicycle. Apprehended and then released, he is as poor as ever, but now he feels the shame of having sunk to the level of the thief.

Plainly there is not enough material here even for a news item: the whole story would not deserve two lines in a stray-dog column. One must take care not to confuse it with realist tragedy in the Prévert or James Cain manner, where the initial news item is a diabolic trap placed by the gods amid the cobble stones of the street. In itself the event contains no proper dramatic valence. It takes on meaning only because of the social (and not psychological or aesthetic) position of the victim. Without the haunting specter of unemployment, which places the event in the Italian society of 1948, it would be an utterly banal misadventure. Likewise, the choice of a bicycle as the key object in the drama is characteristic both of Italian urban life and of a period when mechanical means of transportation were still rare and expensive. There is no need to insist on the hundreds of other meaningful details that multiply the vital links between the scenario and actuality, situating the event in political and social history, in a given place at a given time.

The techniques employed in the *mise en scène* likewise meet the most exacting specifications of Italian neorealism. Not one scene shot in a studio. Everything was filmed in the streets. As for the actors, none had the slightest experience in theater or film. The workman came from the Breda factory, the child was found hanging around in the street, the wife was a journalist.

These then are the facts of the case. It is clear that they do not appear to recall in any sense the neorealism of *Quattro passi fra le nuvole, Vivere in Pace,* or *Sciuscià.* On the face of it then one should have special reasons for being wary. The sordid side of the tale tends toward that most debatable aspect of Italian stories: indulgence in the wretched, a systematic search for squalid detail.

If *Ladri di Biciclette* is a true masterpiece, comparable in rigor to *Paisà,* it is for certain precise reasons, none of which emerge either from a simple outline of the scenario or from a superficial disquisition on the technique of the *mise en scène.*

The scenario is diabolically clever in its construction; beginning with the alibi of a current event, it makes good use of a number of systems of dramatic coordinates radiating in all directions. *Ladri di Biciclette* is certainly the only valid Communist film of the whole past decade precisely because it still has meaning even when you have abstracted its social significance. Its social message is not detached, it remains immanent in the event, but it is so clear that nobody can overlook it, still less take exception to it, since it is never made explicitly a message. The thesis implied is wondrously and outrageously simple: in the world where this workman lives, the poor must steal from each other in order to survive. But this thesis is never stated as such, it is just that events are so linked together that they have the appearance of a formal truth while retaining an anecdotal quality. Basically, the workman might have found his bicycle in the middle of the film; only then there would have been no film. (Sorry to have bothered you, the director might say; we really did think he would never find it, but since he has, all is well, good for him, the performance is over, you can turn up the lights.) In other words, a propaganda film would try to prove that the workman could not find his bicycle, and that he is inevitably trapped in the vicious circle of poverty. De Sica limits himself to showing that the workman cannot find his bicycle and that as a result he doubtless will be unemployed again. No one can fail to see that it is the accidental nature of the script that gives the thesis its quality of necessity; the slightest doubt cast on the necessity of the events in the scenario of a propaganda film renders the argument hypothetical.

Although on the basis of the workman's misfortune we have no alternative but to condemn a certain kind of relation between a man and his work, the film never makes the events or the people part of an economic or political Manicheism. It takes care not to cheat on reality, not only by contriving to give the succession of events the appearance of an accidental and as it were anecdotal chronology but in treating each of them according to its phenomenological integrity. In the middle of the chase the little boy suddenly needs to piss. So he does. A downpour forces the father and son to shelter in a carriageway, so like them we have to forego the chase and wait till the storm is over. The events are not necessarily signs of something, of a truth of which we are to be convinced, they all carry their own weight, their complete uniqueness, that ambiguity that characterizes any fact. So, if you do not have the eyes to see, you are free to attribute what happens to bad luck or to chance. The same applies to the people in the film. The worker is just as deprived and isolated among his fellow trade unionists as he is walking along the street or even in that ineffable scene of the Catholic "Quakers" into whose company he will shortly stray, because the trade union does not exist to find lost bikes but to transform a world in which losing his bike condemns a man to poverty. Nor does the worker come to lodge a complaint with the trade union but to find comrades who will be able to help him discover the stolen object. So here you have a collection of proletarian members of a union who behave no differently from a group of paternalistic bourgeois toward an unfortunate workman. In his private misfortune, the poster hanger is just as alone in his union as in church (buddies apart, that is—but then who your buddies are is your own affair). But this parallel is extremely useful because it points up a striking contrast. The indifference of the trade union is normal and justified because a trade union is striving for justice not for charity. But the cumbersome paternalism of the Catholic "Quakers" is unbearable, because their eyes are closed to his personal tragedy while they in fact actually do nothing to change the world that is the cause of it. On this score the most successful scene is that in the storm under the porch when a flock of Austrian seminarians crowd around the worker and his son. We have no valid reason to blame them for chattering so much and still less for talking German. But it would be difficult to create a more *objectively* anticlerical scene.

Clearly, and I could find twenty more examples: events and people are never introduced in support of a social thesis—but the thesis emerges fully armed and all the more irrefutable because it is presented to us as something thrown in into the bargain. It is our intelligence that discerns and shapes it, not the film. De Sica wins every play on the board without ever having made a bet.

This technique is not entirely new in Italian films and we have elsewhere stressed its value at length both apropos of *Paisà* and of *Allemania Anno Zero*, but these two films were based on themes from either the Resistance or the war. *Ladri di Biciclette* is the first decisive example of the possibility of the conversion of this kind of objectivity to other, similar subjects. De Sica and Zavattini have transferred neorealism from the Resistance to the Revolution.

Thus the thesis of the film is hidden behind an objective social reality which in turn moves into the background of the moral and psychological drama which could of itself justify the film. The idea of the boy is a stroke of genius, and one does not know definitely whether it came from the script or in the process of directing, so little does this distinction mean here any more. It is the child who gives to the workman's adventure its ethical dimension and fashions, from an individual moral standpoint, a drama that might well have been only social. Remove the boy, and the story remains much the same. The proof: a *résumé* of it would not differ in detail. In fact, the boy's part is confined to trotting along beside his father. But he is the intimate witness of the tragedy, its private chorus. It is supremely clever to have virtually eliminated the role of the wife in order to give flesh and blood to the private character of the tragedy in the person of the child. The complicity between father and son is so subtle that it reaches down to the foundations of the moral life. It is the admiration the child feels for his father and the father's awareness of it which gives its tragic stature to the ending. The public shame of the worker, exposed and clouted in the open street, is of little account compared with the fact that his son witnessed it. When he feels tempted to steal the bike, the silent presence of the little child, who guesses what his father is thinking, is cruel to the verge of obscenity. Trying to get rid of him by sending him to take the streetcar is like telling a child in some cramped apartment to go and wait on the landing outside for an hour. Only in the best Chaplin films are there situations of an equally overwhelming conciseness.

In this connection, the final gesture of the little boy in giving his hand to his father has been frequently misinterpreted. It would be unworthy of the film to see here a concession to the feelings of the audience. If De Sica gives them this satisfaction it is because it is a logical part of the drama. This experience marks henceforth a definite stage in the relations between father and son, rather like reaching puberty. Up to that moment the man has been like a god to his son; their relations come under the heading of admiration. By his action the father has now compromised them. The tears they shed as they walk side by side, arms swinging, signify their despair over a paradise lost. But the son returns to a father who has fallen from grace. He will love him henceforth as a human being, shame and all. The hand that slips into his is neither a symbol of forgiveness nor of a childish act of consolation. It is rather the most solemn gesture that could ever mark the relations between a father and his son: one that makes them equals.

It would take too long to enumerate the multiple secondary functions of the boy in the film, both as to the story structure and as to the *mise en scène* itself. However, one should at least pay attention to the change of tone (almost in the musical sense of the term) that his presence introduces into the middle of the film. As we slowly wander back and forth between the little boy and the workman we are taken from the social and economic plane to that of their private lives, and the supposed death by drowning of the child, in making the father suddenly realize the relative insignificance of his misfortune, creates a dramatic oasis (the restaurant scene) at the heart of the story. It is, however, an illusory one, because the reality of this intimate happiness in the long run depends on the precious bike. Thus the child provides a dramatic reserve which, as the occasion arises, serves as a counterpoint, as an accompaniment, or moves on the contrary into the foreground of the melodic structure. This function in the story is, furthermore, clearly observable in the orchestration of the steps of the child and of the grownup. Before choosing this particular child, De Sica did not ask him to perform, just to walk. He wanted to play off the striding gait of the man against the short trotting steps of the child, the harmony of this discord being for him of capital importance for the understanding of the film as a whole. It would be no exaggeration to say that *Ladri di Biciclette* is the story of a walk through Rome by a father and his son. Whether the child is ahead, behind, alongside—or when, sulking after having had his ears boxed, he is dawdling behind in a gesture of revenge—what he is doing is never without meaning. On the contrary, it is the phenomenology of the script.

It is difficult, after the success of this pairing of a workman and his son, to imagine De Sica having recourse to established actors. The absence of professional actors is nothing new. But here again *Ladri di Biciclette* goes further than previous films. Henceforth the cinematic purity of the actors does not derive from skill, luck, or a happy combination of a subject, a period, and a people. Probably too much importance has been attached to the ethnic factor. Admittedly the Italians, like the Russians, are the most naturally theatrical of people. In Italy any little street urchin is the equal of a Jackie Coogan and life is a perpetual *commedia dell' arte*. However, it seems to me unlikely that these acting talents are shared equally by the Milanese, the Neapolitans, the peasants of the Po, or the fishermen of Sicily. Racial difference apart, the contrasts in their history, language, and economic and social condition would suffice to cast doubt on a thesis that sought to attribute the natural acting ability of the Italian people simply to an ethnic quality. It is inconceivable that films as different as *Paisà, Ladri di Biciclette, La Terra Trema,* and even *Il Cielo sulla Palude* could share in common such a superbly high level of acting. One could conceive that the urban Italian has a special gift for spontaneous histrionics, but the peasants in *Cielo sulla Palude* are absolute cavemen beside the farmers of *Farrebique*. Merely to recall Rouquier's film in connection with Genina's is enough at least in this respect to relegate the experiment of the French director to the level of a touchingly patronizing effort. Half the dialogue in *Farrebique* is spoken off-stage because Rouquier could never get the peasants not to laugh during a speech of any length. Genina in *Cielo sulla Palude,* Visconti in *La Terra Trema,* both handling peasants or fishermen by the dozen, gave them complicated roles and got them to recite long speeches in scenes in which the camera concentrated on their faces as pitilessly as in an American studio. It is an understatement to say that these temporary actors are good or even perfect. In these films the very concept of actor, performance, character has no longer any meaning. An actorless cinema? Undoubtedly. But the original meaning of the formula is now outdated, and we should talk today of a cinema without acting, of a cinema of which we no longer ask whether the character gives a good performance or not, since here man and the character he portrays are so completely one.

We have not strayed as far as it might seem from *Ladri di Biciclette*. De Sica hunted for his cast for a long time and selected them for specific characteristics. Natural nobility, that purity of countenance and bearing that the common people have. . . . He hesitated for months between this person and that, took a hundred tests only to decide finally, in a flash and by intuition on the basis of a silhouette suddenly come upon at the bend of a road. But there is nothing miraculous about that. It is not the unique excellence of this workman and this child that guarantees the quality of their performance, but the whole aesthetic scheme into which they are fitted. When De Sica was looking for a producer to finance his film, he finally found one, but on condition that the workman was played by Cary Grant. The mere statement of the problem in these terms shows the absurdity of it. Actually, Cary Grant plays this kind of part extremely well, but it is obvious that the question here is not one of playing of a part but of getting away from the very notion of doing any such thing. The worker had to be at once as perfect and as anonymous and as objective as his bicycle.

This concept of the actor is no less "artistic" than the other. The performance of this workman implies as many gifts of body and of mind and as much capacity to take direction as any established actor has at his command. Hitherto films that have been made either totally or in part without actors, such as *Tabú, Thunder over Mexico, Mother,* have seemingly been successes that are either out of the ordinary or limited to a certain genre. There is nothing on the other hand, unless it be sound prudence, to prevent De Sica from making fifty films like *Ladri di Biciclette.* From now on we know that the absence of professional actors in no way limits the choice of subject. The film without names has finally established its own aesthetic existence. This in no sense means that the cinema of the future will no longer use actors: De Sica who is one of the world's finest actors would be the first to deny this. All it means is that some subjects handled in a certain style can no longer be made with professional actors and that the Italian cinema has definitely imposed these working conditions, just as naturally as it imposed authentic settings. It is this transition from an admirable *tour de force,* precarious as this may be, into an exact and infallible technique that marks a decisive stage in the growth of Italian neorealism.

With the disappearance of the concept of the actor into a transparency seemingly as natural as life itself, comes the disappearance of the set. Let us understand one another, however. De Sica's film took a long time to prepare, and everything was as minutely planned as for a studio superproduction, which, as a matter of fact, allows for last-minute improvisations, but I cannot remember a single shot in which a dramatic effect is born of the shooting script properly so called, which seems as neutral as in a Chaplin film. All the same, the numbering and titling of shots does not noticeably distinguish *Ladri di Biciclette* from any ordinary film. But their selection has been made with a view to raising the limpidity of the event to a maximum, while keeping the index of refraction from the style to a minimum.

This objectivity is rather different from Rossellini's in *Paisà* but it belongs to the same school of aesthetics. One may criticize it on the same grounds that Gide and Martin du Garde criticized romantic prose—that it must tend in the direction of the most neutral kind of transparency. Just as the disappearance of the actor is the result of transcending a style of performance, the disappearance of the *mise en scène* is likewise the fruit of a dialectical progress in the style of the narrative. If the event is sufficient unto itself without the direction having to shed any further light on it by means of camera angles, purposely chosen camera positions, it is because it has reached that stage of perfect luminosity which makes it possible for an art to unmask a nature which in the end resembles it. That is why the impression made on us by *Ladri di Biciclette* is unfailingly that of truth.

If this supreme naturalness, the sense of events observed haphazardly as the hours roll by, is the result of an ever-present although invisible system of aesthetics, it is definitely the prior conception of the scenario which allows this to happen. Disappearance of the actor, disappearance of *mise en scène?* Unquestionably, but because the very principle of *Ladri di Biciclette* is the disappearance of a story.

The term is equivocal. I know of course that there is a story but of a different kind from those we ordinarily see on the screen. This is even the reason why De Sica could not find a producer to back him. When Roger Leenhardt in a prophetic critical statement asked years ago "if the cinema is a spectacle," he was contrasting the dramatic cinema with the novel-like structure of the cinematic narrative. The former borrows from the theater its hidden springs. Its plot, conceived as it may be specifically for the screen, is still the alibi for an action identical in essence with the action of the classical theater. On this score the film is a spectacle like a play. But on the other hand, because of its realism and the equal treatment it gives to man and to nature the cinema is related, aesthetically speaking, to the novel.

Without going too far into a theory of the novel—a debatable subject—let us say that the narrative form of the novel or that which derives from it differs by and large from the theater in the primacy given to events over action, to succession over causality, to mind over will. The conjunction belonging to the theater is "therefore," the particle belonging to the novel is "then." This scandalously rough definition is correct to the extent that it characterizes the two different movements of the mind in thinking, namely that of the reader and that of the onlooker. Proust can lose us in a madeleine, but a playwright fails in his task if every reply does not link our interest to the reply that is to follow. That is why a novel may be laid down and then picked up again. A play cannot be cut into pieces. The total unity of a spectacle is of its essence. To the extent that it can realize the physical requirements of a spectacle, the cinema cannot apparently escape the spectacle's psychological laws, but it has also at its disposal all the resources of the novel. For that reason, doubtless, the cinema is congenitally a hybrid. It conceals a contradiction. Besides, clearly, the progression of the cinema is toward increasing its novel-like potential. Not that we are against filmed theater, but if the screen can in some conditions develop and give a new dimension to the theater, it is of necessity at the expense of certain scenic values—the first of which is the physical presence of the actor. Contrariwise, the novel at least ideally need surrender nothing to the cinema. One may think of the film as a supernovel of which the written form is a feeble and provisional version.

This much briefly said, how much of it can be found in the present condition of the cinematographic spectacle? It is impossible to overlook the spectacular and theatrical needs demanded of the screen. What remains to be decided is how to reconcile the contradiction.

The Italian cinema of today is the first anywhere in the world to have enough courage to cast aside the imperatives of the spectacular. *La Terra Trema* and *Cielo sulla Palude* are films without "action," in the unfolding of which, somewhat after the style of the epic novel, no concession is made to dramatic tension. Things happen in them each at its appointed hour, one after the other, but each carries an equal weight. If some are fuller of meaning than others, it is only in retrospect. We are free to use either "therefore" or "then." *La Terra Trema,* especially, is a film destined to be virtually a commercial failure, unexploitable without cuts that would leave it unrecognizable.

That is the virtue of De Sica and Zavattini. Their *Ladri di Biciclette* is solidly structured in the mold of a tragedy. There is not one frame that is not charged with an intense dramatic power, yet there is not one either which we cannot fail to find interesting, its dramatic continuity apart.

The film unfolds on the level of pure accident: the rain, the seminarians, the Catholic Quakers, the restaurant—all these are seemingly interchangeable, no one seems to have arranged them in order on a dramatic spectrum. The scene in the thieves' quarter is significant. We are not sure that the man who was chased by the workman is actually the bicycle thief, and we shall never know if the epileptic fit was a pretense or genuine. As an "action" this episode would be meaningless had not its novel-like interest, its value as a fact, given it a dramatic meaning to boot.

It is in fact on its reverse side, and by parallels, that the action is assembled—less in terms of "tension" than of a "summation" of the events. Yes, it *is* a spectacle, and what a spectacle! *Ladri di Biciclette,* however, does not depend on the mathematical elements of drama, the action does not exist beforehand as if it were an "essence." It follows from the pre-existence of the narrative, it is the "integral" of reality. De Sica's supreme achievement, which others have so far only approached with a varying degree of success or failure, is to have succeeded in discovering the cinematographic dialectic capable of transcending the contradiction between the action of a "spectacle" and of an event. For this reason, *Ladri di Biciclette* is one of the first examples of pure cinema. No more actors, no more story, no more sets, which is to say that in the perfect aesthetic illusion of reality there is no more cinema.

Vittorio De Sica's Vision of Cycles

GIAN-LORENZO DARRETTA

> Each stands alone on the heart of the earth
> pierced by a ray of sunlight:
> and suddenly it's evening.
> Salvatore Quasimodo, *Ed é subito sera*

Salvatore Quasimodo's celebration of evening and the end of the day reflects the influence of the crepuscular school of Italian poetry, "i crepuscolari," which found its major mood in twilight. The modern Italian poets, not unlike Dante and the earlier Italian poets, were enamored of the endings of things. These poets wrote of evening, the close of the day; Sunday, the end of the week; autumn, the death of the year. But their vision of endings or deaths was never depressing; rather, they expressed a typical form of Italian optimism—with endings and deaths will come new beginnings and new births. They believed that after the night of *Inferno* comes the sunburst of *Paradiso*, that disintegration and degeneration lead to a new wholeness and regeneration. Out of the destruction of war, the new Italians looked toward reconstruction. It was this vision, which has its foundations in the cycles of nature, that was expressed cinematically in the postwar films of such Italian neorealists as Vittoria De Sica and Federico Fellini.

To describe the "twilight" mood of these films as pessimistic is to impose upon them a concept from another country. By the same token, Italian realism has its roots in the romantic and the poetic; it is not the realism of France, Germany, or the United States. So it would be most accurate to describe a film such as De Sica's *The Bicycle Thief* as a work of optimistic, poetic realism. The structure of *The Bicycle Thief* reveals its optimistic theme: man always endures. Bruno and his father walk into a twilight that will lead to a new dawn. The structure of the film is realistic, as it is built around three mornings and three evenings of a weekend. It begins on a sunny Friday and ends on a Sunday at twilight. Inextricable from this basic realism is the poetry that lies beneath its surface: twilight gives birth to a new day; Sunday generates a new week.

Friday. Saturday. Sunday. De Sica's artistic structure is neatly tripartite, which, of course, is the perfect form for any Italian craftsman weaned on Dante's *Commedia*. It allows a dialectical rhythm that expresses futurity, progression, ongoing optimism. It is a cyclical vision that allows for a fusion of opposites, for a synthesis of beginnings and endings that become new oppositions and new beginnings. "Twilight" is the thesis, "dawn" is the antithesis, the "new day" is the synthesis; and the dialectic moves onward to a new procession of days, weeks, months, seasons, years.

Cycles form the major movements of De Sica's film. These movements are exemplified by the bicycles, the rhythms of nature, the revolutions of life. Ricci offers the key to the interpretation of De Sica's cycles when he says, "Everything sorts itself out, except death." To grasp the meaning of this statement the viewer must recall the extremities, the beginning and ending, of *The Bicycle Thief*.

The film begins on Friday morning, with Ricci seeking a job at the government employment office. He is told that he can have a job if he has a bicycle. The formula is neat: Ricci needs a bicycle for the job; he needs the job to survive and to keep his family together. But reality is never that neat. Once Ricci's bicycle has been stolen, it takes on an importance that transcends surface reality, and the film becomes an odyssey as father and son search for their lost property. This journey takes them through realistic scenes in a police station, a political party headquarters, marketplaces, a church, a mission soup-kitchen, a fortune-teller's flat, ghetto streets, a government brothel, the gates of a soccer stadium.

For De Sica, such realism is only a starting point. Like the Italian poets, the neorealist filmmaker moves from stark realism into the forms of poetry. His vision is hierophantic: it always penetrates beneath the surface of things to the mystery below. The real always reveals the supernatural, and mystery is inextricable from matter. Therefore, De Sica needs no extraneous symbolism. His camera observes and uses the mystery of reality that is revealed to it. Within the hierophantic vision, Ricci's bicycle becomes the equivalent of all of Ricci's needs. The bicycle is a "Fides," a popular brand, but "Fides" translates as "Faith." In Ricci and Bruno's odyssey to find the "Fides," they are thwarted by an old man who happens to be carrying a can of tomatoes labeled "Circe," which is also a popular brand name. Ricci's family name itself means more when it is translated: it means "Riches." Beyond all this, De Sica's camera compounds the personal story of one family into a story of many families by showing shelf after shelf of linens in the pawnshop and row upon row of bicycles at the black market, which reveal that the Riccis' plight is the plight of many.

At the end of De Sica's film the major cycle has run its course. Ricci begins and ends with no job. The sheets that had been pawned to redeem the bicycle are also lost. Hence, the family ends with no sheets, no bicycle, no source of income. Yet, the family is still together. Ricci and Bruno walk into the twilight of a Sunday. The family has been stripped of its meager material wealth. But in a cyclical vision this degeneration only presages regeneration. De Sica's camera shows that what breaks down is built up again. In his film day breaks down into night, night breaks down into day. Sunshine gives way to a downpour of rain, but the rain gives way to sunshine. Sunday night yields to Monday morning and a new week. The end of one experience leads to the beginning of another. "Everything sorts itself out, except death." It is only death that can end the cycles of life.

De Sica emphasizes the point that cycles must inevitably run their course with the episode of the fortune-teller, Signora Santona. La Santona mouths trite epigrams: "Your son will rise from his bed before the leaves fall. . . . That means that your son will be better by autumn." She has told Maria that Ricci will find a job, but Ricci's wisdom tells him that life works itself out with no interference from the outside. He says to Maria, "How can you, a woman with two children and with a head on your shoulders, be taken in by this foolishness . . . these frauds. . . . As if these witches had any control over people's lives. . . . It's just idiotic." Eventually, however, out of sheer desperation, Ricci seeks help from the fortune-teller in locating his bicycle. Again, La Santona mouths general-ities: "Your bicycle. . . . What do you want me to tell you, my son? I can't see what I can tell you. . . . I can only tell you what I see. . . . Listen . . . either you will find it immediately or you will never find it. . . . Understand?" Though Ricci has in a sense found a job, La Santona's prophecy that he would proves erroneous, because she cannot help him retrieve the bicycle that is necessary for the job; therefore he still has no job. The natural cycle of life cannot be interfered with from the outside: "Everything sorts itself out."

The father and son motif of De Sica's film is also developed cyclically. At first Bruno has faith in his father. However, when Ricci loses the old man who might have been able to lead them to the thief, Bruno criticizes his father's tactics. Ricci slaps Bruno, temporarily severing their bond. Then, relieved that the drowning boy he hears shouts about is not Bruno, and eager to make amends for the unjust blow, Ricci takes his son to dinner. In the café their bond is reestablished. Ricci treats Bruno as an equal, letting him drink wine and involving him in the family finances by having him add up what Ricci's salary would be if he had a bicycle to work with. It is in this scene, after Bruno's faith in his father has been restored, that Ricci expresses his philosophy: "Everything sorts itself out, except death." Toward the end of the film, when Bruno witnesses his father's attempt to steal a bicycle, he again comes close to losing faith in his father. By now, however, their bond has become too strong to break. The last image is of father and son walking hand in hand into the crowded street as twilight is descending. This scene is a repetition of their walk home after Ricci's bicycle has been stolen, a sequence that had begun at dawn with Ricci and Bruno elatedly setting out for work on the bicycle. With a dawn sky behind them, they ride the bicycle toward the camera. But on the way home on Saturday evening, the bicycle is gone, and Ricci and Bruno walk dejectedly away from the camera into a twilight sky. When the film ends, on Sunday evening, they walk away into twilight again. The rhythms of life are similar to the rhythms of nature: Things come and go, begin and end and begin again.

In accordance with De Sica's vision it would be more accurate, although less euphonious, to translate his Italian title, *Ladri di biciclette*, literally as *The Thieves of Bicycles*. De Sica's film is about "thieves" not "a thief." The story is meant to compound itself, to demonstrate that other people experience cycles similar to Ricci's. In the beginning, there is "a bicycle thief" who steals Ricci's bicycle; in the end, Ricci becomes "a bicycle thief" himself. His attempt at thievery occurs after he has condemned the entire ghetto of Via Panico with the words, "You're all thieves . . . all of you!" Ricci comes to realize that the situation of the young man who stole his bicycle is as desperate as his own. The "thief" is apparently an epileptic; he is poor; he has no job. Ricci—and the viewer—becomes aware that many men in postwar Italy have been reduced to the status of "bicycle thief." The man who is the victim of Ricci's own thievery is also aware of this. He sees the weeping Bruno tugging on his father's leg, sees the plight of a poor, jobless family man, and decides not to press charges against this "thief": "Let's just forget it."

The ending of *The Bicycle Thief*, though it shows Bruno and Ricci walking away with no job and no bicycle, is not in the least pessimistic. The viewer knows that Bruno and Ricci will walk continually in and out of new experiences until death—and only death—ends the cycles. The bicycle is gone, but life is not. The Italian neorealist filmmaker always sees hope for man. Twilight is only the prelude to dawn. De Sica's vision of the cycles in the life of a common laborer reveals that poetry is eternally inextricable from reality.

BERGMAN

THE SEVENTH SEAL

CREdiTs

The Seventh Seal (Sweden, 1957)
Swedish title: *Det sjunde inseglet*
Directed by Ingmar Bergman from the screenplay by Bergman, based on his
  one-act play, *Trämalning (Painting on Wood)*.
Produced by Svensk Filmindustri
Distributor (16 mm): Janus Films

Assistant director: Lennart Ohlsson
Photography: Gunnar Fischer
Sets: P. A. Lundgren
Costumes: Manne Lindholm
Music: Erik Nordgren

Main performers:
Max von Sydow (*The knight,
  Antonius Blok*)
Gunnar Björnstrand (*The squire, Jöns*)
Bengt Ekerot (*Death*)
Nils Poppe (*Jof*)
Bibi Andersson (*Mia*)
Inga Gill (*Lisa*)

Maud Hansson, (*The witch*)
Inga Landgré (*The knight's wife,
  Karin*)
Bertil Anderberg (*Raval*)
Erik Strandmark (*Skat*)
Anders Ek (*The monk*)
Ake Fridell (*The smith*)

Length: 96 minutes

Ingmar Bergman established an international reputation with *The
Seventh Seal* (1957), *Wild Strawberries* (1957), *The Magician* (1958), and
The Virgin Spring (1960). Since then he has become possibly the most
widely respected intellectual artist in the Western cinema. The release of
the annual Bergman film is always regarded as a special occasion in international film circles. Within Sweden, Bergman has always been successful enough commercially so that since his career began at the close of the
Second World War, he has been able to work steadily, averaging more
than one film a year. And he has been fortunate in being able to work
with many of the same performers and crew in several films: thus, even
his lesser films are characterized by the highest levels of acting and
technical proficiency.

Bergman inaugurated a new era for the cinema of ideas with *The
Seventh Seal* and continued to lead the way in such later films as *Through
a Glass Darkly* (1961), *Winter Light* (1963), *The Passion of Anna* (1970),
and *The Touch* (1971), in all of which intellectual characters discuss ideas
in highly literate speech. In spite of his literary skill, his films never ap-

pear to be mere filmed theater. Other directors have, like Bergman, come to the cinema from the theater and have attempted to apply the techniques of dramatic art (which is almost entirely verbal) to film; inevitably, the result seems to be dull, talky films. Bergman's dramatic sense, however, is primarily visual rather than verbal, and each of his several major films is memorable for its visual imagery. In fact, the intellectual framework of his films is sustained more by the imagery than by the dialogue. The basis of Bergman's art is the development of intricate psychological studies and provocative philosophical issues through the presentation of concrete situations.

The Seventh Seal and subsequent films of his "middle period" dealt with the general subject of the search for values in the modern world. What seemed at first so striking about *The Seventh Seal* was its overt theological orientation within a medieval setting so unfamiliar that it virtually demanded allegorical interpretation. Religious motifs have never thrived in the cinema unless they were sentimentalized, as in the epics of Cecil DeMille, which posed no theological problems. Carl Dreyer's rather astounding film, *Ordet* (1955), is one exception, but Dreyer never had Bergman's vast audience. After the initial enthusiastic reception of *The Seventh Seal*, some critics claimed that the theological matters presented were either defects in the film or unintelligible mysteries. Other critics insisted that *Wild Strawberries* had the advantage over the previous film because the setting was contemporary and the ponderous intellectual questioning was not as extensive. Nevertheless, the occasional negative critiques of *The Seventh Seal* have failed to convince very many filmgoers that the undeniable visual power of this film is diminished by the intensity of its intellectual concerns.

The landscape of *The Seventh Seal* is a ravaged world. From the beginning, when the knight and his squire come upon a corpse on a beach as they return from the futile slaughter of the Crusades to a despairing country stricken by the plague, death seems to dominate the spirits of men. Murder, rape, theft, all forms of irresponsible conduct, characterize this as a world calling for judgment; and the reading, toward the end of the film, of the biblical verses about the opening of the seventh seal indicates that a negative judgment has indeed been passed. Within a world of daily disasters, the disillusioned knight desires to know whether any affirmation is plausible, whether any feeling of faith is sensible. His cynical squire has abandoned all hope, but neither man has any intention of disavowing his instinctive humanistic principles, even though he has not discovered any rational basis for a life of honor and integrity. They have wasted ten years in support of the Crusades, a cause they now consider false, but the knight has returned only to begin a new quest: the search for a source of affirmation in a barren world. The negation of life is personified in the character of Death, a traditional figure of allegory, who comes to claim the life of the knight. As dissatisfied as he is, the knight realizes that should he die in his present state, his whole life will have been meaningless; before he dies he must perform some meaningful action that will prove the possibility of positive values even within a world on the verge of ruin. The dramatized conflict between the knight and Death occurs over a game of chess, after the knight convinces his antagonist to give him the chance of saving his life should he win the contest, though a defeat seems inevitable. This delaying tactic eventually enables the knight to succeed in performing an action that saves the lives of two innocent people and thus provides him with the evidence he needs that it is indeed possible within each man's experience to affirm life, even in a world of death.

The resolutions reached in *The Seventh Seal,* as in any other Bergman film, seem tentative rather than final. The structure of his films and their philosophical probings direct our thoughts more toward the intellectual process than toward the solutions of any dilemmas.

Milieu and Texture in *The Seventh Seal*

PETER COWIE

The Seventh Seal (Det sjunde inseglet), is regarded by many critics as an achievement secondary to that of *Wild Strawberries*. Yet in none of his other films does Bergman appear to be so involved in the drama as in *The Seventh Seal*. The intellectual dilemmas discussed in this film seem to reflect the inmost problems of the artist himself. In addition to this, the work has three intrinsic qualities which, to my mind, make it the richest expression of Bergman's genius. As a purely historical film, it convinces to a degree rarely equalled in the cinema, and perhaps only then by the vintage films of the Japanese, Mizoguchi and Kurosawa; as a demonstration of the wedding of technique to content it is also excellent (the dreams which are such a large part of *Wild Strawberries* make it to a certain degree easier to film than *The Seventh Seal*); and the script is both economical and profound, foreboding and poetic. It is drawn from a short play written by Bergman many years before, called "A fresco" (Trämalning). With *The Seventh Seal* Bergman enters a stage of true maturity.

The film opens dramatically with a choir singing very loudly and intensely as a predatory bird hovers against a louring sky. Then it is suddenly quiet and we see a Knight, Antonius Blok (Max von Sydow), and his Squire, Jöns (Gunnar Björnstrand), sprawled asleep on a rocky beach. It is dawn. A voice reads a brief passage from the Book of Revelations, which puts the title of the film into context. The Knight awakes and washes himself in the sea. Bergman's establishment of atmosphere almost defies description here: by using high aerial shots from the cliffs above the beach, by shooting at exactly the right stage of dawn, he achieves a marked feeling of desolation. Suddenly Death (Bengt Ekerot) appears. Bergman escapes theatricality by disguising his arrival on the beach by means of a cut so that the figure is all at once standing a few paces from the Knight, clad in black from head to toe, his face cold and white by contrast. "Are you ready?" he asks the Knight, who replies "My body is, but I am not." The Knight is weary after a decade of futile Crusading. As his wife says when she meets him later, "Somewhere in your eyes, somewhere in your face, is that boy who went away so many years ago." But his spirit is still hopeful: Blok has been disillusioned but he is sure life must evince some significance. He is an acutely sensitive man and this is why—allegorically—he alone (save the visionary Jof) can see Death before

FROM *Antonioni, Bergman, Resnais* (1963) by Peter Cowie, pp. 83–90. Reprinted by permission of A. S. Barnes & Company, Inc.

the Apocalypse. He "is plagued, not so much by the prospect of death, as with the knowledge that he can neither kill God within him nor find a belief that God exists, either now or in an after life."* "We must make an idol of our Fear and call it God", he says in a subsequent scene with Death.

Blok delays Death by challenging him to a game of chess, and this symbolic contest continues at intervals as a theme throughout the film. The scene then dissolves to the hills along which Blok and Jöns ride slowly on their homeward journey (it is now midmorning: the action of the film, like the best of Bergman's works, takes only 24 hours).

> *Between a strumpet's legs to lie*
> *That's the place for such as I*

sings the Squire cynically. Jöns represents the captious and hedonistic among us, who believe that life is short and only occasionally sweet. He provides a fitting contrast to the Knight, even though the attitude of both men at the last is similar. At the start of the film the Squire is jovial and fearless, the Knight troubled at his "inability to get an inner contact with people and with life":† at the end, the former, though still stoical, is profoundly disturbed by the scenes of horror and death he has witnessed; the latter is slightly less anguished because he has recorded one positive victory over Death (cf. below). Jöns stops to ask the way of a man seated beside the path. He is a corpse in a black cowl. This is the first shock for the Squire. He merely tells Blok that the man was "most eloquent"— doubly ironic, for the corpse brings home swiftly to Jöns the ravages of the plague.

The scene changes as the Knight and Squire ride past a caravan, where Jof (Nils Poppe), his wife Mia (Bibi Andersson), small son Mikael, and Skat (Erik Strandmark) are sleeping. They are a troupe of wandering players, and their purpose in *The Seventh Seal* is to contrast with the Knight and his Squire. Jof and Mia (surely the scriptural connotations of their names and that of their child are not accidental) are simple beings who escape Death in the end because they never question God's existence or love. Theirs is an implicit faith in the beauty of life which relates them to other Bergman characters such as Sara in *Wild Strawberries* and Simson in *The Face*. Jof is a visionary who suddenly sees the Virgin walking with her child in an idyllic garden, and later perceives Death playing chess with the Knight. He also dreams that Mikael will be a great juggler and perform the one impossible trick—to make a ball stand still in the air.

The Knight and his Squire meet this family at a small village where they are performing, but beforehand there are two important incidents.

* Colin Young: *Film Quarterly*, Spring, 1959.
† Max von Sydow, quoted by Marie Seton: *Painter & Sculptor*, Spring 1960.

Firstly, Blok enters a church and confesses his doubts and fears to a priest who turns out to be Death. As the Knight realises that he has been duped, he is fired with fresh courage: "This is my hand", he says ardently, "I can move it, feel the blood pulsing through it. The sun is still high in the sky and I, Antonius Blok, am playing chess with Death". It is one of those masterly moments in Bergman's work when in a single image he epitomises a host of feelings and, above all, the unquenchable spirit of man (Töre's uprooting of the birch-tree in *The Virgin Spring* is a comparable instance). As Eugene Archer comments, "Death's deception (as priest) demonstrates the conspiracy of the natural and social world to prevent man from achieving knowledge".* Secondly, a short distance farther on, Jöns discovers a seminarist, Raval [Bertil Anderberg], robbing a dead man and trying to rape a serving-girl (Gunnel Lindblom). Raval—"Doctor Mirabilis, Coelestis et Diabolis" as Jöns calls him sarcastically—had urged the Knight to embark on a Crusade, so that he and his kind could indulge their thieving instincts. He is perhaps the most unattractive ecclesiastical figure in Bergman's *oeuvre,* active, lecherous witness to the unethical advantage which the ministers of the Church took of most men's naïvety in the Middle Ages. It is quite appropriate that Raval should later be stricken hideously by the plague which he and his associates regard as an instrument of divine disfavour.

In the next village, Jof, Mia, and Skat perform a farce which is contemptuously received by the onlookers. While Skat (dressed as Pan) creeps behind the waggon to seduce the wife of Plog, the blacksmith, Jof and Mia are pelted with bad fruit. Artistry is spurned in this doomed age. What frightens everyone is the prospect of hell-fire and this is shown in the ensuing scene, when a band of flagellants stumbles through the village while a Monk screams, "Do you know, you fools, that you will die today or tomorrow, or the next day, because all of you are doomed!" Bergman's fertility of imagination and eye for detail have rarely been in greater evidence than here. The smoke from the censers, the skulls carried aloft, the cross with its anguished, ascetic Christ, the half-naked penitents who lash each other's backs with spasmodic, jerky movements, all fuse into what has been described as a "kind of burlesque horror close to Brueghel,"† but which is probably closer still to Bosch. Bergman shoots some of the scene from a high set-up that lends to the picture the breadth and depth required to emphasise the agony of the procession. Then, as the flagellants move out of the village, their wailing suddenly dies away and by a cunning dissolve Bergman creates the impression that they have disappeared into the barren ground, perhaps symbolising the futility of their superstitious fervour.

---

* *Film Quarterly,* Summer 1959.
† Henri Agel: *Les Grands Cinéastes,* p. 291.

In a nearby inn Raval accuses Jof of being connected with the disappearance of Plog's wife and takes advantage of the drunkenness and latent sadism of the crowd to make him dance like a bear on the table. Again Bergman builds up an atmosphere of unmitigated horror: he uses cuts from close-ups of the various exultant faces around the table (contrasting with the naked fear registered on Jof's features) to low-angle shots of beer-mugs being banged rhythmically on the table, and of firebrands being flicked at Jof's legs to force him to jump higher. One critic has claimed that this "comic dance becomes a crucifixion,"* and although I do not feel that the sequence is at any time comic in tone, the reference to the Crucifixion may have some validity in that Raval, the priest, is driving Jof, a symbol of innocence, to death (also Jof holds out his arms horizontally as on a cross). The scene is interrupted by the entry of Jöns, who brands Raval across the face with his knife as punishment, while Jof escapes.

Now comes a beautiful and tenderly-wrought sequence. The Knight has joined Mia at her caravan outside the village. Jof and the Squire return from the uproar at the inn, and Mia brings them all a bowl of fresh milk and some wild strawberries ("symbolic of the bright days of life").† The peace and simplicity of the scene suddenly gives clarity to the Knight's thoughts (as a similar moment in Wild Strawberries prompts Borg to express his true feelings). Wistfully, he recalls his wife whom he has not seen for ten years, and then describes his doubts with unerring lucidity: "Faith . . . is like loving someone who is out there in the darkness but never appears, however loudly you call". Like Töre in The Virgin Spring, he longs for a sign to justify his faith. The serenity and poignance of this scene on the hillside is most perfectly captured, however, in the Knight's subsequent reflection: "I shall remember this moment, the silence, the twilight, the bowl of strawberries and milk, your faces in the dusk, Mikael sleeping, Jof with his lyre. I'll carry this memory between my hands as carefully as if it were a bowl filled with fresh milk." This is his sign, just as the appearance of the spring is Töre's in the later film. There are brief instances in life which are of such exquisite beauty that they compensate for all the misery and unhappiness. Another magical moment in this vein occurs earlier when Mia tells Jof to stop juggling. He does so and turns toward her. "I love you," she smiles. It is fragile and spontaneous.

This episode in the dusk is the artistic fulcrum of The Seventh Seal. It stimulates the Knight to save Jof, Mia, and their precious son from falling into Death's clutches, and Bergman's juxtaposition of moods is skilful, for directly after Blok has shared the evening meal with the family, he notices Death waiting for him to resume the game of chess. As usual during the scenes with Death, there is absolute silence, which conveys well the uncanny and almost unearthly nature of their encounters.

There are three further climactic incidents in the film. The first is when the Knight and his companions witness the burning of a suspected witch in the depths of the forest. Blok and Jöns had encountered this pathetic creature earlier when they had come out of the church, but now the Knight's doubts are revived once more as he watches the girl die. He asks her with suppressed ardour if she has really been in communion with the Devil, because he wants to ask him about God ("He if anyone must know"), but all he sees is fear in her eyes. When he asks who is responsible for hurting her hands, the soldiers refer him to the "Monk" who sits beside the cart. The "Monk" turns towards him, and is revealed as Death, cold and minatory as ever. It is interesting to note how Death glides into the frame from one side or another in the film, thus arousing a sinister feeling. As the witch dies, the Knight clenches his teeth and cries, "There must be something!" while Jöns at his side comments dryly, "Look at her eyes, my lord. Her poor brain has just made a discovery—emptiness". And though Blok shakes his head vigorously at his Squire's remark, it is obvious that he has now become aware emotionally of what previously he had intellectually realised—that man must rely solely on himself to counter Death. There is in him at this point the essence of the struggle between faith and reason, just as there was in Luther, whom Bergman resembles in many ways, not least in that he is obsessed with the idea of original sin, and that for him here philosophy is the study of death. All that Blok can effect is a very small gesture, and this is made during the penultimate crisis of the film. While Jöns and Mia make their way out of the glade where Death is playing chess with him, the Knight sweeps the pieces off the board and diverts his adversary's attention for a few seconds —all the time needed for the "Holy Family" to escape. "The Knight's caravan takes on the spiritual contours of an ark in a drowning world".* Significantly, the Knight is check-mated as soon as the pieces have been rearranged. Paul Overy has noted that "previously it has been the cynical extrovert Squire who has performed the good acts (saving the girl from rape and rescuing the juggler), but here the Knight . . . seizes his last opportunity to turn moral sentiment into moral action".†

Finally, there is the superbly edited scene at the castle. The Knight leads his companions (Jöns, the young girl whom he had rescued from Raval, Plog and his unfaithful wife) over the moonlit drawbridge and through bare rooms to where his wife Karin (Inga Landgré) greets him rather coolly. "It's over now and I'm a little tired", sighs the Knight, and it is to Bergman's credit that a remark like this bears, in its context, an

---

* Andrew Sarris: *Film Culture,* Number 19.
† *Broadsheet* (Cambridge, May 30, 1962).

232

Bergman

ineffable melancholy and resignation. In fact, the way in which he assembles scenes and incidents so as to arrive suddenly at a moment of overwhelming power and feeling is one of the most effective qualities in Bergman's craftsmanship.

The company sits at table and Karin reads the description of the Apocalypse from the Book of Revelations. There is all at once an immense knocking on the door of the castle. Jöns goes out but returns saying, "I saw no one" (he is disturbed and senses that the end has come, but is still unable to see Death). Then there is a shot of the group at the table suddenly rising to their feet and staring at the door: Bergman cuts to a shot of Death, standing in the shadow of the porch, cloak clutched ready to enwrap his victims. The Knight still prays keenly, hopeful to the last that what his intuition tells him may not in fact be true: "God, you who are somewhere, who must be somewhere, have mercy on us". Jöns submits, "but under protest", whilst Karin's sentence contains what is virtually a note of relief: "I am Karin, the Knight's wife, and I welcome you courteously to my house". Andrew Sarris has aptly called her a "medieval Penelope who seems as weary of life as does her tortured husband".* Jöns' girl drops to her knees and says quietly, "It is the end" (compare Christ's last words on the cross).

The next morning Jof sees the figures dancing away on the dark hills, clinging to each other in a line as Death makes them perform (another frequently depicted ceremony in medieval frescoes), while "the rain washes their faces and cleans the salt of the tears from their cheeks". This is almost a direct quotation from Chapter 7 of Revelations. And the caravan with its errant, innocent owners trundles along the seashore into the sun. This allegorical conclusion is acceptable and hopeful: love can conquer Death (or the fear of Death).

This analysis of *The Seventh Seal* has of necessity omitted many details which are interesting in themselves as well as being tightly interwoven in the general fabric of the film: the major virtue of this work is that nothing is irrelevant. I have also not devoted much space to Bergman's technique because the importance of the film rests primarily in the originality of its scenario. The milieu of the Middle Ages enables Bergman to draw his characters not only in a more stylised manner but also more sharply than usual. Mia, for example, is the one truly good heroine in his *oeuvre*. As he has said, "Whenever I am in doubt and uncertainty I take refuge in the vision of a simple and pure love. I find this love in those spontaneous women who . . . are the incarnation of purity".† But while this is obviously one of the bases of the thought behind *The Seventh Seal*, one cannot altogether overlook the reference to his wife made by the Knight as

* Andrew Sarris: *Film Culture*, Number 19.
† Jos Burvenich: *Thèmes d'Inspiration d'Ingmar Bergman*, p. 40.

he sits with Jof and Mia: "We were newly-married. We played and laughed together. I wrote songs to her eyes, her nose, and her little ears. We hunted, we danced, my house was full of life!" If we take this as describing a happiness equal to that of Jof and Mia *in the present,* and then recall how lacking in emotion is the reunion of Blok and his wife, we cannot help deciding that Bergman does not believe in the endurance of this type of idyllic life. Such a conclusion should be tempered, however, by the corollary that probably what he is really trying to say is that love cannot flourish unless the lovers live together. Karin and the Knight have been separated for ten years and their passion has ebbed away.

The Seventh Seal must, in any evaluation of Bergman's work, be treated as the most revealing of his films. *Summer Interlude* may be closer to his heart, but *The Seventh Seal* is a titanic outburst of all that pervades his mind as well as a work in which the influences of his childhood and his reading are apparent. He has said that Jof's vision of the Virgin was inspired by George Bernanos's descriptions in "The Diary of a Country Priest": and a fundamental situation in Pär Lagerkvist's drama is that of men faced by Death and striving to find some meaning in life. The horror and suffering painted on the walls of the churches which he visited when young are reproduced not only in the frescoes being portrayed by the artist in the porch of the church where Blok confesses to Death, but in the very incidents of the film itself—the corpse on the hills by the sea, the procession of flagellants, the burning of the witch, the final dance against the sky.

The conclusions to be drawn from *The Seventh Seal* are not, as many have inferred, pessimistic. They are best expressed in one of Bergman's most famous remarks: "Somehow life goes on. I believe in life, in this life, a life after death, all kinds of life . . . and death is a part of life".

The Seventh Seal: The Film as Iconography

NORMAN N. HOLLAND

Aside from giving us a masterpiece, Ingmar Bergman in *The Seventh Seal* has created a strange and wonderful paradox: a singularly modern medium treated in a singularly unmodern style—a medieval film. It is medieval in

FROM *The Hudson Review,* Vol. XII, No. 2 (Summer 1959). © 1959 by Norman N. Holland. Reprinted by permission of the author.

the trivial sense of being set in Sweden of the fourteenth century. More important, *The Seventh Seal* is a traditional *Totentanz* in which the allegorical figure of Death, robed in black like a monk, carrying scythe and hour-glass, leads the characters away in a dancing line under the dark, stormy sky. Most important, Bergman shows us, as medieval artists did, an allegorical, iconic reality, in Erich Auerbach's term, a figural reality which can be understood only by seeing that it prefigures something beyond itself. "My intention," Bergman writes in a note to the film, "has been to paint in the same way as the medieval church painter," and lo and behold! he has done just exactly that.

The Seventh Seal deals with a Crusader's quest, not in some faraway Holy Land, but in his own fourteenth-century Sweden. After ten years of holy war, the Crusader has returned home, weary, bitter, and disillusioned. On the shore, the ominous figure of Death steps out of a series of striking dissolves to claim him. The Crusader delays, however; he challenges Death to a game of chess. If the Crusader wins, he escapes Death; so long as the game goes on, he is free to continue his quest for certain knowledge of God and to do one significant act during his lifetime. As Death and the Crusader play at intervals through the film, the knight moves on a pilgrimage through Sweden, the land itself ravaged by the Black Death.

Bergman has in mind some obvious modern parallels to his medieval characters. "Their terror is the plague, Judgment Day, the star whose name is Wormwood. Our fear is of another kind but our words are the same. Our question remains." Our plague is intimate, as theirs was, and we too have our soldiers and priests, or as Bergman has called them, "communism and catholicism, two -isms at the sight of which the pure-hearted individualist is obliged to put out all his warning flags." Yet it would unnecessarily limit the universality of Bergman's achievement to call *The Seventh Seal* merely a necroterpsichorean parable for modern times. All men everywhere have always lived with death. Bergman is going beyond the *Totentanz*, trying to answer the further question: if death is the only certainty, where is God?

The Crusader's quest gives us the answer, though the knight himself seems never to learn it—or to learn that he has learned it. Accompanied by his positivistic, materialistic squire, a foil to his own abstractly questioning nature, he looks for certainty about God, for "to believe without knowledge is to love someone in the dark who never answers." Yet what the Crusader finds at first are people who believe in God only as a scourge, the cause of plagues and death, and who respond in kind. Religion for them becomes suppression, cruelty, persecution, the burning of innocent girls as witches, the terrifying realism of the crucifixes in the peasants' churches. In one of the most horrifying scenes ever put on film, Bergman shows us a procession of flagellants: a line of half-naked men lashing one another; monks struggling under the weight of huge crosses or with aching arms holding skulls over their bowed heads; the faces of children who wear crowns of thorns; people walking barefoot or hobbling on their knees; a great gaunt woman whose countenance is sheer blankness; slow tears falling down the cheeks of a lovely girl who smiles in her ecstasy of masochism. The procession interrupts the gay skit of a group of strolling players and halts while a mad priest screams abuse at the ugliness of his audience, long nose or fat body or goat's face. Glutted with hate, he joyfully proclaims the wrath of God, and the procession resumes its dogged way over the parched, lifeless soil.

Such is religion, Bergman seems to say, to those who see God as hater of life. Art (as represented by a surly, tippling church painter) becomes the representation of death to gratify the people's lust for fear. Living, as shown in a grotesque scene in an inn, becomes a sardonic "Eat, drink, and be merry." Cinematically, Bergman identifies this side of the ledger by great areas of blackness in the film frame and often by slow, sombre dissolves from shot to shot. Musically, the sound track treats even scenes of merrymaking with the *Dies Irae* theme.

In his notes to the film, Bergman tells how,

> As a child I was sometimes allowed to accompany my father when he traveled about to preach in the small country churches . . . . While Father preached away . . . I devoted my interest to the church's mysterious world of low arches, thick walls, the smell of eternity, . . . the strangest vegetation of medieval paintings and carved figures on ceiling and walls. There was everything that one's imagination could desire: angels, saints . . . frightening animals . . . . All this was surrounded by a heavenly, earthly, and subterranean landscape of a strange yet familiar beauty. In a wood sat Death, playing chess with the Crusader. Clutching the branch of a tree was a naked man with staring eyes, while down below stood Death, sawing away to his heart's content. Across gentle hills Death led the final dance toward the dark lands.
>
> But in the other arch the Holy Virgin was walking in a rose-garden, supporting the Child's faltering steps, and her hands were those of a peasant woman . . . I defended myself against the dimly sensed drama that was enacted in the crucifixion picture in the chancel. My mind was stunned by the extreme cruelty and the extreme suffering.

The Seventh Seal finds God for us—or at least another certainty than Death—not in the wormwood-and-gall institutional religion of suffering and crucifixion, but in the simple life of a strolling actor and juggler named Jof (Joseph), his girl-wife Mia (Mary), and their baby. As if to make the parallel to the Holy Family even more clear, Jof plays the cuckold in the troupe's little Pierrot-Columbine skit. Jof is also the artist. He is given to visions, and Bergman shows us one, of "the Holy Virgin . . . supporting the Child's faltering steps." Except for the Crusader, Jof is the only one who can see the allegorical figure of Death. (To the Crusader's materialistic squire, for example, Death appears not as an iconic figure, but as a grisly, rotting corpse.) Jof is a maker of songs whose simple melodies provide the sound track for this side of the religious ledger. Cinematically, Bergman gives us the certainty and holiness of life represented by Jof's family in light, airy frames; quick cuts tend to replace the slow dissolves used for the religion of death.

Yet even innocent Jof can be converted to a thief and a buffoon by the death-forces. In the grotesque comic scene at the inn, he is tortured with flames, forced to jump up and down on the board table in an exhausting imitation of a bear, parodying his own ability to leap beyond the ordinary human. An artist stifled in his art, he responds by becoming a rogue; he steals a bracelet as he makes his getaway.

This grim *reductio ad absurdum* proves, as it were, that death and the religion of death cannot be the only certainty. As a mad young girl about to be burned for a witch tells the Crusader, you find God (or the Devil who implies God) in the eyes of another human being. But the abstractly questioning Crusader says he sees only terror. He seems for a moment to find his certainty of God in a meal of wild strawberries and cream handed him by the gentle Mia, in effect, a communion of life as opposed to the bread and wine consecrated to Death. (Strawberries are associated with the Virgin in some late northern iconography.) The Crusader seems also to find his "one significant act": he performs the service of the knight traditional to medieval art, not the colonizer of the Holy Land, but the protector of the Holy Family. He leads Jof, Mia, and the child through the dark wood. As he plays chess with Death, he sees that the visionary Jof has recognized the Black One, seen his family's danger, and is trying to escape. To help him, the knight busies Death by knocking over the chessmen, incidentally giving Death a chance to cheat and win. By losing the game, the knight gives up his life to let Jof and Mia escape (in a tumultuous, stormy scene like paintings of the flight to Egypt).

And yet, though the Crusader has pointed the way for the audience, he seems not to have found it for himself. He goes on in his quest for abstract answers. He leads the rest of his now doomed band, a smith, the smith's venereous wife, the squire, and the squire's mute "housekeeper" to his castle. There, in a curiously emotionless scene, the Crusader distantly greets his wife whom he has not seen for ten years, shows her his disillusionment, but says he is not sorry he went on his quest. With the chess game lost and Death near, he knows it is too late for him now to act out the importance of the family himself, but he has learned its worth, though he does not realize its full godly significance. As his wife reads the lurid images of Revelation viii: "And when he had opened the seventh seal," Death, whom they all seem to await, appears. The Crusader asks once more that God prove himself. The mute girl opens her mouth and speaks, "It is finished," the sixth of the seven last words from the Cross. Death gathers them all in, his cloak filling the screen with black.

In short, then, the film answers its question, If Death is the only certainty, where is God? by saying, You find God in life. The opening shots of the film set up the contrast: first a blank empty sky; then the same sky but with a single bird hovering against the wind. Life takes meaning from its opposition to death, just as Jof and Mia's simple love of life takes meaning from the love of death around them—or as a chess game takes form in a series of oppositions.

The chess game is the central image of the film. It dictates much of the incidental imagery such as the knight's castle or the "eight brave men" who burn the witch. The playing (*spela*) of chess matches the playing (*spela*) of the strolling troupe. Both are traditional images for the transitoriness of life: Death robs us of our roles; Death jumbles the chessmen back in the box. (The two images are juxtaposed, for example, in *Don Quixote*, II. xii.) The characters themselves and the points of view they represent are played off against one another much like pieces in a game.

There are also some particular correspondences (somewhat confused for an English audience by the Swedish names for the chessmen). The Crusader, distinguished by his cross, is the king of the chess game: when he is lost, all the rest are lost, too. It is the juggler Jof who is the knight (in Swedish, *springare*, the "leaper"). Only these two men have visions that go beyond reality, just as only the king and knight can go beyond the chess board. The juggler-knight (the "leaper") is free at all times to jump out of the two dimensions of the board—Jof's powers as a seer are almost exactly parodied by his tormentors' forcing him to jump up and down on the board table in the grotesquerie at the inn. The only other chessman who can rise off the board during the game is the king, and then only when he is *castling*, i.e., returning home, like this Crusader. All the pieces or characters, of course, in their own moment of death when they are taken from the board can see beyond it. Yet their visions beyond the physical reality of the board, and the Crusader's, are limited to the allegorical figure of Death; the "leaper" can see not only Death, but also the holy life of the Mother and Child.

In other words, it is the artist who has the vision the Crusader seeks in answers to abstract questions. As the church painter (whose murals prefigure the scenes of the film) says, the artist can conceive God with his senses, giving "not the reality you see, but another kind." Jof the juggler is this kind of artist: he hopes his Christ-like infant will grow up to achieve what he calls "the impossible trick," keeping the juggled ball always in the air, above the board, as it were. And Bergman himself is this kind of artist: he has called himself "a conjurer" working with a "deception of the human eye" which makes still pictures into moving pictures.

In short, in *The Seventh Seal*, as in any great work of art, theme and medium have become one. "Art lost its creative urge," Bergman writes, "the moment it was separated from worship," and, by creating in the iconographic manner of medieval art, Bergman has turned the film back to worshipping (though not God, but life). He depicts the real world objectively, with tenderness and joy, but he shows reality as signifying something beyond itself. And in doing so, Bergman has established himself as one of the world's great and original directors. He has lifted the film out of mere physical realism and made his audience of chessmen with tricked eyes see in their own moves something beyond the board.

The Role of Jöns in *The Seventh Seal*

JORN DONNER

The Seventh Seal is built on a one-act play by B,* *Painting on Wood*. The action in this short piece is more taut, more concentrated than in the film. Many critics have regarded it as B's foremost dramatic work. Strindberg has earlier treated similar subjects, especially in *The Tale of the Folkungs*, regarded by some as a prototype.

The film's action is very simple. The Knight Antonius Block returns, after a long crusade, to the Sweden of the fourteenth century, devastated by the Black Death. He is accompanied by his squire, Jöns. On a desolate shore, he engages in a game of chess with Death. The prize for the Knight's victory is to be his life. While the game is in progress, the Knight manages to perform a meaningful act. He saves a couple of traveling jugglers, Jof and Mia, from death. The Knight arrives home and finds his wife. Then enters Death. All present are compelled to join in his dance, while the jugglers look on.

The most interesting figure is Jöns, a refutation of the often advanced statement that "The only villains in any of his films are always men of

FROM *The Personal Vision of Ingmar Bergman* (1964) by Jorn Donner, pp. 139–46, 149–51. Reprinted by permission of Indiana University Press.

* Donner usually refers to Bergman as "B".

science and intellect."[*] It has been maintained that B has one-sidedly presented an irrational philosophy. It has been said that his penetration into the world of women is an expression of this, since to live seems more important to women than to think, to act. I cannot entirely accept this theory, because that would mean to deny the root and origin of B's art: the Swedish community. The questions of society have not been finally settled, to be sure, but in most cases they have been changed into queries that concern the technical application. B emphasizes the irrational in man's nature. He turns attention inward, to the individual. This seems to correspond to a tendency in the community itself, that the Swedish citizen "is able to devote too much spare time on self-reflection, which often leads to confused eschatologies or an abuse of moral freedom."[†] Perhaps B is seeking a consolation which is too simple for one who, like Freud, wants to heal civilization. But to regard him exclusively as an irrationalist does not correspond to the image his films give us.

In *The Seventh Seal* Jöns acts and lives in conscious opposition to the other persons in the film. The Church is busy with persecutions and witch-burning. The Knight unceasingly asks questions, which rebound against emptiness. When the Knight's game with Death begins, Jöns is asleep. He then "opens his eyes, and grunts pig-like, yawns widely, but rises and saddles his horse, lifts up the heavy pack. The Knight rides slowly away from the sea, through the forest by the shore, up toward the road. He pretends not to hear the squire's morning prayer." This morning prayer is a particularly blasphemous song, which Jöns recites to the Knight's rising indignation. The riders pass a human form. Jöns dismounts. But when he takes hold of it, an empty skull is grinning at him. He wasn't mute, Jöns answers to the Knight's question. He was highly eloquent.

One of the clearest scenes takes place in a church where the Knight is at his prayers. Jöns begins to talk to the painter while he is waiting for his master. He becomes so shaken by the artist's tale of mankind's self-torment and stupidity that he asks to have a little brandy. This is interwoven with the Knight's questions. The parallel action in B's films is always illuminating, as, for instance, in *The Naked Night*. The Knight's questions remind us of the confession the minister Tomas Ericsson delivers in *Winter Light:* "How are we going to believe in the believers, when we ourselves do not believe? What will happen to us who wish to believe but cannot? And what will become of those who neither wish to nor can believe?" The Knight demands an answer: knowledge, not faith. In a moment of fright he discovers that the unknown who stands behind the bars is Death himself. In the meantime Jöns continues his conversation with the painter.

[*] Carolina Blackwood, "The Mystique of Ingmar Bergman," *Encounter*, XVI, No. 91 (April, 1961), p. 55.
[†] Antonio Napolitano, "Dal settimo sigillo alle soglie della vita," *Cinema Nuovo*, No. 151 (May–June, 1961).

In his description of the crusade, he renders the background to the Knight's questions:

"Ten years we sat in the Holy Land and let the snakes bite us, insects prick us, wild animals nip us, heathen slaughter us, the wine poison us, women give us lice, fleas feed on us, and fevers consume us, all to the glory of God. I'll tell you, our crusade was so stupid that only a real idealist could have invented it."

Jöns has not much use for the doctrines of the Church. Outside the church he spies a young woman who has had "fleshly intercourse with the Evil One." She will be burned. Critics have offered the information that no witches were burned in medieval Sweden, and have advanced this as an artistic argument against the film.* Strindberg's historical dramas could very well be condemned with the same argument. His portrait of *Master Olof*, which is historically inexact and faulty, has become the prototype for the picture the Swedish people have made for themselves of the great Reformer.

In a shop Jöns runs into Raval, a thief and a grave robber. Raval was the doctor from the theological seminary in Roskilde who ten years earlier convinced the Knight of the "necessity to go to the Holy Land on a splendid crusade." Jöns announces that he has suddenly come to understand the purpose of the wasted years. "We were too well off, we were too satisfied, and the Lord wanted to chastise our contented pride. Therefore he came and spewed his celestial venom and poisoned the Knight." Jöns is a materialist and a skeptic. He doubts that the big questions have a meaning. Still he is not insensible to the sufferings of others. The Knight continues his questioning. But Jöns helps other people.

Juggler Jof has entered the Tavern Embarrassment. Suspected by the smith Plog of having seduced his wife, Jof is forced by Raval to execute a bear dance on the table. These dark pictures are frightfully, nauseatingly cruel. There is a directness there which otherwise is expressed too seldom in the film. The sequence in the tavern is perhaps the best in the film. It brings to mind the exposure and the absence of disguise that we find in *The Naked Night*,† Jöns has promised to get Raval if they ever meet again. Jöns enters the tavern and rescues Jof.

Once more Jöns appears as a helper, when he tries to console the smith for the loss of his wife. But Jöns' words are then spoken on a level that would be more justified in some of the cynically tired train-sequences in *A Lesson in Love*. On their way through the nocturnal forest the group meets eight servants who are taking the witch to be burned. The Knight wants to see the face of the Devil to ask him about God. He, if any, should know. Ironic before the servants, Jöns is trying to think up a prac-

---

* Ivar Harrie, "Ingmar Bergman vill vara Sveriges Kai Munk" (Ingmar Bergman wants to be the Kaj Munk of Sweden), *Expression*, March 2, 1957.
† Andrew Sarris, *"The Seventh Seal," Film Culture*, No. 19 (1959).

tical plan to rescue the girl. He is moved in her presence. But he does not want to use his stirred-up emotions as an excuse for propounding his own questions. The person is the main issue, regardless of how much he tries to hide his sympathy behind a mask of cynicism.

The group meets one more person (aside from Death, with whom the Knight finishes his chess game). It is Raval, now infected by the plague. He wants something to drink, Jöns holds back the girl who accompanies him, not because of hatred toward Raval, but because help is futile. Raval is doomed to die in any case. Jöns' actions are practical. The Knight performs his actions as if there were another task beyond that of living. Jöns is prepared to enjoy life as long as possible. He curses his fate. Jöns is no philosopher: to live is to live is to live. Viewed in this perspective, the foolishness is not found in Jof and Mia ("the golden virgin and her idiot husband"*) but in the Knight, because he went on a crusade, and because he is still asking his meaningless questions.

Jöns has been called "a modern agnostic, himself not a little cruel, but not indiscriminately so, skeptical toward everything and everybody, not least himself, at the same time candid with his fellow man, aware of his inadequacy, passive up to a certain point, but beyond that full of energy and responsibility."† The difference between Jöns and the rest finds its clearest expression in the final sequence. The group has reached the home of the Knight. The morning gets lighter. Karin receives her husband. When seated at their breakfast she reads from Revelation, eighth chapter. Death enters. He is the unknown one who has come to take them away. They speak to Death. The Knight continues to call upon the God that *must* exist. Jöns remains sarcastic. All he knows is that his body exists, that he himself is. The girl whom he has saved from Raval, bids him to be silent. And he answers: "I shall be quiet, but under protest."

Jöns is a realist. We are reminded of the ballet master's admonition to Marie in *Illicit Interlude*. The dance is her profession. We remember the laborious and masterly cinematographic strategy that makes possible the final picture in *The Naked Night*. The solution, that of protest and action, that Jöns chooses does not appear as the film's only ideal, but as its most dignified. The persons who remain alive are Jof and Mia and their son Mikael. Their solution is in privacy, in the happiness of marital communion. They find their satisfaction in the knowledge that the family will perpetuate itself. But in any world at all, a Jof and a Mia have the chance to escape. Jöns, on the other hand, is a character who aims at a militant, active relationship with the world around him.

The squire's part is played by Gunnar Björnstrand, who by now has appeared in more than a dozen of B's films. In *Torment* his role was very

* Carolina Blackwood, "The Mystique of Ingmar Bergman," *Encounter*, XVI, No. 91 (April, 1961), p. 55.
† Harry Schein, "Poeten Bergman," *BLM*, No. 4 (April, 1957).

small, while in *A Lesson in Love* he was one of the dominating figures. The most typical portrait was delineated in *The Magician,* as the medical counselor Vergérus, who proposees to prove the sorcerer's incompetence, but becomes frightened by the unknown powers. With B's conception of the film medium, it is obvious that he has preferred to use the same actors in picture after picture, for instance, the romantic hero Birger Malmsten during the forties, or Harriet Andersson from *Monika* on. (In *While the City Sleeps* she has a walk-on bit.)

B wants to create an artistic instrument which he can fully master. He has seldom changed cameramen, designer, cutter, composer. He has worked in the same surroundings, with a crew he knows well. This analysis of his films is built on the conception that he is one of few artists who has succeeded in realizing his personal vision. He has achieved this through the intermediary of closely associated artists and technicians. The films are analyzed here as the final result, the completed work. It is evident that a great deal of the credit for this result, for the film's inner richness of meaning, belongs to B's collaborators. They are instruments in his hand, nothing more, nothing less.

> There are many film makers who forget that the human face is the starting point in our work. To be sure, we can become absorbed by the esthetic of the picture montage, we can blend objects and still lifes into wonderful rhythms, we can fashion nature studies of astonishing beauty, but the proximity of the human face is without doubt the film's distinguishing mark and patent of nobility. . . . In order to give the greatest possible power to the actor's expression, the movement of the camera must be simple and uncomplicated, in addition to being carefully synchronized with the action. The camera must appear as a completely objective observer and should only on rare occasions participate in what is going on. We must also consider that the actor's finest means of expression is his eyes.[*]

The choice of actors corresponds to the change and the shading that have taken place in B's films. The romantic heroes were superseded by persons with greater intellectual complications. The idea content in B's pictures achieved a deeper form and was interpreted by such actors as Ingrid Thulin, Max von Sydow, and Gunnar Björnstrand. Still it seems to me a grossly mechanical conception to lump together, for instance, Gunnar Björnstrand's roles and consider that his character remains the same in film after film, as Béranger has done in his book about. B. The artist's creative imagination works with the material of reality. A part of the reality that surrounds B is the world of the film, his actors. It is obvious

---

[*] Ingmar Bergman, "Varje film är min sista film" ("Every Film Is My Last Film"); *Filmnyheter,* No. 9–10 (May, 1959).

that he creates his characters and writes his parts with a consideration, among other things, of the qualifications he finds among his inter-
preters. Perhaps the squire Jöns has something of Gunnar Björnstrand, a
dignity and a vulnerability found in this actor. This is, however, as irrelevant to the analysis of films as to combine the facts of private life with the
fiction of art. It suffices to note the importance of Jöns to the action of
The Seventh Seal.

> Here we perceive the outline of Camus' modern hero, a symbol of
> man's, of the individual's, integrity. The portrait is not fully
> rounded. Bergman apparently has not dared to give it the central
> place it deserves in modern drama. But the fate of the squire
> intimates in any case modern man's dramatic relationship to the
> world around him. Man's sluggish hopelessness is contrasted with-
> out any religious embellishment with his courage and dignity.
> This is more than social consciousness: this is the most urgent
> social message.*

The film's main parallel action is between the Knight-Jöns and Jof-Mia.
These are the poles around which the action revolves. Jof dreams that
his son Mikael will achieve the impossible: that is, to make the juggling
balls stand still in the air. Their story begins with the awakening, shown
in another light than Albert Johansson's awakening in *The Naked Night.*
Albert, too, has sons, but they do not wish to join the circus. While Albert
must pass through darkness and suffering before he is freed, Jof slips
away from all questions despite the moments of terror he experiences in
the tavern.

It is the Knight's meeting with the jugglers that changes his action and
gives these characters another meaning. Before this, however, the jugglers'
appearance in the market place has been interrupted by the passing procession of the flagellants, a vision of man's folly and the Last Judgment.
The scene takes place on a sunny slope. At first, Mia is alone with Mikael.
Jof is at the tavern.

The scene, in B's construction, has the simple, magnificent seriousness
of a consecration, a religious rite. The play of light in *The Seventh Seal*
shows plainly the contrasts between the contemporary patterns of action.
In the lighting of the Knight's story, the dark, the black, dominates. Above
Jof and Mia there almost always hovers a brightness of grace, as if the
action took place in another reality. Jos Burvenich† believes that the
image B makes for himself of a God represents a higher being to whom

---

* The conception that an art which discusses man's conditions for existence is the
social art of our time is advanced with great brilliance by Villy Sörenson in his collection of essays, *Hverken-eller* (Copenhagen: Gyldendal, 1961). I have not, however, been able to work it into my book.
† Jos Burvenich, "Ingmar Bergman à la trace de Dieu," *Art d'Eglise,* No. 113 (1960).

one should dedicate himself with pain, like a sacrifice. The dream of paradise and purity in *The Seventh Seal* cannot become dramatically (Catholic) correct before B speaks of evil by its rightful name, which is the sin that lives in the hearts of men. Accordingly, one should not seek a religious interpretation of the film outside of Jof and Mia: their mutual love is God. The Catholic interpretation presupposes that the paradise of innocence cannot be found here on earth in the momentary, but only in God's love, which is the Realm, the Kingdom.

As I look at the film, I find it an exact expression of earthly dreams of paradise, of a philosophical materialism. One may answer Burvenich, with Colin Young, that both the Knight and Jöns are, "by their philosophical positions, unable to dispatch the problems presented by death, but Mary and Joseph never commit themselves to this argument and are, in fact, aloof from it and from the double scourge of pestilence and a reactionary church. Calm and serene, they are the only ones who in the end are saved."* If we place Jof's and Mia's fate in a social connection, the solution is unsatisfactory. It is just about as purposeful as to flee to a desert island to escape a nuclear war. Philosophically, however, the solution is the right one. The juggler couple ask only the small questions. Their existence acquires depth from the power of being together.

.   .   .

We know that the picture ends in the death of everybody except the juggler family. The first one to succumb is the actor Skat, who in a grotesquely comical scene manages to do away with his tormentor, the smith Plog. Skat has eloped with Plog's wife. This happens in the forest during the night. Skat climbs up in a tree, but Death saws it off. On the stump appears a squirrel, to indicate life's continuity. Skat is a failure, and all except the jugglers have at some time in their lives failed.† The Knight has left his wife for a meaningless crusade. He goes with Jöns to the clearing in the woods where the servants have built a pyre for Tyan, the woman we saw outside the church. He interrogates Tyan. Since the Devil is with her, perhaps he knows something about God. He sees the emptiness in her eyes, nothing else, and receives no answer. He consoles her; she cannot console him. She goes calmly to her death, for the Devil will protect her from all evil.

"I believe at times that to ask questions is the most important thing," says the Knight in the frightful scene with Tyan. He thereby intimates his faith in intellectual aspiration. But what remains purposeful in his life is still the one action, namely, that he saves Jof and Mia. The Knight, in other words, gets a chance for a creative action. His life has had a meaning.

---

* Colin Young's review of the film in *Film Quarterly*, XIII, No. 3 (Spring, 1959), pp. 42 ff.
† Andrew Sarris, *"The Seventh Seal," Film Culture*, No. 19 (1959).

The Seventh Seal opens itself slowly to the viewer. This is partly due to the many planes the story touches on, the polyphonic structure of the work. The framework of the narrative is, of course, the chess game with Death, a threatening vision, underscored by the desolate seashore, where the game begins. *The Seventh Seal* has a plastic effect which few of B's films possess, a harmonious rhythm, in spite of the fact that one may detect such different stylistic sources as German expressionism, the Japanese film (Kurosawa), and the Swedish tradition.

B's greatness lies in the fact that he is able to give to terror and insecurity such a dramatic and urgent molding. That I find Jöns to be the film's most interesting and commanding figure is a subjective evaluation, since *The Seventh Seal* "will continue to be a source of discussion for many years to come and—this concerns all the classics of thought—the interpretations will change with the ideas and the era of the critics."[*] In order to survive, man must be able to conquer death. It is a matter of escaping both the inner death of feeling and the threat that looms from without. The film lets this attempt end in success and failure, but the important element is the salute to human dignity, the longing for justice, for life in peace, which constitute the movement of the film. The picture contains a great wisdom and a great naïveté. However:

> it is a naïveté that characterizes the eras in art—here the Middle Ages—the spirit of which Bergman has succeeded in transmitting, without spoiling it with pedantry, thanks to his incomparable artistry when it comes to transferring to the language of the film the motifs in the iconography that has inspired him. The shape and forms he shows us are never insignificant, but the fruit of a constantly original creation. His art is so genuine, so new, that we forget art for the questions' questions and the endless series of conclusions. Seldom has the film managed to aim so high and so completely realize its ambitions.[†]

[*] Andrew Sarris, *"The Seventh Seal," Film Culture,* No. 19 (1959).
[†] Eric Rohmer in *Arts,* April 23, 1958.

HITCHCOCK

VERTIGO

CREDITS

Vertigo (United States, 1958)
Directed and produced by Alfred Hitchcock
Screenplay by Alec Coppel and Samuel Taylor, based on the novel *D'Entre les Morts* by Boileau and Narcejac.
Production/release: Paramount

Photography: Robert Burks
Art directors: Hal Pereira, Henry Bumstead, Sam Comer, Frank McKelvey
Special effects: John P. Fulton
Music: Bernard Herrmann
Editor: George Tomasini

Main performers:
James Stewart (*John "Scottie" Ferguson*)
Kim Novak (*Madeleine Elster, Judy Barton*)
Barbara Bel Geddes (*Midge*)
Henry Jones (*The coroner*)
Tom Helmore (*Gavin Elster*)
Raymond Bailey (*The doctor*)

Length: 128 minutes

During his fifty years of directing, from the late silent film era to the present, Alfred Hitchcock has turned out as notable a body of films as any filmmaker, most of which are stylistically so recognizable for their witty juxtapositions of humor and terror that even casual moviegoers have come to associate his name with a film genre. Today we often see advertisements for films by lesser directors with such tags as "in the Hitchcock tradition" or "better than Hitchcock," which indicates that his work is the accepted standard for all new films in the suspense genre. A cult figure in Europe and a commercially successful filmmaker everywhere, Hitchcock has only begun to attract serious critical study in the United States in recent years. In this country his reputation for technical virtuosity and skillful handling of suspense stories has long obscured his merit as one of the cinema's presiding geniuses and most reflective artists. Like Griffith in an earlier era, Hitchcock, in films like *Vertigo*, was too entertaining and too proficient a craftsman to be always credible as an artist. For more than a decade following his widely acclaimed *Psycho* (1960), Hitchcock was regarded primarily as a filmmaker in decline—until the extraordinarily impressive achievement of *Frenzy* (1972) reversed the critical trend and provoked many viewers to reexamine the other recent films.

If such a decline had in fact occurred, surely it was to a level seldom attained by other directors at the height of their careers: it consisted of *The Birds* (1963), *Marnie* (1964), *Torn Curtain* (1966), and *Topaz* (1969). All these films are remarkable and all are strikingly experimental, though overtly designed within the dominant narrative tradition of the cinema. They are experimental in the sense that in them, as in all his films, Hitchcock has striven to create new modes of cinematic expressiveness and to clarify, in an increasingly complex way, the relationship of the camera to the subject. Hitchcock's artistry is preeminent in his communication of vivid insights into people's reactions to situations of peril or emergency. In Hitchcock's world, we *suddenly* see, we *suddenly* confront, we *suddenly* understand. The camera thrusts us into settings that are both familiar and attractively strange: the British Museum in *Blackmail* (1929), a vaudeville show in *The Thirty-Nine Steps* (1935), a tennis court in *Strangers on a Train* (1951), the United Nations in *North by Northwest* (1959). Enticed by the filmmaker's swift and telling selection of images, we absorb a number of amusing and perplexing incidents; and then the combinations of images unexpectedly collide in a moment of visual clarity that forces us to reinterpret the information we had been receiving so passively from the previous shots in the sequence. A gun is fired or a body discovered, and immediately the amusement and confusion of the preceding scene becomes an ironic counterpoint to a situation of jeopardy. The camera leads us through a maze of details as the characters are brought to a new consciousness of their vulnerability. The Hitchcock world is particularly susceptible to the intrusion of terror or fear, which is often juxtaposed comically with some absurdly incongruous event— perhaps this is why it is so striking a metaphor of the modern environment.

Vertigo is one of Hitchcock's most intriguing visualizations of the intrusion of evil into a man's ordinary existence. The world of the hero, an ex-policeman retired from the force because he suffers from vertigo, reverberates with intense psychological undertones that make us particularly aware that Hitchcock's real goal is to establish the mental landscape of man in a universe that is uncontrollable, alien, and antagonistic. The perspective is not just the protagonist's but ours. We experience the vertigo, the confusion of the senses overwhelmed by a variety of images, and we participate vicariously in the visualized projections of the hero's guilt. We are constantly required to perceive the main character's experiences from a double perspective, both from his own subjective interpretation and from a more objective, detached view. As the hero attempts to reconstruct his life after having a breakdown, we share in his tentative probing of the meanings behind the surfaces he encounters. Once we discover that the woman he virtually recreates, Pygmalion-fashion, into the woman he had lost is in fact the same person, we grasp the sinister nature of the situation that is beyond the hero's knowledge, and yet we

Narrative Viewpoint in *Vertigo*

DAVID THOMSON

Essential to every Hitchcock film is this awareness the director has of his spectator. It conceives of the spectator as an economic generalization and there is an element of sadism in the devices inflicted. In one way Hitchcock's films are un-cinematic: his images are most effective when most contrived. At the same time his work defines the nature of cinema more than any other director's. The chief contribution to this definition is the similarity of treatment he offers to his audience and to the characters in his films. And if Hitchcock evokes the voyeur in one it is, I think, because he regards his own characters in this way.

Speaking about his confessed inclination to torture his characters, Hitchcock said, 'That scene in *Vertigo* where James Stewart forces Miss Kim Novak to alter her whole personality by altering her lipstick, hairstyle, even hair-tint—for me it has the compulsion of a striptease in reverse. The woman is made insecure by being forced to make up, not take-off.'*

The setting of *Vertigo* is San Francisco and Hitchcock emphasizes the sheerness of that city. This is clearly relevant to vertigo—the complaint of the private detective played by James Stewart—but it is an image Hitchcock has already made us familiar with: the cliff-top and the staircase of Manderley in *Rebecca;* the steep streets of Quebec in *I Confess;* the staircase, guarded by a dog, that Farley Granger ascends in *Strangers on a Train.* More than specific instances of steepness there is Hitchcock's use of high-angle camerawork at moments of crisis and judgment. At the conclusion of the court proceedings in *The Paradine Case,* for example, the camera towers above Gregory Peck. Height is a metaphysical symbol for Hitchcock just as the fact that so many of his characters have 'fallen' is a sign of their moral condition.

In *Vertigo* Stewart is hired by a friend, Tom Helmore, to keep a watch on his wife, Kim Novak. There is a long sequence in which he trails her through San Francisco and into the Californian countryside as she visits places associated with her Spanish grandmother. The grandmother committed suicide and Helmore has told Stewart that he fears his wife's own depression may be leading to this end. Ostensibly, the terms on which the film opens are those of a thriller, and the method of narration transmits these terms to the audience. But Hitchcock is not content that Ste-

FROM the book *Movie Man* by David Thomson. Copyright © 1967 by David Thomson. Reprinted with permission of Stein and Day/Publishers and Martin Secker & Warburg Limited.

* *Evening Standard,* 24th March, 1965. Interview with Alexander Walker.

wart should be simply the ingenious and heroic detective of tradition or that we should be allowed to enjoy the thrills unaffected. Both Stewart and the spectator follow Novak in the same degree of ignorance, and when Stewart's interest grows into sympathy and love it is an expression of what many of the spectators may feel. Stewart rescues Novak from an attempt to drown herself and the pattern of pursuit changes to their travelling together. It is a love affair, but blighted by Novak's remoteness and the emphasis this gives to Stewart's original role as detective and watcher. When they visit the monastery where the grandmother died a distraught Novak runs away from Stewart up the bell tower. When he tries to follow vertigo disables him. He reaches the top only to see Novak's body in the courtyard below. Stewart is quietly condemned for negligence at the inquest and he has a breakdown.

Several months later, when his recovery seems good, he sees a girl in the street who resembles Kim Novak. At this point the difficulty of distinguishing the two Kim Novaks from the two characters she is playing is such that I must divulge the device behind the film. Hitchcock himself waits a little longer but still reveals it half an hour before the end of what started as a thriller, the twist of which one might have expected would be reserved for the last minute. The throwaway shows how little the 'detective story' interests him compared with the moral psychology. The two Kim Novaks are, as our eyes tell us, one. More than that, Novak has not been Helmore's wife, but only part of a conspiracy with him to accomplish the killing of his real wife. She had not been an unknowing object of pursuit but a decoy. Helmore had been waiting at the top of the tower with his unconscious wife whom he had thrown down; he had hidden with Novak and escaped when Stewart collapsed. To impersonate the wife Novak had been blonde, now she is a brunette.

Just as Helmore has deceived Stewart, so Hitchcock has misled the spectator by ensuring that he gains information in exactly the same way as Stewart. Stewart's assignment to follow and the subsequent attraction he feels towards his object are the equivalents of the cinematic method. Because the central character is a detective and because the movie's main purpose seems to be the solution of a mystery, which on the available evidence presupposes a supernatural intervention in man's affairs, *Vertigo* progresses by what appears to be a factual gathering. The facts can be related to the ideal of pure cinema: what a person looks like, what she does, the manner of her gestures. It is in these terms that Stewart watches Novak and the entire visual material is directed to this information; cuts separate fact from fact rather than allowing them to elide with each other so that their certainty might be undermined by context. And, of course, Novak is behaving to the order of this method through her conspiracy with Helmore, which is the equivalent of her co-operation with her director.

The appearance of the second Novak is a crucial indication of *Vertigo's* real nature, for Stewart's obsession with the Novak face and the associations of guilt he has with it override the detective in him. He attempts, as Hitchcock indicated in his interview, to recreate the appearance she had as Helmore's wife. When the transformation is complete and the second Novak stands in a sexually-charged and quite non-naturalistic green light, the exact image of her earlier self, and the camera tracks a full circle of vortex round them while they kiss, we can see how deranged Stewart is. He notices only that his dream has been reincarnated and that it is possible for him now to exercise the desire he had felt earlier but which had been suppressed by the nature of his job. For Novak the position is ontologically precarious. She has herself fallen in love, but while in her first character the mechanism of deceit kept her from being frank, she now recognizes how far Stewart is obsessed. Finally she confesses to the trick. Furiously Stewart takes her back to the monastery and chases her to the top of the tower. Novak is startled at the top by the sudden appearance of a nun—black robes appearing from black shadow—and falls to her death. This death is accident, punishment and suicide of remorse and identification, so involved have the layers of duplicity become. For Stewart, left at the top of the tower, there is no prospect but madness. Hitchcock has even intimated that he expects Stewart might throw himself down. Vertigo has been made the symptom of delusion, indecision, guilt, sexual obsession and, finally, chaos.

I have found it more necessary to detail the sequence of events in *Vertigo* than in any other film. As in *Psycho* the movement of plot hypnotizes; at the same time the overtly narrative aspect is a pretext for Hitchcock to uncover spiritual responses. The height of his plots is when the mystery is most inexplicable, so that the rational processes the characters have been following break into psychological fantasy. Cary Grant, stranded in a mid-West desert in *North by Northwest*, is in such a position; the whole idea of *The Birds* is perhaps Hitchcock's boldest juxtaposition of the real and the abstract. It is this talent that enables him to appeal more than any other director to the most general and most exclusive of film audiences. The cynical use of *doubles ententes* is the director's own awareness of his width of appeal. When Anthony Perkins remarks to Janet Leigh in *Psycho* that taxidermy is his hobby, the horrible pun is a dare to the audience: how can such artifice coexist with a tension so compulsive? Why, in fact, do the most old-fashioned plots work in his hands?

Basically, the effectiveness lies in the paradox that Hitchcock's films purport to be a sequence of factual statements, but that these 'facts' are subsequently revealed to be false. Because the method filters a continuum of experience into discrete items, the real source of disorientation is the insinuation of the film's form with the natural processes of watching a movie, particularly a movie from Hollywood in a circuit cinema. While involve the spectator: before the film proper has begun, we are made aware that the vertigo of the title is to be more than a literal fear of heights. This credit sequence is linked by the music that accompanies it to the scene of Judy's metamorphosis into Madeleine in the beauty salon: the only scene where the same music returns, again as accompaniment to a close-up of a woman's face—a face that is being transformed into a mask.

The first image is of a horizontal bar standing out against a blurred background: a single solid object against an undefined mass. The shot is held for a moment, then two hands grab the bar, the camera moves back, the focus deepens, to reveal a city spread out beneath the night: suggestions of clinging and falling set against a great wilderness of roof-tops. There follows the accident, with Scottie (James Stewart) clinging to a collapsing gutter while a policeman, trying to save him, plunges past him to his death hundreds of feet below. The sensation of vertigo is conveyed to the spectator by the most direct means, subjective shots using a simultaneous zoom-in and track-back that makes the vast drop telescope out before our eyes; we watch, from Scottie's viewpoint, the policeman hurtle down. The sensation has been explained, I believe, by psychologists as arising from the tension between the desire to fall and the dread of falling—an idea it is worth bearing in mind in relation to the whole film. In any case, we, with Scottie, are made to understand what it feels like to be so near death, and to have death made so temptingly easy, yet so terrifying, a way out of pain and effort: to live, he must hold on desperately to the gutter, his arms and body agonisingly stretched, his fingers strained, his mind gripped by unendurable tension; to die, he has only to let go. When we next see Scottie, he is sitting in the apartment of Midge (Barbara Bel Geddes). We do not see, and are neved told, how he got down from the gutter: there seems no possible way he *could* have got down. The effect is of leaving him, throughout the film, metaphorically suspended over a great abyss.

Midge and her apartment (that contrasts markedly, we see later, with Scottie's own, which is furnished largely with antiques) represent one of the possibilities before Scottie. The assessment of Midge herself is made with that complexity and economy so characteristic of Hitchcock (though it is only completed by the contrast offered by Madeleine); it is an assessment not only of a clearly defined character but of a whole milieu, even of modern culture itself. It is a very sympathetic portrait: Midge is practical, realistic, emancipated, eminently sane, positive and healthy in her outlook: but from the outset the inadequacies revealed later are hinted at. A trained artist, she devotes her energies to sketching advertisements for brassières. In her cluttered studio-cum-living-room, Miros on the wall are juxtaposed indiscriminately with fashion designs. Entirely devoid of mystery or reserve, the kind of sexuality she represents is suggested by her smart sex-chat about corsets and brassières ("You know about those things, you're a big boy now"), she reduces everything to the same matter-of-fact level. Yet one senses already a discrepancy between what she is and what she might be: a depth of feeling, of constancy, is hinted at, more visually than verbally, which is at odds with the superficiality of the cultural environment her flat evokes. Her look at Scottie when he reminds her that it was she who broke off their three-week-long engagement is one of those moments that reveal the basic strength of the cinema, because it suggests things not really formulable in words: one could say that the rest of the film defines why she broke it off. If there is something a little boyish about her, there is also something—Scottie actually uses the word —"motherly". She reminds one a little of that other sympathetic young-mother figure, the Doris Day of *The Man Who Knew Too Much:* she disapproves of Scottie's leaving the police, she supervises his attempt to "lick" his vertigo (by climbing her portable steps) as a mother might help a child to master a bicycle, alternately urging and restraining.

He tells her, in his habitually non-committal manner, that he is still available—"That's me, available Ferguson"; the phrase recalls his decision to "do nothing" to give us the full extent of his "availability" and suggests one aspect of that metaphorical suspension: he is suspended both in work and in personal relationships. That characteristic Hitchcockian economy and directness in organisation connects this "availability" with Elster, whom Scottie goes on at once to mention. The scene ends with the attempt to overcome the vertigo, culminating in the startling subjective shot of the street over which Scottie hung, which he sees again when he looks down from the top of Midge's steps. In the foreground of the shot, we see ornaments and a bowl of flowers that keep the reality of Midge's room before us; but that reality—Midge's world, charming, uncomplicated, safe, superficial—is shattered by the vision. Scottie has seen death, and the experience has undermined all possibility of his accepting Midge and the life she represents as adequate fulfillment. It is Midge's room that becomes unreal, the vision (a great abyss apparently in the middle of that room) that is "real". Hitchcock cuts from her "motherly" frightened comforting of him to the exterior of Elster's offices.

What I have called the *thematic* organisation of the film can be seen in the transition from the smart modernity of Midge's apartment to the discussion about the past in Elster's office. Behind Elster we see shipbuilding in progress, and there is a model ship in the room, carrying a suggestion of escape. The walls are covered with prints of San Francisco in the "old days": Scottie and Elster examine one as they talk. Elster bears a clear thematic relationship to Scottie. Shipbuilding—modern development—bores him; he has a nostalgia for the past, where a man had "freedom" and "power": the words are echoed twice later in the film, in the bookshop (linking Elster with the man who destroyed Carlotta Valdes) and at the end. There is in Elster a hint of the inexplicable—of the diabolical—in his intuitive understanding of Scottie's psychological traits (the metaphorical, as well as the literal, vertigo), in his fastening on them and *using* them: at the end of the film, Scottie's insistent question, "Why did you pick on me? Why *me?*" never gets an explicit answer. Elster, like other Hitchcock villains (Bruno Anthony [in *Strangers on a Train*], for example), besides being a clearly defined character in his own right, is related to a weakness in the hero. We shall see how important for Scottie are a nostalgia for the past and a desire for "freedom" and "power".

The long expository dialogue between the two men is given tension by the sense conveyed of Elster's control of Scottie's responses, and by the exactness in the use of cutting and camera-movement to express that control. In a cut to close-up we see the effect on Scottie of Elster's abrupt, unobtrusive "Someone dead" (in answer to Scottie's question as to who may harm Elster's wife); then the camera immediately moves back to take in Elster standing over him, dominating, *imposing* his story. Scottie rejects it: he is "the hard-headed Scot": but rejects it, with his insistent reiteration that all the wife needs is a psychologist, too emphatically. We are very much aware of the tension in him between natural scepticism and an attraction towards the fantastic story, with its associations of Elster's wife with the past and with death. Madeleine, Elster tells him, sits by a lake looking at pillars across the water, pillars that are called "The Portals of the Past." The "wandering" theme—picked up both verbally and visually many times later in the film—the theme of being lost in life, of having no clear aim—is stated here by Elster ("She wanders—God knows where she wanders"). It is natural to link it with Scottie's expressed lack of purpose (his "doing nothing") and hence with the "vertigo" idea. He is sufficiently intrigued to agree at least to see Madeleine before he rejects the case.

There follows about quarter of an hour without dialogue, showing us the growth of Scottie's obsession with Madeleine. She herself is introduced by a camera-movement different from any that has preceded it, that sets a new mood, maintained throughout the ensuing sequences up to Scottie's next meeting with Midge. We are in Ernie's, the restaurant where Scottie is to see Madeleine. Close-up of Scottie seated at the bar, looking across. The camera swings over in a slow, graceful movement disclosing the *décor* of the restaurant, which evokes immediately the gracious living of the past, then tracks slowly in towards a table, gradually focussing our attention on the bare back of a woman in evening dress leaning in a graceful attitude, almost statuesque. Then, in a subjective shot from Scottie's viewpoint, we watch her cross the restaurant with an easy, gliding motion, and pause near him so that her face is clearly visible, beautiful, smooth, without definable expression.

The fascination Madeleine exerts over Scottie—and over us—is complex. One is immediately aware of the contrast between her and Midge. Where Midge is an entirely known quantity, Madeleine is surrounded by an aura of mystery. She is always remote from Scottie and from us: we see her only as Scottie sees her. When she goes to a flower-shop, she enters by a back door, down a side street, passing through dingy, cobwebby store-rooms; later, she apparently disappears from a house: she may be herself a ghost. She represents a completely different sexuality from Midge's: one has only to compare Midge's demonstrating the latest brassière "based on the principle of the Cantilever Bridge", with Madeleine's hesitant grace of movement and attitude later as she comes to stand in the doorway of Scottie's sitting-room wearing his dressing-gown: Madeleine is so much more erotic because of this combination of grace, mysteriousness and vulnerability. She is from the start the representative of another world, of experience beyond the grasp of the cards-on-the-table reality of Midge. A higher reality, or an illusion? Or, to shift to the Keatsian terminology, "vision", or "waking dream"? It seems more reasonable to adduce *Lamia* or the Nightingale Ode in this connection than to make the conventional classification of *Vertigo* as "mystery-thriller"; and it is worth pointing out that we find in Hitchcock a far more secure and mature balance of sympathy and interest between the real world and the visionary, and certainly a no less complex awareness of the issues, than Keats was capable of. If it be objected that Madeleine does in fact turn out to be pure illusion, I shall answer that the matter is by no means so simple.

Madeleine certainly is presented as a dream, in some sense; and she becomes our dream as well as Scottie's. If her own movements, in their grace, their air of remoteness, are dream-like, the effect of dream is intensified by Hitchcock's use of the camera. Leisurely, steady-paced subjective tracking-shots characterize the sequences in which Scottie follows Madeleine; we are placed behind the windscreen of his car in the driver's seat as he follows her around the streets of San Francisco, pursuing a dream through modern surface-reality; we wander at his walking-pace round the graveyard; we watch Madeleine continually through his eyes, her distance, her silence, his and our inability to understand her, help her, protect her, are all a part of the fascination. The effect of romantic dream is especially strong in the churchyard sequence, everything steeped in hazy sunlight as Madeleine stands, statue-like, minute in long-shot, over an unknown grave.

The settings to which she leads Scottie (Spanish church, graveyard, art gallery, old house) in and around San Francisco, seem nonetheless not to belong to the city, they are little pockets of silence and solitude, another world. She leads him back always to the past—the grave, the portrait, the house of a long-dead woman. Finally, and perhaps most important of all, she is continually associated with death, and the fascination she exerts is the fascination of death, a drawing towards oblivion and final release; the yearning for the dream, for the Ideal, for the Infinite, become logically a yearning for death: Scottie's and our vertigo.

This death-wish—or more exactly, in "vertigo" terms, the simultaneous longing for and fear of death—culminates in the scene among the sequoia trees: "the oldest living thing". The dialogue stresses the fear:

> SCOTTIE: "What are you thinking about?"
> MADELEINE: "All the people who were born and died while the trees went on living. . . ."
> SCOTTIE: "Its real name is Sequoia Semperviva".
> MADELEINE: "I don't like it. . . . Knowing I have to die".

They examine a cross-section of a felled tree. The camera moves across it, outwards from the core, taking us through centuries in seconds; Madeleine puts her fingers tentatively near the circumference, murmuring, "Somewhere here I was born, and there I died. It was only a moment for you, you took no notice". She moves off, and disappears among the trees. Disappears, as she previously disappeared in the Carlotta Valdes house: Scottie follows but can't find her, and we get a slow, sinuous tracking-shot of "ever-living" tree-trunks and sunlight which precisely realises the significance of the quoted dialogue, the pitiful brevity and transience of the individual life most beautifully and disturbingly conveyed. The whole scene is bathed in an atmosphere of romantic dream—its great visual beauty intensified by the emotional overtones, by the whole context—which counterpoints the dread of death expressed in the dialogue with a sense of yearning for peace and oblivion.

The sequence culminates in the kiss by the sea, the mutual capitulation to love. From Scottie's point of view, the significance of this *as* a culmination is clear—his love for Madeleine becomes identified with his death-yearning. Earlier, gazing in his car at a reproduction of the Carlotta Valdes portrait, he saw the dead woman and Madeleine as interchangeable (in terms of film, dissolve from the portrait to Madeleine and back). On one level there is a strong element of romantic cliché in the image of the lovers embracing against a background of crashing waves, an effect which crystallises for us another aspect of the film: for many spectators, the cinema itself is a kind of dream, an escape-world in which reality can be evaded and forgotten. In one way Hitchcock is throughout the first half of *Vertigo* using his audience's escapist expectations, the fact that they go to the cinema in order to see a "hero" with whom they can identify, involved in romantic wish-fulfilments: hence at this climactic moment dream and romantic cliché merge. But, at a deeper level, the sea as the culmination of this part of the film has another significance: if the sequoia trees are "the oldest living thing", the sea is older still, beating eternally against the rocks, eroding, wearing down; and it is against such sea-associations that the two embrace on the cliff-edge, a tiny, precarious moment placed against eternity. But this is perhaps merely to suggest why the cliché itself still has emotional validity.

Before this sequence there has occurred the nearest to a meeting between Midge and Madeleine that ever takes place: Midge, driving up to
Scottie's apartment, sees Madeleine drive away. That the two women
never appear, beyond this, in the same scene brings home to us the in-
compatibility of the worlds they represent. Midge's reappearance immediately after the beautiful, sensitive, tentative groping towards a relationship between Scottie and Madeleine, makes us aware of her exclusion
from certain levels of experience and her inadequacy to combat the sort
of rivalry Madeleine offers; yet at the same time it makes us aware of her
as representing a healthy normality to set against the element of neurotic
sickness in Scottie's attraction to Madeleine. Now, after the sequoia sequence, we have the scene in Midge's apartment where she shows Scottie
the parody-portrait of herself as Carlotta. She is trying to make him see
her, to substitute herself for the woman who obsesses him, at the same
time making the obsession ridiculous by satirizing it, and the attempt reveals both her anti-romantic down-to-earth normality and her inadequacy.
It finally destroys Scottie's connection with her: he resents the attempt to
shatter the dream. There is a marvellous shot, superbly balanced between
pathos and humour, of Midge seated beside her self-portrait, the two
images in the same attitude, the Carlotta portrait with Midge's unglam-
orous, bespectacled face; but the figure in the portrait holds the posy
Madeleine carried with her through the graveyard and the art gallery,
and Midge's hands are empty. The portrtait is Midge's attempt at an
"alienation effect", its purpose the breaking of an involvement; but its
effect is to alienate Scottie from *her.* We recall the moment in his car when
the image of Madeleine was superimposed on the portrait reproduction.
Reality is defeated, the dream is too strong; and Midge is left tearing her
hair, alone with her sense of inadequacy.

There follows the sequence at the Mission of San Juan Baptista, culminating in Madeleine's suicide. Here, in the livery-stable, amid the *décor*
of the past, Scottie makes his last effort to explain the dream, to make it
reality. The suicide itself has a shattering effect on the spectator which
is by no means to be explained solely in terms of visual impact, strong as
this is—the bell-tower, the unnerving "vertigo" shots down the stair-well,
the body falling past the aperture then spread out lifeless on the roof
below. On one level, again, we have Hitchcock capitalising on audience
expectations by abruptly defeating them: no one, I think, seeing *Vertigo*
for the first time unprepared, thinks that Madeleine is going to die halfway through. She is the heroine of the romance, the medium through
which the escape-wishes are to be fulfilled: we are prepared for a happy
ending, or perhaps for final grand tragedy, but not for this brutal mid-way
rupture. But Madeleine, as I have suggested, represents wish-fulfilment
on a deeper and more valid level than that normally offered by the Hollywood film: by this point in the film she has evoked in us all that longing

for something beyond daily reality which is so basic to human nature. We are in fact by this time so thoroughly identified with Scottie that we share his shock, and the resulting sense of bewildered desolation, in the most direct way, just as we share his sense of helplessness, even of responsibility. We are stunned, the bottom is knocked out of the world, we cannot at all see where the film is going, what possible sequel this event can have: all is chaos. It is an effect that Hitchcock is to match, two films later, in *Psycho* with the shower-bath murder.

We have already been placed, then, in a position to understand, sympathetically, Scottie's breakdown. It is preceded by the inquest, in which a brutal coronor places the responsibility for Madeleine's death on him, and which closes with the shot of his leaving the courtroom, a vast expanse of ceiling seeming to weigh down oppressively over the tiny figures in long-shot.

.   .   .

Much popular discontent with the film can be traced to [the] premature revelation [that the supposedly dead Madeleine has adopted a new identity, Judy], and in terms of audience-reaction it was certainly a daring move on Hitchcock's part. Yet our feelings of being cheated, if we analyse them, reveal a deeper cause. We have been, up to the revelation, very largely identified with Scottie, we have involved ourselves deeply in his weaknesses and his desires, in his longing to fulfil a dream as a means of escaping from or of rising above daily reality. We experienced directly his shock at Madeleine's death; now we experience a further, and worse shock: not only is she dead—she never existed. The effect is not merely of discovering that we have been deceived by an ingenious murder plot: one of our most vulnerable moral spots, our discontent with reality, has been penetrated, we have been caught off our guard. Some of the best films that have come from Hollywood, films as different in tone and in overt subject-matter as Howard Hawk's *Monkey Business* and Nicholas Ray's *Bigger Than Life,* have had as their core this theme of discontent with the actual world, but none has explored it as profoundly or brought it home to the spectator by such direct, inescapable means, as *Vertigo.* The revelation cuts the ground away from under our feet, and makes us painfully aware of the degree of our previous involvement in what is now proved to be a cheap hoax.

Yet this reaction, which the film certainly provokes at this point, has to be modified on reflection. If we re-see the film, or carefully reconstruct the first two-thirds, we shall see that we have not yet taken the full measure of the subtlety and complexity of Hitchcock's conception. For such a re-viewing or reconstruction will show us that the illusion is not *just* an illusion: Judy was not *merely* acting Madeleine—up to a point she *became* Madeleine. Our very incredulity that the Judy we see could ever have been trained to act the part of Madeleine works for Hitchcock here. Judy—on her first appearance, and in her treatment of Scottie when he follows her to her hotel room—appears hard and vulgar, over made-up, her attitude at once defiant and cheaply provocative; she is playing up the tartiness to deceive him, and her underlying vulnerability is gradually exposed, yet she is never depicted as intelligent. But she was, as Scottie tells her at the end of the film, "a very apt pupil". If we mentally juxtapose her stance and manner in the doorway of the hotel room—her way of holding her body, her expression, her intonation, her vulgarised version of what is in part their love story—with, again, Madeleine's entry from Scottie's bedroom, her way of moving and standing, her hesitant words, her reticence and *pudeur,* we shall see that Madeleine was not just an acted role but another *persona.*

It is not difficult to see that the pretence partly became reality. Most obviously, there is the point that Judy was to make Scottie fall in love with her by pretending to fall in love with him, and then she really *did* fall in love. Her behaviour before the "suicide" is full of obvious ambiguities ("It wasn't supposed to happen this way. . . . If you love me, you'll know I loved you and I wanted to go on loving you"—the remarks mean something quite different depending on whether we think of them as spoken by Madeleine or by Judy), and if we look further we shall see that in fact every moment of the relationship is ambiguous, it is impossible to distinguish pretence from reality. Is her nervousness during the car journey to San Juan Baptista real or feigned—Judy pretending to be Madeleine becoming distraught, or Judy becoming distraught as she gets nearer to what she has agreed to do? Her scream as Mrs. Elster falls, the scream Scottie so insistently questions her about at the end: is it the scream that was (presumably) planned to accompany the fall, or the scream of a woman trying, too late, to prevent an outrage at which she has connived?

Madeleine says to Scottie, "One shouldn't live alone. . . . It's wrong": Judy lives alone. Later, by the sea, telling Scottie her fragments of memory: ". . . . A room. I sit there alone—always alone". The room in the McKittrick hotel, of course. Or Judy's hotel room? We see Madeleine once when Scottie can't see her—as she watches him from her car going to close the door of his apartment before they drive out to the sequoias: she is watching him tenderly, sadly, as if attracted to him—is she still acting? When he trie to make her tell him, under the trees, why she jumped into the Bay, she appears to panic, reiterating "Please don't ask me, please don't ask me": again, Judy pretending to be a woman on the verge of breakdown, or Judy falling in love and terrified at the situation she is in? And the fears of death: when Madeleine says, "I don't want to die—there's someone within me says I must die", she could be speaking for Judy, for all of us; she is not only Judy pretending to be Madeleine possessed by

Carlotta. Yet Judy, we feel (the Judy of the last third of the film), is not a girl who would ever allow herself to become explicit about, perhaps even conscious of, such fears: she hasn't the intelligence, the self-awareness, or (despite her evident capacity for suffering) the depth. The fears can only be released in her through her being Madeleine: in a sense, it is Madeleine who is the more "real" of the two, since in Madeleine all kinds of potentialities completely hidden in Judy find expression. The pretence was that Carlotta was taking possession of Madeleine; in reality, Madeleine has taken possession of Judy. Scottie and Madeleine are linked verbally—at many points—by the fact that both are "wanderers" (with all the overtones the word accrues in the course of the film). In fact, it becomes clear that Judy as well, in surrendering to the Madeleine identity, is abandoning herself to the fulfilment of a dream. There is, up to the revelation, only one subjective shot from Judy/Madeleine's viewpoint, and it clinches this thematic connection between her and Scottie: the shot, as she stands by the water before flinging herself in, of the torn flowers drifting away on the current—the disintegration-symbol of Scottie's dream. The shot can also be taken as an imaginative-subjective shot from Scottie's viewpoint: he can't *see* the flowers drifting away, from where he is standing, but he can see Madeleine tearing and throwing them. So the shot links the two consciousnesses, and we are made to feel that the image has much the same significance for both. With this, and Judy's absorption in Madeleine, in mind, it is an easy step to see an *element* of reality in all her supposedly artificial behaviour. We cannot say that Madeleine's attempted suicide, her fears of madness, express nothing of Judy. The painfully limited, enclosed Judy, in fact, becomes articulate in Madeleine, whose *potential* reality to some extent validates the dream she represents. The theme of unstable identity is reflected in Scottie, the "wanderer" who is going to "do nothing": he is "Johnny" or "Johnny-O" to Midge, "John" to Madeleine, "Scottie" to Judy: the identity is created in part by the relationship.

The "vertigo" of the title, then, expands from one man's fear of heights into a metaphysical principle, and the metaphysic of the film is "peculiarly terrifying". I am thinking of T. S. Eliot's remarks about Blake, where he speaks of Blake's "peculiarity" as revealing itself as "the peculiarity of all great poetry. . . . It is merely a peculiar honesty which, in a world too frightened to be honest, is peculiarly terrifying." (He also remarks that this honesty "is never present without great technical accomplishment".) The world—human life, relationships, individual identity—becomes a quicksand, unstable, constantly shifting, into which we may sink at any step in any direction, illusion and reality constantly ambiguous, even interchangeable. To such a response to life, Hitchcock's authoritarian attitude to film-making, each film predestined down to the smallest detail before shooting starts, each camera-movement and camera-angle rigorously thought out, the actors strictly controlled, nothing left to chance, is clearly relevant.

Why did Hitchcock divulge the solution so early? Clearly, the decision entailed sacrifices, and not only on the "popular thriller" level: if the spectator's identification with Scottie had been preserved to the end, so that we identified throughout his attempt to re-create Madeleine from Judy, the fascination of the "dream" would also have been preserved, and only at the very end would we have been left stranded with "reality", to leave the cinema in some perplexity. Imagine the last half-hour of the film with the "revelation" scene cut out: we would be in a position to share Scottie's feelings towards Judy very exactly, our interest in her restricted to the lurking suggestion there of Madeleine. We would have shared (as she undergoes her transformation) Scottie's wonder at her resemblance to Madeleine, and like him we would have been torn between surrender to the re-created dream and suspicion of the possibility of some cruel fraud. The Hitchcockian "suspense", in short, with its characteristic under-current of moral division, would have held us to the end. Yet the very act of imagining the film without the revelation will convince the spectator of the rightness of Hitchcock's decision.

First, more obviously, the effect of the revelation is to detach us from Scottie's consciousness: suddenly, and for the first time in the film, we know something about Madeleine that he doesn't know. From here on we shall be watching him as much as watching *with* him. But our involvement with him has been such that this is in essence like watching ourselves, and what we see is again, right up to the final clarification, deeply ambig-uous: simultaneous drives towards sickness and towards health. As Scottie re-creates Madeleine, is he impelled by a desire to rebuild a dream in which he can lose himself, or by an undeviating (though obscure) deter-mination to reach the truth? If the former is the more obvious, the latter is, as we shall see, indisputably expressed in the film, which offers a par-ticularly beautiful example of that Hitchcockian sense of the inextrica-bility, in human life, of good and evil. Like Jefferies in *Rear Window* Scottie can achieve health (or, if you prefer, enlightenement) only by fol-lowing through to the end an obsession that has its source in a spiritual sickness. We could have been made (as we were in *Rear Window*) to share in this process; Hitchcock elected to have us study it.

Why this is in this case the better alternative arises from the second difference the revelation makes. Without it, Judy would remain, neces-sarily, as inscrutable as Madeleine had been; with it, we are constantly made aware of her feelings as well as of Scottie's. The gain in richness and complexity is great; the sacrifice in "suspense" is compensated for by a gain in poignancy that makes this last part of the film profoundly dis-turbing to watch, by a tension set up in the mind of the spectator between conflicting responses. Knowing the truth, we also have far more opportunity, during the last part of the film, to consider the implications of what we see.

The detachment itself is achieved with a startling abruptness: some find the introduction of the flashback very clumsy, but it seems to me that the abrupt brutality is essential to the effect. Throughout the middle part of the film—since Madeleine's "death"—we have been feeling increasingly at sea. We can't see where the film is going—where Scottie is going. There seems no firm ground, no sense of direction: in fact, we are being made to share Scottie's state of mind once again. Then, suddenly, we are in the room alone with Judy: the withdrawal of Scottie from the scene is like the withdrawal of our own consciousness, we have nothing to cling to. Then the screen darkens around Judy and the flashback begins. Few moments in the cinema produce a greater *frisson:* this rather cheap, shallow-seeming girl is suddenly associated with Madeleine's dash up into the church tower. We experience a moment of total bewilderment in which all sense of reality seems terrifyingly to dissolve; then, abruptly, the vertigo is over for us: over, anyway, until we begin to reflect on the quicksand of reality and illusion the film presents.

.   .   .

The ending of the film perfectly knots all the strands. Scottie's vertigo is cured, not by forcing himself to go higher, nor by the "emotional shock" that Midge told him might do it (he had that the first time Madeleine died), but by finally learning the whole truth: after he has forced the confession from Judy, he can look down the well of the tower without dizziness: the symbolic nature of the vertigo is thus finally emphasised. Judy's death, on the face of it an accident, contains elements both of murder and suicide. It is clear, as he drags her up the tower stairs, that he wants to kill her—he takes her by the throat and shakes her violently. He hates her for not being Madeleine—for destroying for him the possibility of escape into fantasy. Even after he knows the whole truth, he can still cry out bitterly, "I loved you so, Madeleine", without being aware of the name he is using. As for Judy, she protests frantically and yet allows herself to be dragged up the stairs. During and after her confession, we have a terrifying sense of watching a personality disintegrate before our eyes: she talks sometimes as Madeleine, sometimes as Judy. We remember Madeleine's cry to Scottie after the sequoia sequence: "If I'm mad, that would explain it". She is already quite broken before she falls. . . .

The film ends with the magnificent image of Scottie looking down from a great height to where Judy has fallen: magnificent, because it so perfectly crystallises our complexity of response. Scottie is cured: yet his cure has destroyed at a blow both the reality and the illusion of Judy/Madeleine, has made the *illusion* of Madeleine's death real. He is cured, but empty, desolate. Triumph and tragedy are indistinguishably fused.

Vertigo seems to me of all Hitchcock's films the one nearest to perfection. Indeed, its profundity is inseparable from the perfection of form: it is a perfect organism, each character, each sequence, each image, illuminating every other. Form and technique here become the perfect expression of concerns both deep and universal. Hitchcock uses audience-involvement as an essential aspect of the film's significance. Together with its deeply disturbing attitude to life goes a strong feeling for the value of human relationships. To object that the characters' motives are not explained in terms of individual psychology is like demanding a psychological explanation of the sources of evil in Macbeth: Hitchcock is concerned with impulses that lie deeper than individual psychology, that are inherent in the human condition. The film's only blemish is the occasional inadequacy of Kim Novak as Judy. Her performance as Madeleine, lovingly moulded by Hitchcock, is flawless, but there are moments when one wants more inwardness from her Judy. The taxing long take of her composing the letter reveals this slight inadequacy: one becomes uncomfortably aware of the director behind the camera telling her "Now you do this. . . . Now you do that. . . ." But this weakness is not serious enough to detract from the poignancy of these last sequences. In complexity and subtlety, in emotional depth, in its power to disturb, in the centrality of its concerns, *Vertigo* can as well as any film be taken to represent the cinema's claims to be treated with the respect accorded to the longer-established art forms.

Vertigo: The Cure Is Worse Than the Dis-Ease

DONALD M. SPOTO

Since the publication several years ago of Robin Wood's searching analysis of the screenplay and direction of Alfred Hitchcock's *Vertigo*, there has been very little critical work on this important film. While Wood's observations are profound, enlightening, and entertaining, he does not discuss two aspects of the film that may provide a rich field for further investigation. These are, first, the psychic effect of several scenes in which explicitly archetypal symbols and themes emerge and, second, Bernard Herrmann's brilliant score. My remarks about these two aspects are intended to be provocative rather than probative.

The Emergence of Symbols of Dis-Ease

Carl Jung defines archetypal symbols as forms or images of a collective nature that occur practically everywhere on earth both as constituents of myths and as products of the individual unconscious. Any modern analysis of literature, drama, or cinema that tries to reveal archetypal symbols and themes must emphasize that what is termed "archetypal" is not intended to elucidate some recondite meaning of the creator. Even if one postulates that Hitchcock was ignorant of archetypal images (a dubious postulate at best), there is little purpose in attempting to demonstrate that the revelation of such images entered his conscious mind as a filmmaker. But that they do indeed appear in his films is undeniable.

We should recall at the outset, too, that it has always been popular to present scenes of horror in films in order to produce feelings of fright, repulsion, or psychic disturbance—what might be called dis-ease—in the viewer. Regardless of the intention of the filmmaker (and intentions range from the apparently esthetic schemes of James Whale and Fritz Lang to the clumsy pandering of directors of "spaghetti" westerns), certain images have enormous inherent power to affect an audience.

An awareness of the power of images is, of course, not new to film-making. It stands at the basis of all intelligent cinema. But Alfred Hitchcock has succeeded especially well at image-composition. He breaks cinematic clichés like so many unworthy ikons. As Robin Wood has indicated, it is precisely the absurdity of the bird attacks in *The Birds* (1963) that causes dis-ease. We are confronted with some great, elusive force whose very boundaries seem to defy us. In such a situation we are not in control, and the awful possibility slowly dawns that perhaps we are not in control of most of life. (In this regard, incidentally, Hitchcock seems to be far less Catholic than some of his followers would have him: most of what happens to his characters is determined by inner and outer forces or by chance—over all of which they have little or no control. Here, the influence of Hitchcock's Jesuit education seems to have waned with the passage of years.)

To use examples of archetypal images from another Hitchcock film, in *Psycho* (1960) the imposing shots of the house on the hill and the shadow-throwing stuffed birds in Norman Bates' office upset us just as much as the murder in the shower or the discovery of the corpse in the fruit-cellar. In fact, the first two images have perhaps a more awesome power. We can effectively distance ourselves from corpses and stabbings because they are identifiable, objective realities that are rather fantastic but can safely be seen as just part of the "story." But the house and the stuffed birds—precisely because they are ordinarily familiar and unthreatening—cause us to shudder when put in atmospheres where a latent, malevolent force seems to emanate from them. It is with this sort of image that Hitchcock most effectively breaks clichés. It is at this point, too, that the common object becomes the conveyor of a most uncommon sensation. House and birds become archetypes that are deliberately ambiguous: security/flight, life/death, appearance/reality.

The archetypal images in *Vertigo* are many and varied, and they are most evident in two major sequences. These are awe-ful images, images of a nameless power at once destructive and constructive, and hence most suitable as authentic images of life. The churchyard sequence following Madeleine Elster's "death" and the sequence at Dolores Mission at dusk are scenes of exquisite emotional power, largely as a result of the skillful use of color filters. The Golden Gate Bridge, used as background, is an image of the attempt to link opposites—here, life and death. The giant redwood trees suggest the disparity between man and nature, and the brevity of one man's life as compared with the life span of the ancient trees. The unused antique carriage near the mission is a relic from the past that is madly wrenched into the present and is linked by association with the painting of Carlotta Valdes in the museum. In terms of specific actions in the film related to water, San Francisco Bay symbolizes both life and death. The eye, a favorite Hitchcock image that not only begins and ends the film but provides a structural link for various important elements within it, becomes, finally, the eye of the audience. These are some devices used in the film to re-create the psychic state of Scottie Ferguson in the viewer. Such images, in other words, present a clash of opposites and a sense of the unknown, of psychic grotesquerie, and of the tyranny of time, all of which cause a dis-ease in the viewer far more profound than the terror that could be caused by vampires or mummies. This may be the reason that Hitchcock chose to play down the "mystery story" elements of the Boileau-Narcejac novel. In order for him to arouse an authentic sense of suspense, he had to sacrifice the element of surprise. And because the images are so compelling, the plot and its resolution become less important. Instead, the psychic aspects of Scottie Ferguson's experiences are stressed, and these are relentlessly communicated to the viewer throughout the film: the precarious balance between life and death; the slow, painful realization of the death-in-life process (represented by the roof-top accident at the beginning, the church murder, the accidental death at the end, and the scenes filmed amid the trees and waves); and the dawning awareness of the tenuous, illusory, and basically imperfectible nature of human relationships. The dis-ease, presented symbolically in terms of a fear of heights, is, paradoxically, healthy, and can lead to the reflective balance without which no life has meaning.

In the way it used images *Vertigo* served as a harbinger of later works such as John Schlesinger's *Sunday, Bloody Sunday,* Peter Bogdanovich's *The Last Picture Show,* Harold Pinter's play *Old Times,* and even Stephen

Sondheim's acerbic musicals *Company* and *Follies.* All these works shatter the clichés of romantic idealism, proclaiming without smugness that there is no "whole thing" in what e. e. cummings has termed "this so-called world of ours" and rejecting a dreamy nostalgia for an easier, safer past. They all accomplish this mainly through the power of their images. In *Vertigo,* one example of this viewpoint is an image in the nightmare sequence that precipitates Scottie's breakdown: the real flowers turn to paper flowers, suggesting that the ideal represented by Madeleine Elster is a fraud. Things are not what they seem. Our concepts of the real, the concrete, and the absolute are far less real than what we often call the world of the imaginary.

The Importance of Bernard Herrmann's Score

A consideration of Bernard Herrmann's brilliant score for Vertigo will disclose further examples of the above ideas.

The film contains seven clearly defined episodes, each of which is reflected in the music.

1. *The titles and opening sequence* The initial music is an elusive series of chords that accompany the camera as it spirals into anonymous eyes. Thus, at the outset, two important themes in the film are suggested: the notion of a journey and the problem of reality and illusion. These opening measures convey a real sense of terror, a fear of something ineffable. Even when the strings are prominent, the tempo arouses an apprehension of malevolent interruption.

For the rooftop sequence, Herrmann has written more than the usual "chase music." There is a shattering finale, the notes of which are repeated at two important junctures later in the film. Harp, strings, and trumpets seem to go berserk, and the drum-roll at the fade-out of the sequence is a particularly brilliant touch, made all the more haunting by a light echo-chamber effect. From the beginning, therefore, it is apparent that *Vertigo* will be more than just a good story, and the music conveys this impression as much as does the cinematography.

2. *Madeleine and the portrait of Carlotta* With the introduction of Madeleine Elster and the plot involving the "late" Carlotta Valdes, there is a romantic musical theme that is broken up into minor keys and triads throughout the film, and through this, every suggestion of romance is turned inside out, made fragile and suspect. The music for Carlotta's portrait, which is also used for Scottie Ferguson's silent journey through the (archetypal?) city and at the flower shop, at the museum, and in the forest, is mysterious and apprehensive. Subtle as it is, however, we cannot

resist the music's power. We must go along on this terrible psychic journey and learn, with Scottie, that to re-create the past is to invite decadence and death.

3. *The beach* In this sequence the music that accompanies the swell of the waves—and of passion—is almost unbearably poignant, and then becomes spiritual, thus reflecting the theme of the contrast of opposites. Like the beach sequences in Fellini's *La Strada* and 8½, where shore and sea become images of the elemental forces of life and death battling for and within every individual, this sequence has an unresolved musical finale that holds great importance: it prevents us from being seduced into thinking that the great mysteries posed by both the film and the music can be readily understood.

4. *The farewell and the tower* The music accompanying this episode portrays obstacles that are almost metaphysically insurmountable: the pitiable frailty of human effort and the awful finale—death—that may ultimately terminate a man's most obsessive attempts to pursue an ideal. Scottie's obsessions have led him nowhere, and the music here, which begins languorously and culminates in frenzied chords and irrational timing, forms perhaps the musical highpoint of the film. We get an impression of a frantic journey ending in nothingness, as the music takes us back to where we started at the beginning of the film: the theme of emptiness and death. The same chords again create a picture of a bottomless well of madness and destruction.

5. *The nightmare and dawn* The fifth episode of the film, containing Scottie's nightmare, begins with subtle musical scoring. It is almost reverent, with measures reminiscent of the beach scene. But the calm is quickly destroyed, and the music takes on a mad life of its own; in fact, the impression conveyed is that not even the composer or the conductor has control of it. Castanets horribly satirize Carlotta's Spanish origins, and we (through Scottie) go back to the Spanish church, the carriage now darkened and grotesque, the flowers falling away in decay, the courtroom dissolving during the coroner's inquest. We finally become aware (again, through Scottie) of falling headlong into a grave. We are drawn into this awful confrontation with life-and-death forces as his head, detached, careens toward us and, ineluctably, we follow. We cannot even escape from his screaming directly at us as he awakens from the nightmare, on the brink of psychosis.

Dawn brings no surcease: a lugubrious cello passage and a string obbligato give a feeling of sad emptiness.

6. *The love sequence* In the next episode, Herrmann's music unravels for us (there is very little dialogue) the Madeleine/Judy riddle. At the same time, however, the music is so startling in its complexity that it heightens our sense of awe at the mystery of life and death. Musically, it is an arresting meditation.

7. *The necklace, the return, and the finale* The last episode, cinematically one of the most haunting film conclusions of the last two decades, is also enhanced by Herrmann's sensitive scoring. The important element here seems to be the constant series of notes—almost serially arranged—that spiral in and out, up and down, interlaced with string tremolo. The effect recalls the "Liebestod" from Wagner's *Tristan und Isolde,* a comparison that, in its ironic inversion, is intriguing in itself.

Both the real and the apparent resolution of the problem of Madeleine's death can be nothing else but Judy's death and the reenactment of Scottie's loss, the third and most profound loss. The music written for the climb to the bell-tower is dark and fearsome. Moments of calm only signal a regrouping of musical forces, the real (if minimal) delicacy of which is used not to sweeten a harsh pill, but to inform us that beauty may be illusory and that a man, cured of his vertigo, may also be cured of his sense of life.

ANTONIONI

THE RED DESERT

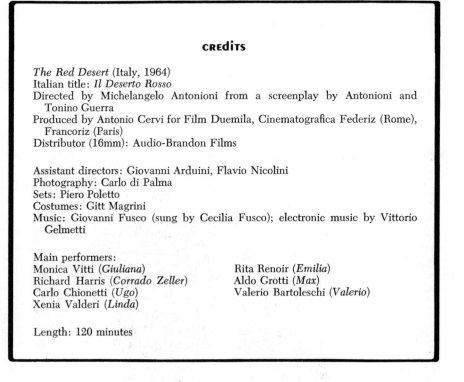

Michelangelo Antonioni has exerted an enormous influence on the development of the structural patterns of the modern cinema. Prior to the
controversial public response to, and the widespread critical acclaim for,
his film *L'Avventura* (1960), other reputable directors had departed from
the conventional narrative mode, as had Antonioni himself, but these earlier
films had not received comparable international attention. The French
"New Wave" had already begun and was to depart even further from the
recognized tradition of cinematic narrative than did Antonioni, but even
Truffaut's *The 400 Blows* (1959) and Godard's *Breathless* (1959) did not
seem, at least on the surface, to be such complete departures from the
familiar film patterns as was *L'Avventura*.

What Antonioni did here and in such later films as *La Notte* (1960),
Eclipse (1962), *The Red Desert* (1964), and *Blow-Up* (1966), was to re-
define the relationship between action and characterization in a manner
already popular in modern fiction: instead of illustrating character primarily as a person's reaction to a new or critical situation, Antonioni
prefers to depict action as resulting almost casually from the personalities
of the main characters. This approach is the opposite of that found in

such films as *Vertigo* and *The Seventh Seal,* in which the pressure of events or incidents is what determines the protagonists' course of action. When Aristotle established plot as the major element in drama, he began the tradition wherein a particular character's essential traits are either shaped by or revealed through certain incidents. What made Antonioni seem particularly difficult to follow in 1960 was his apparent neglect of plot; actually, his films usually do contain some identifiable elements of plot, but they evolve out of a conversation or a personality trait, so that the action itself can seem fortuitous or random. In short, his work is not governed by the old dramatic rules, the logical order of beginning, middle, and end that Aristotle sanctioned for narrative structure.

In *The Red Desert,* Antonioni expands his typical story structure to a new dimension, or at least affords us a new level of awareness only partially apparent in his preceding film, *Eclipse.* The malaise of the heroine—related to that of his previous heroines as dramatized through the motif of restlessness, unfulfillment, and aimlessness—is very firmly connected to the particular malaise of the modern world. Thus, Giuliana's suffering is continually related to the question of how anyone who is sensitive to the spiritual oppressions of modern living can cope with the world. Her neurosis, dramatically heightened and certainly more extreme than that of most people, is manifested through her reactions to her environment, the visualization of which constantly clarifies the general problem presented by the film: the industrialized world overwhelming the isolated individual, technology encroaching upon human identity.

The accomplishment of *The Red Desert* in depicting the interaction of Giuliana and her environment results from Antonioni's impressive use of the camera and handling of color. Seldom before had a moving camera displayed so much of a film's tone by its persistent exploration of background; the camera sometimes seems to be prowling for external signs that might serve as metaphors for either the mental state of a character or the spiritual state of society, as when it travels along the metallic surfaces of a factory or ship, pursuing a maze of twisting tubular shapes that are overtly meaningless but vaguely threatening and impossibly complicated. The camera makes even the insides of homes seem disorienting by its movements or intimidating by its continual emphasis on meticulously functional rooms, stairways, and furniture. At one point the camera watches a toy monster rushing back and forth in a child's bedroom, its senseless, unregulated motion serving as a reminder of a technology outpacing human control.

Even before it was released, *The Red Desert* began to attract notice for its special use of color. The public read stories of the director's spray-painting of grass and other natural objects to achieve predetermined color effects. With the film's appearance, many filmgoers became aware for the first time of the distinction (once made by Carl Dreyer) between a film that happened to be shot in color and a true color film. *The Red Desert* makes deliberate use of colors to shape our perceptions of the heroine's world. The encroachment of industry upon nature, with its subsequent dislocation of the human element in nature's landscape, is one of the visually developed themes in the film. Huge yellow clouds of industrial pollution create a weird beauty when seen against a drab, gray background. Colors, or the surfaces of reality, are used as points of psychological reference; for instance, in the shack, where a group of people try feebly but fail to establish an arena for their sexual fantasies, the glaring red walls become a sign of sexual disillusionment. Colors also suggest the modern trend toward the dominance of machine over man; machines are taking over the brightly colored areas of the landscape—factories and homes—and leaving men with nothing but an industrial wasteland, decaying shacks, and visionary dreams (like Giuliana's escape to an uninhabited island). In its elaborate and complex use of color to suggest meaning, *The Red Desert* reveals a source of expressive power seldom before applied in the cinema.

The Achievement of *The Red Desert*

STANLEY KAUFFMANN

With Michelangelo Antonioni's *Red Desert,* the art of the film advances. This masterly creator has, in all his films shown here, opened new possibilities. Now, with his first use of color and with other elements, he further enlarges our vision of what a film can be and do.

The story chiefly concerns Giuliana, the young wife of Ugo, an electronics engineer in Ravenna. They have a boy of four or five. Corrado, another engineer, visits Ugo to recruit skilled workers for a job in South America. Ugo tells him that Giuliana has recently been in an auto accident, was not badly hurt, but is still suffering from shock. (In fact, as we learn, it was a suicide attempt, and the "shock" is her explanation to Ugo of her state of mind.) During Corrado's stay in Ravenna, he visits a shop that Giuliana is going to open, to occupy herself; asks her to accompany him when he drives out to interview a worker; goes on a party in a seaside shack with her and Ugo and friends. All through this, Giuliana is living on her nerve-ends, trying desperately to become "normal," to become *something.* Ugo has to leave for some days on business, and during this time their little boy has a short episode of fancied paralysis. When this passes, Giuliana's disquiet does not pass. She goes out, more or less purposefully to Corrado's hotel. They make love. Later, after they part, she wanders aboard a ship, encounters a Turkish sailor, has a brief, pathetic, disconnected conversation with him, neither one understanding the other. In the last scene she is walking with her little son outside Ugo's factory. The boy asks her why the smoke from a certain chimney is yellow. She says it is a warning that it is poisonous. Doesn't it kill birds? he asks. By now, she says, the birds know all about it and don't fly through it. They walk out of the film, and it ends.

The story is both dry and full, austere and intense. It is a series of incidents with sufficient but minimal connection, not cumulative drama of well-made scenes; yet each of these terse incidents is more than a skin-and-bones gesture (à la Bresson), it is implicative and revealing. Antonioni has always been interested in symbology. His method here is not—as it has been—first, to try to move us in new ways and, second, to have the symbols beneath the emotion resonate within us: it is to hold us, to fascinate us into reading the hieroglyphics he has unearthed, dating from the mid-twentieth century. The figures on these tablets suffer, embrace, reject, but their actions weave a second symbolic language that is the primary meaning and effect.

Or, in another figure, the story is not placed in the usual dramatic topography of valleys and mountains. It takes place entirely on the heights of character and action; thus the gradations, as in any view above the clouds, are only the relatively slight ones among peaks. Though these gradations are thus more subtle than if one were looking up from far below, they are nevertheless there. But a film that begins and continues at this high altitude makes assumptions between you and itself—about the valleys of character detail and the slopes of plot cumulation. Admittedly the atmosphere of the heights is perhaps a bit chilly, but it stings and clarifies.

The setting of the new industrial town and Giuliana's neurotic state help to illuminate each other. The Ravenna we see is a manufacturing seaport. (All through the film, ships pass in the background.) But by his vistas of factories, inside and out, of new dwellings, of radar installations, even of slag heaps, Antonioni is not making any trite charge of ugliness in the modern world. He is searching out the new life in it, the means of living in it. He has jarred Giuliana into a state of shock to make her hyper-sensitive—like a clairvoyant of change, of a means to accept life as it is and as it is going to be. In his press conference at the 1964 Venice Festival (where *Red Desert* won the Golden Lion) Antonioni said: "The story was born when I went to Ravenna, which I had not seen for some time. The film was born on the spot and the color was born with it—the industrial ambience of the film." In an interview (with Jean-Luc Godard) in the November 1964 *Cahiers du Cinéma,* he says further:

> My intention . . . was to express the beauty of this world where even the factories can be very beautiful . . . The line, the curves of the factories and their chimneys are perhaps more beautiful than a line of trees, of which the eye has already seen too much. It is a rich world, lively, useful. For me, I try to say that the sort of neuroticism which one sees in *Red Desert* is entirely a question of adaptability. There are some people who adapt themselves and others who have not yet been able to do so, for they are too tied to structures or rhythms of life which are now bypassed. This is the case with Giuliana. . . . If I had chosen a normally adaptable woman, there would not have been any drama.

This can be expanded to say, also, that if he had made the film in black and white, the urgency and immediacy of the neuroticism would have been lessened. The color serves several ends. First, quite simply, it is the best use of color I have ever seen in a film, exquisite in itself. It would be a quite wrong emphasis, but one could say that the film is worth seeing for its color alone. (And also that there is a buried history of modern painting in it, from the Impressionists through Mondrian to Hopper and Wyeth.) Second, the color underscores the color in the new world, a usually disregarded facet. The age of plastic and mold-injection and die-stamp is an age of heightened colors. Third, he has used color subjectively. Antonioni has said that he had an entire marsh painted a certain shade of gray because that is the way Giuliana and Corrado felt when they looked at it. A small room of the seaside shack, where a lot of sexual teasing and talk goes on, is painted a shade of red, off which, so to speak, the talk can rebound. "It is necessary to intervene in a color film," he says, "to take away the usual reality and replace it with the reality of the moment." Yet this subjectivism is gently handled, is complementary, is never carried to musical-comedy lengths. Fourth, color makes the environment a character in the drama. I know of no film in which a greater tension exists between the movement of the story and the places through which it moves.

As the film begins, we hear electronic music; then, over it a woman's voice vocalizing. It is an apt overture. These juxtaposed elements separate, and we hear the *vocalise* again later, in an interpolated idyl. Giuliana is the exponent and victim of these two themes. She is very much herself, a woman in crisis, but she also has something of the abstracted quality of a masque figure. (Those who have noted that Antonioni builds his films around female characters may also note that he has Monica Vitti to build them around. It is one of those happy occurrences in the performing arts when the advent of the right executant evokes the best work of a creator.) A recurrent method used to open a sequence is a shot of a background in slightly blurred, diffused focus in which Miss Vitti then appears, very close, in sharp focus. Thus the world is made the scenery of her stage, both in the sense of the author's use and the sense of Giuliana's own neurotic egocentricity. I would concede, however, that both senses are given a bit too much play; something less of Giuliana's gazing out of windows or backing herself into corners would have heightened the impact of both.

The film is susceptible of considerable textural and thematic analysis. Here I can deal with only two moments. The first is a small skillful device. In the opening scene, outside the strike-bound factory, Giuliana, suddenly ravenously hungry, buys a sandwich from a worker who has already taken a bite out of it. Her insistence on buying a sandwich already "begun" is a small arresting gesture, unextravagant, just odd enough to make us wonder about her at once. The episode of the child's paralysis, which turns out to be spurious, is a painful mirror-image of the mother's troubled state. Psychiatrists know that young children apprehend and reflect neurosis in their parents; when a child is disturbed, the physician often asks that the parents (at least the mother) be treated. Suddenly one morning this little boy cannot walk or stand. During this siege, while waiting for the doctor's diagnosis, the mother distracts her son with a story, which we see as she tells it: about a young girl and a lovely, deserted pink beach (the closest we come to a literal substantiation of the film's title). This girl swims in the transparent water in the bright sun, sees birds and rabbits, is alone and happy. One morning she spies a sailing ship, unlike any other that passes by. She swims out to it and finds that, mysteriously, it is unmanned. It turns about and sails away. She swims back to the beach and hears a woman singing (the *vocalise* we heard under the titles of the film). She cannot find the woman. "One mystery is all right, two is too much," says Giuliana. "But who was singing?" asks the boy. Giuliana replies, "Everything. Everyone." The story is finished; and when she returns to his room, a little later, she finds the boy unconcernedly walking about.

The obvious contrast of the idyllic spot with the factory milieu is certainly not the prime point of the episode. (Anyway, whenever Antonioni approaches an obvious point, he always redeems it with fresh vision.) The episode is a qualified adieu to that girl's world of sailing ships and wilderness and untrammeled freedom: qualified, not because there is the slightest doubt that such a world is almost gone but because it is sheer romanticism to think that such a world was free of mystery, of unanswerable questions. Giuliana says of the ship, "The girl was used to the strangeness of men and she was not surprised." The strangeness of men was and will be—in the natural world, in the machine-monitored world. Thus Giuliana is telling *herself* the story, with that perception of her trouble that neurotics often have rationally as they try to make their way toward health emotionally. In her mind, her best mind, she knows that it is rankly sentimental to think of our times as deterioration.

A personal example: When I walk through the New York neighborhood where I lived as a child and which is now a forbidding canyon of glass-and-steel apartment houses twenty stories high, I am tempted to sigh, until I think that in 2065 men will walk through these streets, then lined with fifty-story buildings, and will yearn for the bygone "human" days of twenty-story buildings.

It is worth noting, for argument, that the Italian press is to some extent anti-Antonioni. Some of their critics seem to resent the fact that he is Italian: as if he does not fit their conception of the Italian character, which is not much different from the travel-poster stereotype. After the Venice premiere a Milanese paper predictably referred to *Red Desert* as "*ancora una volta il 'michelangiolesco' giochetto*"—once more the "michelangelesque" little game. (By contrast, and again predictably, some of the French press went to the other extreme and immediately hailed it as an imperishable masterpiece. The film has been a success in Paris.) But if there is anything that this film is not, it is "once more" of anything. The same artist left the same highly personal imprint on it, but it is different both in style and subject from his trilogy [*L'Avventura, L'Eclisse,* and *La Notte*].

In style there is small trace in it of the distention of time that was germane to the trilogy, immersion in the extended moment. The handling of scenes is much more theatrically elliptical, and the editing, with rare exceptions, is pared. There are no marked lingerings on scenes, as if the pedal were being held down after the chord was released—a device often, and effectively, used in the trilogy.

As for subject matter, the trilogy was concerned with differing aspects of love as the medium of hope in our world. This film is stripped to naked essence—hope or nonhope unadorned: the prospect of human life in the midst of whirling changes. We live, as we know, in the age of the swiftest transition in history, and all indications are that the speed of change will increase: in everything from household appliances to concepts in philosophy, the whole architecture of thought. Antonioni seems to be saying, without effervescent cheeriness, that what was valuable can be preserved or can be transmuted to a new viability: that the future may contain new, at present inconceivable, values.

His film reaches no grand resolution. The affair with Corrado does not "cure" Giuliana. Her isolated dialogue with the Turkish sailor is not a "come-to-realize" scene. There is no guarantee that she is on the Road to Happiness. But she has finally accepted what has been no secret from her all along: that "what happens to you is your life"; and the very story that she herself tells her son evidences that she has within her a treasury of truth on which she may some day have courage to draw.

There are only three important characters. As Ugo, Carlo Chionetti has the right face and voice; not much more is asked of him. Miss Vitti is, as noted, the perfect Giuliana. She is asked to carry the film and she succeeds. Her vocabulary of uncertainty, in speech and gesture, is rooted in the certainty of her distress, her shame at her distress, her shameless display of it, her anger at the strength of others.

The principal and, to me, only serious flaw in the film is the casting of Richard Harris as Corrado. What he does is suitable enough; he has affecting ease and unexpected gentleness. But (this is a persistent Antonioni habit) what point was there in using a non-Italian who had to be dubbed? (At times rather perceptibly.) In Venice, when Antonioni was asked why he used Harris, he replied wryly that he chose Harris because he was thirty. "In Italy we have many actors of forty, like Gassman and Mastroianni, but we don't have any of thirty." I took this small joke as an oblique statement of regret. I hope I was right and that the practice can be discontinued.

I have now seen *Red Desert* three times, and each succeeding time it has not only seemed lovelier in color, it has had an increased sense of motion forward: in thematic penetration and artistic refinement. But pre-eminent in this sense of forward motion is a conviction that, as in his other recent films, Antonioni is not only making art of a high order, he is finding ways to help keep art itself alive. In these days of chance music, action painting and pop art, aesthetic idiocy in prose and poem, monolithic monomania in architecture, in these days when good artists question by act and statement the necessity for art, Antonioni continues to keep the film fresh and relevant: fresh without inane novelty, relevant without facile nostalgic reference. He has often been accused of being literary; if that is an indictment, he has perhaps been guilty, but here he is more purely cinematic than ever. There are few living directors who can be compared with him in level of achievement; there is none who is his peer in shaping the film form itself to the needs of contemporary men.

The Red Desert: The Triple Split

RICHARD ROUD

The Triple Split

As part of her attempts to "reintegrate herself with reality," Giuliana, heroine of *The Red Desert*, has decided to open a small shop. When a friend drops by, he finds her trying out various samples of paint for the walls and ceiling. Giuliana has nearly decided on a light green—it will be less distracting. Distracting, echoes Corrado? Yes, from what I'm sell-ing, the things . . . . There is a pause, and suddenly Giuliana wheels on Corrado: What do you think I should sell?

Antonioni may not have intended this scene as a reference to the vexed problem of form and content, but the image of Giuliana carefully decorat-ing a shop before she knows what—if anything—she is going to sell in it, underlines very early in the film that rift in *The Red Desert* between what it is *about*, and what it *is*. Actually, there is a three-way split between what Antonioni says his film is about, what it is about, and most important of all, what it is as film.

As film, it is a remarkable achievement. All the more reason, then, for a

FROM *Sight and Sound*, Vol. 34 (Spring 1965), pp. 76–80. Reprinted by permission of *Sight and Sound* and the author.

close examination of why—as a statement—it is something less than satis-factory. Antonioni has proclaimed that this film is a new departure for him, that everything he has done so far no longer interests him. And yet there are enough elements of the past in *The Red Desert* partially to belie this claim, enough of the past to undermine it.

The Undistributed Middle

May, 1960: La Napoule. At a press conference the day before the presenta-tion of *L'Avventura* at the Cannes Festival, Antonioni read the now famous statement: "There is today a very serious split between science on the one hand—completely projected towards the future and ready each day to repudiate its past if by so doing it can conquer even the smallest fraction of its future—and, on the other hand, a static, rigid morality, to which Man, fully aware of its obsolescence, nevertheless continues to cling." Antonioni then proceeds to deplore the contrast between man's conformism to his moral heritage and his willingness, in the scientific domain, to try any likely hypothesis. He offers no solution to the problem, saying only that *L'Avventura* is neither sermon nor denunciation: simply a statement of the problem. He concludes, however, with a query. Why is it that, knowing the old Tables of the Law no longer offer us anything more than an all too chewed-over message, we none the less remain faithful to them? Why is the man who is not afraid of the scientific unknown still afraid of the moral unknown?

At the time, there seemed little reason to ponder deeply on this state-ment, partly because it appeared irrelevant to *L'Avventura,* and partly because one discounts general philosophical pronouncements from film directors. But now, in *The Red Desert,* Antonioni seems finally to have attempted a dramatisation of this statement. So perhaps it is time we took it seriously, especially as Antonioni declared, in a recent interview in *Cahiers du Cinéma,* that only by adapting ourselves to the new techniques of life can we find a solution to our moral problems.

Taking Antonioni's La Napoule statement seriously, then, we can see immediately that it betrays a certain degree of confusion. It implies that while science has made enormous progress in the last hundred years, morality has remained where it was in 1860. This, I believe, is untrue—at least in England and America. So manifestly untrue is it that there is little need to offer proof: one has only to read the newspapers and keep one's eyes open. In any case, Antonioni assumes that it is possible to make a valid comparison between science and morality. This seems to me as untenable as his statement that, in *La Notte,* he was trying to show that his characters did not live up to the beauty of the modern architecture in which they lived. But architecture, like any art, is an idealisation, a concentration, an incarnation of life: one cannot "live up" to the Pirelli build-ing any more than the Greeks "lived up" to the Parthenon or the twelfth century French to Chartres.

One does not want to maintain that "human nature never changes." It does. But it changes much more slowly than science and for different reasons. Surely the difference between science and morality is that science is . . . scientific: i.e., it deals with matters that can be empirically mea-sured or ascertained. But how could one prove that monogamy is inferior to polygamy?

Travellers on the Red Desert

Giuliana (Monica Vitti): Giuliana is happily married to an engineer; to-gether with their boy they live in Ravenna. Two years ago she tried to commit suicide, but managed, with the help of the doctors, to pass it off as a car accident. In spite of prolonged treatment, she still has great diffi-culty adjusting to reality. Her husband is very kind to her, but this does not seem to help. His colleague, Corrado, finds her extremely attractive; perhaps he will be able to protect her from all the things of which she is afraid. After a particularly violent crisis, she goes to him for help. They end up in bed together, but the experience is inconclusive. Somehow she manages to achieve a kind of stability thereafter, but for how long, we do not know.

Ugo (Carlo Chionetti): Ugo is an engineer, happy in his work and happily married. After the shock of his wife's automobile accident (which occurred while he was in London: he did not, however, return) he found her rather difficult to live with. On the other hand, he gets much pleasure from teaching his son the rudiments of science. Were it not for Giuliana's neuroses, he would be very happy indeed. The only cloud is the inordinate interest she seems to be showing in his colleague, Corrado Zeller. But Zeller is off to South America soon.

Corrado (Richard Harris): Corrado came to Ravenna to recruit work-men for the factory he is going to run in Patagonia. The task takes him much longer than he expected, but in the meanwhile he becomes very attracted to Giuliana. He is pleased that she seems to like him, too, but disturbed by her rather peculiar behaviour. When she finally tells him that she has tried to commit suicide, he begins to understand her a little better. She demands from him, however, more than he, or perhaps any man, can give. One night she goes to his hotel in a particularly disturbed state; they end up by going to bed together. The experience is not very satisfactory for either of them. Corrado feels that he must complete his arrangements for the expedition; at the same time he experiences a cer-tain lassitude, an unwillingness to keep moving, as he has done for years, from one place to the next.

Objective Correlative?

To judge from the reasonably objective statements I have invented for each of the three leading characters, *The Red Desert* would seem to be a film about a neurotic woman. And Antonioni admits in the *Cahiers* interview that it is not the milieu in which Giuliana lives that provokes her crisis: it only makes it explode. Her husband and her lover do seem to be happy enough, and reasonably well adjusted.* If Ugo and Corrado have come to terms with their world, and Giuliana and the other women have not, would not this seem to indicate that the moral of the film is really the same one that moralists have preached for centuries: the Devil finds work for idle hands.† This is further borne out by Antonioni's personal statement that if he could not work, could not make films, life would not be worth living.

But this is not at all what Antonioni claims he is saying. Throughout the film, Giuliana's tangled neuroses are contrasted with the clean forms and austere beauty of industrial architecture. Further, her life is compared with the slag heaps, the rusted iron, the refuse: the waste products of industrial civilisation. We see her first in the waste land surrounding the factory, crouching grotesquely amidst the brush and the waste, against the belching yellow poisonous exhaust from the factory, devouring a half-eaten sandwich which she has just bought for 2,000 lire from an astonished workman.

Antonioni might reply that women are simply more sensitive, and react more strongly than men to the contagion that menaces us all. And it is true that the cry (*il grido*) which heralds the arrival of the plague ship is heard only by Giuliana and Linda: the men hear nothing. And yet, the ship arrives, flying its yellow flag.

The problem is not entirely philosophical, however. Perhaps Antonioni might have succeeded with another actress in rendering significant Giuliana's neuroses. But it must be said, with all respect, that Monica Vitti is inadequate for this purpose. From her first appearance, slouched inside her coat, her fingers jammed in her mouth, staring wildly from right to left, she looks more like a Monica Vitti character who has finally taken complete leave of her senses than the result of the split between science and morality.‡ The problem remains: whether because of the way she is played, or because of the action of the film, Giuliana remains a pathological case. Therefore, when Antonioni assures us that, because Corrado

---

* Antonioni denies this in part: he maintains that Corrado's meeting with Giuliana unhinges him; perhaps because of the inadequacy of Richard Harris in the role, this is never visible.

† True, there is the worker at Medicina who was in Giuliana's clinic, but he remains a shadowy symbol, rather than a character, expressly put in to show that workers can be neurotic too. In any case, when we see him he is happily back at work, and only his wife displays neurotic tendencies.

‡ This is neither his nor her fault: it would seem that the only way he can get a film set up is with the commercial guarantee of the presence of Miss Vitti.

sleeps with her when she comes to him for help, she is consequently the victim of her own outmoded world of sentiments, one can but demur. If she had gone to someone really well adapted like Ugo, Antonioni says, he would have tried to cure her rather than "profit" by her dismay. But as the character is played by Miss Vitti, any "treatment" other than the most basic would seem to be of little use.

But this remark of Antonioni's demands investigation, for it displays an unexpected attitude towards sexual relations. If he is against our out-moded morality, why then does he feel it so beastly of Corrado to have slept with Giuliana? And why does "Nothing Happen" in the so-called orgy scene? One hopes Antonioni is saying that the fact that nothing happens is another proof of how these people are prisoners of their morality. But the arrival of a worker (seen in a heroic low-angle shot from the point of view of the entangled mass of bourgeois limbs on the floor) may signify a condemnation of these wicked, if abortive, upper middle class goings on. The meaning of the scene remains vague, perhaps because of a confusion between Antonioni's old left-wing sympathies (corruption and decadence of the bourgeoisie) and his current view that it is the rising engineer class who—adjusted to science and technology—will inherit the earth. One could say that it is precisely this confusion which is the subject of the film, but it would have been more convincing had Antonioni seemed clearer in his own mind.

There are other examples of basic uncertainty in the film: the husband (admirably played by Carlo Chionetti, a non-professional) is supposed to be the only character approaching Antonioni's ideal, and yet we are astonished to learn that he did not come back from London when Giuliana had her "accident." Corrado (and we) cannot help but find this reprehensible. Is this because we are tied to the old morality, too? This seems hard to believe; if it is not true, then perhaps well-adjusted Ugo is *too* well-adjusted?

One could go on picking holes in the film's message, but as Antonioni admits, he is not a philosopher, and these considerations have little to do with what he calls the "invention" of his film. Not being a philosopher (or a scientist) has taken its toll, none the less. Antonioni has been a victim of that deductive reasoning abhorred by scientists: he has imposed an idea or a belief on his materials, rather than inducing one from them. This is a fault of which he was rarely guilty in his previous three films (except, perhaps, for the party scenes in *La Notte*). But the specific virtues of *The Red Desert* were largely absent from these films, too.

Figure or Carpet?

These virtues are purely cinematographic, or, to put the fat in the fire, abstract. How can this be, you cry? We all know that films deal with human relationships, not spatial relationships. But do they? I defy anyone to deny that *The Red Desert* is a "great" film. And yet anyone could—as I have done—pick gaping holes in it as drama, as statement. Ergo: its virtues must be non-intellectual, and, in a measure, non-dramatic. The colour, one anxiously suggests? Yes, it is beautiful. But that's not it. At least, that's not all of it. To go back to the old argument, is it simply that a painting is, before being a battle scene or a nude, first of all an arrangement of lines and colours in a certain order? There is much in *The Red Desert* to justify this view.

This is not an entirely new departure for Antonioni: his early *Cronaca di un Amore* and *Signora senza Camelie* were distinguished by an autonomous and non-functional use of camera movements, a formal choreography which accompanied the film, providing a non-conceptual figure in the carpet, an experience in pure form. But about the time of *L'Avventura,* he seemed to abandon all this; declaring, in fact, that he had tired of what he called experiments in film syntax. None the less, in *La Notte* (particularly the great sequence of Lidia's walk) one found him experimenting again. Now, in *The Red Desert,* non-representation is well to the fore. Antonioni says that it was the use of colour which prompted a certain modification of his style. But it goes deeper than that: he has quite consciously foregone realism. For example, he says, he has made much use of a telephoto lens precisely in order to avoid that depth of focus so indispensable to realism. In fact (perhaps because of near-by Ravenna?) many shots have a Byzantine two-dimensionality, a lack of perspective which comes close to creating purely painterly effects.

Then, too, landscape and even people are treated as elements to be arranged and placed in a frame: people are inserted into landscape, inserted into frame; surging up from the bottom, sliding in from the side. The arrival of Corrado at Giuliana's shop in the Via Alighieri begins with the irruption from the right of an abstract white form along the bottom of the frame: a second later we see that this is the roof of his car.

Because he has treated the film abstractly, or rather, concretely as film—something which is made up of frames arranged in a certain order—he has also paid more attention to the problem of the cut. But the cut used not for dramatic purposes (to reinforce the action), but almost autonomously for its own sake. For example, the early scenes of Giuliana with the strikers: the camera pans down over her, then cuts to an empty frame into which she slides from the bottom. In the old days, Antonioni used to say that his camera followed his characters "beyond the moments conventionally considered important for the spectator." In *The Red Desert,* he pays as much attention to objects and landscape as to the characters. Only a moment after the characters have walked out of frame does he cut to a bit of landscape; seconds later, the characters reappear in frame. Landscape was used extensively in *Il Grido,* too, but here its use is not so much expressive as formal. Not completely, of course: there is obviously a relationship, however tenuous, between the emotional mood of the film and the objects, the trees, the fragments of landscape. But it is tenuous. It approaches the pure beauty of, say, the opening sequence of *Marnie*, which also has little to do with the plot or theme of the film, but everything to do with cinema.

If the Hitchcock reference is too shocking, one might further compare *The Red Desert* to [Alain Resnais'] *Muriel*. Apart from a few superficial resemblances (the use of a singer in the music score, the relatively choppy montage, the fascination in rendering beautiful the essentially ugly, like the Medicina housing estate), both films are alike in their espousal of a construction which is dictated more by formal considerations than by dramatic relevance or expression.

Meaning and Image in *The Red Desert*

JOHN S. BRAGIN

. . . *The Red Desert:* "His most static film to date, a series of picture post-cards replaying a by now worn out theme." One hears this kind of criticism from those critics who decry the movement away from good, solid films to simple agility and pyrotechnics with the medium. I think a closer look will reveal that *The Red Desert*, as well as others like it, is a good deal more in the groove of the film art than it is given credit for by many critics and reviewers, and that it traces its roots back to the birth of the film, to the techniques used by the Lumière Brothers: the directness and wonder of reality in movement. No more is the old vocabulary of shot angles, coverage, and scene editing valid to present these men's ideas. No more is the film-maker a translator of the script into visual terms, but he is beginning, in Antonioni's words, to write the film as it is actually being photographed. Sequences, events, ideas, and objects are no longer objective correlatives, symbols, allusions, or metaphors to things outside the film itself. No more than the brush stroke of a painter stands for anything but itself. As film leaves literature and the theater behind, it cleaves to its closer kin: poetry and music. Antonioni and Resnais have a close relation-

FROM "Notes on *Muriel* and *The Red Desert*" by John S. Bragin, Film Culture, Vol. 41 (Summer 1966), pp. 24–29. Reprinted by permission of *Film Culture*.

ship to Chaplin and Hitchcock, respectively, but they are ridding themselves of the story and plot structure which, in its conventions, is laid over
the works of these two masters of movement. Resnais, in his marvelous
fluidity, and Antonioni, in his strength and density, are asking us to throw
ourselves into the stream of life, and to abandon ourselves to the ebb and
flow of the film, as we do with music. In the twenties and early thirties
many artists from other fields came to the cinema to try and create what
we now call the abstract or art film. Each one tried to build a film around
the successive photographing and editing of objects and symbolic events
into an abstract ballet. Léger's *Ballet Mechanique* and Clair and Picabia's
Entr'acte are two major examples. But all these lacked the existence of
human consciousness as the factor which makes the image incisive and
gripping. Without this the films fall prey to gadgetry. Antonioni has made
the remark that he has a great deal of sympathy for objects, that he learns
much from them, but that his primary concern is with man. It is the
defining and ordering power of man which he investigates. Man's emotional reactions to the world because of his ever increasing consciousness
are presented to us in terms of movements and variations of the images
with which he works. Resnais, talking about *Last Year at Marienbad,*
said that he was in agreement with Truffaut that a good film could be
summed up in one word. The effect of this is to destroy the old ideas of
dramatic structure, and the literary and theatrical qualities of a film-play,
and to bring all the elements in the film to a level which is the film's
overriding tone. Resnais with the slickness in *Muriel* shows us a woman
whose greatly accelerated pace of life comes from her insecurity in relation to the world around her. She frantically glides from situation to
situation, and literally runs out of steam by the end of the film. Antonioni
gives us a woman whose greatly reduced state of movement is caused by
each instant of reality weighing so heavily on her that all things, people
as well as objects, become overburdening to her. She no longer seems to
be able to filter reality so that there are crests and troughs, so that her
being is not drowned in a sea of overwhelming perceptions, but *all* reality
seems to penetrate her being as a wave of constantly rising crests.

In *The Red Desert* the first three shots are arranged in exactly the opposite order from what traditional cutting would imply. The first cut, after
the titles, is made on the explosive burst of an exhaust flame, seemingly
unsupported, from the bottom frame line. The second shot is a wider
angle revealing, on the second burst of flame, the chimney and the top
part of its concrete support. In the third shot the flame is a tiny yellow
spurt, in the upper left of the frame, from a very high factory chimney.
On the right side of the frame this chimney is balanced by a large concave cylinder, the same height as the chimney. The smaller buildings and
forms around the factory are seen at the base of these two giant structures.

The first cut rivets our attention to the screen. With the next cut we are still looking at the flame with the same intensity, and with an otherwise empty frame. And when the third shot appears we are still compelled to the same level of attention, even though, this time, we are forced to look at more objects in the frame. It is the hard-hitting compulsion of the first cut which determines our emotional reactions to the two following, and to the film as a whole. Usually the Master Shot, which the third cut reveals, is used to establish location or geography so that later, closer shots will not throw the viewer into confusion as to the physical layout of the scene. A rule of thumb is to save the most important items to be shown in closer shots. But here we are told in what manner we must view the film on an emotional level, there is not the intellectual giving of information, the traditional use of coverage is giving way to a texture so dense that absolute attention is required at all times. This is, of course, the way in which Giuliana views reality: with everything in the world having become oppressive with a super-thereness. Thus, even though Giuliana is not yet seen in this prologue, we are plunged into her consciousness of reality.

Immediately following this abstract prologue comes the second sequence, at the beginning of which we are given a mild expository look at "la vie quotidienne" which surrounds the other people who work and make their living in and through the factory. It is a quite comprehensible world until Giuliana enters. With her coming the lesson of the prologue comes into play. When we first see her she is shot with a normal lens from a distance. She and Valerio, her son, are walking forward at the right edge of the frame, she seems to be just another person around the factory at the time of the strike. The next shot of her, a close-up, is shot with a very long lens, and she is framed with her eyes along the center of the frame, with people passing back and forth between the camera and her. She seems immersed in a sea of people moving over and around her. The rest of the film is her point-of-view.

The last two sequences of the film can be fruitfully compared with the first two. Giuliana talking to the Turkish sailor is speaking to someone who cannot possibly either understand her language or her state of mind. Throughout the film she has been trying to communicate this state of mind to the people who surround her; by the end she is speaking out loud to herself. Her speaking of her sickness in this way is the turning point in her relations with reality. The setting is one which appears very artificial, like an exterior reproduced on a sound stage, as if Antonioni were giving his character a stage from which to speak. The speech is divided into three parts: A medium close shot of her telling about her sickness: the background is out of focus and both our center of attention and the film's center of attention are focused on her. The next, when she loses the thread of her thoughts, is a full shot with the background held in focus; she has relapsed back into her old world. When she finally regains her thoughts we cut back to a shot identical with the first one. There are no reaction shots of the Turk, or point-of-view shots of Giuliana. She stands and delivers in the most sustained speech she gives in the film. This is her summing up. Repeating out loud the instructions of her doctors and friends, she finishes with the Italian word "Ecco," or "here it is!" just as the characters of the Old Testament use the Hebrew "henini" as they present themselves naked before God. With this she comes to an equilibrium of sorts, a certain acceptance of herself and her life, but there is no guarantee that this will endure or grow stronger. Antonioni shows us her new relation to the world about her by photographing in long shot Giuliana's decisive move out of this setting. She is seen in full figure, about half the height of the frame, as she exits making a bee-line from frame right to frame left. We see her in profile, and she seems all the more decisive because the scene around her is very still. The ship, dock, piping, and the rest form a very static composition.

The last sequence is again in front of the factory, it is day, and the area is completely deserted except for Giuliana and Valerio. Because she is now able to explain about the poisonous flame, she is able to communicate with Valerio in much the same manner as her husband, Ugo, explains the scientific principles behind his toys. It is a little step, and on a simple plane it is an allusion to her own problem, but, more than this, she begins to act, to relate fruitfully to the world and to her son, who is so much the greatest part of her world. She and Valerio exit frame and we hold on a scene of the factory, which is deserted. Somehow, this scene, so terrifying and oppressive at the film's beginning, has lost most of its terror. Giuliana, whose ego had been swallowed whole, is beginning to pull herself out, replacing her fear and passivity with an initiative of her own. She does this in much the same way, emotionally, as did primitive man discard the animistic myths and come into relation with the world on a level above mere magic and exhortation.

. . .

From *Il Grido* through *The Red Desert* each film of Antonioni's has marked both the culmination of a set of formal ideas, and the beginning of a still newer set. Basically, the whole development has been the gradual but steady approach to the investigation of movement on a more and more minute scale. It is an approach to absolute zero. This begins with the effect that both *Il Grido* and *L'Avventura* are a continuous tracking shot, which allows Antonioni to concentrate and to bring detailed movement to a very high level. As the pace slows down and movement becomes more and more concentrated, we are pulled into an ever thickening texture. Each image is brought closer and closer to us for very careful consideration. With *L'Eclisse* he begins to rid himself of social and caste ideas dominating his characters, and begins a more psychological and individual investigation. *The Red Desert* is about only one person, much more so than even *Il Grido* was. With his use of color Antonioni has a very powerful partner for this concentrated attention. He seems to be right on the threshold of making a film dealing simply with color and form in move-ment—thus succeeding, because it has grown out of human consciousness, in making the abstract film which many had striven for before him.

In our first view of the control room of the factory where Ugo is working we are shown a scene which seems to be right out of a science-fiction film. It is not until Ugo, speaking on the phone, moves to a medium shot frame right, that we have a balance between him and his environment. In the following sequence of shots, which show us other offices and workers, this feeling continues, but the other workers, like Ugo, fit right in among their surroundings. This holds true when Ugo and Corrado leave the control room and walk amongst the huge machines. But, as Giuliana enters the same complex of machinery, as she appears and disappears on her way to her husband, we feel that she is being swallowed up by the plant. The abstract design in black and yellow tile which is at one end of the raised walking platforms, and which Ugo and Corrado pass, is the first of a series of forms on which the camera lingers, a device which Antonioni uses throughout the rest of the film. As Ugo and Corrado walk by this form and leave the frame, the camera remains in full shot on this design.

This is the use of clean exits and entrances. Formerly films used the device in order to allow people to familiarize themselves with a setting so that they would not become confused when the action moved into this area. This is somewhat analogous to the French Scene, where a different scene number is given any time a character leaves the stage, or a new one enters. As we watch the film and a new scene appears empty of characters, this abstract feeling is very neutral, but with the appearance of the char-acter the scene takes on depth, and after the pause in the action which this clean entrance causes, we again resume the action. It is the same with a clean exit. Many times it is the back of Giuliana's head which appears in frame, and this view over or to the left or right of her head changes the tone with which we view the scene. The back of her head is even more expressive than one would think. Since we do not see facial expres-sions, what is it that gives this heightened emotion to the scene? It is the tacit realization that we are looking directly at the same thing that she is. She is facing in the same direction that we are, and forms a direct line or pointer from our eyes through hers to the scene. Thus our attention is directed, rather than with an empty frame, with the normal point-of-view shot, when our eyes simply wander back and forth across the screen. Antonioni has said that one of the techniques he used in *L'Avventura* was to keep his camera on the actors for a few seconds after they had finished their lines or business. In this way he gained the extra emotional residue left in the scene, the extra bit of truth which came when prescribed events had settled down. In *The Red Desert* he has taken this idea a step further. After the actors have performed their lines or action they linger a moment, then exit frame; thus we are left with this emotional residue from both the actors and the tone which the actors have given to the setting. From *Il Grido* to *The Red Desert* there has been a steady coming forward of the background and geography, so that finally, with this use of clean exits and entrances, it has become an equal partner in the film.

Throughout his other films Antonioni has eschewed the reaction shot and the point-of-view shot. Several times he uses these in *The Red Desert,* but they are less successful than the method of placing someone in the frame as a pointer. Instead of increasing the emotional intensity, they open up the view and diffuse the scene. There are two occasions, however, when the camera becomes neutral or represents the point-of-view, mentally, of a character which are quite successful. The first is the scene in Max's shack, where, for a time, all the characters become as important as Giuliana, and Antonioni investigates the emotions which prevail over the whole group. This is shattered when Giuliana becomes afraid of the epidemic, and forces the others to follow her. The second is the illustration of the story which Giuliana tells Valerio. The scene in Max's shack is an exquisite ballet, especially when the characters are crowded together on the bed behind the red partition. Here we find the camera alternating regularly in its emphasis on one or another character, and in its emphasis on the group as a whole. Throughout the sequence there are many emotional moods, each one breaking in suddenly on the one before it: The argument about the scream, the scene with the quail eggs, the discussion of ointments and herbs which prolong sexual potency, and the destruction, almost in a fit of madness, of the partition by Corrado. This all leads, in an extraordinarily beautiful way, to the trauma of Giuliana almost plunging the car into the sea; the fear of the epidemic is just the trigger which releases the emotions pent up in her. The mist, revealing and concealing the characters, along with the very long lens close-ups of everyone except Corrado, gives one the feeling of a series of mug shots, or a line-up—this because of the extreme flattening of the image. After watching their antics in the shack, we are given one last, concentrated portrait of them as Giuliana sees them. To Giuliana they all become neutral beings who cannot help her, so she runs desperately to the car.

The second time the camera is used directly as an instrument to illustrate the story which Giuliana tells to Valerio. The clarity and crispness of these scenes, especially in comparison with the rest of the film, represents the clarity of Giuliana's inner vision. Why should Antonioni want to place this illustrated fairy tale among the rest of the film, which is so stark and realistic? It is because the rest of the film is not just realistic; the nature of Giuliana's vision is artistic. The artist must view reality with an intensity comparable to Giuliana's, but, where the thereness or isness

BUÑUEL

belle de jour

CREdiTS

Belle de Jour (France, 1968)
Directed by Luis Buñuel from a script by Buñuel and Jean-Claude Carrière,
  based on the novel by Joseph Kessel
Produced by Henri Baum for Paris Film Production (Robert and
  Raymond Hakim)
Distributor (16mm): Hurlock Cine World

Photography: Sacha Vierny
Décors: Robert Claval

Main performers:
Catherine Deneuve (*Séverine*)
Jean Sorel (*Pierre*)
Michel Piccoli (*Husson*)
Geneviève Page (*Anaïs*)
Francisco Rabal (*Hyppolite*)

Pierre Clementi (*Marcel*)
Georges Marchal (*The Duke*)
Brigitte Parmentier (*Séverine as a child*)

From the beginning of his career as a director, Luis Buñuel has revealed
two seemingly contradictory stylistic tendencies: surrealism (*Un Chien
Andalou*, 1928 and *L'Age d'Or*, 1930) and naturalism (*Land Without
Bread*, 1932). Although his instinctive skill for fastening on disturbing
images that shock the viewer into an immediate awareness of a situation's
potential for horror is apparent in both aspects of Buñuel's style, for
many years it remained difficult to evaluate the direction of his genius
or even to see any consistent perspective from one film to another. After
1932 he worked on films in Spain and France and was Director of Documentaries for the Museum of Modern Art in New York, but he directed no
feature films of his own until he began working in the artistically
nebulous Mexican industry in 1947. There, for another dozen years, he
turned out a series of good, bad, and indifferent films. The twentieth film
of this period, *Viridiana* (Spain, 1961), proved to be an international success—enhanced perhaps by the controversy that ensued when Spanish
authorities banned and even tried to confiscate it, and Catholic or-
ganizations in other countries attempted to prevent it from being shown.
It was this film that marked the turning point in Buñuel's reputation; it
made audiences aware that he possessed an extraordinary power to penetrate the façade of the familiar world. By using the most grotesque and
psychologically suggestive images and symbols, Buñuel immediately
moves us beyond the perceptions of our senses into the highly imaginative
surrealistic universe that seems to be permanently associated with his

vision of the real world. *Belle de Jour* is the culmination of this film-maker's dual vision; it is a film that proceeds with perfect equanimity on both levels, leaving critics to debate vehemently the particular level on which a particular sequence takes place.

Buñuel's style exhibits an affinity with that of Hitchcock, though their subject matter and thematic material are overtly quite different. Both men are the supreme metaphysical poets of the cinema—metaphysical in the sense of Samuel Johnson's famous definition: "The most hetero-geneous ideas are yoked by violence together." Their ability to associate the gruesome and the comic has often seemed perverse to critics, who usually prefer a separation of terror and wit, as if art should strive for a purity that belies the complexity of real life. In *Viridiana* a little girl is seen playing with the rope just used by a man to hang himself; in *Tristana* (1970) the heroine sees the head of her oppressive uncle as the clapper of a huge church bell. The basic concept of *Belle de Jour* encompasses the yoking together of the heterogeneous ideas of prostitution and chas-tity, visualized in the paradoxical appearance of the heroine, a combina-tion of worldly experience and perpetual innocence. Like Hitchcock, Buñuel draws disparate elements together, often in a shocking way, for the purpose of instructing us in the perception of reality: the world is an uncertain place, and we should not let calm surfaces mislead us into an easy assurance of stability. Buñuel has devoted entire films such as *The Milky Way* (1968), *The Exterminating Angel* (1962), and *The Discreet Charm of the Bourgeoisie* (1972) to undermining our faith in surfaces, wittily revealing the hollowness and dangers that lie beneath.

Although *Belle de Jour* contains some of Buñuel's typical motifs of terror, sadism, and cruelty, it strikes most viewers, even those who dis-like its subject matter, as a thoroughly beautiful film. It opens with a marvelously colored autumnal scene: a magnificent horse-drawn carriage appears, driving slowly through a wooded area. The carriage stops and the occupants descend, and then, with tranquil indifference, the husband proceeds to order his coachmen to flog and rape his wife. The fact that the sequence turns out to be a daydream hardly reassures us, for elsewhere in the film we may have difficulty in distinguishing apparent fantasy from Buñuel's vision of the modern world in which the grotesque is inextricably united with the beautiful. *Belle de Jour* sustains this vision, in spite of its continuous effect of tension, without damage to the integrity of its artistic form. The film awakened many of Buñuel's admirers to the fact that, like every other great director, Buñuel is a master craftsman. The myth of Buñuel as a speedy worker, careless of the procedures of filmmaking and indifferent to the art form, has in large measure been propagated by his own remarks made in interviews. His working habits, however, mean little in the evaluation of his finished products, which are obviously designed with considerable care. No doubt minor filmmakers occasionally

Buñuel

achieve felicitous effects by accident, but never the effects characteristic of Buñuel, which are marked by a rapid movement from an explicit image to a concisely implicit relevation about the situation. In other words, after *Belle de Jour*, only the most naive viewer could still believe that Buñuel's art exploits meaning at the expense of cinematic form, or that his style evolves by chance from merely functional filming and editing techniques.

Fantasy and Reality in *Belle de Jour*

RAYMOND DURGNAT

Sévérine (Catherine Deneuve) is married to Pierre, a young doctor who is not merely successful, but handsome, loving, considerate. Her frigidity pains him, but hardly ruffles the surface of his goodness. The film begins in the middle of a frequent daydream of Sévérine's, in which Pierre punishes her by having her dragged from a carriage, tied, gagged, flogged and raped by his obedient coachmen. Later, an eerie family friend, Husson, happens to let drop the address of a clandestine brothel, to which Sévérine, smoothly encouraged by its young Madame, Anaïs, subsequently returns each afternoon, under the name of Belle de Jour. Her regulars include an ugly young thug, Marcel, who falls in love with her, and, when she's slow to elope with him, threatens to force her hand by telling Pierre. She persuades him to refrain, but he shoots her husband, crippling him for life, before being himself shot down by a passing gendarme. Sévérine spoonfeeds her paralysed spouse, like a good wife. But Husson mesmerises her into letting him tell Pierre the truth about her past escapade.

So far the film has developed its story in a straightforward, linear narrative, interspersed with obviously relevant daydreams, nightdreams and flashbacks. Fantasies are clearly signalled, either by their intrinsic improbabilities, or by the jingling of carriage bells. But after Husson's departure, Sévérine goes in to Pierre. His face is bedewed with tears; his hand opens, and falls back, in the conventional screen gesture for death. But abruptly he rises from his chair, miraculously cured, and ever-loving. The jingling carriage of Sévérine's fantasies passes under their window, empty, and, it seems, no longer needed.

The equal realism of these climactic contradictions—Pierre dead, Pierre well—seems to place both in the same order of reality, and cannot but throw doubt on the reality or otherwise of every scene in the film. Buñuel, with one twist, has rendered his whole film as riddled with alternative realities as Robbe-Grillet's *L'Immortelle*.

In the course of discussing the film with several art students, innumerable permutations emerged, which will here have to be simplified into four main alternatives.

1. The synopsis above represents the commonsense interpretation. The general drift of the action clearly indicates that Pierre's revival is a fantasy and the question is not whether it's real, but why it seems so real.

FROM *Luis Buñuel* (1968) by Raymond Durgnat, pp. 139–46. American edition published by the University of California Press; reprinted by permission of The Regents of the University of California. Copyrighted by Movie Magazine Limited, 1967.

2. The two scenes are only apparently contradictory. Husson, by telling Pierre the truth, almost kills him, but provides the traumatic shock which enables him to throw off his paralysis, which must have been psychosomatic. He can come to terms with Séverine's sins, since they suit the suppressed guilts which made him so gentle. So now they can live happily ever after.

3. At the other extreme, there is the view that if the frontiers between reality and merely mental reality become paradoxical, this must be because the film isn't about reality on any level. Buñuel's film is primarily a practical joke which propels us, *Marienbad*-style, out of any mental reality into non-sense, and a consciousness of *sheer* film. There is no particular meaning to this effect; it's just a surprise, a gimmick. A more sophisticated variant sees it as a neo-Dada twist which, nonetheless—and this is the crux—absolves us of the necessity of trying to make sense of the film as a whole.

4. The climactic contradiction suggests that what we took for a real story is more extensively fantasy than we had realised. Some see the shift from reality to fantasy beginning when Marcel calls on Séverine, for this act links the two social worlds which she has kept apart. Others feel that Séverine never really went to the brothel. Perhaps nothing happens at all, except that Pierre and Séverine are sitting quietly in the same room. Séverine has told herself a frightening but rewarding story, to escape from a reassuring, though empty, reality. Her dreaming and daydreaming may be part of her story, or may be parallel fantasies.

All of these interpretations are challengeable. The first collapses if, as some maintain, the coachmen in Pierre's fantasy carriage also turn up as coachmen in the Duke's real carriage. The second seems contradicted by the improbable rapidity of Pierre's volte-face. The third accounts for the coachmen, but it disposes of too much, solving the whole set of riddles too easily, too glibly, writing off most of its content. The fourth, though leaving the film with more dignity of content than the third, lacks the clear framework of the first, and dissolves into an infinite number of equivalent alternatives, making deeper thought almost impossible.

One advantage of the commonsense interpretation is that it is the one which first presents itself. Other interpretations only appear after this has been felt through. Even if we don't want to settle for it, we can't avoid it, and shouldn't forget it. Even more important, though, is the gradual shift from *differences* of reality (physical, mental, etc.) to a virtually ambiguous reality. That this evolution is profoundly Surrealist is indicated by André Breton's dictum: 'Everything leads us to believe that there exists a certain point of the spirit at which life and death, the real and the imaginary, the past and the future . . . cease to be perceived as opposites. It is vain to see in the Surrealists' activity any motive other than the location of that point.' The contradictory scenes, it would seem, represent the attainment of such a point; though whether it represents a Surrealist liberation is another question.

But if the film works so well on this plane, why does the film seem to outrage it? The carriage-and-coachmen motif we have already noted. There are other oddities: for example, as the whips are raised, Séverine shrieks a nonsense-sentence about cats, echoed later by the Duke's unpleasant major-domo. One can imagine reality inspiring fantasy; but here, it seems, fantasy precedes reality. Again, though, an answer lies in Surrealist theory. Breton discusses just that sort of coincidence at length in 'Nadja', in 'Les Vases Communicants', and in 'L'Amour Fou', suggesting that a certain kind of passionate clairvoyance might reveal occult parallels in the universe, particularly between dream and reality. The impossibilities may also have a Dadaist meaning, but the joke is a secondary aspect of a metaphysically subversive meaning. Or such is the power of Séverine's libido, that she is controlling the film of which she is part. The ultimate change of level has taken place. This is an experiment with film, like J. M. W. Dunne's 'An Experiment with Time'.

This respects the switch between orders of reality which accounts for many of the film's tensions. It even begins in the middle of a daydream, thence returning to reality. The principal levels are 1) reality, 2) daydreams, the most rational of which are distinguished from 1) by the jingling of bells, and 3) dreams (the scene with the cattle, and the duel) distinguished from 2) by their more 'poetic', enigmatic material, and by a more richly textured and earthier visual style. A puzzling fantasy, about an orgy proceeding under the table at the restaurant where Séverine is undoubtedly sitting, represents level 4), of hypnagogic visions (the scenes or patterns which flow before our eyes when we are half-awake and, according to psychologists, honeycomb our waking hours rather more than most of us remember). Buñuel's view of the mind is more sophisticated and scientifically more accurate than rationalism's summary division into the conscious and the unconscious. Between rationality and deep dream are many strata, each constantly irrupting into the interstices of the other. Such a merging is achieved with Buñuel's very, very slow dissolve, virtually a superimposition, between the streets and the forests, the stonily civilized and the dreamily organic. The presence of so conspicuous an optical at this one point only in the film suggests that a major breakthrough has been made in Séverine's mind—that contrarieties are ceasing to be mutually exclusive.

Other fantasies interact with Séverine's, sometimes producing secondary ambiguities. The incestuous, necrophiliac Duke's pick-up of Séverine is almost too smooth to be true. But perhaps there was a curious rapport between them? Or was it all prearranged, via Anaïs? Or was the whole thing Séverine's fantasy, since it involves that carriage? (The second interpretation is this critic's preference.)

The film is a pattern of fantasies. The Duke needs Sévérine as a prop. The gynaecologist plays at being a valet, but brusquely and briefly emerges from his trembling servitude to give his pretty tyrant angry orders as to the exact timing of the ceremony. An Asiatic client tries to interest the girls in a buzzing object in a box—which terrifies Sévérine's colleagues and profoundly satisfies her, but which we never see. (One suggestion is that the box contained a wasp tied to a thread.) Anaïs's fantasy-game is that the brothel is a gay, spontaneous place.

If the fantasies are puzzling, ambiguous or elliptic, the characters are no less so. Despite her masochistic daydreams, Sévérine's self-degradation never takes such masochistic forms. She threatens to leave Marcel if he hits her, and doesn't seem to be shamming. Neither can she take the sadistic part. She is too hesitant to satisfy the gynaecologist (inverting a Prévert *boutade* in *Les Visiteurs du Soir:* 'two hangmen without a victim! what melancholy!') And while spying on the other girl's handling of him, she soon turns away, wondering how anyone could degrade himself so. Catherine Deneuve beautifully catches the vague sullenness of such a character: her beautiful eyes glaze over, suddenly clicking back to reality, disappointedly; her jaw becomes mournfully set, giving her face a skull-like quality under its soft whiteness. In her secret violence and hesitant docility, Sévérine is halfway between the heroines of *Repulsion* and *Les Parapluies de Cherbourg*.

Many a critic has seen Pierre as Marcel's innocent victim. But there is a significant scene when Sévérine, already working for Anaïs, asks Pierre to confide in her about his premarital experience in brothels. Immediately he launches into the classic 19th-century line (compare Max Ophuls' *La Ronde*) that gentlemen, unwilling to corrupt nice girls, go to certain women for a purely physical relief, and feel melancholy for the rest of the day. Not only are his delusions about Sévérine as grave as her fantasies about him, but he wants to keep her in a fantasy world. When she puts him off, pleading frigidity but dreaming of rape, he suffers, yes, but just turns his back on her. He might instead have pressed her, not more roughly, but with more frankness of passion, even admitting to paroxysmic emotions of dependence, insistence and reassurance conjoined, so that she can feel loved and safe even while being overwhelmed by his dangerous authority. Passive as he is, he shows much greater strength of will when, after her spell in the brothel, she goes on holiday with him, feels her frigidity weakening, and wants to stay with him until it dissolves. But no, he absolutely insists on mistaking her thoughtfulness for boredom, and returning her to Paris. Without pretending that complicated girls like Sévérine aren't tough nuts to crack, one might well suspect him of complicity in his own frustration, or a secret determination to be the pure, passive victim. Several students were reminded of a crucifixion by the opening of his dying palm. Pierre's politeness masks a secret wish to be Jesus—using the word in its derogatory sense.

How Pierre should have behaved is demonstrated by Anaïs, who is experienced and friendly, firm and seductive, prepared to reject her, and also to forgive her, but not willing to stand any nonsense. Anaïs, alas, is a woman. The girls make a Lesbian experiment. First, Anaïs, then, later, Séverine, affectionately disconcerts the other by taking the male role, and Séverine's final 'mastering' of Anaïs marks the end of the latter's ability to help her.

Marcel is the anti-gentleman. Not only is he a thug, with a concealed blade in his walking stick, but it is stressed that he utterly rejects not only honour among thieves but the most primitive duties of friendship. He is as outside any possible law as Jaibo in *Los Olvidados,* whom he physically resembles; he too dies like a dog. He also defiantly parodies the gentleman, with his gold-riddled upper gums, his dandy affectations, and a splendid gesture of extravagant fastidiousness: he makes the immaculate Séverine strip, then, on finding a birthmark, disappointedly requests her to dress. But Séverine satisfies, civilizes, and outwits him. He loves her, brings her flowers, and, intelligently, wants to force her hand by telling the truth and to free her. Even when she conquers him, sending him away, he is capable of a last savage gesture: he will kill the man she loves, and perhaps she will *then* come. If she doesn't, he has paid her back as Heathcliff did Cathy. But the policeman shoots him so that only his negative purpose survives.

What he fails to do is done by the even more mysterious Husson. Quiet, wealthy, outwardly respectable, seductively corrupt, he boasts of being a masochist and sadly cherishes being rejected by Séverine. He seems to enjoy half-corrupting her, and in fact sets her feet on the primrose path to the roses and raptures of vice. But he also has a tender concern for his own well-being: on entering the brothel, almost his first words are 'Is the central heating turned full on?' When he has his chance of humiliating Séverine, he just shrugs, having lost his erotic interest in her when he found she was impure. His apparent corruption was only inverted idealism. He respects her plea not to inform Pierre until, hearing that Pierre is crippled, he persuades her that it is her duty to tell him the truth. She can't, but he can, perform the cruellest act in the film. His apparent idealism now in telling the truth is only destructiveness—he is a bourgeois anagram of all that is gratuitously destructive in Marcel, but his concern with purity mirrors Pierre's. He has the idealistic passivity of the one, the devious viciousness of the other. He reads Séverine's mind better than any character in the movie, better even that Anaïs, and spots her spiritual cruelty. As he enjoys destroying peace of mind, he is almost a rebel. Failing to be one, he is a creep.

His intervention is climactic. From the beginning, Séverine has felt, and it may be true, that it is Pierre whom, spiritually, she loves; after Marcel, she very nearly loses her physical frigidity, achieving a complete love. Conversely, she isn't frigid with Marcel, nor masochistic, except in so far as he is what he is, and it seems possible to us, as to him, that she loves him. But once Marcel has crippled Pierre, her reactions take on a new complexion. She seems suspiciously serene with the *utterly* impotent Pierre. She is happily anticipating a lifetime of frigidity (almost of maternal sadism) and of masochistic self-immolation. But Husson, the tempter, facilitates her passage from devotion to cruelty. It's true that she doesn't watch as Husson 'enlightens' Pierre. No doubt she can't bear to, but also, she won't deign to involve herself frankly. She doesn't need to, for, immobile, alone, her heart is, perhaps, undergoing its most convulsive horror-pleasure in the entire film. All through the film she has believed she would have to pay for her sins, but now her beloved Pierre has become the scapegoat for her sado-masochism. Hence the flagellatory carriage appears, for the last time, empty. Her eroticism has been overwhelmed by a sado-masochistic frigidity. Now her daydreams can become normal, i.e. switch round to a banal sentimentality. Her crippled husband is seductive again, because she will always remember their happy times. That memory is the biggest lie of all. But it's a memory, which fools Séverine, of a superficial reality. Hence the last fantasy doesn't need its quotation marks. Séverine has fooled herself, immolated herself, become a devoted wife, a monster, a living lie.

Hence also it is a carriage which links Séverine's and the Duke's fantasies. Both are necrophiliacs, masturbating over the surfaces of a vanished, falsified past.

Thus the film reveals its true bitterness. It is a circle of near-liberations by Séverine, by Pierre, by Marcel, by Husson, none of which can be completed, all of which frustrate one another.

But if Husson best understood her, the real soul-mate of all that was best in Séverine was the man who, at first, understood her least (threatening to beat her), and whose outcast status matched her wealth. She dreamed endlessly of flagellations. He had lost all his front teeth at one blow. She broke free from society to gratify her *nostalgie de la boue* but kept her anonymity, alas, only too well. He enjoyed his dandy-aesthete pose, though with grotesque wrongness. She lost her frigidity to him. He defied the gangster fraternity and let her civilize him. He tried to play the game by her rules, but she was more determined by her social status than he. The outlaw didn't understand how deep were her roots in her class. They are parted, like Heathcliff and Cathy, by social status, which in our fluid, 'classless' society, works through the characters which it forms.

The film is, in the end, a comedy of manners—of an astounding and deeply tragic kind. We remember, too, how many of the brothel fantasies involved money and class fantasies. There is the curious interplay between the gracious Duke and the sour manservant, who not only breaks into his fantasies, as if to ruin them, but throws Séverine callously into the rain—a sort of anti-Barratt, actuated by envious spite. And Séverine's sisters-in-sin could never forget the fact that she was from a higher class than theirs. It's significant, too, that, though she sends Marcel away, she lets Husson in, for Husson is of her class. The film asserts the astonishingly intricate tenacity with which, even in what appears to be a purely erotic obsession, class is intimately mingled with Séverine's sense of identity.

Considered as a Freudian character-analysis, the film's conspicuous omission is the nexus of ego-formation and unconscious guilt. Séverine seems, indeed, to be beautifully schizophrenic about actual guilt—shame worries her more. Guilt reappears only in the chastisement fantasies. But there are hints of these processes: she assumes a false name; she expects punishment; she dreams of cattle whose names are expiation and remorse; she remembers moments of guilt from her childhood—significantly it's a workman who is caressing her.

The film abounds in typical Buñuel motifs: one need hardly relate Marcel to Jaibo, Pierre to the weak but well-meaning advocates of progress, the little daughter of the plain maid in the brothel to the little girl whom Celestine in *Le Journal d'une Femme de Chambre* befriends, the plain maid to Célestine's fellow-servant. Just as Célestine saw her own innocence in the little girl, so the girl here looks sufficiently like Séverine as a child that several spectators mistook the flashbacks for cutaways to the little girl's story. Motifs of shiny shoes, dirty socks, and dung or tar appear. While on her way to sell her body, Séverine remembers how she refused to accept the gift of Christ's body. Shot from a high angle, Pierre's writhing on the pavement, watched by Séverine from her window, recalls the fallen cyclist in *Un Chien Andalou*. The daydream bells are from the *L'Age d'Or* mirror. The parody in *Viridiana* of The Last Supper is echoed by a parody of Millet's 'The Angelus', which, of course, is also a parody of Dali. The office whose bankroll Marcel and his friend steal is that of the film's producers, the Hakim Brothers. There are two references to the untypically Buñuelian motif of cats, which may be a little joke to fool serious critics, like this one.

Buñuelian, too, is the film's moral order. So smoothly and painlessly is decency replaced by erotic fulfilment that, as Séverine on her way to the brothel hesitates, every spectator urges her: 'Go on!' Its picture of vice is the very antithesis of a 'Fleurs du Mal' fascination. The brothel is run on lines, and in a spirit, very like that of the boutique as which it is camouflaged, and the people there are very much like other people of their class, mainly because they are the same people. The little girl doing her homework may soon be corrupted, or may not; it doesn't matter too much. We probably hope she'll *choose* prostitution by her 'aunts'' happy example, rather than be seduced by the sly, snide gentleman offering financial advantage. But even then why shouldn't she enjoy her little secret adventures, like Séverine?

The film's bland, pellucid line, its almost Lubitschian mood, beneath which a vicious tragedy develops, is part of its moral order. People often remain unaware of their own tragedies. Since it's a comedy of manners, the interplay between characters is observed in the traditional tennis-match style, stroke by stroke—he says, then she says, then he says. . . . But, on reflection, the ellipses, mysteries, oddities, depths are there.

Several critics have spoken of a *stilted* reality, and either disparaged it on those grounds, or, like Marcel Martin, ingeniously excused it on the grounds that it's only a girl's fantasy and ought therefore to be unreal. As he regretfully insists, this defence is also a condemnation, since it asserts that this is a stilted film. In a finer variation of the same approach, a student described it as a fairy-story—a fairy-story which Séverine is telling herself, as so many young women tell themselves romantic fairy-stories. It has the simplicity of a fairy-story; throughout it, Séverine is seeking to put herself in situations in which she is a child, in which she has no choice. Even the bright, enamelled colour is childlike.

By liberal standards, the film *is* a fairytale, its psychology is strange indeed. But its serene indifference to liberal notions is the condition of its insidious freshness. It can treat a psychopathic case in the Lubitsch style because bourgeois manners are psychopathic anyway.

Buñuel's Golden Bowl

ELLIOT STEIN

Most of all, Buñuel wanted to go back to work in Spain again. He had been encouraged by reports that the brouhaha over *Viridiana* had calmed, that censorship there had been relaxed. He returned. Then, after months of preparation, in the summer of 1963, Franco's government refused the shooting authorisation for his version of Galdos' *Tristana*. Later that year, in France, he made one of his finest films, *Le Journal d'une Femme de Chambre*. When shown in Paris, in 1964, it was coolly received. A year later, one of his old pet projects, an adaptation of Lewis's *The Monk*, was finally about to take shape. At the last minute the production company was dissolved, and it too had to be written off. The Hakim Brothers then approached Buñuel to ask him to consider a screen version of Joseph

FROM *Sight and Sound*, Vol. 36 (Autumn 1967). Reprinted by permission of *Sight and Sound*.

Kessel's novel, *Belle de Jour*. He accepted, and cloistered himself in an ultra-modern building in Madrid with Jean-Claude Carrière (co-scenarist on *Le Journal* and *The Monk*). They finished the script in five weeks. The shooting schedule for this, Buñuel's 27th film, was ten weeks. He brought it in in eight.

Belle de Jour is a masterpiece, technically Buñuel's most accomplished, free-flowing work. It is unique, the only one of his films in which his obsessions, his purity, and his convulsive spirit have all been fully, satisfactorily organised into an architectonic whole. It unfolds so smoothly, with such sustained legato, that there is no chance to catch a breath. *Viridiana* was a step in this direction, the underrated *Journal* a near-arrival. *Belle* is the many-faceted and perfect Golden Bowl which crowns a life's work. When released in Paris recently, it was greeted with shock, reticence, and disappointment by most of the critics for the daily and weekly papers. The great man, tired, deaf, 67 years old and alcoholic (his own admission), now only wants to return to Mexico and rest.

Joseph Kessel's novel, published in 1929, whipped up a fair *succès de scandale* at the time. Although Buñuel has said of it: "La novela no me gusta nada," it is a far from uninteresting book, firmly in the tradition of the French *roman psychologique*, and a precursor of the post-war, but already classic *Histoire d'O*. It concerns a beautiful young *grande bourgeoise*, Séverine Sérizy, wife of a handsome young surgeon (Pierre) whom she deeply loves. She has every reason to be happy, but of course isn't. She learns that an acquaintance, a woman of her own class, is working in a brothel. Séverine gradually becomes obsessed by the thought of such a situation, finds out the address of one of these bagnios, and applies for a job there. She only works afternoons from two to five—thus her sobriquet, Belle de Jour. Frigid in the arms of her kindly, well-behaved husband, she is impelled by a masochistic urge for humiliation which leads her to seek out 'rough trade'. Marcel, a doting young gangster, falls in love with her; she soon becomes very fond of him. The devoted hoodlum attempts to kill a friend of her husband who is about to inform Pierre of Séverine's double life. The murder misfires when Pierre intervenes, and it is *he* who is seriously wounded. He recovers, but is paralysed, condemned to a wheelchair. Overcome by guilt, Séverine confesses everything. Pierre never speaks to her again.

Kessel elevates this novelettish plot through a convincing portrayal of the frightening divorce between the heart and the senses. In 1936, Philippe Hériat adapted the book for the stage. The play was rejected by sixteen theatre directors and as many actresses. It is a sentimental watering-down of the novel, with an unconvincing happy ending. It has never been performed; with luck, it never will be.

Although Buñuel does not fancy the novel (he didn't like Defoe's *Robin-*

son Crusoe much either), he stated: "I found it interesting to try to make something I would like, starting from something I didn't. . . . I enjoyed complete freedom during the shooting of *Belle,* and consider myself entirely responsible for the result." He took pains with the editing, modifying several sequences in the process—a procedure rare for him. Hindered often in the past by tight budgets, his only inconvenience here was the producers' insidious autocensorship; several cuts were made by them before *Belle* was sent to the censors.

Buñuel's last great film is close in spirit to his first great film, *L'Age d'Or.* Indeed, one of the things in *Belle de Jour* which seems to have bothered people is its fidelity to what can only be called the true spirit of surrealism: not the tacky Surrealism to be found in the moth-eaten commemorative art shows which have popped up from time to time in Paris, London, or New York art galleries since the war, but the invigorating, positive, liberating surrealism which marked *L'Age d'Or,* caused riots when that film was first shown, and resulted in its being banned for a generation. The result is more mellow, less overtly aggressive than *L'Age d'Or,* even calm, But it is all there.

Buñuel: "*Belle de Jour* is a pornographic film. . . . by that I mean *chaste* eroticism."

The film contains threads of events from Kessel's book. But Buñuel has turned the book inside out, ripped the surface from it, and stitched inside to outside with such invisible mending that much of the time the heroine's real life, her fantasies and childhood memories, are integrated as a fluent story in which past, present, and the merely possible form a solid block of narrative. With her, we fall through trapdoors of consciousness, and then with relief, fall out of them—but only into new ones.

Buñuel did not like the novel's ending, "because morality is saved." The climax of his film is simply the most astonishing 'open ending' in the history of the cinema. It is the meanest trapdoor of them all (half open?— half shut?), a renewal of the beginning; but once seen, it fastens the entire film into a writhing subliminal image, that of an admirable circular serpent, forever catching its own tail in its own mouth.

The film's motifs are not those of the book. Kessel tells the story of a woman who loves one man with her heart, and a few dozen others with her body—and feels badly about it. Buñuel sidesteps sin and guilt; for him they are obviously luxuries the human race has been burdened with for too long. His film (the theme is far from new to him) tells the story of a liberation from the moral handcuffs of social caste by means of a personal *sacerdoce,* a self-fulfilment.

During the main credit titles, an open landau trots down a pleasant country lane towards the camera. Inside it, Pierre (Jean Sorel) and Sévérine (Catherine Deneuve) are cosily enlaced. She tells her husband that she loves him more each day. Suddenly, he orders the coachman to stop and his wife to descend. The lackeys drag her through the woods. At Pierre's command, she is gagged, bound to a tree, whipped, etc. by the servants. "What are you thinking of?" an offscreen voice asks. "Of us," Séverine replies to Pierre. "We were in a landau." They are in the bedroom of their Paris apartment.

A few days later, at a mountain ski resort, they meet Pierre's friend (Father Lizzardi from *La Mort en ce Jardin* and Monteil from *Le Journal d'une Femme de Chambre*), here called Husson (Michel Piccoli). "He's rich and lazy. That's his sickness," a woman friend remarks. Returning from her holidays, Séverine learns that a young married woman of her 'group' works in a clandestine brothel. (Clandestine because Kessel's novel, like France, has been modernised, and *maisons de rendezvous* are no longer legal.) Husson, met one day at the country club, insists on supplying her with details about 'the houses' he has known. After days of hesitation spent obsessed by troublesome thoughts, Séverine goes *chez* Madame Anaïs (Geneviève Page), and as she climbs the stairs to the brothel for the first time, we come upon a little girl in church (Séverine as a child?) refusing the host. The priest is impatient: "Get it down you!" Séverine does get herself enrolled in the brothel, and returns that very afternoon to begin work—all gleaming patent leather shoes Buñuelian style on the stairs.

She is recalcitrant with her first customer, an obese bonbon magnate, but when he and Anaïs get tough with her, she becomes joyfully submissive. One busy day, her list of clients includes a truckling gynaecologist, who has come *chez* Anaïs for the same reason as Séverine—to be humiliated. She cannot cope with him, but is pleased to be manhandled by a huge Japanese who tries to pay with a Geisha Diner's Card. We then see her seated demurely, enjoying the fresh air in an elegant outdoor café near the Cascade in the Bois de Boulogne, where Bresson's *Dames* were wont to meet. (At the next table, too thin to be Hitchcock, is a Spanish tourist, Señor Buñuel, talking business with one of the Hakim Brothers.) She is approached by the one-time leading man of *La Mort en ce Jardin* and *Cela s'appelle l'Aurore* (Georges Marchal). He is wearing no make-up and looks like a weird old French Duke. He asks Séverine if she likes money, and tells her that, indeed, he is a rich Duke. He invites her home for "a very moving religious ceremony." They are driven to his château by the two footmen who had whipped her at Pierre's command right after the main credit titles. The Duke dresses her up as his dead daughter, covers her with asphodels, mutters something about "the inebriating odour of dead flowers," then disappears under the coffin for a part of the service which the producers removed before submitting the film to General de Gaulle's censor board. When the ceremony is terminated, she is paid for her pains and kicked out into the rain.

One day at the brothel, the Nazarin (Francisco Rabal), who has become a Bolivian gangster, arrives with a young protégé, Marcel (Pierre Clementi). They have just robbed a bank messenger (bringing the profits from the latest Vadim film?) in the lift leading to the Hakim Brothers' office, 79 Champs-Elysées, and are loaded with money to spend on pretty women. Marcel falls in love with Séverine and returns often to see her. She develops a strong physical passion for the hysterical punk, although she still loves her husband.

Marcel discovers Belle's secret identity, invades her home, shoots her husband, and is pursued and killed by the police. Pierre recovers. He is paralysed, has lost the power of speech, and will spend the rest of his days in a wheelchair. One beautiful autumn afternoon. Séverine is seen giving her husband his medicine. Then, looking out of the window of her splendid Paris apartment, she sees in the pane the reflection of the pleasant country lane (leading to the Duke's château?) where the landau was driving in the opening sequence. "I don't dream any more—since your accident," she lies to Pierre lovingly. She then hears Buñuelian cowbells (first heard in 1930 in *L'Age d'Or* when Lya Lys, on discovering a huge cow on the bed of her splendid Paris apartment, chased the *vache* off the *lit,* looked into a mirror, and saw moving clouds and a vision of *her* lover). Pierre rises from his wheelchair. He is no longer a cripple, he can speak, he pours a drink. "Let's take a vacation, go to the mountains." "Do you hear?" she replies, and looking out of her Paris window we see the open landau in the country landscape. The coachmen from the opening scene are driving it down the country lane, towards Pierre and Séverine. It has come to take them to the château?

This summary does even less than skeletal justice to the complex enchantments of *Belle de Jour.* . . . Here, at random, is a brief of particulars which after three viewings of the film stand out strongly:

—Geneviève Page as Madame Anaïs: one of the great performances of the screen in recent years; and most uncanny it is, since the role, as written, is rather one-dimensional.

—None of the film's 'fantasies' are in the book—the girl refusing the host is of course plumb Buñuel. He discards, however, a ferociously Buñuelian item which occurs at the beginning of Kessel's novel. During the last days at winter sports, Séverine falls ill; by the time she returns to her Paris home, a near-fatal case of pneumonia has developed. And it is at *this* point that she begins to be aware of her disquieting sensuality, after the doctors "have delivered her body to the bites of leeches."

—When the bonbon magnate (Francis Blanche) invites the girls at the house to drink a bottle of champagne with him, the sequence is so superbly articulated, although unostentatiously edited, that its climax, as the cork pops (a miraculously 'right' placed high-angle group shot), physically imposes itself as a major moment in the film, even though the scene itself is of relatively little importance. There is no precedent in Buñuel's work for such a purely formal 'state of grace'.

—It is early in the film. Sévérine returns home, after the disturbing taxi ride during which brothels were discussed. Flowers are brought in, sent by Husson. She drops the vase. "What's the matter with me today?" she mutters. Until this point, colour in the film has been cool and non-committal. Now, the visual shock of the red roses sprawled on the floor is tremendous—out of all proportion to the apparent seriousness of the incident. A chromatic premonition. As if she had opened a tin of sardines and a live cobra had popped out.

.   .   .

Indeed, it is impossible and unnecessary to decide whether the end of *Belle de Jour* conveys a shift from fantasy to reality or vice versa. The ambiguity is as immanent in the film, as deliberately Buñuel's, as the tranquil nobility of his point of view—a decent neutrality which condemns no one. He does not side with Sévérine, nor can he regard her as a pervert. She has her reasons; but so does everyone else. Neither he nor his heroine wastes a minute worrying about Divine punishment. In accepting herself, Sévérine liberates herself. She is no longer *une grande bourgeoise,* but a human being who has undergone a shattering and enchanting apprenticeship. But instead of a Hollywood style clinch at fade-out time, we and she can content ourselves with visions of Sévérine, joyful handmaiden at her husband's wheelchair-side *and* (or) riding with Pierre in the magic lantern of her mind down a beautiful country lane, where at any moment he may stop the carriage and deal her the merely divinely human punishment which to her is another name for love.

The Beauty of *Belle de Jour*

ANDREW SARRIS

Luis Buñuel's *Belle de Jour* has evoked in many critiques that all-purpose adjective "beautiful." Catherine Deneuve is undeniably beautiful, never more so than in this context of Buñuelian perversity, and almost any meaningfully designed color film seems beautiful if only because the vast subconscious sea of the cinema is safely gelatinized within the frames of an academic painting. Describing a film as beautiful is unfortunately too often a device to end discussion, particularly nowadays when irrationality and hysteria have become institutionalized as life styles. *Elvira Madigan*

FROM *Film 68/69* (1969) by Andrew Sarris, pp. 43–49. Reprinted by permission of *The Village Voice.* Copyrighted by The Village Voice, Inc., 1968.

is beautiful in the way flowery poems are poetical, not through functional expressiveness but through lyrical excessiveness. *Bonnie and Clyde* is beautiful when its luminously lyrical close-ups involve the audience with the killers, but the film is equally beautiful when its concluding slow-motion ballet of death and transfiguration takes the audience off the hook by distancing the characters back into legend and fantasy. The fact that the close-ups contradict the distancing is immaterial to the film's admirers. *Bonnie and Clyde* is beautiful, and consistency is the hobgoblin of little minds.

I would argue that *Belle de Jour* is indeed a beautiful film, but not because of any anesthetizing aesthetic of benevolently mindless lyricism. Nor is the film beautiful because its director's visual style transcends its sordid subject. The beauty of *Belle de Jour* is the beauty of artistic rigor and adaptable intelligence. Given what Buñuel is at sixty-seven and what he has done in forty years and twenty-seven projects of film-making and what and whom he had to work with and for, *Belle de Jour* reverberates with the cruel logic of formal necessity. From the opening shot of an open carriage approaching the camera at an oblique ground-level angle to the closing shot of an open carriage passing the camera at an oblique overhead angle, the film progresses inexorably upward, an ascent of assent, from the reverie of suppressed desires to the revelation of fulfilled fantasies. But whose desires and whose fantasies? Buñuel's? His heroine's? Actually a bit of both. The exact proportion of subjective contemplation to objective correlative can best be calculated by comparing Joseph Kessel's basic anecdotal material with what appears on the screen.

In his preface to *Belle de Jour*, Kessel writes: "The subject of *Belle de Jour* is not Séverine's sensual aberration; it is her love for Pierre independent of that aberration, and it is the tragedy of that love." Kessel concludes his preface with a reprovingly rhetorical question for those critics who dismissed *Belle de Jour* as a piece of pathological observation: "Shall I be the only one to pity Séverine, and to love her?"

The "sensual aberration" of which Kessel writes undoubtedly seemed more shocking in 1929, when the first French edition was published, than it would seem in the current period of erotic escalation. Séverine Sérizy, happily married to a handsome young surgeon, goes to work in a house of ill-repute, actually less a house than an intimate apartment. The money involved is less the motivation than the pretext for her action. Pierre, her husband, provides for her material needs handsomely, but his respectfully temporizing caresses fail to satisfy her psychic need for brutal degradation, a need first awakened by a malodorous molester when she was a child of eight. To preserve a façade of marital respectability, Séverine works at her obsessive profession only afternoons from two to five, the mystery of her matinée schedule causing her to be christened Belle de Jour. Kessel's novel, like his heroine, is fatally divided between clinical ob-

servations on sexual psychology and novelistic contrivances to overcome
the innate lethargy of a woman of leisure. Husson, a weary sensual-
ist in her husband's circle of friends, is a particularly intricate contrivance in that he triggers much of the novel's intrigue. It is Husson who
first alerts Séverine to her own frustrations by his unwelcome advances.
It is he who inadvertently supplies her with the address of her sensual
destiny, and who, discovering her double life, poses such a threat to her
non–Belle-de-Jour existence that he precipitates, almost innocently, the
final catastrophe.

Marcel, a gold-toothed gangster infatuated with Belle de Jour, provides
a violently melodramatic climax to the novel, by agreeing to murder Husson to preserve Séverine's secret and Belle de Jour's respect. Irony is piled
upon irony as Marcel's assault on Husson is deflected by Pierre, who is
so grievously wounded that he is confined for life to helpless paralysis in
a wheelchair. Marcel and Husson remain silent about Belle de Jour, thus
enabling Séverine to escape a public scandal and even prosecution, but,
perverse to the end, she confesses everything to Pierre, and is rewarded
not with his forgiveness but with his stern silence.

Buñuel and his co-scenarist Jean-Claude Carrière retained most of the
characters of the novel. Séverine goes to work for Madame Anaïs in both
novel and film, and Belle de Jour's colleagues are Charlotte and Mathilde
in both versions. The most striking variation between novel and film is in
the elaborately structured dream apparatus of the film. Kessel's Séverine
never dreams the concrete images of Buñuel's surreal reveries of feminine
masochism. There are no floggings in the book as there are in the film, no
binding of hands with ropes, no sealing of mouths, no splattering with
mud. Kessel's Séverine never really dreams at all; she merely recollects
the past and anticipates the future. If the novel had been filmed in the
thirties or the forties by a French director trained in the Tradition of
Quality, a Marcel Carné or Claude Autant-Lara perhaps, Séverine would
probably have been played with many shimmering close-ups to dramatize
the desperate conflict between her feelings and her senses. The background music would have been exquisitely sentimental. Except for the
bells that signal the movement of the horse-drawn carriage, Buñuel uses
no music whatsoever. No Simon and Garfunkel, no Beatles, no Donovan,
not even the realistically based music of radios and record players. There
is no radio or television in the modern world of Belle de Jour, but there
is a Geisha Club credit card. Buñuel has stripped modernity of its speci-
ficity. Thus we are not bothered so much by the suspicion that horse-
drawn carriages are not as likely to figure in the reveries of Séverine's (or
Catherine Deneuve's) generation as in the memories of Buñuel's. The fact
that Buñuel does not employ music in *Belle de Jour* is not significant as a
matter of general aesthetic policy. Buñuel himself has derived ironic
counterpoint from the musical backgrounds of such recent films as *Viri-*

diana and *Simon of the Desert*. He must have felt that he didn't need music to underscore the fundamental irony implicit in a woman with the face of an angel and the lusts of a devil. Still, *Belle de Jour* overcomes an awesome handicap of affect by disdaining the facile frissons of music.

Many of the script changes were dictated by the differences in the media. Pierre emerges through Jean Sorel as a much duller character than in the book, but it is difficult to see what any director can do with the character of the Noble Husband in such a grotesque context. The changes in Husson's character are more meaningful. Kessel's Husson was more mannered in his ennui, but he takes advantage of Séverine's degraded status as Belle de Jour to possess her body. Buñuel's Husson (Michel Piccoli) is more fastidious; he loses interest in Séverine at precisely the instant she becomes available to him as Belle de Jour. But it is Buñuel's Husson who tells Pierre of Belle de Jour after the accident; Kessel's Husson never seriously contemplated such a course of action before or after.

Kessel wants us to love Séverine by identifying with her; Buñuel wants us to understand Séverine by contemplating the nature of her obsession. Instead of indulging in Kessel's sentimental psychology by staring into Catherine Deneuve's eyes, Buñuel fragments Deneuve's body into its erotic constituents. His shots of feet, hands, legs, shoes, stockings, undergarments, etc., are the shots not only of a fetishist, but of a cubist, a director concerned simultaneously with the parts and their effect on the whole. Buñuel's graceful camera movements convey Deneuve to her sensual destiny through her black patent-leather shoes, and to her final reverie through her ringed fingers feeling their way along the furniture with the tactile tenderness of a mystical sensuality. Séverine's, Deneuve's or Buñuel's, it makes little difference.

The beauty of the filmed version of *Belle de Jour* arises from its implication of Buñuel in its vision of the world. It is Buñuel himself who is the most devoted patron of *chez* Madame Anaïs, and the most pathetic admirer of Catherine Deneuve's Séverine–Belle de Jour. Never before has Buñuel's view of the spectacle seemed so obliquely Ophulsian in its shy gaze from behind curtains, windows, and even peepholes. Buñuel's love of Séverine is greater than Kessel's, simply because Buñuel sees Belle de Jour as Séverine's liberator. The sensuality of *Belle de Jour* is not metaphorical like Genêt's in *The Balcony* or Albee's in *Everything in the Garden*. Most writers, even the most radical, treat prostitution as a symptom of a social malaise and not as a concrete manifestation of a universal impulse. Buñuel reminds us once again in *Belle de Jour* that he is one of the few men of the left not afflicted by puritanism and bourgeois notions of chastity and fidelity. The difference between Buñuel and, say, Genêt is not entirely a difference between a man of images and a man of words. What distinguishes *Belle de Jour* from most movies is the impression it gives of having been seen in its director's mind long before it was shot.

There is a preconceived exactness to its images that will inevitably disconcert middlebrow film critics, especially those who are highbrows in other cultural sectors. It is only the specialist in film who can fully appreciate the directness of Buñuel's image above and beyond the novelistic nuances he sacrifices on the altars of shock and laughter.

The ending of *Belle de Jour* is tantalizingly open as narrative. Husson has told Pierre about Belle de Jour, or at least we presume so. Buñuel does not show the scene, and we are not obliged to believe anything we do not see, but there is no particular reason to believe that Husson has not carried out his stated intention. Buñuel does not cast his audience adrift in a sea of ambiguity at every opportunity; he is simply not that interested in dramatic suspense. Séverine enters Pierre's room, and for the first time in the film Buñuel's technique obscures the flow of action. Buñuel breaks up the spatial unity of the scene with alternative sights and sounds to indicate a range of possibilities. Cut to Jean Sorel's tear-stained face. Pierre Knows All and Feels Betrayed. Cut to his crumpled upturned hand. Pierre Is Dead from the Shock of His Grief. Cut on the sound track to the bells of a carriage, and to Sorel's voice asking of Deneuve's pensive face what Séverine is thinking. Everything Turns Back to Fantasy.

Or does it? Some critics have suggested that Séverine has been cured of her masochistic obsession by becoming Belle de Jour. Hence the empty carriage at the end of the film. She will no longer take *that* trip. One French critic has argued that the entire film is a dream, but the big problem with such an argument is Buñuel's visually explicit brand of surrealism. Earlier in the film, Husson calls on Séverine at her home and is rudely rebuffed. Buñuel cuts immediately to a shockingly "cute" Boy-Girl-profile two-shot of Séverine and Husson at the ski lodge. As the camera pulls back, we see Jean Sorel and Macha Meril at the same table. It must be a dream, we assure ourselves, while Séverine and Husson slip out of sight under the table to perform some unspeakable act of sacrilege against bourgeois society. The table begins to bump up and down, but the deserted partners, Sorel and Meril, are only mildly concerned. Buñuel has transported *Belle de Jour* back to *L'Âge d'Or*, but the effect of the scene is unsettling if we accept it as occurring in Séverine's mind. Here I think Buñuel slipped into a sadistic attitude of his own toward Pierre, since this is the only scene in the film in which Pierre is made to look completely ridiculous. The key to the scene, however, is not Séverine's characterization but Buñuel's satiric attitude toward Hollywood sentimentality. The profile shot more than the table-bumping gives the show away, but audiences would never "get" the joke without the table-bumping, and Buñuel does not disdain vulgarity as one of the strategies of surrealism.

Actually we are such Puritans that we talk of surrealism almost exclusively in the solemn terms of social defiance. Humor is only a means to an end, but not an end in itself. No, never? Well, hardly ever. And in Buñuel's case laughter serves to disinfect libertinism of its satanic aura.

If we can laugh at the prissiness of perversion and the fastidiousness of fetishism, not with smug superiority, but with carnal complicity, we become too implicated to remain indifferent. Buñuel's masochist, unlike Genêt's in *The Balcony*, satisfies his devious lechery by stroking the thighs of his professionally cruel mistress. Buñuel's brothel is a brothel and not one of Genêt's microcosms, and Buñuel's sensuality turns in upon itself as an enclosed experience devoid of allegorical signification.

Similarly, the entire film turns in upon itself by ending with the same question with which it began: "Séverine, what are you thinking of?" And Séverine tells the truth in her fashion. She thinks of places and conveyances and trips and herds of Spanish bulls named Remorse except one named Expiation. At the end, she is still dreaming, and who is to say that the dream is any less real or vivid than the reality it accompanies? Certainly not Buñuel's probing but compassionate camera. There are several possible interpretations of Buñuel's ending, but the formal symmetry of the film makes the debate academic. Buñuel is ultimately ambiguous so as not to moralize about his subject. He wishes neither to punish Séverine nor to reward her. He prefers to contemplate the grace with which she accepts her fate, and Buñuel is nothing if not fatalistic. Even the hapless husband is granted a mystical premonition when he sees an empty wheelchair in the street. It is destined for him, and the concreteness of Buñuel's visual imagery is so intense that we feel that the wheelchair is as destined for Pierre as Pierre is destined for the wheelchair.

Buñuel's fatalism actually undercuts the suspense of the narrative to the extent that there is no intellectual pressure for a resolved ending. Between the fatalism and the formal symmetry, *Belle de Jour* seems completely articulated as a Buñuelian statement. We do not have to know what we are not meant to know, and Buñuel establishes a precedent within his film for the ambiguity of his ending. This precedent involves Madame Anaïs, after Séverine the most absorbing character in the film. Alone of all the characters, Madame Anaïs is the truth-seeker, and she is inevitably far from the mark. She misunderstands the motivations of Belle de Jour from the outset, and she misinterprets Belle de Jour's departure. Still, she is always staring at Belle de Jour as if it were possible to peel away layers of lacquered flesh to the raw impulses underneath. The scenes in which Geneviève Page's Madame Anaïs gazes with loving curiosity at Catherine Deneuve's Belle de Jour gleam with a psychological insight not customary with Buñuel, or, as rigorously empirical aestheticians would have it, the scenes gleam with the appearance of a psychological insight, the very beautiful appearance derived from two extraordinary screen incarnations.

The great irony of *Belle de Jour* is that a sixty-seven-year-old Spanish surrealist has set out to liberate humanity of its bourgeois sentimentality only to collide with the most sentimental generation of flowery feelings in human history.

FELLINI

SATYRICON

CREdiTS

Satyricon (Italy, 1969)
Original title: *Fellini's Satyricon, Fellini-Satyricon*
Directed by Federico Fellini from a screenplay by Fellini and Bernardino
    Zapponi, based on the *Satyricon* of Petronius Arbiter
Produced by Alberto Grimaldi for United Artists
Distributor (16mm): U.A. 16 (division of United Artists)

Assistant director: Maurizio Mein
Photography: Giuseppe Rotunno
Scenery and costumes: Danilo Donati (sketches by Fellini)
Scenery architect: Luigi Scaccianoce
Music: Nino Rota, Ilhan Mimaroglu, Tod Dockstader, Andrew Rudin
Editor: Ruggero Mastroianni

Main performers:

Martin Potter (*Encolpius*)	Alain Cuny (*Lichas*)
Hiram Keller (*Ascyltus*)	Capucine (*Tryphaena*)
Max Born (*Giton*)	Lucia Bose (*The matron*)
Fanfulla (*Vernacchio*)	Joseph Wheeler (*The suicide*)
Salvo Randone (*Eumolpus*)	Hylette Adolphe (*The slave girl*)
Mario Romagnoli (*Trimalchio*)	Tanya Lopert (*The emperor*)
Magali Noel (*Forturata*)	Luigi Montefiori (*The minotaur*)
Giuseppe San Vitale (*Habinnas*)	Marcello Bifolco (*The proconsul*)
Elisa Mainardi (*Ariadne*)	Donyale Luna (*Oenothea*)
	Carlo Giordana (*The captain*)

Length: 120 minutes

Federico Fellini has one of the most impressive visual imaginations of all modern filmmakers. In spite of his background and ability as a writer, he does not rely on either dialogue or an implicit intellectual framework to establish ideas or themes in his films; rather, he embodies the ideas in strikingly bold visual images and (like De Sica) in carefully selected faces that can continually suggest symbolic values beyond the immediate dramatic situation. His films are filled with the sort of images that sum up the essence of a character (for example, the hero's absurd and naive presence on a giant swing in *The White Sheik*, 1952) or even of an entire civilization (for example, the ludicrous juxtaposition of the modern mechanized society with the old other-worldly spirituality as a helicopter transports a large statue of Christ over Rome at the beginning of *La Dolce Vita*, 1960).

The philosophical humor of Fellini's imagination, at least in regard to its wide-ranging associations, produces the effect of a cosmic comedy:

a world viewed with both love for the limitations of its inhabitants and pity for the almost continual degradation and perversity of the human spirit. Although continually critical and often pessimistic, Fellini's films—in line with the conventions of great comic art from Aristophanes' plays to Chaplin's *Monsieur Verdoux*—are deliberately imbedded in that humanistic tradition. He attacks all the false, life-denying values of contemporary society and reaffirms the individual's right to be respected and his need to be loved. At the end of *La Strada* (1954), this attitude is epitomized in the image of the grief-stricken strongman, Zampano, weeping at the discovery of the love he has destroyed. And the dehumanized world of *Satyricon* abounds in images of spiritual deprivation and bankrupt values.

Ever since the release of *8½* in 1963, Fellini has avoided strictly realistic presentation, a tendency foreshadowed in "The Temptation of Dr. Antonio," the episode he directed in *Boccaccio '70* (1962). Nevertheless, the world of Fellini's films, though populated mostly by grotesque characters engaged in raucous entertainments, is always recognizably our world. If his specific locale is not exactly identifiable with our everyday world, it is at least readily perceivable as the landscape of our contemporary intellectual anguish: the decadence manifest in the "high society" of *Satyricon's* Rome—in the banquet scenes, mock funerals, and sadistic theatricals—is a sardonic parallel of similar (if more polite) forms of contemporary decadence seen in *La Dolce Vita* (1960) and *Juliet of the Spirits* (1965). Fellini's tendency toward the surreal or the dreamlike is controlled; the basic image is highly representational, capturing the sense of tedium, ambiguity, and purposelessness in modern life. In its symbolic aspect, the environments of *Satyricon* are a comic version of hell in which lost souls assemble in brothels or colosseums or banquet halls. Bored as they are, the inhabitants exhibit an unremitting commitment to their present life-styles, which makes them truly unregenerate inhabitants of a dead world. All their energy can find no outlet other than that of repetitive dissipations, for Fellini's Romans are near relatives of Dante's Italians, who insisted on endlessly pursuing their trivial fates in the various circles of the *Inferno*. (It is worth remembering that the *Inferno* is part of a poem entitled *La Commedia;* it was not the view of life as a tragedy enacted in a vale of tears, but as an epic comic spectacle, that attracted both Dante and Fellini.)

Although the structure of *Satyricon* is deliberately contrived around patterns of decadent behavior, it appears to be almost as formless and fragmentary as its ancient literary source, Petronius' *Satyricon*. But the film's seeming lack of form is deceptive. In spite of the visionary or fantasy elements in his later films, Fellini's roots are in Italian neorealism, with its focus on man's journey through an indifferent or hostile environment. This neorealistic approach affects the structure of his films in that the plots tend to be circular rather than linear. On such a journey, either the protagonist is observed as he becomes involved in a series of events (as in *Nights of Cabiria*, 1957) or a group of incidents is displayed to illuminate a central moral situation (such as the decadence of the Roman world in *Satyricon*). But with Fellini, we never return to where we began; instead, we move to a position of far greater understanding, as each new incident illuminates another facet of the basic situation. Still, the central vision of *Satyricon* is not easy to grasp. Lacking the usual protagonists or spokesmen for any point of view, it is very much a film experience, a visual feast of selected images that work on our minds, somewhat in the style of the mosaic of Trimalchio shown in the film (which is said to have been made of pieces of candy). *Satyricon* is a tour through Fellini's imagination too, of course, but it is not just the subjective ambiguity of an artist drawing solely upon his own dreams of ancient Rome. Rather, it is an interpretation of historical patterns: a world abandoned to luxury, losing contact with its traditions and motivating values, and heading gradually but inevitably toward self-destruction. The loss of direction and the dissipation of energy are not unique to ancient Rome. Fellini extends his vision of a civilization in decline through history to reflect parallel modern cultural phenomena: the lessons of the past, the problems of today. His *Satyricon* serves as a myth for modern times.

Preface to the Screen Treatment of *Satyricon*

FEDERICO FELLINI

Many years ago at school I read the *Satyricon* by Petronius for the first time, with all the energy and greedy curiosity a schoolboy can muster. That reading has remained with me as a vivid memory, and its interest has evolved to become a constant and mysterious challenge.

After the lapse of many years I reread the *Satyricon* recently, with perhaps a less greedy curiosity but with the same enjoyment as before. This time more than just a temptation to make a film out of it, there was a need, an enthusiastic certainty.

The encounter with that world and that society turned out to be a joyful affair, a stimulation of fantasy, an encounter rich in themes of remarkable relevance to modern society.

In fact it seems we can find disconcerting analogies between Roman society before the final arrival of Christianity—a cynical society, impassive, corrupt and frenzied—and society today, more blurred in its external characteristics only because it is internally more confused. Then as now we find ourselves confronting a society at the height of its splendor but revealing already the signs of a progressive dissolution; a society in which politics is only the sordid, routine administration of a common affluence and an end in itself; where big business intrudes at all levels in the brutality of its instruments and the vulgarity of its ends; a society in which all beliefs—religious, philosophical, ideological and social—have crumbled, and been displaced by a sick, wild and impotent eclecticism; where science is reduced to a frivolous and meaningless bundle of notions or to a gloomy and fanatical elitism. If the work of Petronius is the realistic, bloody and amusing description of the customs, characters and general feel of those times, the film we want to freely adapt from it could be a fresco in fantasy key, a powerful and evocative allegory—a satire of the world we live in today. Man never changes, and today we can recognise all the principal characters of the drama: Encolpius and Ascyltus, two hippy students, like any of those hanging around today in Piazza di Spagna, or in Paris, Amsterdam or London, moving on from adventure to adventure, even the most gruesome, without the least remorse, with all the natural innocence and splendid vitality of two young animals. Their revolt, though having nothing in common with traditional revolts—neither the faith, nor the desperation, nor the drive to change or destroy—is never-

FROM *Fellini's Satyricon* (1970) by Federico Fellini, pp. 43–46. Published by Ballantine Books, Inc., New York. Reprinted by permission of Mario De Vecchi, Agent.

theless a revolt and is expressed in terms of utter ignorance of and estrangement from the society surrounding them. They live from day to day, taking problems as they come, their life interests alarmingly confined to the elementaries: they eat, make love, stick together, bed down anywhere. They make a living by the most haphazard expedients, often downright illegal ones. They are drop-outs from every system, and recognize no obligations, duties or restrictions. Their ignorance, except for the few scraps of scientific knowledge they have picked up, can be disconcerting. They are totally insensible to conventional ties like the family (usually built less on affection than on blackmail): they don't even practice the cult of friendship, which they consider a precarious and contradictory sentiment, and so are willing to betray or disown each other any time. They have no illusions precisely because they believe in nothing but, in a completely new and original way, their cynicism stays this side of a peaceful self-fulfillment, of a solid, healthy and unique good sense.

Disconcerting modernity, we said, in the work of Petronius; but I intend to give the film a more varied composition, drawing episodes in a wholly arbitrary way, guided only by the choices of fantasy, from some of the other beautiful texts of classical antiquity: *The Golden Ass* of Apuleius for example, with its flair for the fabulous in the metamorphoses —the part where Lucius peeps through a keyhole and surprises the sorceress Pamphile in the act of changing herself into an owl, then hissing a strident lament she spreads her wings and flies off. *The Metamorphoses* of Ovid, the *Satires* of Horace. Horace himself would be a fascinating figure to portray, the hoary poet in exile, half-blind, his face disfigured by a granuloma in the eye.

And then that cruel, degenerate and crazy Roman world described by Suetonius in his lives of the twelve Caesars. A gallery of stars, fabulous figures, impudent and boastful, tyrannical and pleasure-loving, whose modern incarnations are no less numerous or crazy, even if more irrelevant, and giving performances of frank self-irony. Another very tempting aspect of this cinematic procedure is one of evoking this world not through the fruit of a bookish, scholastic documentation, a literal fidelity to the text, but rather in the way an archeologist reconstructs something alluding to the form of an amphora or a statue from a few potsherds. Our film, through the fragmentary recurrence of its episodes, should restore the image of a vanished world without completing it, as if those characters, those habits, those milieux were summoned for us in a trance, recalled from their silence by the mystic ritual of a séance.

What is important, it seems to us, is not descriptive precision, historical fidelity, the complacently erudite anecdote, or elegant narrative construction, but that the characters and their adventures live before our eyes as though caught unawares. They should be as free as the beasts of the jungle when they move about, wrestle with each other or tear each other to pieces, give birth and die, all without being aware of their observers.

Sometimes the customs of these characters must appear to us as totally incomprehensible, some of their extravagant gestures as indecipherable: grimaces, winks and other codes whose meaning we have lost. We no longer know the allusions behind them, as if we were a foreigner gradually discovering the meanings and connotations of all those facial gymnastics the Neapolitans indulge in, or as if we were watching a documentary on some Amazon Basin tribe.

The film should suggest the idea of something disinterred: the images should evoke the texture of ashes, earth and dust. Thus the film will have to be made of unequal segments, with long, luminous episodes joined by far-out, blurred sequences, fragmentary to the point of never being reconstructed again—the potsherds, crumbs and dust of a vanished world.

Certainly it is difficult to wipe two thousand years of history and Christianity off the slate, and square up to the myths, attitudes and customs of peoples who came long before us, without judging them, without making them the object of a moralistic complacency, without critical reserves, without psychological inhibitions and prejudices; but I think the effort will be precisely one of evoking this world then knowing how to sit back, calm and detached, and watch it all unfold.

This it seems to us is the most honest and fascinating way of getting it together. Encolpius, Ascyltus, Eumolpus, Giton, Lichas, Tryphaena . . . make their fabulous adventures relive, without glamourizing them as sadistic or erotic. Even if their adventures were sometimes so cruel as to be revolting by our standards, if they were obscene in such a grand and total way as to become innocent again, yet beyond their ferocity, their eroticism, they embody the eternal myth; man standing alone before the fascinating mystery of life, all its terror, its beauty and its passion.

A Film from Fellini's Mythology

MARSHA KINDER and BEVERLE HOUSTON

In *Satyricon,* blond and earnest Encolpius (played by Martin Potter) moves through a series of episodes, often accompanied by Ascyltus (Hiram Keller), his dark and sneering friend, in almost all of which his life or freedom is threatened. He is able to survive because, unlike Ascyltus, he knows himself, offers no disguises, and can acknowledge his weakness and vulnerability. When the Minotaur is about to kill him in the laby-rinth, he weeps and says, "There should be a gladiator here, not I, who am a student. . . . I don't know how to use a sword as one needs to use it here. Have pity on Encolpius." As Lichas is about to squeeze him to death on a ship, his very helplessness and beauty inspire Lichas' love, and he is spared. Yet events in his bitter universe are charged with irony. The Minotaur saves him only for the terrible shame of sexual failure, and Lichas spares him so that he must endure the humiliation of a mock mar-riage. And Ascyltus, whose code of expediency ("Friendship lasts as long as it is convenient") would seem to assure his survival, is murdered in the most unpredictable, almost offhand way. The camera glances briefly out the window to see someone assaulting him. Though the murderer can be identified as the boatman who brought them to the dwelling of the witch Oenothea, this recognition requires a second viewing of the film and careful attention during the few seconds of the action. The boatman's motives are never revealed. Encolpius recognizes the irony of Ascyltus' death as he comments, "Where is all your joy now, all your arrogance. . . . You who only a little time ago were showing off for us your thoughtless bravery." Thus Fellini makes a nondiscursive statement about the random power of violence in this universe through his choice of victim (the adap-tive "modern" boy) and through the pacing, which offers only the most fleeting glance at this matter of life and death, as it is to dwell unevenly on events throughout the film. We get only brief or fragmented revela-tion about things like the gallery, the murder of young Caesar, and En-colpius' restorative encounter with Oenothea, but spend a great deal of time on the banquet scene at Trimalchio's, the encounter with the Mino-taur, and the elaborate failure at the Garden of Delights.

The uneven use of time heightens the baffling quality of experience in this surreal vision and emphasizes the fragmented and bizarre in ironic contrast to the most mundane and realistic details. The structure is char-acterized by extreme narrative discontinuity. The film cuts from one major

FROM *Close-up* by Marsha Kinder and Beverle Houston, pp. 313–19. © 1972 by Har-court Brace Jovanovich, Inc., and reprinted with their permission.

episode to another with almost no expository linking, confusing movement in time and space. For example, after Encolpius and Eumolpus talk dreamily of nature while lying in a field, the film cuts suddenly to Encolpius awakening, bound and a prisoner, on a beach where a boat awaits him. After the encounter with the Hermaphrodite, we suddenly find Encolpius being pushed down a dirt slide into an arena. Though Encolpius acts as narrator, only occasionally does he give us information, apparently at random. We are more baffled by such narration than we would be by none at all. Fellini said, "I want to take all the narrative sequence of traditional cinema out of the story, to give it an unremitting harshness."*

As sequences neither unfold nor conclude but rather start and stop, almost nothing is complete or whole. We see the huge head of a broken statue being drawn through the streets at night, and later, in the Minotaur's arena, Encolpius' impotence is displayed before the statue of a female figure whose head is broken off. People, particularly the leader in the Minotaur sequence, laugh in short bursts and screams that end suddenly. Bodies are dismembered, appearing without heads and limbs. In the gallery, paintings and sculptures are partial and broken; there is an unfinished mosaic on the wall of Trimalchio's house, and the film ends with the camera fixed on fragmented murals of the main characters. The discontinuities and fragments heighten our sense of the bizarre and abstract, making it extremely difficult to determine the mode of reality in which events take place and creating a deep sense of disturbance, which underlies the fantastic visual texture dominating the film.

Seldom in the history of cinema have plastic effects—particularly make-up and setting—been developed with such innovative brilliance. The characters' faces painted bright red, blue, green, yellow, gold, and white, the women's hair piled high in fabulous arrangements—these extremes reassure us that we are watching a fantasy, a decadent circus going mad. But not all the make-up is so extreme. Prostitutes and upper servants often wear a cruder, less elaborate version of the aristocrats' embellishment, and streets, kitchens, and galleys are full of the unadorned poor. This range awakens the uneasy sensation that a whole culture is being represented with historical accuracy. Fellini emphasizes the artful, nonrealistic face of Lichas by peering at it through cracks in a wall and shadowing it carefully, arousing our curiosity before he gives us the chilling shock of the glass eye. But what do we know of the treatment of such wounds in Roman times, especially in this vision designed to enhance mystery? Perhaps such apparitions walked the streets of Rome. The film offers a catalogue of grotesques such as might inhabit a sideshow designed by Hieronymous Bosch: midgets, cripples, and hunchbacks, the hugely fat and painfully thin, those without arms and legs, old toothless whores with darting tongues and young ones with whips or tattooed faces, the oversexed, the

---

* Federico Fellini, quoted in *Fellini's Satyricon* (New York: Ballantine Books, 1970), p. 20.

sexless, and the androgynous—the population of a nightmare, combining the grotesques of the earth with those of fantasy. Yet along with their extreme, bizarre characteristics, these people are often given business to do that is at once realistic and more mystifying than their appearance. When Giton leaves with Ascyltus before the collapse of the Insula Felicles (the apartment-like building at the beginning of the film), his stylized hand gestures suggest some commonly known Roman form of communication, but their meaning is completely inaccessible to us. Giton repeats these gestures in the hold of Lichas' ship when he meets other prisoners. At the feast, Trimalchio's wife Fortunata receives a female friend who makes similar gestures. This repetition causes the audience to speculate like archeologists or historians—perhaps this is a form of greeting authentic to the period and with a range of variations—and enhances the surreal mix of styles. The list of details exhibiting this mysterious realism can be drawn from anywhere in the film. In the prologue and throughout, words and numbers of graffiti and advertising appear scrawled on the walls; two painted, costumed little boys play and scuffle at Trimalchio's mock funeral, the strange context rendering artificial their commonplace behavior; Fortunata and her visitor peck at each other's lips in some unfathomable version of a kiss, whether of lust or greeting is unknown; Giton plays a strange little instrument that might or might not have really existed. One of the most successfully jarring of these effects is the film's mixture of languages, including forms of German, French, Latin, Greek, Italian, and a gloriously bizarre clicking tongue spoken by a slave girl at the suicide villa.

These people act out their strange realism in a physical universe that is at best inhospitable and at worst frightfully hostile. Again the effects are achieved through a mix of the bizarre and realistic. Lichas' ship and the one that conquers it are covered with huge metal anchors and other strange instruments bristling with steel points and spikes. In Oenothea's cave, we see a sculptured figure studded with large nails or spikes. After Lichas' defeat, we see a montage of cruel, smoking machines of war and torture, crucifixions, spears, and severed heads. (This montage is followed by the only welcoming environment in the film, the suicide villa, enhancing the ironic structure just described.) These nightmare props exist side by side with the realism of an unhealthy and repellent world; many people are crowded into small spaces, especially in the hold of Lichas' ship, where ledges and openings are too small or too oddly shaped to allow comfort. Such is the sense of confinement that it is a surprise to see the open skylight of the Insula Felicles. The air is fetid with pollution, as in Trimalchio's house. Nature itself is hostile, offering the burning sun of the valley and the stinging wind of the plains.

The artificial sets, perhaps more than any other characteristic, lift *Satyricon* out of time and space, distorting its mode of reality as Fellini ignores film conventions for his special purpose. Large budgets, technical improvements, and a popular taste for verisimilitude have accustomed us to a high degree of realism in film. If a scene takes place outdoors, we expect the contemporary filmmaker to go outside and shoot it. While several exterior sequences are indeed filmed outdoors, many more are shot before highly artful backdrops, making a surreal contrast with the strange signals of realistic behavior. The sequence in Vernacchio's theater (which is the first to follow Encolpius' prologue) makes good metaphoric reference to this relationship. Before a crudely artificial backdrop, dressed in bizarre masks and costumes, the players suddenly and actually (in the play within the play) cut off a man's hand. The visual shock of Fellini's realistic treatment of the actual severing is deepened by the dawning notion that Roman theater indeed included such actions. After Encolpius and Eumolpus leave the gallery, the film cuts to the overripe red of a painted sunset before Trimalchio's house, its exaggerated coloring enhanced by the flickering golden light of candles held by scores of bathers in steaming pools. After the feast, poet and hero lie in a plowed field offering one of the closest horizons since the invention of perspective. Barren sticks, unaccountably planted in orderly rows, stand behind the wagon of the nymphomaniac. Even the pinks, grays, and beiges of the suicide villa, while suggesting the soft, pleasing colors of certain rocks and sand, are too clean to be natural, the setting of the waterfall too perfect, and the greenish shrubbery not quite recognizable. The sound track also seems too clean, offering only the faintest chirp of birds and trickle of water. The frank artifice of setting is frequently complemented by the composition of scenes. In the foreshortened depth of the cannibal sequence, Eumolpus' body, lying on a platform, is surrounded by his heirs, who carefully distribute themselves in back, middle, and foreground, as if making conventionally correct use of stage space.

The narrative discontinuity, fragmentation, and combination of the frankly bizarre and mysteriously realistic together lift the film out of time and space and call into question the mode of experience being presented. This ambiguity is the basis of one of the film's strongest effects: It permits an analogy with contemporary life that is strongly felt but in a way not seen. Freed from the bonds of authenticity and verisimilitude, the film invites us to seek causes, motives, and values from our own culture. In other words, like a vacuum, it demands that we rush in with what we know to occupy a kind of allegorical space left vacant by the mystery. Though the film can be experienced primarily as a visual artifact, the vacant spaces allow us to receive certain cultural signals in the subject matter. Like the Romans who worship freaks and corrupted gods, we live in a time of bizarre cultism where God is said to be dead, as he had not yet made himself felt in the Rome of *Satyricon;* his presence looms outside the film, anticipated by the audience but unfelt by the characters. The fragmented state of art and the harkening back to Greek culture remind us of our own apprehension about the health of the arts. The episodic life style of Encolpius and Ascyltus suggests not only the lives of many traveling and uncommitted young people today; the two of them embody conflicting moral attitudes in the contemporary world. Life is controlled by the money-hungry and corrupt (Eumolpus: "By means of little swindles and little deals I've become master of the town."), who seem eminently recognizable to a civilization that may itself be dying of imperialism, vandalism, warmaking, and other ills that many blame on exclusive dedication to the profit motive. Fellini (like Swift in "A Modest Proposal") renders explicit this cannibalism in the final sequence, where the heirs cannot inherit Eumolpus' fortune unless they consume his corpse. Like civilized men, they justify their horrific action with a too-familiar argument: So has man always been, and so shall I be:

First Heir: In certain races, even today, it's usual for the defunct to be eaten by his relatives.

Fat Heir: I'm not worried about my stomach turning. It'll follow orders if, after an hour of nausea, it is promised such a heap of good things.

Wise Heir: When the Sagutines were besieged by Hannibal, they ate human flesh and they weren't waiting for an inheritance.

Young Heir: I am ready to conform.*

The Distancing Perspective in *Satyricon*

NEAL OXENHANDLER

All of Fellini's films have been constructed around performances, from the feats of Zampano in *La Strada* to the dreams of Juliet in *Juliet of the Spirits;* his characters are all in some way theatrical, playing either on literal stages or in the theater of the mind. In *Satyricon* once again, theatricality is a central theme: there is the literal theater of Vernacchio, there is the pyramidal brothel, where all kinds of performances are available, there is the gladiatorial performance of Encolpius against Lichas or against

FROM *Film Quarterly*, Volume XXIII, Number 4, pp. 38–42. © 1969 by The Regents of the University of California. Reprinted by permission of The Regents.

* *Ibid.*, p. 272.

the Minotaur; and there are other, more implicit kinds of performance, such as Trimalchio's feast, where all the banqueteers are performers, vying with each other for their host's favor, or the suicide of the patrician and his wife, staged to look like the sequence of events in a series of faded Pompeian frescos. For Fellini the situation of the actors is a profoundly suggestive archetype, one to which he constantly returns and from which he draws philosophical implications.

Critics of *Satyricon,* such as Alberto Moravia (*New York Review,* March 26, 1970) and John Simon (*New York Times,* May 10, 1970) fault the film for its dreamlike quality and the corresponding mechanization of its characters, who repeat the same actions over and over instead of freely evolving in new configurations. In rebuttal of this quite gratuitous attack, I would like to point out that in such a picaresque or episodic film character *must* be unified, since character provides the continuity that holds the film together.

Neither Moravia nor Simon has seen how the monolithic consistency of character contributes to the expression of the film's theme nor how, under an ever-changing surface of shapes and colors, Fellini has given coherent expression to one of his principal themes. This theme, which might be called the fable of the monster, appears in a host of forms in *La Strada, La Dolce Vita,* and *Juliet of the Spirits;* it revolves around the ambiguity of the monstrous, and expresses itself in the proposition that man is inherently monstrous but can be redeemed by love (*La Strada*), or by understanding (*Juliet*), or perhaps cannot be redeemed (*La Dolce Vita*). In *Satyricon,* we have a series of theatrical representations in which the banally beautiful young heroes, quite ordinary young men who represent (Fellini has told us) the youth of today, encounter a series of monstrous creatures or events, only to triumph over them not by strength or wits but by beauty. The monster is rendered harmless: Lichas is tamed, the Minotaur repents, the hermaphrodite proves to be not a god but a mortal, etc. Over and over the monstrous, the threatening, the overwhelming, the terrible is cleansed of its threatening aspect by the gaiety and spontaneity of Encolpius and Ascyltus. On this level, the film becomes the wish-fulfillment dream of the adolescent who, confronting a terrible world, finds that he can wander through it unscathed, thanks to his youth and beauty.

. . .

Looking at *Satyricon* is like nothing we have ever done before. There is a sense of wandering in a new zone of inner geography; and we understand why Fellini stated, in a recent interview, that the film was "science fiction." As we wander past the most unusual collection of faces that has ever been assembled in a film (including many monsters), the conviction grows that the film is *strange,* that indeed its strangeness is what we are pointing at when we call it "dreamlike" or "subjective" or "expressionistic" or "unreal."

The faces, and there are hundreds of them—of pimps, of actors, of slaves and Caesars, of banqueteers, of nymphomaniacs, of gods—are distortions of typical Mediterranean types (even though the cast is in fact international); the gestures—smacking of lips, winking of eyes, shaping of hands— are enlargements of idiosyncrasies we have seen in Roman crowds or in Parisian back-alleys or at bullfights in Madrid; and yet to recognize them is still not quite to understand them. Because they *are* strange. They speak of a world that is both familiar and unknown, both near and remote; it is not our world and yet, somehow, at the same time, it is. We are implicated in the obscene spectacle of Vernacchio's theater, in the casual amorality of Giton, in the cruelty of Lichas of Tarentum. The monumental city is our own city, the people who flow through its streets our compatriots. The film is therefore a fable for our own times, a commentary on our own society. Fellini himself admits the parallel: "I could say that declining Rome was quite similar to our world today, the same fury of enjoying life, the same violence, the same lack of moral principles and ideologies, the same despair and the same self-complacency."

Yet the strangeness which implicates us in the film also distances us from it, forces it away from us, provides us with a sense of historical perspective so that we see these people as different from and alien to ourselves. This too is part of Fellini's intention: "What interests me is the pagan attitude to life before the coming of the Christian conscience. One discovers this in Petronius and it is the chief thing that I will borrow from the text, which otherwise is but the fragment of a narrative."

No doubt Fellini has taken total liberty with the text of Petronius, often changing the order of events (for example, he puts the break-up of the two friends at the start instead of after the banquet; and he puts the Lichas incident, much changed, after the banquet instead of before) and interpolating scenes either of his own invention or lifted from other classical sources (the "marriage" of Lichas and Encolpius, the fight with the Minotaur in the maze, the episode with the hermaphroditic demigod); but he has captured the bitter sarcasm of the original and its powerful unmasking of the ugliness of Roman life in the time of Nero. It is a partial view, of course, biased in favor of the horrible, the ugly, the grotesque, but not less true for that. To underline the ugliness Fellini has invented the scene, previously mentioned, in which a virtuous patrician and his wife bid farewell to their children and then commit suicide. They are an improvisation, like the other non-Petronian elements I have mentioned, brought in for an obvious contrast.

Throughout the film one feels the vigorous competition of Fellini's imagination with the original. Fellini never hesitates to place his own inventions on a par with those of Petronius; and we accept this because *La Dolce Vita* and 8½ place him directly in the line of the earlier satirist. Fellini here shows himself as inventive an artist as Petronius who drew on his knowledge of Roman life under Nero (by whom he was condemned to death after serving the Emperor, the legend says, as sometimes procurer).

The film's strangeness places it at the proper historical distance (since history is always alien and strange); this distancing effect allows us to see *Satyricon* as if it were, truly, in the past. True history, the discovery of temporality (hence decay and death), is always terrifying. We look into *Satyricon* as we might look into the hermaphrodite's pool, and there we see other human beings who ate, talked, loved, fought, bled, and died just as we do. The past, their past, is validated. It is not a figment of our imagination, it happened. Those others, now vanished, were once as substantial as we are today. In this way authentic historical awareness fills us with dread of our own death. This may help account for the film's ability to upset and even terrorize some spectators.

In its ability to capture the mythical dimension of the past, and despite any disclaimer Fellini may have made in regard to its historical *vraisemblance,* the film is historically cogent and expressive: it is true history because it is true art.

Style is another aspect of the film's strangeness. It is obvious that Fellini has a personal style which reaches its zenith in *Satyricon;* but what this style is remains difficult to say. Perhaps more than anything else style is control of the mimetic devices by which the artist conveys his inner vision; it is the ability to model shapes and forms, to regulate the flow of images, to orchestrate sounds; it is the ability to control powerful characters so that they express a precise meaning; it is the ability to make the work determinate and specific while at the same time allowing it to be indeterminate and free. The style is as strange as a new language which we hear for the first time. It is true, as Vincent Canby points out, that there is considerable continuity between this work and other Fellini films; but it is also true that Fellini has never gone so far toward the stylization of his materials and the creation of an arcane visual language.

.   .   .

Eventually the film's strangeness brings us to the cluster of images surrounding the notion of the monstrous. These include the sense of the vast, of the gigantic, of the monumental, and the terrifying. All of these interrelated archetypes fuse together in the atmosphere given off by the film, an atmosphere that is oppressive and preeminently strange. Any criticism of the film's artistic unity runs counter to this knot of subjective impressions, generated in the viewer. The film is not an idle, arbitrary dream, as Moravia and Simon contend, but rather a carefully drafted masterwork designed to produce a specific gamut of responses. The sharpness, the clarity, the vividness, the power of the images convey no dreamlike essence. The images do not have the compulsiveness, the random distortion, the timelessness, the floating quality of dream images; rather they have the contour, color, and rhythm of authentic poetic expression. True, the depth and resonance of these images make it clear that they emanate from the artist's prereflexive experience; and the unconscious adds its necessary component in their generation before they are shaped by artistic craft and narrative genius. But the whole spectacle unfolds with a rhythm and logic that testify to the highest degree of conscious control. Fellini has been less dominated by his materials in *Satyricon* than in any of his other films. He stands at a greater distance from it, shapes it with greater assurance.

The film is not a dream but a poetic meditation on the great currents of human history: on love, on slavery, on pleasure, on terror, on the rise and fall of monarchs. We embark on this meditation with characters who are transparent as glass, so that while we see them we at the same time see through them. In the cosmic evolution of their lives (and Fellini is at bottom a stoic who sees human destiny as part of a natural process of decay and renewal) we experience the world in the immediacy of Fellini's own experience of it. It is given for us just as it is given for him, a creation of colors, movements, and elemental forces: for the two hours of its unfolding the film is existence itself. Than which nothing is more strange.

Fellini's Demythologized World

JANET C. DOSS

Hermaphrodite is dead. That is the message of *Satyricon,* Fellini's symbolic exploration of the human condition. The child of Mercury and Venus, Hermaphrodite, who is both man and woman, is the representation of inspiration in *Satyricon's* world of abandoned myth and dehumanized ritual. Without Hermaphrodite's intercession, life would be governed entirely by the satyr: unless inspiration exists to mediate between reason and emotion, existence becomes a meaningless debauch.

In *Satyricon* the ancient myths that once gave meaning to life have been reduced to grotesque parodies. For example, consider the scene in which Encolpius, the Odysseus-like main character, reenacts the myth of Theseus, the Greek hero who rescued Ariadne from the Minotaur's labyrinth.

Encolpius is pushed down some steps inside a provincial amphitheater
by a group of people with dark skins and white robes, who yell, "Go on!
. . . It's your turn. . . . You must!"* The sun is hot, the arena dusty. A
withered old man hands Encolpius his weapons: a lighted torch and a
phallus-shaped glove with thorny projections. Encolpius approaches a
labyrinth with bare, peeling walls in the center of the arena, in the middle
of which a seductive Ariadne awaits her Theseus. The crowd above yells
contradictory directions: "Go to the right, Theseus. . . . No! Turn back."
Encolpius then encounters a Minotaur, a man with the mask of a bull
and a bestial stance. The Minotaur attacks, and the battle continues until
Encolpius retreats. The monster is angry, the crowd silent. Trapped,
Encolpius begs for mercy: "I'm not a Theseus worthy of you. Dear
Minotaur, I will love you if you will let me off with my life. . . ." The
speakers laugh. The proconsul exclaims, "Go meet your Ariadne; she, at
least, you will overcome. . . ."

The classical myth of Theseus' defeat of the Minotaur with the help of
the virtuous Ariadne has here been denigrated to a ritual celebration of
the god Laughter, which the townspeople celebrate by playing a sadistic
joke on a stranger. Their laughter, however, is not hearty and spontaneous:
it erupts only on cue from their leader and thus is just one more aspect of
the ritual. We see that Ariadne is a prostitute. She lounges on a platform
beneath a fertility statue while attendants pamper and perfume her.
Encolpius mounts her, but he is impotent, and at this the crowd first
howls, and then stones him.

In another sequence, glass-eyed old Lichas, who roams the seas in
search of unusual treasures for Caesar, has captured Encolpius; then he
falls in love with Encolpius and decides to marry him. Lichas dons the
garments of a bride, including a veil, and summons his wife, Tryphaena,
who chants:

> The gods approve this matrimony. . . . Let the new Bride take
> her husband by the hand. . . . remember that you are united
> with him forever. . . . And you, Bridegroom . . . you must
> dedicate yourself totally to your bride . . . May you ever be
> happy and content, and ever in accord . . . Now, the ritual
> words, please. . . .

The death of Eumolpus provides the occasion for an equally perverse
ritual. The poet-pretender and wealthy opportunist lies wrapped in burial
gauze, mummy fashion, on a bier at the seashore. The camera lingers on
the slightly smiling Eumolpus, as the elders read his will:

---

* All quotations are taken from the screenplay *Fellini's Satyricon,* translated by Eugene
Walter and John Matthews (New York: Ballantine Books, 1970), edited by Dario
Zanelli.

> All those who are mentioned in my testament, with the exception
> of the freed slaves, can enter into immediate possession of what I
> have left to them on the condition that they cut my body into
> pieces and eat it in full sight of everybody. I exhort my friends
> not to refuse my invitation, but to devour my body with that same
> ardor with which they consigned my soul to Hell.

There is a moment of shocked silence; the heirs express incredulity, disgust, surprise, but then a wizened old man begins to speak reassuringly:

> Certainly, there are examples . . . When the Sagutines were besieged by Hannibal, they ate human flesh and they weren't
> waiting for an inheritance. . . . The Petelines did the same . . .
> and when Numanzia was wiped out by Scipio he found mothers
> holding onto the half-eaten bodies of their children. . . .

In response, a piggish young man steps to the bier: "I am ready to conform." He draws a knife and prepares to carve the body while the old man mumbles, "Everything that happens is necessary."

Where the original myths portrayed immortal virtues—courage, purity, respect for the individual and for the dead—these rituals uphold greed and lust as human ideals. Fellini's explanation for this state is that life here is lived without inspiration. The Romans have misused affluence and luxury: life's fulfillments have been replaced by destructive entertainments. Even emotions do not arise from within the individual spirit, but, like the laughter in the arena, have become a matter of social convention; and intellect is relegated to providing the rational basis for these diversions.

Since the symbol of inspiration is the male-female Hermaphrodite, this demigod embodies the virtues of each sex and provides an ideal to which man can aspire, but which he can never achieve. Hermaphrodite lies in the ruined temple of Ceres, sickly and helpless, cared for by a single old man. Before him, in postures of supplication, are the ill, the wounded, and the poor: among them, an armless and legless war hero borne on a litter, a sick child, a hunchback, and a midget—the refuse of humanity. But Hermaphrodite is incapable of hearing their pleas. He occasionally speaks, perhaps as a result of delirium, but he is unintelligible. As the worshipers consider this a sign, however, they are prepared for a lengthy stay until he awakes.

Encolpius and two companions wait until night, then attack the guards and seize Hermaphrodite, planning to make a fortune by demanding money from future worshipers of the demigod. But as they drag him through the desert, the sun proves too brilliant for his frail flesh to endure. Even the shrubs he passes are blanched, and the stench from his decaying teeth is dispersed as his tongue stretches out for that precious tear, that enlightened emotion that will stimulate his body to go on. But he dies, and the last vestige of hope dies with him. With hope, the desire to be, inspiration, the desire to become, dies also; and as they did in the Roman world, they both have slipped from our grasp.

Satyricon makes little use of the sophisticated cinematic techniques found in many contemporary films. Camera movement is limited, and optical effects are few. Fellini cuts directly from one sequence to another, rarely using the customary transitional devices. For example, immediately after Trimalchio and Fortunata are shown dancing heatedly, they are suddenly sitting serenely on a divan. There are even occasional sunspots on the camera lens. The film sometimes appears noncinematic, a throwback to the early days when feature films were essentially stage plays viewed by a stationary camera.

But *Satyricon* maintains a fluidity, a continuity that is achieved by the film's impact on the viewer's inner consciousness. *Satyricon* is intended to be absorbed unconsciously, like a dream or a flight into a phantasmagorical world, where images and impressions dominate over plot and characters. To accomplish this effect, Fellini resorts to certain distancing techniques: the sound track is out of synchronization with the actors; the music is weird and sometimes inappropriate; and the scenes are sometimes disconnected, one shot having no apparent link with its predecessor. The viewer, as dreamer, is discouraged from making connections.

Detachment on the part of the viewer is encouraged throughout the film. For example, before Trimalchio's dinner, the Overseer makes a financial report in order to impress the guests; but though he gestures dramatically, the camera rarely portrays the luxury objects to which he points. Like the eyes of a bored and surfeited guest, the camera sometimes follows the Overseer and sometimes looks off to something else. An old man leans over to speak into the camera, as though in confidence. The camera pans over the guests, who react as though offended by the camera's staring. Tryphaena looks sensuously into the camera. Yet the relationship between the characters *en scène* and the viewer is veiled through soft-focus, muted colors, and a scarcely perceptible mist that always keeps the viewer on the outside peering in.

In fact, the viewer is prevented from traditional cinematic involvement from the opening shot: Encolpius is facing a reddish wall; he turns, discovers a listener (the camera), and delivers a soliloquy. It is not clear throughout the film who is peering at whom, or what is real. In the Theater of Vernacchio, who are the actors and who is the audience? With whom does the viewer identify? Sometimes, extraneous characters, neither participating in the action nor connected with the scene, will stare at the viewer from the background. As Eumolpus and Encolpius are talking in an art gallery, a floating scaffold with a group of peasants passes them. They stare fixedly, not at Eumolpus and Encolpius, but directly into the camera. These devices give the audience an omniscient view of the situation, but provide no character with whom to empathize. Reaction shots are rarely used. The camera and the viewer often move on a frontal, flattened plane, without perspective. Space is linear, but time is not.

The few optical effects used also prevent us from gaining insight. Encolpius, who has become impotent, visits the sorceress Oenothea, who is both sex object and mother figure. As he climbs upon this massive woman, eyes gleaming, the camera holds on his face, while massive matronly breasts loom in the foreground. As he thrusts, the lens zooms in and out in time with his movements. With this, Fellini points to still another way in which man can create perversity: the film itself becomes a perversion of cinematic technique of exposition.

Fellini's use of dialogue presents another noteworthy departure from conventional cinema: it is a mood-setting and expository device. Rather than showing action, Fellini sometimes violates the first premise of filmmaking by having his characters tell about it. In the opening scene Encolpius relates:

> And who was it who condemned me to this solitude. A young man with every vice, worthy of punishment himself: Ascyltus. . . . And Giton. A boy who played the whore in prison. . . . Like a woman in heat he sells everything for the space of one night. And now they lie locked in each other's arms . . . and certainly they must laugh at me. Left out in the cold . . . and alone . . . I love you, Giton. I must fiind you, no matter what.

A few scenes later Ascyltus, too, addresses the audience in soliloquoy:

> While he [Encolpius] was sleeping, dazed with wine, I dragged Giton out from under him and passed a most sweet night with the boy. Friendship lasts as long as it is useful.

If Fellini had chosen to portray these events dramatically, the effect might have been that of arousing the audience's interest in and empathy with the characters: they would have appeared to be caught off-guard by the camera, behaving naturally and in accordance with their standards. In this film, however, the actor tells the story, and thus the truth is veiled by all the masks and defenses of a character who knows he is subject to public view. In this manner Fellini maintains the atmosphere of detachment, the estrangement between man and meaning.

Sets and props are also used to enhance the effect of estrangement. They are designed to appear infinitely detailed, but in fact, heavy shadows, low lighting, and a static camera prevent overview and close examination. These factors contribute to the film's dream-like quality. Exotic food is served at Trimalchio's dinner, but to the viewer it remains indistinct. Encolpius studies the frescoes that line the Garden of Delight, but the audience can merely glimpse them. Aboard Lichas's ship, where are the various quarters in relation to each other? Where is the field in which Eumolpus and Encolpius lie? Graffiti cover the red wall before which Encolpius stands for his opening soliloquoy, but what do they say? Although glimpses of things create the impression of detail, the actual images will remain unclear.

With production techniques such as these, Fellini paints a grim portrait of a world without inspiration, and the parallels between the culture of pre-Christian Rome and today's post-Christian era are evident. His characters discuss such things as crass commercialism, the decay of ethics, the perversion of myths and rituals, decadence in the arts, and their own boredom and feelings of uselessness. With this film Fellini has killed the gods of greed and lust and has made ready to build a new temple. He has turned the camera on the void, on the viewer, and on an uninspired world. But this detached, intellectual examination of what happens to man deprived of hope contains the implied message that action—creation of a new ideal—is the means by which a *raison d'être* will be restored to man.

Although the film does not elaborate on this ideal, it does provide us with clues for hope and for the regeneration of mankind. One instance of this is found in the sequence at the Villa of the Suicides, in which there is both rich development and the use of traditional cinematic techniques. A beautiful villa, surrounded by a lush garden in which children are playing, opens the scene. Closeups include a stone fawn dripping water, birds singing in the trees, peacocks exploring the flowers, and a sundial that reads *Sicot Umbra Dies Nostri.* Behind the villa we see two carts prepared for travel. The sad and noble master and mistress of the Villa, clothed in white robes, are conducting a last rite. The master first turns to the assembled slaves and announces their freedom. Then the couple embraces each child in farewell and the children's cart moves away down a dusty, winding road. As they pass, the cart awning flaps in the wind, the little girl eats a bun, the slave pulls the reins, wooden wheels turn slowly, and the mistress murmurs, *"Animula Vagula blandula hostes comesque corporis."*

In the garden the master prepares for the final rite. As he punctures first one wrist, then the other, reaction shots portray the expressions of his subdued, saddened wife. The master reminisces as the blood gushes onto his white garments, the divan, and the ground. The camera provides an in-depth study of the suicidal pair; it dollies and turns. Tight editing provides revealing images. In this sequence, perspective, details, and editing techniques that follow action allow the viewer to examine and to participate.

These two suicides are figures of a world in which meaning was found in stability, and order was sustained by observing the old myths and rituals. Fellini is not suggesting a return to these outmoded values: they, like the patricians, have died. But whatever form it takes, the new order should contain the same inner stability. What must occur is a conscious rejection of the perverted myths and rituals and a concomitant search for a new ideal. Encolpius rejects the ultimate ritual of eating the flesh of his friend Eumolpus, the sole conscious and affirmative act in his adventures. It is prompted by the understanding that the myth is a convenient contrivance and by the reawakening of natural emotion. Embodied in the words of Eumolpus' will—"to devour my body with that same ardor with which they consigned my body to Hell"—is the key to an existence dominated by a lack of feeling and an intellectual dishonesty. Encolpius abandons the old cannibals and joins the other young men who have not eaten the flesh. They set sail to continue their adventures with a sense of inner direction, in search of the new ideal.

For an instant the face of Encolpius is held in tight close-up; then it is fragmented until it becomes part of a decaying mosaic. The dream dissolves. The picture fades out. The audience sits alone, conscious, and . . . waiting.

APPENDIX

filmographies and
selected bibliographies

Dates of films are release dates; however, there is no authoritative list of release dates, and thus different sources will vary within a year or two. Short films and documentaries are omitted except as noted.

The lists of additional readings are limited to five items in English on each film and omit the materials reprinted in this book.

D. W. GRIFFITH (1875–1948)

1914 Judith of Bethulia; The Battle of the Sexes; The Escape; Home Sweet Home; The Avenging Conscience
1915 The Birth of a Nation
1916 Intolerance*
1918 Hearts of the World; The Great Love; The Greatest Thing in Life
1919 A Romance of Happy Valley; The Girl Who Stayed at Home; Broken Blossoms; True Heart Susie; Scarlet Days; The Greatest Question
1920 The Idol Dancer; The Love Flower; Way Down East
1921 Orphans of the Storm; Dream Street
1922 One Exciting Night
1923 The White Rose
1924 America; Isn't Life Wonderful?
1925 Sally of the Sawdust
1926 That Royle Girl; Sorrows of Satan
1928 Drums of Love; The Battle of the Sexes
1929 Lady of the Pavements
1930 Abraham Lincoln
1931 The Struggle

Additional Readings

Brownlow, Kevin. *The Parade's Gone By.* . . . New York: Alfred A. Knopf, 1968.
Eisenstein, Sergei. *The Film Form.* New York: Harcourt Brace Jovanovich,

---

* In later years, *The Mother and the Law* and *The Fall of Babylon* were borrowed from *Intolerance* and released as separate features.

1949. (Particularly important is the essay entitled "Dickens, Griffith, and the Film Today.")

Geduld, Harry M., ed. *Focus on D. W. Griffith*. Englewood Cliffs, N.J.: Prentice-Hall, 1971.

Henderson, Robert M. *D. W. Griffith, His Life and Work*. New York: Oxford University Press, 1972.

Kael, Pauline. "A Great Folly, and a Small One," *Going Steady*. Boston: Atlantic–Little, Brown, 1970.

Screenplay: Huff, Theodore. *"Intolerance," the Film by David Wark Griffith, Shot-by-Shot Analysis*. New York: Museum of Modern Art, 1966.

ROBERT WIENE (1881–1938)

1914   Arme Eva (*codirected with A. Berger*)
1915   Die Konservenbraut; Er Recht, sie links
1916   Die Ehe der Luise Rohrbach; Die Räuberbraut
1919   The Cabinet of Dr. Caligari
1920   Genuine
1921   Höllische Macht
1923   Raskolnikov (Crime and Punishment)
1924   I.N.R.I.
1925   The Hands of Orlac; Der Rosen Kavalier
1926   The Guardsman; Die Königin von Moulin Rouge
1927   Die Berühmte Frau; La Duchesse de les Folies; Die Geliedte; Die grosse Adenteurerin
1928   Die Frau aut dem Folter; Amori Contrasto; Leontines Ehmänner; Un fug de Liebe
1931   Panik in Chikago; Der Liebesexpress
1932   Der Andere
1934   Polizeiakte 909; Eine Nacht in Venedig
1938   Ultimatum (*completed by Robert Siodmak*)

Additional Readings

Clarens, Carlos. *An Illustrated History of the Horror Film*. New York: Capricorn Books, 1967.

Fulton, A. R. *Motion Pictures: The Development of an Art from Silent Films to the Age of Television*. Norman, Okla.: University of Oklahoma Press, reprint of 1960 edition.

Kinder, Marsha, and Beverle Houston. *Close-Up: A Critical Perspective on Film*. New York: Harcourt Brace Jovanovich, 1972, pp. 26–30.

Rotha, Paul, and Richard Griffith. *The Film Till Now*. Reprinted by Hamlyn House, Feltham, England, 1967.

Solomon, Stanley J. "The Symbolic Representation of Inner Reality: Wiene's *The Cabinet of Dr. Caligari*," *The Film Idea*. New York: Harcourt Brace Jovanovich, 1972, pp. 168–72.

SERGEI EISENSTEIN (1898–1948)

1924   Strike
1925   Potemkin
1927   October (Ten Days That Shook the World)
1929   The General Line (Old and New)
1931   Que Viva Mexico (*fragments of an incomplete project*)
1936   Bezhin Meadow (*unfinished*)
1938   Alexander Nevsky
1945   Ivan the Terrible, Part I
1958   Ivan the Terrible, Part II (*completed in 1946*)

Additional Readings

Eisenstein, Sergei. *Notes on a Film Director,* ed. S. Yurenev. London: Lawrence and Wishart, 1959.

Knight, Arthur. *The Liveliest Art.* New York: Macmillan, 1957.

Lawson, John Howard. *Film: The Creative Process.* New York: Hill and Wang, 1967.

Moussinac, Leon. *Sergei Eisenstein.* New York: Crown, 1970.

Wollen, Peter. *Signs and Meanings in the Cinema.* Bloomington, Ind.: University of Indiana Press, 1969.

Screenplay: Mayer, David. *Sergei M. Eisenstein's "Potemkin."* New York: Grossman, 1972.

CHARLES CHAPLIN (b. 1889)*

1914   Making a Living; Kid Auto Races at Venice; Mabel's Strange Predicament; Between Showers; A Film Johnnie; Tango Tangles; His Favorite Pastime; Cruel, Cruel Love; The Star Boarder; Mable at the Wheel; Twenty Minutes of Love; Caught in a Cabaret; Caught in the Rain; A Busy Day; The Fatal Mallet; Her Friend the Bandit; The Knockout; Mabel's Busy Day; Mabel's Married Life; Laughing Gas; The Property Man; The Face on the Barroom Floor; Recreation; The Masquerader; His New Profession; The Rounders; The New Janitor; Those Love Pangs; Dough and Dynamite; Gentleman of Nerve; His Musical Career; His Trysting Place; Getting Acquainted; His Prehistoric Past; Tillie's Punctured Romance
1915   His New Job; A Night Out; The Champion; In the Park; The Jitney Elopement; The Tramp; By the Sea; Work; A Woman; The Bank; Shanghaied; A Night in the Show
1916   Carmen; Police; The Floorwalker; The Fireman; The Vagabond; One A.M.; The Count; The Pawnshop; Behind the Screen; The Rink

* The complete filmography of Chaplin given here includes the films he appeared in but did not direct prior to *Caught in the Rain*, his first directed film. Thereafter, he directed or codirected all the films listed except *A Busy Day* (which may have been made earlier) and *Tillie's Punctured Romance,* both directed by Mack Sennett. All the films before *A Woman of Paris* are shorter than feature length except *Tillie's Punctured Romance* and *The Kid.*

Appendix

1917	Easy Street; The Cure; The Immigrant; The Adventurer
1918	Triple Trouble; A Dog's Life; The Bond; Shoulder Arms
1919	Sunnyside; A Day's Pleasure
1920	The Kid; The Idle Class
1922	Pay Day
1923	The Pilgrim; A Woman of Paris
1925	The Gold Rush
1928	The Circus
1931	City Lights
1936	Modern Times
1940	The Great Dictator
1947	Monsieur Verdoux
1952	Limelight
1957	A King in New York
1967	The Countess from Hong Kong

Additional Readings

Bazin, André. *What Is Cinema?*, Vols. 1 and 2, tr. by Hugh Gray. Berkeley: University of California Press, 1967, 1971.

Huff, Theodore. *Charlie Chaplin*. New York: Schuman, 1951.

McCaffrey, Donald W., ed. *Focus on Chaplin*. Englewood Cliffs, N.J.: Prentice-Hall, 1971.

Solomon, Stanley J. "Accumulation as a Unifying Style: Chaplin's *The Gold Rush*," *The Film Idea*. New York: Harcourt Brace Jovanovich, 1972, pp. 326–34.

Wilson, Edmund. "The New Chaplin Comedy," *The New Republic* (Sept. 2, 1925), pp. 45–46.

CARL DREYER (1899–1968)

1919	The President
1920	Leaves from Satan's Book
1921	The Parson's Widow; The Marked Ones (Love One Another)
1922	Once Upon a Time
1924	Mikaël
1925	Master of the House; The Bride of Glomdale
1928	The Passion of Joan of Arc
1931	Vampyr
1943	Day of Wrath
1945	Two People
1955	Ordet
1964	Gertrud

Additional Readings

Bowser, Eileen. *The Films of Carl Dreyer*. New York: Museum of Modern Art, 1964.

Kelman, Ken. "Dreyer," *Film Culture,* Vol. 35 (Winter, 1964–65).

Kinder, Marsha, and Beverle Houston. *Close-Up: A Critical Perspective on Film.* New York: Harcourt Brace Jovanovich, 1972, pp. 44–48.

Neergaard, Ebbe. *Carl Dreyer: A Film Director's Work.* London: British Film Institute (New Index Series, No. 1), 1950.

Stanbrook, Alan. *"The Passion of Joan of Arc,"* *Films and Filming,* Vol. 8 (June 1961), pp. 11–13, 40–41.

Screenplay: Dreyer, Carl. *Four Screenplays.* Bloomington, Ind.: Indiana University Press, 1970. (Contains *The Passion of Joan of Arc.*)

FRITZ LANG (b. 1890)

1919	Halbblut; Der Herr der Liebe; Der Goldene See *(Part One of* Die Spinnen); Harakiri (Madame Butterfly); Das Brillanten Schiff *(Part Two of* Die Spinnen)
1920	Das Wandernde Bild
1921	Vier um die Frau; Der Müde Tod
1922	Dr. Mabuse, der Spieler *(Part One of* Dr. Mabuse, der Spieler); Inferno *(Part Two of* Dr. Mabuse, der Spieler)
1924	Siegfried's Death *(Part One of* Die Nibelungen); Kriemhild's Revenge *(Part Two of* Die Nibelungen)
1926	Metropolis
1928	Spione; Frau im Mond
1931	M
1932	The Testament of Dr. Mabuse
1933	Liliom
1936	Fury
1937	You Only Live Once
1938	You and Me
1940	The Return of Frank James
1941	Western Union; Manhunt
1942	Hangmen Also Die
1943	Ministry of Fear
1944	The Woman in the Window
1945	Scarlet Street
1946	Cloak and Dagger
1948	Secret Beyond the Door
1950	House by the River; An American Guerrilla in the Philippines (I Shall Return)
1951	Rancho Notorious; Clash by Night
1952	The Blue Gardenia
1953	The Big Heat
1954	Human Desire
1955	Moonfleet
1956	While the City Sleeps; Beyond a Reasonable Doubt
1958	Der Tiger von Eschnapur; Das Indische Grabmal*
1960	The Thousand Eyes of Dr. Mabuse

* The two films of this year were combined and cut into *Journey to the Lost City* (*The Tigress of Bengal*).

Appendix

· Additional Readings

Bogdanovich, Peter. *Fritz Lang in America*. New York: Frederick A. Praeger, 1969.

Eisner, Lotte H. "The German Films of Fritz Lang," *Penguin Film Review*, No. 6 (April, 1948).

Ferguson, Otis. "Fritz Lang and Company" and "Behind the Camera: Lang," *New Republic*, Vols. 104, 105 (1941).

Lennig, Arthur. *Classics of the Film*. Madison, Wis.: Wisconsin Film Society, 1965.

Solomon, Stanley J. "Sound and Drama: Lang's *M*," *The Film Idea*. New York: Harcourt Brace Jovanovich, 1972, pp. 193–203.

Screenplay: Lang, Fritz. *M*. New York: Simon & Schuster, 1968.

JEAN RENOIR (b. 1894)

1924	La Fille de l'Eau
1926	Nana
1927	Charleston; Marquitta
1928	La Petite Marchande d'Allumettes (*codirected with Jean Tedesco*); Tire au Flanc
1929	Le Tournoi; Le Bled
1931	On Purge Bébé; La Chienne
1932	La Nuit du Carrefour; Boudu Sauvé des Eaux
1933	Chotard et Compagnie
1934	Toni; Madame Bovary
1935	Le Crime de Monsieur Lange
1936	La Vie Est à Nous; Une Partie de Campagne; The Lower Depths
1937	Le Marseillaise; Grand Illusion
1938	The Human Beast
1939	Rules of the Game
1940	La Tosca (*codirected with Carl Koch and Luchino Visconti*)
1941	Swamp Water
1943	This Land Is Mine
1944	Salute to France (*allegorical documentary*)
1945	The Southerner
1946	The Diary of a Chambermaid
1947	The Woman on the Beach
1950	The River
1952	The Golden Coach
1954	French Can-Can
1956	Paris Does Strange Things
1959	Picnic on the Grass
1960	The Testament of Dr. Cordelier
1961	The Elusive Corporal

Additional Readings

Braudy, Leo. *Jean Renoir: The World of His Films*. Garden City, N.Y.: Doubleday, 1972.

Cowie, Peter. *Seventy Years of Cinema.* New York: A. S. Barnes and Co., 1969.
Pechter, William. *Twenty-Four Times a Second: Films and Film-makers.* New York: Harper & Row, 1971.
Thomson, David. *Movie Man.* New York: Stein and Day, 1967.
Whitehall, Richard. *"La règle du jeu,"* Films and Filming, IX, 2 (1962), pp. 21–25.

Screenplay: Renoir, Jean. *Rules of the Game.* New York: Simon & Schuster, 1970.

ORSON WELLES (b. 1915)

1941	Citizen Kane
1942	The Magnificent Ambersons
1943	Journey into Fear (*credited to Norman Foster*)
1946	The Stranger
1947	The Lady from Shanghai
1948	Macbeth
1952	Othello
1955	Mr. Arkadin (Confidential Report)
1958	Touch of Evil
1963	The Trial
1966	Chimes at Midnight
1968	The Immortal Story

Additional Readings

Bessy, Maurice. *Orson Welles.* New York: Crown Publishers, 1971.
Bogdanovich, Peter. "The Kane Mutiny," *Esquire* (October, 1972), pp. 99–105.
Cowie, Peter. *The Cinema of Orson Welles.* New York: A. S. Barnes and Co., 1965.
Gottesman, Ronald, ed. *Focus on "Citizen Kane."* Englewood Cliffs, N.J.: Prentice-Hall, 1971.
McBride, Joseph. *Orson Welles.* New York: Viking Press, 1972.

Screenplay: Included in Pauline Kael's *The Citizen Kane Book.* Boston: Atlantic–Little, Brown, 1971.

VITTORIO DE SICA (b. 1902)

1940	Rose Scarlatte
1941	Maddalena Zero in Condotta; Teresa Venerdi
1942	Un Garibaldino al Convento
1943	I Bambini ci Guardano
1944–46	La Porta del Cielo

Appendix

1946	Shoeshine
1948	The Bicycle Thief
1951	Miracle in Milan
1952	Umberto D
1953	Stazione Termini (Indiscretion of an American Wife)
1954	The Gold of Naples
1956	The Roof
1960	Two Women
1962	Il Giudizio Universale; La Riffa (*episode in* Boccaccio '70)
1963	The Condemned of Altona; Il Boom
1964	Yesterday, Today, and Tomorrow; Marriage Italian Style
1965	Un Monde Nouveau; After the Fox
1966	Una Serata come le Altre (*episode in* Le Streghe)
1967	Woman Times Seven
1968	A Place for Lovers
1969	Sunflower
1970	*episode in* Le Cottie
1971	The Garden of the Finzi-Continis

Additional Readings

Brown, John M. "Struggle for Survival," *Saturday Review,* Vol. 33 (January 7, 1950).

Crowther, Bosley. *The Great Films.* New York: G. P. Putnam's Sons, 1967.

Riondi, Gian L. *Italian Cinema Today.* New York: Hill and Wang, 1966.

Rotha, Paul. "Neo-Realism," *Rotha on the Film.* Fair Lawn, N.J.: Essential Books, 1958.

"Shoeshine and Bicycle Thief," *Hollywood Quarterly,* Vol. 4 (1949–50).

Screenplay: De Sica, Vittorio, and Cesare Zavattini. *The Bicycle Thief.* New York: Simon & Schuster, 1968.

INGMAR BERGMAN (b. 1918)

1946	Crisis; It Rains on Our Love
1947	A Ship to the Indies
1948	Night Is My Future; Port of Call; The Devil's Wanton
1949	Three Strange Loves
1950	To Joy; It Can't Happen Here
1951	Illicit Interlude
1952	Secrets of Women
1953	Monika; The Naked Night (Sawdust and Tinsel)
1954	A Lesson in Love
1955	Dreams; Smiles of a Summer Night
1957	The Seventh Seal (*completed in 1956*); Wild Strawberries
1958	Brink of Life; The Magician (The Face)
1960	The Virgin Spring; The Devil's Eye
1961	Through a Glass Darkly
1963	Winter Light; The Silence
1964	Not To Speak About All These Women
1966	Persona

1968 Hour of the Wolf; Shame
1969 The Ritual (*made for television*)
1970 The Passion of Anna
1971 The Touch
1972 Cries and Whispers; The Lie (*made for television*)
1973 Scenes Out of a Marriage (*six-part television series*)

Additional Readings

Archer, Eugene. "The Rack of Life," *Film Quarterly*, Vol. 12 (Summer, 1959), pp. 3–16.
Gibson, Arthur. *The Silence of God*. New York: Harper & Row, 1969.
Sarris, Andrew. "*The Seventh Seal*," *Film Culture*, Vol. 19 (1959), pp. 51–61.
Steene, Birgitta, ed. *Focus on "The Seventh Seal."* Englewood Cliffs, N.J.: Prentice-Hall, 1972.
Wood, Robin. *Ingmar Bergman*. New York: Frederick A. Praeger, 1969.

Screenplay: Bergman, Ingmar. *Four Screenplays of Ingmar Bergman*. New York: Simon & Schuster, 1960. (Contains *The Seventh Seal*.)

ALFRED HITCHCOCK (b. 1899)

1925 The Pleasure Garden
1926 The Mountain Eagle; The Lodger (A Story of the London Fog)
1927 Downhill; Easy Virtue; The Ring
1928 The Farmer's Wife; Champagne
1929 The Manxman; Blackmail
1930 Juno and the Paycock; Murder
1931 The Skin Game
1932 Rich and Strange (East of Shanghai); Number Seventeen
1933 Waltzes from Vienna (Strauss's Great Waltz)
1934 The Man Who Knew Too Much
1935 The Thirty-Nine Steps
1936 Secret Agent; Sabotage
1937 Young and Innocent (The Girl Was Young)
1938 The Lady Vanishes
1939 Jamaica Inn
1940 Rebecca; Foreign Correspondent
1941 Mr. and Mrs. Smith; Suspicion
1942 Saboteur
1943 Shadow of a Doubt
1944 Lifeboat
1945 Spellbound
1946 Notorious
1947 The Paradine Case
1948 Rope
1949 Under Capricorn
1950 Stage Fright
1951 Strangers on a Train
1953 I Confess
1954 Dial M for Murder; Rear Window

Appendix

1955	To Catch a Thief
1956	The Trouble with Harry; The Man Who Knew Too Much
1957	The Wrong Man
1958	Vertigo
1959	North by Northwest
1960	Psycho
1963	The Birds
1964	Marnie
1966	Torn Curtain
1969	Topaz
1972	Frenzy

Additional Readings

Bogdanovich, Peter. *The Cinema of Alfred Hitchcock*. New York: Museum of Modern Art, 1963.

Durgnat, Raymond. Series of articles in *Films and Filming*, Vols. 16, 17 (March, 1970–November, 1970).

Houston, Penelope. "The Figure in the Carpet," *Sight and Sound*, Vol. 32 (Autumn, 1963), pp. 159–64.

LaValley, Albert J., ed. *Focus on Hitchcock*. Englewood Cliffs, N.J.: Prentice-Hall, 1972.

Truffaut, François. *Hitchcock*. New York: Simon & Schuster, 1967.

MICHELANGELO ANTONIONI (b. 1912)

1950	Cronaca di un Amore
1952	I Vinti
1953	La Signora senza Camelie; Tentato Suicidio (*episode in* Love in the City)
1955	Le Amiche
1957	Il Grido
1960	L'Avventura; La Notte
1962	Eclipse
1964	The Red Desert
1965	Prefazione (*episode in* I Tre Volti)
1966	Blow-Up
1970	Zabriskie Point
1972	Chung Kuo (*television documentary*)

Additional Readings

Baumbach, Jonathan. "From A to Antonioni: Hallucinations of a Movie Addict," *Man and the Movies*, ed. W. R. Robinson. Baton Rouge, La.: Louisiana State University Press, 1967.

Cameron, Ian, and Robin Wood. *Antonioni*. London: Movie Magazine Limited, 1968.

Houston, Penelope. "The Landscape of the Desert," *Sight and Sound*, Vol. 36 (Spring, 1965), pp. 80–81, 103.

Solomon, Stanley J. "Modern Uses of the Moving Camera," *Film Heritage* (Winter, 1965–66), pp. 19–27.

Strick, Philip. *Antonioni*. Loughton, England: Motion Publications, 1963.

LUIS BUÑUEL (b. 1900)

1928	Un Chien Andalou (*short*)
1930	L'Age d'Or
1932	Land Without Bread
1947	Gran Casino
1949	El Gran Calavera
1950	Los Olvidados (The Young and the Damned)
1951	Susana; Daughter of Deceit; A Woman Without Love; Ascent to Heaven
1952	El Bruto; Robinson Crusoe; El
1953	Wuthering Heights; Illusion Travels by Streetcar
1954	The River and Death
1955	The Criminal Life of Archibaldo de la Cruz; Cela S'Appelle L'Aurore
1956	La Mort en Ce Jardin
1958	Nazarin
1959	La Fièvre Monte à El Pao
1960	The Young One
1961	Viridiana
1962	The Exterminating Angel
1964	Diary of a Chambermaid
1965	Simon of the Desert
1967	Belle de Jour
1968	The Milky Way
1970	Tristana
1972	The Discreet Charm of the Bourgeoisie

Additional Readings

Armstrong, Marion. "Plausible Fantasy," *The Christian Century,* Vol. 85 (July 31, 1968), pp. 969–70.

Harcourt, Peter. "Luis Buñuel: Spaniard and Surrealist," *Film Quarterly* (Spring, 1967).

Kyrou, Ado. *Luis Buñuel.* New York: Simon & Schuster, 1963.

Mast, Gerald. *A Short History of the Movies.* Indianapolis, Ind.: Bobbs-Merrill, 1971.

Taylor, John Russell. *Cinema Eye, Cinema Ear.* New York: Hill and Wang, 1964.

Screenplay: Buñuel, Luis. *Belle de Jour.* New York: Simon & Schuster, 1972.

FEDERICO FELLINI (b. 1920)

1950	Variety Lights (*codirected with Alberto Lattuada*)
1952	The White Sheik
1953	I Vitelloni; Matrimonial Agency (*episode in* Love in the City)
1954	La Strada
1955	Il Bidone
1957	Nights of Cabiria
1960	La Dolce Vita
1962	Temptation of Dr. Antonio (*episode in* Boccaccio '70)
1963	8½

Appendix

1965   Juliet of the Spirits
1967   Tony Dammit (*episode in* Histoires Extraordinaires)
1969   Satyricon
1971   The Clowns
1972   Fellini's Roma

Additional Readings

Cox, Harvey, Jr., "The Purpose of the Grotesque in Fellini's Films," *Celluloid and Symbols*, ed. John C. Cooper and Carl Skrade. Philadelphia: Fortress Press, 1970.

Highet, Gilbert. "Whose· *Satyricon*—Petronius's or Fellini's?" *Horizon,* Vol. 13 (Autumn, 1970), pp. 43–47.

Hughes, Eileen. *On the Set of the Fellini "Satyricon."* New York: Morrow, 1971.

Solmi, Angelo. *Fellini.* New York: Humanities Press, 1968.

Solomon, Stanley J. "Structuring an Expanding Visual Idea: *Fellini Satyricon,*" *The Film Idea.* New York: Harcourt Brace Jovanovich, 1972, pp. 370–76.

Screenplay: Fellini, Federico. *Fellini's Satyricon.* New York: Ballantine Books, 1970.

INDEX

À *Nous la Liberté*, 180
Adventures of Dolly, The, 4
Alexander Nevsky, 125
Alexandrov, Grigory, 71n., 72–73
All Quiet on the Western Front, 63n.
Allemania Anno Zero, 212
America, 13
Andersson, Harriet, 242
Antonioni, Michelangelo, 8, 9, 181, 274–94
Antonov, A., 71n.–72n.
Arnold, Edward, 197
Artaud, Antonin, 118, 121
Astaire, Fred, 41, 192

Ballet Mécanique, 289
Bambrick, Gertrude, 21
Barsky, Vladimir, 71
Battle Cry of Peace, The, 17
Bel Geddes, Barbara, 255
Belle de Jour, 9, 295–316
Bergman, Ingmar, 8, 9, 110, 181, 223–45
Berkeley, Busby, 181
Bernhardt, Sarah, 58
Bête humaine, La, 153–55, 162
Bicycle Thief, The, 8, 199–221
Big Heat, The, 131
Big Parade, The, 63n.
Bigger Than Life, 261
Birds, The, 9, 249, 253, 267
Birth of a Nation, The, 5, 7, 13, 15, 24, 25, 58, 85, 87
Björnstrand, Gunnar, 227, 241–43
Blackmail, 249
Blackton, J. Stuart, 4, 17
Blanche, Francis, 310
Blood of a Poet, 183
Blow-Up, 274
Blue Angel, The, 134, 136
Boccaccio '70, 319
Bogdanovich, Peter, 268
Bonanova, Fortunio, 193
Bonnie and Clyde, 312
Boudu Sauvé des Eaux, 154, 164, 166
Breathless, 274

Bresson, Robert, 115, 118, 120, 170, 181, 277, 309
Buñuel, Luis, 9, 296–316

Cabinet of Dr. Caligari, The, 7, 39–69, 130, 135, 173, 183
  Janowitz-Mayer script for, 41, 43–45, 47, 51
  sets for, 46–48, 51–57, 182
  Wiene and, 41, 45–47, 52, 53, 62
Chaplin, Charles, 7, 20, 212, 289, 319
  compared with Keaton, 104–05, 107
  and *The Gold Rush*, 90–107
Chien Andalou, Un, 183, 296, 305
Chienne, La, 154, 164, 166
Chimes at Midnight, 179
Chinoise, La, 185
Chionetti, Carlo, 281, 284, 286
Cielo sulla Palude, Il, 214, 217
Circus, The, 90, 92
Citizen Kane, 22, 91, 147, 171–97
City Lights, 90, 100, 101
Civilization, 17
Clair, René, 8, 181, 189, 289
Clementi, Pierre, 310
Cocteau, Jean, 148, 170
Cooper, Miriam, 16, 28, 33
Cotton, Joseph, 193
Crime of Monsieur Lange, The, 150, 154
Cronaca di un Amore, 287
Cure, The, 95

Day, Doris, 256
Day of Wrath, 110, 117–18, 122, 124–27
De Broca, Philippe, 170
DeMille, Cecil B., 16, 225
Dempster, Carol, 21
Deneuve, Catherine, 299, 302, 308, 311, 314–16
De Sica, Vittorio, 8, 200–21, 318
Destiny, 133
Diary of a Chambermaid, The (*Le Journal d'une Femme de Chambre*), 165–66, 305–07, 309
Dietrich, Marlene, 134n.

Discreet Charm of the Bourgeoisie, The, 297
Dr. Mabuse films, 131, 137, 139, 145–48
Dolce Vita, La, 318, 319, 329, 330
Dreyer, Carl, 7, 58, 170, 173, 225, 275
    and *The Passion of Joan of Arc,* 110–27
Dupont, E. A., 7
Dwan, Allan, 20

Eclipse (L'Elisse), 274, 275, 281, 291
8½, 9, 270, 319, 330
Eisenstein, Sergei, 6, 7, 16, 59, 65–88, 124–26, 166, 173, 189, 201
    casting methods of, 83–84
    montage technique of, 70, 72, 80, 82–88, 118, 182
Elena et les hommes, 166
Elusive Corporal, The, 151
Elvira Madigan, 312
Entr'acte, 289
Exterminating Angel, The, 297

Face, The, 228
Fairbanks, Douglas, 41, 91
Falconetti, Marie, 35, 111–14, 116–19, 123
    See also *Passion of Joan of Arc, The*
Fall of Babylon, The, 17, 18
    See also *Intolerance*
Farrebique, 214
Fellini, Federico, 9, 181, 218, 270, 318–38
Film, 105
Flaherty, Robert, 84, 106
Folie du Dr. Tube, La, 53
Ford, John, 8
400 Blows, The, 274
Frankenheimer, John, 148
French Cancan, 166
Frenzy, 248
Freshman, The, 97
From Paris to Monte Carlo, 2
Frozen North, The, 98
Fury, 138, 141, 145

Gance, Abel, 16, 53, 118
Garden of the Finzi-Continis, The, 200
General, The, 7, 101, 105
Genina, Augusto, 214
Genuine, 41
Gertrud, 110, 115
Gish, Lillian, 17, 18
    on Griffith at work, 19–24
Godard, Jean-Luc, 8, 118, 148, 170, 181, 274, 278
Gold Rush, The, 7, 89–107
Golden Coach, The (Le Carrosse d'Or), 154, 155, 166

Gomorov, M., 72*n.*
Grand Illusion, 150, 153, 161–63, 165
Grant, Cary, 214, 253
Great Dictator, The, 90
Great Train Robbery, The, 3, 7, 15
Greed, 7, 106
Grido, Il, 287, 291–94
Griffith, David Wark, 2, 4–7, 58, 181
    editing techniques of, 5–6, 13, 15, 16, 23–25, 66, 86, 88, 90–91, 118, 182
    Gish on, 19–24
    influence of, on Eisenstein, 16, 66, 86, 87
    and *Intolerance,* 5, 7, 11–37, 86, 87
    sequence concept of, 5–6

Hardy, Oliver, and Stan Laurel, 41
Harris, Mildred, 20
Harris, Richard, 281, 284, 285*n.*
Harron, Robert, 16, 28
Hart, William, 91
Hawks, Howard, 187, 261
Henry V, 85
High and Dizzy, 100
Hitchcock, Alfred, 6, 8, 9, 124, 140, 148, 175*n.*, 181, 289, 297
    and *Vertigo,* 8, 248–71
Homunculus, 49, 55
Hour of the Wolf, 9
Huston, John, 172

I Confess, 251
Illicit Interlude, 241
Immigrant, The, 101
Ince, Thomas, 17, 91
Intolerance, 5–7, 11–37, 86, 87, 118
    See also *Fall of Babylon, The; Mother and the Law, The*
Ivan the Terrible, 59, 124–25

Jannings, Emil, 134*n.*
Jourdan, Louis, 124
Judith of Bethulia, 16
Juliet of the Spirits, 9, 319, 328, 329

Keaton, Buster, 7, 98, 101, 104–05, 107, 181
Keller, Hiram, 324
Kid, The, 91, 92
Korda, Alexander, 35
Krauss, Werner, 56
Kubrick, Stanley, 148, 196
Kurosawa, Akira, 227, 245

Ladd, Alan, 180*n.*
Lady from Shanghai, The, 177
L'Age d'Or, 296, 305, 308, 310, 315
Land Without Bread, 296

Lang, Fritz, 7, 8, 16, 44–45, 53, 181, 189, 267
  and *M*, 130–48
Last Laugh, The, 7, 41
Last Picture Show, The, 268
Last Year at Marienbad, 289
L'Atalante, 163, 164
Laurel, Stan, and Oliver Hardy, 41
L'Avventura, 274, 281, 283, 287, 291, 292
Léger, Fernand, 289
Lesson in Love, A, 240, 242
Limelight, 90, 105
L'Immortelle, 299
Lloyd, Harold, 41, 100
Lorre, Peter, 134, 136, 137, 145
Losey, Joseph, 137, 148
Lower Depths, The, 166
Lubitsch, Ernst, 8
Lumière, Louis and Auguste, 1, 182, 183, 189, 288

M, 8, 129–48, 189
Madame Bovary, 166
Maggiorani, Lamberto, 201
Magician, The, 224, 242
Magnificent Ambersons, The, 173, 175n., 197
Malmston, Birger, 242
Man I Killed, The, 63n.
Man Who Knew Too Much, 256
Marchal, Georges, 309
Marnie, 249, 288
Marseillaise, La, 161–63, 165
Marsh, Mae, 16, 17, 23, 25, 28, 35–36
  on her role in *Intolerance*, 29–30
Master of the House, 115, 117
Mayakovsky, Vladimir, 73–74
Meinert, Rudolf, 52, 53
Méliès, Georges, 2–3, 5, 88, 182, 183, 189
Metropolis, 130, 137, 139, 142, 145–47
Meyers, Carmel, 10
Milky Way, The, 9, 297
Mizoguchi, Kenji, 227
Modern Times, 90
Monkey Business, 261
Monsieur Verdoux, 90, 92, 319
Mother, 7, 215
Mother and the Law, The, 15, 17, 27, 30
  See also *Intolerance*
Muriel, 288, 289
Murneau, F. W., 181

Naked Night, The, 239–41, 243
Nana, 120, 164, 166
Napoléon, 118
Navigator, The, 97, 101

Nibelungen, Die, 130, 133, 138
Nights of Cabiria, 320
Ninth of January, 69, 73
North by Northwest, 249, 253
Notte, La, 274, 281, 283, 286, 287
Novak, Kim, 251–53, 266

Open City, 200, 209
Ophüls, Max, 302
Ordet, 110, 225
Orphans of the Storm, 13
Ossessione, 200
Ozu, Yasujiro, 170

Page, Geneviève, 309, 310, 316
Paisan (Paisà), 200, 209, 212, 214, 215
Paradine Case, The, 124, 251
Pasolini, Pier Paolo, 9, 181
Passion of Joan of Arc, The, 7, 109–27
  See also Falconetti, Marie
Pawnshop, The, 105
Perkins, Anthony, 253
Persona, 9
Piccoli, Michel, 309, 314
Pickford, Mary, 91
Porter, Edwin, 3–7
Potemkin, 6, 7, 15, 65–88, 118, 125
  Eisenstein on, 70–71, 75–82
  Mayakovsky and, 73–74
  Tisse and, see Tisse, Eduard
Psycho, 248, 253, 261, 267
Pudovkin, V., 7, 16, 183, 201

Quattro passi fra le nuvole, 210
Queen Elizabeth, 58

Rambeau, Marjorie, 30
Ray Nicholas, 261
Ray, Satyajit, 170
Rear Window, 264
Rebecca, 175n., 251
Red Desert, The, 8–9, 273–94
Reed, Carol, 148
Renoir, Jean, 6, 7, 58, 181, 191–92
  and *Rules of the Game*, 149–70
Rescued from an Eagle's Nest, 4
Resnais, Alain, 288–89
Rivette, Jacques, 170
Robbe-Grillet, Alain, 299
Rogers, Ginger, 192
Ronde, La, 302
Rope, 6
Rossellini, Roberto, 200, 209, 215
Rouquier, Georges, 214
Rules of the Game, 7, 149–70

Safety Last, 100
Satyricon, 9, 317–38
Scarlet Street, 131, 145

Index

Schlesinger, John, 268
Sennett, Mack, 90, 91
Seventh Seal, The, 8, 9, 223–45, 275
Seventh Veil, The, 195
Shoeshine, 200, 209, 210
Siegfried's Death, 130, 145
Signora senza Camelie, 287
Simon, Michel, 164
Simon of the Desert, 9, 314
Sorel, Jean, 308, 314, 315
Spiders, The (Die Spinnen), 44–45, 53
Sternberg, Josef von, 134n.
Stewart, James, 251–53, 255
Strada, La, 270, 319, 328, 329
Strangers on a Train, 249, 251, 257
Street, The, 135
Strike, 6, 66, 69, 70, 75n.
Stroheim, Erich von, 7, 173
Student of Prague, The, 135
Sunday, Bloody Sunday, 268
Swain, Mack, 94–95
Sydow, Max von, 227, 242

Tabu, 215
Talmadge, Constance, 20–21
"Temptation of Dr. Antonio, The," 319
Teorema, 9
Terra Trema, La, 200, 214
Testament of Dr. Mabuse, The, 131, 137, 145, 148
Thirty-Nine Steps, The, 249
Thulin, Ingrid, 242
Thunder Over Mexico, 125, 215
Tisse, Eduard, 71, 72, 82, 85, 86
Todd, Ann, 124
Toni, 154, 165
Trial of Joan of Arc, The, 118, 120
See also Bresson, Robert

Trip to the Moon, A, 2, 88
Triple Trouble, 95
Tristana, 297, 306
Truffaut, François, 8, 170, 274, 289
2001: A Space Odyssey, 196

Valli, Alida, 124
Vampyr, 110, 121
Variety, 48
Veidt, Conrad, 56
Vertigo, 8, 185, 247–71, 275
Vigo, Jean, 164
Virgin Spring, The, 224, 229, 230
Viridiana, 296, 297, 305–07, 313–14
Visconti, Luchino, 200, 214
Vitti, Monica, 279, 281, 284–86
Vivere in Pace, 210
Vivre Sa Vie, 120, 170

Wajda, Andrzej, 148
Warrick, Ruth, 193
Way Down East, 13, 118
Welles, Orson, 6, 22, 91, 172–74
Whale, James, 267
White Sheik, The, 318
Wiene, Robert, 41, 45–47, 52, 53
Wild Strawberries, 224, 225, 227, 228, 230
Wilson, Richard, 180n.
Winter Light, 224, 239
Woman in the Moon, The (Die Frau im Mond), 137

Year 1905, see Potemkin
You Only Live Once, 138

Zabriskie Point, 9